Michael Grinberg

Feature-Based Probabilistic Data Association for Video-Based Multi-Object Tracking

Karlsruher Schriften zur Anthropomatik
Band 35
Herausgeber: Prof. Dr.-Ing. habil. Jürgen Beyerer

Eine Übersicht aller bisher in dieser Schriftenreihe erschienenen Bände finden Sie am Ende des Buchs.

Feature-Based Probabilistic Data Association for Video-Based Multi-Object Tracking

by
Michael Grinberg

KIT Scientific Publishing

Dissertation, Karlsruher Institut für Technologie
KIT-Fakultät für Informatik

Tag der mündlichen Prüfung: 12. Dezember 2017
Referenten: Prof. Dr.-Ing. habil. Jürgen Beyerer
Prof. Mohan M. Trivedi

Impressum

KIT Scientific Publishing

Karlsruher Institut für Technologie (KIT)
KIT Scientific Publishing
Straße am Forum 2
D-76131 Karlsruhe

KIT Scientific Publishing is a registered trademark
of Karlsruhe Institute of Technology.
Reprint using the book cover is not allowed.

www.ksp.kit.edu

Print on Demand 2018 – Gedruckt auf FSC-zertifiziertem Papier

ISSN 1863-6489
ISBN 978-3-7315-0781-9
DOI 10.5445/KSP/1000081430

Feature-Based Probabilistic Data Association for Video-Based Multi-Object Tracking

zur Erlangung des akademischen Grades eines

Doktors der Ingenieurwissenschaften

der Fakultät für Informatik
des Karlsruher Instituts für Technologie (KIT)

genehmigte

Dissertation

von

Michael Grinberg

aus Kiew

Tag der mündlichen Prüfung:	12.12.2017
Erster Gutachter:	Prof. Dr.-Ing. habil. Jürgen Beyerer
Zweiter Gutachter:	Prof. Mohan M. Trivedi

Abstract

The aim of object tracking is continuous localization of objects (cars, people, airplanes, ships, etc.) in an environment by processing data of sensors such as sonars, radars, lidars, or video cameras. In general, this task is divided into four subtasks: object detection, measurements generation, data association, and dynamic state estimation (filtering). Object detection processes raw data and generates hypotheses (detections) using pattern recognition methods, such as thresholding, foreground-background segmentation, clustering, motion detection, etc. The second subtask includes the extraction of characteristic features (measurements), like size and position, from the detections. Data association is responsible for the correct interpretation of the collected observations, i.e., for the creation of an internal representation of tracked objects (tracks), assignment of the new sensor observations to the existing tracks and deletion of obsolete tracks. The state estimation task deals with evaluation of the current dynamic state (e.g., kinematics) of the tracked objects from a sequence of associated (noisy) measurements.

Most classical object tracking algorithms start with the assumptions that there is a one-to-one correspondence between detections and tracks, i.e., that a detection fully describes a tracked object, and that a measurement can be modeled using a sensor model with an additive Gaussian noise component. Often, however, these assumptions are violated. This is particularly true in the case of applications aimed at tracking extended objects that obtain object detections based solely on a foreground-background segmentation or on clustering individual measurement points in 3D space without being able to use any prior knowledge about object appearance. Sensory or algorithmic restrictions, limited field of view of the sensors, as well as occlusion situations may lead to partial, split (fragmented) or missed detections. Multiple objects may be detected as a single segment. Clutter may lead to bloated (i.e., falsely augmented) or phantom detections. In combination with uncertainty about the existence and the number of tracks in the perceived scene, as well as about their dynamics, this leads to ambiguities in data association and, as a consequence, to severe tracking errors.

However, unlike radar or lidar, video sensors offer a great potential for re-identification of objects and their parts. In this work, re-identification and tracking of image points (feature points) is utilized for realization of a novel feature-based probabilistic data association and object tracking concept which solves the aforementioned problems in a globally optimal way. This is done by explicitly modeling object existence, occlusions, detectability, noise and clutter, which are represented by means of probability distributions, and by considering different obtainable joint data association events. Introduction of a probabilistic point-to-track assignment scheme and a grid-based object representation allows for a feature-based reconstruction of object measurements and for a correct data association and track state update even in case of corrupted detections – leading to a significant improvement of the tracking performance.

This work adds the following contributions to the state-of-the-art:

- Introduction of a probabilistic point-to-track assignment scheme
- Distinction between a detection and a measurement in the context of object tracking
- Feature-based data association using detections instead of measurements
- Feature-based reconstruction of object dynamics in case of corrupted detections
- Grid-based object extent representation for refined occlusion modeling
- Grid-based object extent reconstruction in case of occlusions
- Consideration of different object constellations and the corresponding association events with explicit modeling and probabilistic incorporation of object existence, observability, and detectability
- Realization of a Track-Before-Detect track management on a solid probabilistic footing

The effectiveness of the proposed approach is demonstrated on a prototypical implementation in the context of a stereo-video based automotive side pre-crash application. Besides, parts of this approach have been successfully used in such fields as Wide Area Motion Imagery analysis and maritime surveillance applications.

Kurzfassung

Das Ziel der Objektverfolgung ist eine durchgängige Lokalisierung von Objekten (Personen, Fahrzeugen, Flugzeugen, Schiffen etc.) durch Verarbeitung der Beobachtungen von Sensoren wie z.B. Radar, Lidar, Ultraschall oder Videokameras. Diese Aufgabe kann in vier Unteraufgaben unterteilt werden: Objektdetektion, Generierung von Messungen, Datenassoziation und dynamische Zustandsschätzung (Filterung). Die Objektdetektion beschäftigt sich mit der Verarbeitung von Rohdaten und Generierung von Objekthypothesen (Detektionen) mit Hilfe von Mustererkennungsmethoden wie z.B. Schwellwert-Bildung, Vordergrund-Hintergrund-Segmentierung, Ballungsanalyse, Bewegungsdetektion etc. Innerhalb der zweiten Teilaufgabe werden aus den erhaltenen Detektionen charakteristische Merkmale (Messungen) wie Objektgröße und Position extrahiert. Die Datenassoziation ist für eine korrekte Interpretation der erhaltenen Messungen verantwortlich, d.h. für die Erstellung einer rechnerinternen Repräsentation der Objekte (Tracks), Zuordnung der Sensormessungen zu den existierenden Tracks und Löschung überflüssiger Tracks. Die Aufgabe der Zustandsschätzung besteht in der Schätzung des aktuellen dynamischen Zustandes der Tracks (z.B. Positionen und Geschwindigkeiten) ausgehend von einer Reihe von zugeordneten (verrauschten) Messungen.

Die meisten klassischen Objektverfolgungsansätze gehen von der Annahme aus, dass eine Detektion jeweils einem Objekt entspricht und dass die entsprechende Messung mittels eines Sensormessmodells mit additivem Rauschanteil modelliert werden kann. Diese Annahme ist jedoch oftmals verletzt. Insbesondere ist dies der Fall bei Anwendungen zur Verfolgung von ausgedehnten Objekten, die ihre Detektionen durch eine Vordergrund-Hintergrund-Segmentierung oder durch Ballungsanalyse einzelner Messpunkte erhalten und sich auf diese stützen müssen, ohne dabei Vorwissen über das Objektaussehen verwenden zu können. In solchen Anwendungen kann es vorkommen, dass aufgrund sensorischer und algorithmischer Einschränkungen sowie aufgrund von Verdeckungseffekten Objekte unvollständig, aufgeteilt in mehrere Segmente oder überhaupt nicht detektiert werden. Außerdem können mehrere Objekte als ein einziges Segment detektiert werden. Stördaten können zu fälschlich aufgeweiteten oder gänzlich stördatenbasierten Detektionen (Phantome) führen. In Kombination mit der Unsicherheit über die Existenz und die Anzahl der Objekte in der Szene sowie deren Sichtbarkeit führt dies zu Mehrdeutigkeiten bei der Datenassoziation, die oft grobe Fehler bei der Objektverfolgung bewirken.

Im Gegensatz zu Radar oder Lidar bieten Videosensoren ein großes Potential für die Wiedererkennung von Objekten und deren Teilen. In dieser Arbeit wird die Wiedererkennung und Verfolgung von einzelnen Bildmerkmalspunkten ausgenutzt, um ein neuartiges Konzept zur Datenassoziation und Objektverfolgung zu realisieren, das für eine Stereo-Videokamera die obengenannten Probleme mittels einer probabilistischen Entscheidung auf eine global optimale Weise auflösen kann. Hierfür werden verschiedene Objektkonstellationen betrachtet und die damit erzielbaren Datenassoziationsereignisse (Joint Events) gebildet, wobei Objektexistenz, Verdeckungen, Detektierbarkeit und Stördateneinflüsse modelliert und durch Wahrscheinlichkeitsverteilungen repräsentiert werden. Durch die Einführung eines probabilistischen Punkt-zu-Track Zuordnungsschemas sowie einer gitterbasierten Objektrepräsentation wird eine merkmalsbasierte Rekonstruktion von Objektmessungen ermöglicht und dadurch auch im Fall von gestörten Detektionen eine korrekte Datenassoziation und eine Aktualisierung der Tracks erlaubt, was zu einer signifikanten Verbesserung der Objektverfolgungsleistung führt.

Im Einzelnen weist diese Arbeit folgende Neuerungen gegenüber dem Stand der Technik auf:

- Einführung eines probabilistischen Punkt-zu-Track-Zuordnungsschemas zur Herstellung einer Beziehung zwischen den einzelnen verfolgten Merkmalspunkten und den verfolgten Objekten,
- Differenzierung zwischen Detektion und Messung im Kontext der Objektverfolgung,

- Merkmalsbasierte Datenassoziation, die Detektionen anstelle von Messungen verwendet,
- Ermöglichung einer merkmalsbasierten Rekonstruktion der Objektdynamik bei gestörten Detektionen,
- Einführung einer lokalen gitterbasierten Objektrepräsentation, dadurch
  - detaillierte Modellierung von Objektbeobachtbarkeit,
  - Rekonstruktion der Objektausdehnung im Falle von Verdeckungen,
- Betrachtung verschiedener Objektkonstellationen und der dabei erzielbaren Assoziationsereignisse, wobei Objektexistenz, Verdeckungen, Detektierbarkeit und Stördateneinflüsse modelliert und durch Wahrscheinlichkeitsverteilungen berücksichtigt werden
- Realisierung einer Track-Before-Detect Trackverwaltung, die auf einer soliden probabilistischen Basis beruht.

Die Effizienz des Verfahrens wird anhand einer prototypischen Implementierung im Rahmen eines Stereo-Video-basierten Pre-Crash-Systems für Automobile demonstriert. Teile des vorgestellten Ansatzes wurden bereits erfolgreich in anderen Anwendungsbereichen angewendet, wie z.B. bei Analyse von Wide Area Motion Imagery Daten sowie in maritimen Überwachungsanwendungen.

Acknowledgments

I wrote this thesis at the Vision and Fusion Lab (IES) of the Karlsruhe Institute of Technology (KIT) in close cooperation with the Fraunhofer Institute of Optronics, System Technologies and Image Exploitation (Fraunhofer IOSB) in Karlsruhe. I would have not been able to complete this work without the fruitful cooperation with the many great people whom I met during my time here.

I would like to express my sincere thanks to my advisor Prof. Dr.-Ing. habil. Jürgen Beyerer for giving me the opportunity to work, learn and grow at the Vision and Fusion Lab and at the Fraunhofer IOSB. His ability to quickly immerse into most complicated scientific problems will forever be an example to imitate. I also very much appreciate his ability to always find time and encouraging words for his staff members, despite the great responsibility and busy schedule as a KIT professor and the head of Fraunhofer IOSB.

I would also like to thank Dr. Dieter Willersinn for greatly supporting me during my first years at the Fraunhofer IOSB.

I am very grateful to my second advisor Prof. Mohan Trivedi for hosting me as a visiting researcher at the Computer Vision and Robotics Research Lab (CVRR) at the University of California, San Diego (UCSD) and for traveling to Karlsruhe in order to serve on my committee. While visiting CVRR I learned a lot and could find a new focus for my research. I also would like to thank the Karlsruhe House of Young Scientists (KHYS) for helping fund this visit.

I am grateful to Prof. Dr.-Ing. Rainer Stiefelhagen, Prof. Dr. Wolfgang Karl, Prof. Dr. Hartmut Prautzsch, and Prof. Dr. Bernhard Beckert for serving on my PhD examination committee.

I am very grateful to all my colleagues at both the Vision and Fusion Lab at the KIT and the department Video Exploitation Systems (VID) at Fraunhofer IOSB for the comfortable working atmosphere and many fruitful discussions.

I would have not been able to complete the research described in this thesis without contributions of the members of the APROSYS Task Force at Fraunhofer IOSB who were involved in creation and evaluation of parts of the APROSYS data processing framework.

I would also like to thank my colleagues from APROSYS SP6 team for the great time we had when conducting the project.

I am very grateful Dr. Dieter Willersinn, Dr. Christian Frese, Dr. Michael Teutsch, Dr. Alexey Pak, Dr. Sebastian Stücker, Raphael Spraul, Felix Pyatkov, Alisa Myazdrikova and Ron Tal for proof-reading parts of this thesis.

My special thanks go to Dr. Tobias Schuchert and Prof. Kristian Kroschel who strongly supported me during the final phases of this work.

Finally, I would like to thank my dad of blessed memory, my mom, Marina, Tanja and Ron, and all my friends for their patience and their encouragement throughout all phases of my doctorate.

Contents

Appendix

Notation

This chapter introduces the notation and symbols which are used in this thesis.

General notation

Scalars	italic Roman and Greek lowercase letters	x, α
Sets	calligraphic Roman uppercase letters bold Greek uppercase letters	$\mathcal{D}$, $\boldsymbol{\Theta}$
Vectors	bold Roman lowercase letters	$\mathbf{x}$
Matrices	bold Roman uppercase letters	$\mathbf{F}$
State spaces	bold calligraphic Roman uppercase letters	$\boldsymbol{\mathfrak{X}}$
Random variables	italic Roman uppercase letters	E
Multi-dimensional random variables	bold italic Roman uppercase letters	$\boldsymbol{E}$

In multidimensional sets of elements related to time series, the first index denotes time.

Distributions

$\mathcal{N}$	Gaussian normal distribution
χ_n^2	n-dimensional chi-square distribution

Numbers and indexing

$\mathbb{N}$	natural numbers
$\mathbb{N}_0$	natural numbers including zero (non-negative integers)
k, t	discrete points in time
i, j, ℓ, q	indexing for objects, measurements and points
m, n	number of detections/measurements, number of tracked objects

Geometry (coordinates, vehicle, and camera modeling)

x, y, z	world coordinates
u, v	image coordinates
b	stereo base line
f	focal length
Δu	displacement in the image, disparity
$\mathbf{d}$	displacement vector
$d(\cdot)$	distortion function
κ_1, κ_2	radial distortion parameters
ρ_1, ρ_2	tangential distortion parameters
l, w, h	length, width, height
r	radius
A	area
V	volume
v	velocity
a	acceleration

α	steering angle
φ	orientation angle
$\dot{\varphi}$	yaw rate
$\mathbf{p}$	point in 2D and 3D space
$\mathbf{p}_q$	q^{th} point
$\mathbf{p}_{k,q}$	q^{th} point at time k
$\mathbf{o}_\text{C}$	camera projection center
$\mathbf{c}$	principle point
$\check{\mathbf{p}}$	point in homogeneous coordinates
$\mathbf{R}$	rotation matrix
$\mathbf{t}$	translation vector
$\mathbf{C}$	camera matrix (containing intrinsic camera parameters)
$\mathbf{E}$	extrinsic camera matrix

Object state modeling and probabilities

$\mathfrak{X}$	state space
$\mathfrak{Z}$	measurement space
$\boldsymbol{X}_k$	object state at time k (random variable)
$\boldsymbol{Z}_k$	measurement at time k (random variable)
$\mathbb{E}[\boldsymbol{X}_k]$	expectation value
$\mathbf{x}$	object state vector
$\mathbf{x}_k$	object state at time k
$\hat{\mathbf{x}}_k^-$	predicted object state at time k (a-priori estimation of $\mathbf{x}_k$)
$\hat{\mathbf{x}}_k$	updated object state at time k (a-posteriori estimation of $\mathbf{x}_k$)

$\hat{\mathbf{x}}_k^{(i)}$	a-posteriori estimation of $\mathbf{x}_k$ after i^{th} iteration
$\mathbf{x}_{k,i}$	state of the ith track at at time k
$\mathcal{D}$	detection set
$\mathcal{D}_k$	set of detections at time k
$\mathcal{D}_{1:k}$	set of detections that have been obtained from the beginning of the observation and up to the time step k
$d_{k,j}$	j^{th} detection at time k
$\mathcal{Z}$	measurement set
$\mathcal{Z}_k$	set of measurements at time k
$\mathcal{Z}_k^{\mathbf{x}}$	set of measurements falling into the gate of the track $\mathbf{x}$ at time k
$\mathcal{Z}_{1:k}$	set of measurements that have been obtained from the beginning of the observation and up to the time step k
$\mathbf{z}$	measurement vector
$n_{\mathbf{z}}$	number of dimensions of the measurement vector
$\hat{\mathbf{z}}_k^{\mathbf{x}}$	predicted measurement for track $\mathbf{x}$ at time k
$\mathbf{z}_{k,j}$	j^{th} measurement at time k
$\tilde{\mathbf{z}}$	innovation (difference between predicted and obtained measurement)
$\mathbf{P}$	covariance matrix
$\mathbf{P}_{\mathbf{x}_k\mathbf{x}_k}$	state covariance matrix
$\mathbf{P}_{\mathbf{z}_k\mathbf{z}_k}$	measurement covariance matrix
$\mathbf{P}_{\tilde{\mathbf{z}}_k\tilde{\mathbf{z}}_k}$	state covariance matrix calculated under the assumption that the innovation is performed with the correct measurement
$\widetilde{\mathbf{P}}_k$	matrix incorporating the measurement association errors
$\mathbf{u}_k$	vector with control parameters

$\boldsymbol{W}_k$	system noise (random variable)
$\boldsymbol{V}_k$	measurement noise (random variable)
$\mathbf{Q}_k$	system noise covariance matrix
$\mathbf{R}_k$	measurement noise covariance matrix
$f(\boldsymbol{X}_k, \mathbf{u}_k, \boldsymbol{W}_k)$	system evolution function (system model)
$h(\boldsymbol{X}_k, \boldsymbol{V}_k)$	measurement model
$\mathbf{F}$	system matrix of the Kalman Filter
$\mathbf{G}$	control matrix of the Kalman Filter
$\mathbf{H}$	measurement matrix of the Kalman Filter
$\mathbf{K}_k$	Kalman gain at time k
$P_{k\|k-1}$	a-priori probability
$P_{k\|k}$	a-posteriori probability
$p(\mathbf{x}_k)$	probability density function (pdf)
$P(\mathbf{x}_k)$	probability mass function (pmf)
$P(\mathbf{x}_{k+1}\|\mathbf{x}_k, ...)$	transition probability
$p(\mathbf{x}_{k+1}\|\mathbf{x}_k, ...)$	transition density
$P(\mathbf{z}\|\mathbf{x})$	emission probability
$p(\mathbf{z}\|\mathbf{x})$	emission density
$f_{z_k^{\mathbf{x}}}$	probability density function of predicted measurement position of the track $\mathbf{x}$ at time k
c	cell
$c_r^{\mathbf{x}_i}$	r^{th} cell of the ith object
$c_{k,r}^{\mathbf{x}_i}$	r^{th} cell of the ith object at time k

Object existence and observability, data association

$\exists$	existent
$\nexists$	not existent
$\supset$	observable
$\not\supset$	not observable (occluded)
$\emptyset$	no detection due to sensor failure
Ⓑ	birth source
Ⓒ	clutter source
$\mathbf{x}_0$	unknown object: aggregation of the clutter source Ⓒ and birth source Ⓑ
d_0	missed detection: aggregation of $\emptyset$ and $\not\supset$
$\mathbf{z}_0$	missing measurement due to missed detections
$V_k^{\mathbf{x}}$	validation gate: volume around predicted measurement of the track $\mathbf{x}$ at time k
$\Gamma_k^{\mathbf{x}}$	gating region of the track $\mathbf{x}$ at time k
γ	gating threshold
P_G	gating probability
P_D	detection probability
μ	probability mass function for the number of clutter-based measurements
λ	mean clutter density
$i \prec \{j\}$	split detection event for the track $\mathbf{x}_i$ leading to multiple detections
$\{i\} \succ j$	merged detection for the set of tracks $\{\mathbf{x}_i\}$

$\theta^{\mathbf{x}_i \mapsto d_j}$	association between i^{th} track and j^{th} detection
$\theta^{\mathbf{x}_i \mapsto \mathbf{z}_j}$	association between i^{th} track and j^{th} measurement
β	association weight
$\beta^{\mathbf{x}_i \mapsto \mathbf{z}_j}$	association weight between i^{th} track and j^{th} measurement
t_j	index of the track associated to the jth detection
$\mathcal{T}$	ordered set of possibly repeating track numbers including 0
Θ	joint association event
$\boldsymbol{\Theta}$	set of feasible joint association events
$\boldsymbol{\Theta}_k^{\mathbf{x}_i \mapsto \exists}$	set of joint association events Θ that assume existence of the track $\mathbf{x}_i$ at time k
$\boldsymbol{\Theta}_k^{\mathbf{x}_i \mapsto d_j}$	set of joint association events Θ that assume that at time k the jth detection is evoked by the ith track
Ω	binary validation matrix with elements $[\omega_{ji}]$
ω_{ji}	element of the binary validation matrix Ω
$\vartheta_i(\Theta)$	binary indicator: indicates whether in the joint association event Θ the ith track has been assigned a detection
$\tau_j(\Theta)$	binary indicator: indicates whether in the joint association event Θ the jth detection has been assigned to a track
$\phi(\Theta)$	number of clutter-based measurements in the joint event Θ
$E_{k,i}(\Theta)$	binary random variable defining existence of the track $\mathbf{x}_i$ within the joint association event Θ at time k
$B_{k,j}(\Theta)$	binary random variable defining birth of a track from the jth detection within the joint association event Θ at time k
$O_{k,i}(\Theta)$	binary random variable defining missed detection for the track $\mathbf{x}_i$ within the joint event Θ at time k due to an occlusion

$S_{k,i\mapsto\{j\}}(\Theta)$	binary random variable defining split detection for the track $\mathbf{x}_i$ within the joint event Θ at time k
$M_{k,\{i\}\mapsto j}(\Theta)$	binary random variable defining merged detection for the set $\{i\}$ of tracks $\mathbf{x}_i$ within the joint event Θ at time k
$N_{k,i}(\Theta)$	binary random variable defining missed detection for the track $\mathbf{x}_i$ within the joint event Θ at time k due to a sensor failure
$C_{k,j}(\Theta)$	random variable defining clutter-based origination of the jth detection within the joint event Θ at time k
$\boldsymbol{E}(\Theta)$	multi-dimensional random variable defining existence of tracks within the joint event Θ
$\boldsymbol{B}(\Theta)$	multi-dimensional random variable defining birth of tracks within the joint event Θ
$\boldsymbol{O}(\Theta)$	multi-dimensional random variable defining occlusion of tracks within the joint event Θ
$\boldsymbol{S}(\Theta)$	multi-dimensional random variable defining split detections within the joint event Θ
$\boldsymbol{M}(\Theta)$	multi-dimensional random variable defining merged detections within the joint event Θ
$\boldsymbol{N}(\Theta)$	multi-dimensional random variable defining non-detection of tracks within the joint event Θ
$\boldsymbol{C}(\Theta)$	multi-dimensional random variable defining clutter-based origination of tracks within the joint event Θ
M_A	appearance mask
M_P	appearance probability mask
M_T	transparency probability mask
$M_\supset$	observability probability mask
$M_{\not\supset}$	occlusion probability mask

1 Introduction

The increased need for mobility over the last several decades has led to a growing traffic density. The rising number of fatalities and injuries due to preventable causes related to human error and driver fatigue has become a major public health concern. Efforts of auto-manufacturers and policy makers have led to the development of many ***Advanced Driver Assistance Systems (ADAS)*** that improve the safety of passengers and reduce human error by assisting drivers and, ultimately, replacing them both in regular driving situations as well as in critical situations. Examples of such systems are anti-lock braking systems, lane departure warning and lane keeping systems, adaptive cruise control systems, and emergency braking assistants. With recent technological improvements the conversation has shifted to autopilot applications and fully autonomous vehicles, completely immune to human error as demonstrated in many projects, such as DARPA Urban Challenge [Bue09] and the Google self-driving car [Gib29]. However, with the elimination of human error, the implications of system error has become more severe and thus the importance of the safety systems robustness will only grow.

A vital component of many driver assistance systems is environment perception. All ADAS systems use sensors in order to detect a critical situation and to trigger an appropriate reaction. The task of the environment perception system is to scan the vehicle's surroundings by means of sensors and to extract appropriate information about the environment elements, traffic participants and their behavior out of the acquired data (measurements). For example, depth data from a stereo camera can be used to gain information about the course of the road as well as position and size of other road users. An important task in the context of environment perception is the detection and tracking of objects. Here and in the following the term "object tracking" does not only mean a classical highlighting of objects in the consecutive images, i.e., a temporal concatenation of detections (as it is often done in surveillance tasks), but additionally an object state estimation in 3D space which allows for a prediction of the object motion and thus e.g., for a collision prediction. In this case, object tracking consists of three main components: extraction of the relevant object parameters out of the detections (measurement generation), data association (object re-identification), and state estimation (filtering) based on the associated measurements. A consistent internal representation of the tracked objects (tracks) is maintained by means of track management, an additional component that is responsible for the creation of new and deletion of obsolete tracks.

Both sensor measurement process and object detection process, as well as the following processing stages that have to derive a scene and situation description out of the detections have underlying uncertainties. For example, in the case of a stereo camera there is an uncertainty of the depth measurement due to sensor noise and quantization effects which strongly increases with object range. But also the object texture has a great impact on formation and quality of detections. Ambiguity errors in case of periodical patterns lead to gross depth measurement errors (outliers). Spatial concentration of such outliers ("clutter") may under certain circumstances lead to detection of nonexistent objects ("false positives") and cause generation of phantom tracks. Concentration of outliers in the interspace of two closely spaced objects may lead to merged detections.

The lack of texture also poses a great problem to stereo vision. In such a case most algorithms are unable to find unambiguous correspondences between the pixels of the left and right images, which makes a correct depth measurement impossible. This leads to holes in the depth data and consecutively to incomplete, split or even missing detections. A fatal accident with the autopilot equipped Tesla car in May 2016 has clearly demonstrated the danger of such effects [Bou19].

Another uncertainty in the context of detection formation is object observability. Aside from the already mentioned problem of poor texturing, the mutual position of the camera and objects in the scene may be the reason for incomplete, split, and missed detections. In particular, this might happen when a foreground object occludes background objects or when an object enters or leaves the field of view of the camera.

Most state-of-the-art object tracking algorithms make the assumption that there is a one-to-one correspondence between detections and tracks, i.e., that a detection fully describes a tracked object. In this case, object tracking may be performed by filtering the centroids of associated detections. However, in general this assumption is untenable due to the aforementioned effects. In many applications there is no a-priori knowledge about the existence and number of objects in the field of view of the sensors, as well as about their dimensions and dynamics. Therefore, there is often no full evidence about the realness and integrity of the obtained detections. Maintaining the centroid filtering strategy for object tracking in case of corrupted detections often leads to severe corruption of the results.

A correct object state estimation is essential for properly fulfilling many vehicle environment perception tasks. Thus, one needs a possibility to perform data association and track updates even in case of incomplete and corrupt detections. This thesis introduces a concept which offers such a possibility and allows for a robust handling of the aforementioned effects. The concept is called Feature-Based Probabilistic Data Association and Tracking Algorithm (FBPDATA) and is a combination of the following subconcepts:

- World model with a mechanism for propagation of uncertainties regarding object existence, dynamics, and observability.
- Detailed object extent representation for refined occlusion modeling and propagation.
- Detection-by-tracking instead of tracking-by-detection paradigm. Measurements are derived ("reconstructed") from detections utilizing low-level information gained by tracking dedicated feature points.
- Affiliation of the tracked feature points to a certain object is modeled by means of affiliation probability which is updated each frame.
- Point-to-track affiliations are utilized for both data association and state estimation procedures.

The proposed concept will be demonstrated by means of an implementation in the context of a driver assistance system for side collision detection. It has been implemented as a module in a stereo-video based object tracking framework which had been developed by the author as a part of a novel integrated lateral pre-crash safety system in the course of the EU funded project APROSYS [APR10].

The remainder of this chapter will give an overview of the context of this thesis. In Section 1.1 we provide a tabular taxonomy of the lateral driver support systems. and list several approaches to video-based object detection and tracking that have been developed specifically for side-looking systems in the 90s and early 2000s – prior to and during the execution of the APROSYS project. Section 1.2 provides a short overview and background knowledge regarding the APROSYS project and particularly subproject SP6 that has delivered the context for this research. Section 1.3 declares the main goals of the video system design and introduces the implemented system framework. Section 1.4 summarizes the challenges of object tracking and defines the main focus of the thesis. Finally, Section 1.5 gives an overview of the remainder of the thesis.

1.1 Lateral Advanced Driver Assistance Systems and video-based object detection and tracking for lateral ADAS

Depending on the car automation level, lateral driver support functions require performing various perception tasks in different areas around the car. First systems aimed at supporting the driver in the lane keeping and lane changing tasks (lane departure warning systems and blind spot warning systems). The next generation aimed at assisting the driver in parking and overtaking. Today the trend goes towards fully-automated driving, making lateral perception and lateral control systems an inevitable part of the ADAS architecture. Table 1.1 gives an overview of the different categorization criteria for lateral driver support systems. The categories of the video-based environment perception system developed by the author within the APROSYS subproject SP6, which provide the context for this thesis, are highlighted in bold.

While lane keeping tasks can be solved using front-looking sensors, other tasks require side-looking sensors which deliver information about presence of objects in the adjacent lanes (e.g., for blind spot monitoring), their range (e.g., for lateral collision detection), extent (e.g., for parking lot measurement), and dynamics (lane change assistance, pre-crash applications, autonomous driving).

Driver assistance type	informing / warning / **control intervention** / fully automatic control (autonomous driving)
Collision avoidance vs. impact mitigation	active safety / passive safety / **integrated safety**
Application area	highway / **urban** / off-road
Field of view	**side** / side-front / side-back / blind spot
Perception task	lane departure detection / lateral and rear area monitoring (including blind spot hazard detection) / **lateral collision detection** / parking lot measuring
Problem to be solved	**detection** / **tracking** / simultaneous localization and mapping (SLAM) / classification / fusion / situation + risk assessment
Sensors used	mono camera / **stereo camera** / omnidirectional camera / time of flight camera / radar / lidar / laser scanner / sonar / multi-sensor

Table 1.1: Categorization of driver support systems. The categories of the video-based environment perception system developed by the author within the APROSYS subproject SP6, which provide the context for this thesis, are highlighted in bold.

In the literature, a bunch of approaches were proposed for performing each of these tasks utilizing information from different sensors, such as radar, lidar, laser scanner, sonar, as well as omnidirectional and classical mono and stereo video cameras [Tid07]. Many current state-of-the-art approaches include Car-To-Car communication in order to better coordinate groups of vehicles and perform co-operative maneuvers [Bat09, Fre11, Wat12]. In the following we focus on vision-based sensors and the task of object detection and tracking for side-looking systems. An extended overview of related work and state-of-the-art regarding object tracking is given later, in Section 3.2.

The first cars with lateral perception were developed in the course of the PROMETEUS project [Wil88]. While the VaMoRs-P vehicle [Dic94] had only front and rear looking cameras and had to "keep in mind" overtaking and overtaken vehicles after they had left the field of view of those cameras, the VITA2 vehicle [Ulm94] used two arrays of three cameras on each vehicle side to monitor the neighboring lanes. Optical flow in combination with inverse perspective mapping was used for detection of hazardous objects in adjacent lanes [Bra94].

In 2002, Lakshmanan et al. presented an approach for side collision probability estimation using optical flow and time-to-collision calculation [Lak02]. A method for computing the so called Collision Threat Index (CTI), which could allow side collision warning, was described there, although neither theoretical nor practical consideration of system / method boundaries were made.

In 2003, detection of overtaking vehicles based on optical flow classification has been proposed in [Día03, Día08] (ECOVISION project). A bio-inspired classification of optical flow patterns has been used for discrimination of the static background and approaching overtaking vehicles.

In 2004, Achler and Trivedi proposed vehicle detection based on wheel detection using 2D filterbanks [Ach04b, Ach04a]. This approach can identify vehicles driven in parallel to the sensor-carrying vehicle.

In 2004 and 2005 Gandhi & Trivedi demonstrated a system for performing vehicle surrounding analysis that was capable of detecting objects in adjacent lanes using an omnidirectional camera which was mounted on the roof of the vehicle [Gan04, Gan05]. In 2007, this approach was enhanced to using two omnidirectional cameras [Gan07b].

In 2005, an approach for overtaking vehicle detection using dynamic and quasi-static background modeling was presented in [Wan05]. The authors utilized homogeneous sparse optical flow and eigenspace modeling to model background as consisting of dynamic and quasi-static regions. Dynamic background regions are regions with rich texture allowing good optical flow estimation while quasi-static regions are regions with lacking texture such as homogeneous road regions etc. and can be modeled using block-based eigenspace approach. After subtraction of the dynamic and quasi-static background regions, hypotheses generation and tracking can be performed to detect overtaking vehicles in the image.

The "LATERAL SAFE", a subproject of the EU funded project PReVENT, which has been carried out from 2004 to 2008, addressed problems of lateral/rear area related accidents [Amd06, Amd08]. The main focus was laid on the blind spot areas and applications that enhance driver's perception and reduce the risk of unintended road departures and maneuver-related collisions during lane changes and merges.

In 2006, utilization of the optical flow and the concept of Focus of Expansion (FOE) have been proposed in [Met06] for detecting dangerous objects and computing the time to collision (TTC) for perpendicularly approaching objects. In 2007, the concept of FOE was utilized for the blind spot detection application in [Son07].

Utilization of the Structure-from-Motion (SfM) concept for side-looking cameras in the context of the lateral safety systems has been tackled in [Woo07] and [Ung11] in 2007 and 2011 respectively. A system based on optical flow has been presented in [Mic11].

1.2 Research context: A novel automotive integrated pre-crash safety system developed within APROSYS SP6

The stereo-video based object tracking framework for side collision detection, which provides the context for this thesis, has been developed by the author during his work on the subproject 6 (SP6) of the EU funded project APROSYS. APROSYS (which stands for "Advanced PROtection SYStems") was a part of the 6th framework program (FP6) of the European Commission. It aimed at improving passive safety for European road users "in all relevant accident types and accident severities". The subproject SP6 of APROSYS was titled "Intelligent Safety Systems". It was one of the first projects that addressed the issue of closing the gap between active and passive safety systems. ***Active safety*** systems aim at preventing accidents by issuing a warning to the driver, helping him or her better control the situation or even by performing autonomous maneuvers such as braking or steering when a critical situation emerges. Examples of active safety systems are anti-lock braking system (ABS), lane departure warning system (LDWS), Emergency Brake Assist (EBA), etc. In contrast, ***passive safety*** measures target at mitigation of accident severity with respect to passenger injuries and reduction of fatalities. Typical passive safety systems are safety belts and airbags.

1.2.1 Goal of APROSYS SP6: Feasibility study of an integrated safety system

Active safety systems operate prior to an accident whereas passive safety systems are activated during the accident progression. The goal of SP6 was a feasibility study of an ***integrated safety system***, i.e., a system which would combine both aforementioned concepts. In the course of the project it has been shown that there was a great potential for such a system, especially in a side collision scenario [Tan08b]. Figure 1.1 shows top view snapshots of Euro NCAP crash tests in two typical side collision scenarios: pole impact and barrier impact. As one can imagine, doors area is the least protected zone of a car. Due to the very thin crumple zone at the vehicle side, energy absorption by classical passive safety elements is often insufficient, which leads to severe injuries of the car passengers. A remedy can be provided by additional proactive measures of passive safety that are able to better protect passengers but need more activation time and action space. This can be achieved, if one could detect an imminent collision in advance using methods of active safety systems.

These thoughts led to the development of the novel integrated side pre-crash safety system concept that has been designed and prototypically implemented within the scope of APROSYS SP6. The developed system consists of two parts – an environment perception part (sensing system) and an active part (actuators). In case of an imminent collision the sensing system would trigger the actuators.

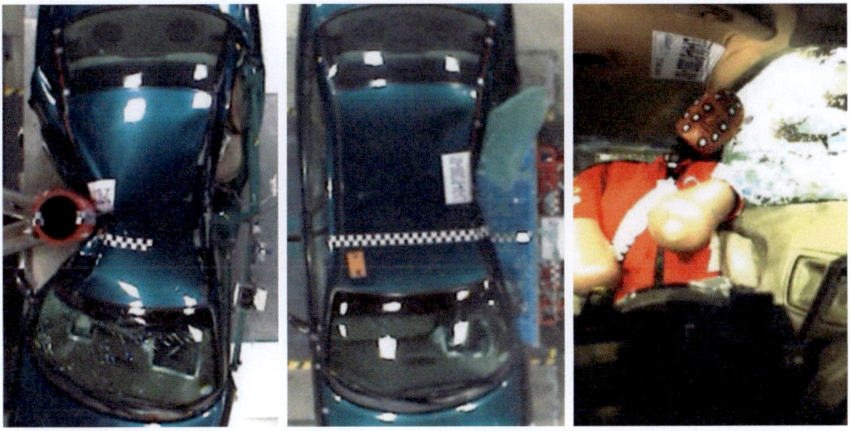

(a) Top view snapshot of a Euro NCAP pole impact crash test.

(b) Top view snapshot of a Euro NCAP crash test with a mobile deformable barrier (MDB).

(c) Snapshot of the vehicle interior during the barrier impact.

Figure 1.1: Snapshots of Euro NCAP crash tests with a Chrysler Neon car in two typical side collision scenarios: pole impact and barrier impact. Source: APROSYS SP6 presentation video. Original crash test videos were provided by Cidaut.

1.2.2 Actuator concepts

The working principle of the actuators should aim to modify the car structure in a way that would facilitate better energy absorption and reduction of intrusion depth. Besides, the actuator functionality should be reversible for the case of false alarms. For this purpose, several actuator concepts have been investigated. The idea of the first one which is shown in Figure 1.2 (a) was based on firing additional bolts between the doors and the car body. This would better connect the doors to the car body and prevent the doors from gaping.

The second concept is aimed at reinforcement of the doors and energy dissipation by means of an active "***friction beam***" devised as a link chain with adaptive stiffness. Different layers of the chain are bolted together by means of piezoceramic actuators as shown in Figure 1.2 (b). The energy absorption is achieved through friction instead of bending. Depending on the accident type the bending stiffness of the "beam" can be dynamically controlled before and/or during the crash by changing the friction coefficients of the connecting elements.

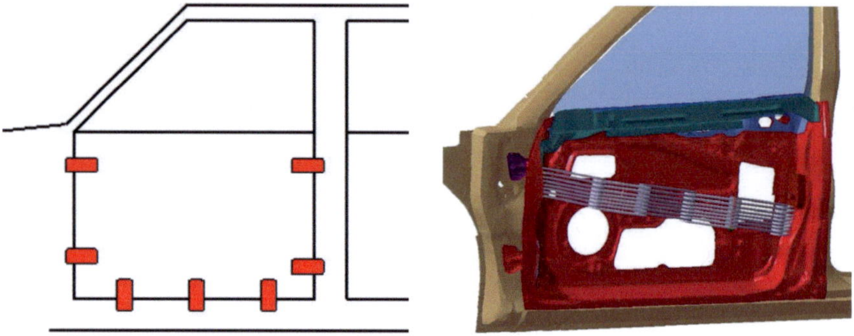

(a) (b)

Figure 1.2: Possible location of the door locking actuators **(a)** and possible placement of a friction beam actuator **(b)**. Source: [Sei05]

After performing crash simulations, both concepts had to be abandoned since it turned out that reinforcing and locking the doors would not solve the main problem, namely caving in of the center pillar (B-pillar).

The third concept proposes a structural door-seat coupling and the creation of a continuous connection from the outer door hull on the struck car side to the stiff car body regions on the unstruck side. The actuator should close all existing gaps between the outer sheet metal and the seat and redirect the loads to uncritical regions on the unstruck side, namely to the region, where the rocker meets the crash box and the floor. In normal driving conditions, the space between the seats and the doors as well as inside the door boxes is needed for the comfort controls. However, in case of an imminent accident, this space can be utilized for the purposes of safety. Simulations have shown that the new load path would unload the B-pillar from the first contact phase on and considerably reduce intrusion depth. Hence, the last concept has been selected for the prototypical implementation.

The working principle of the implemented actuator concept is depicted in Figure 1.3 and Figure 1.4. It consists of two active parts. The first one is a rotating door beam which is located in the door. In Figure 1.3 it is depicted as an orange block. It must stand upright during normal driving operation not to hinder the traveling of the glass. When triggered, it rotates into a horizontal position, thus filling the complete door box. The second part is a tube actuator. It is transversely integrated into the seat, just below the passenger's knees. In Figure 1.3 it is depicted in green.

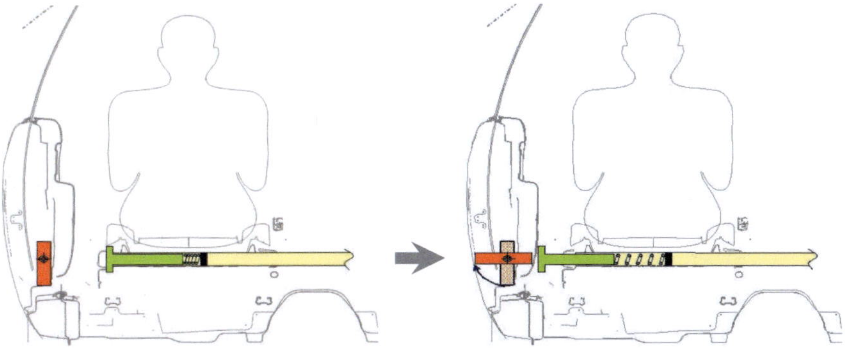

Figure 1.3: Working principle of the actuator with a structural door-seat coupling. Source: APROSYS SP6 presentation video.

In normal driving conditions, the space between the seat and the door must be free to allow the normal comfort functions. When triggered, a bolt pops out to meet the rotating door beam. As a result, all existing gaps between the outer sheet metal and the seat are closed. In this way, the actuators fulfill their safety function to occupy space which otherwise is needed for comfort applications.

Figure 1.4 (b) shows the prototypical implementation that has been evaluated in simulations and in real crash tests. The new load path is drawn in red. A possible implementation in future cars is illustrated in Figure 1.4 (a). As one may see in Figure 1.5, implementation of this concept led to a significant reduction of the intrusion depth in critical regions of the passenger cell, namely at the B-pillar and in the passenger seat area.

Other concepts for reducing the impact of side collisions on car passengers (both reversible and irreversible) are conceivable. They include (seat) belt pretensioning, inflating the air chambers in the seat's side bolsters of the backrest [Ric15] and side airbags (which have proven to reduce the collision force by 30%) [Bob16].

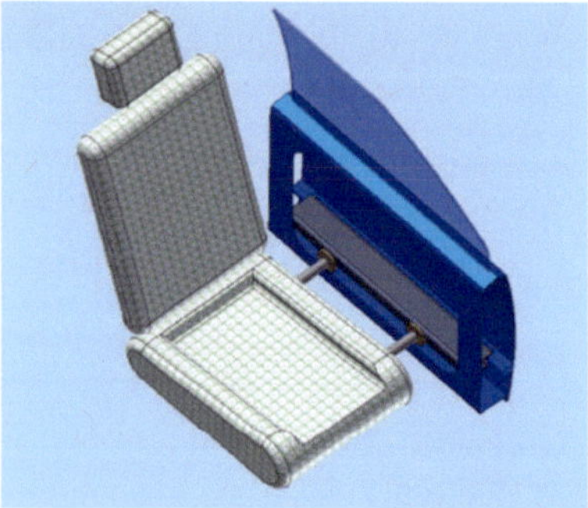

(a)

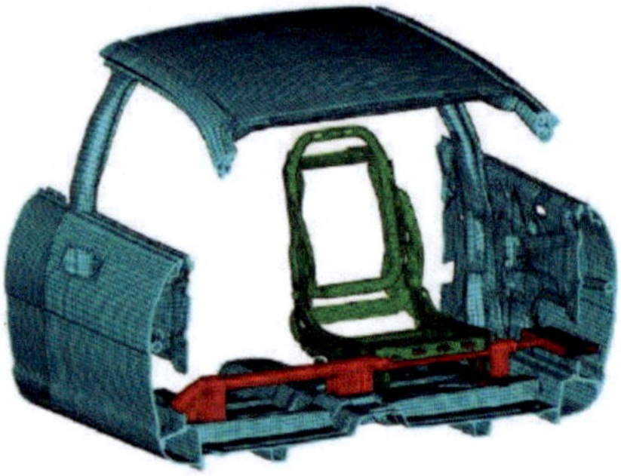

(b)

Figure 1.4: **(a)**: Possible actuator implementation. **(b)**: Implemented prototypical realization for the driver side. The new load path is depicted in red. Source: APROSYS SP6 presentation video.

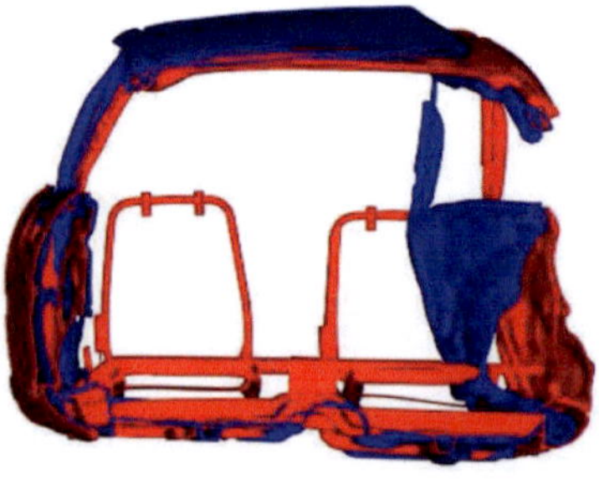

(a)

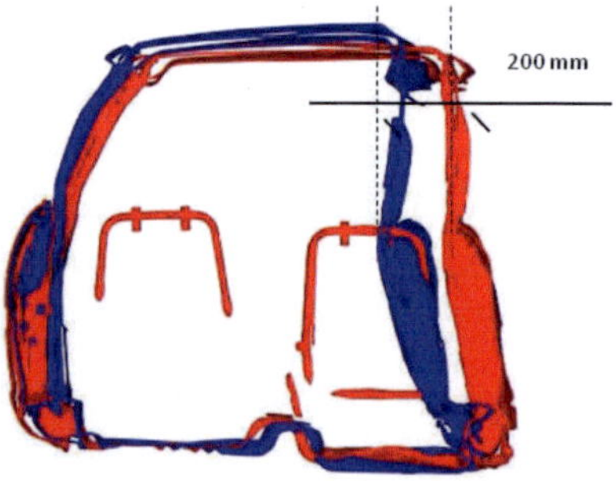

(b)

Figure 1.5: Effect of the actuator integration: simulated intrusion reduction at the B-pillar (a) and in the passenger seat area (b) in a car with deployed actuator (red) compared to a reference car without any modifications (blue). Source: [Tan08b].

For the system developed within the APROSYS SP6, the actuator system has to be triggered 200 ms in advance in order to react in time [Tan06]. This means that the sensing system should be able to provide an activation decision at least 200 ms before the impact.

1.2.3 Sensing system

The sensing system incorporates a stereo-video subsystem and a radar subsystem. Radar sensors provide reliable information about the radial distance and velocity of objects. However, their large angular uncertainty and the limited information about the measured radar reflex points do not allow for a sufficiently reliable classification. In contrast, video sensors allow for object detection with high angular resolution but with a rather high depth uncertainty. Hence, in order to increase the overall accuracy and reduce the number of false alarms, the output of both subsystems is combined within a fusion module. Resulting object hypotheses are passed to the subsequent risk assessment module. This module evaluates possible driving maneuvers of both ego-vehicle and potential bullet vehicles and estimates the probability of a collision. In case of an unavoidable collision the risk assessment module fires the actuators.

Figure 1.6 (a) shows placement of the video and radar sensors. Figure 1.6 (b) depicts the respective fields of view (FoV).

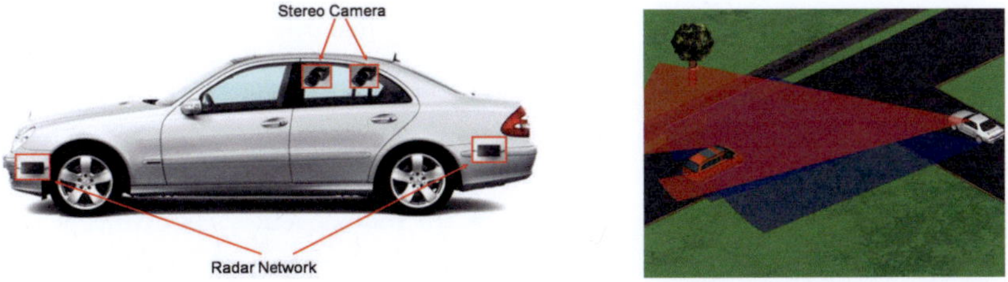

(a) (b)

Figure 1.6: (a) Placement of the sensors in the experimental vehicle. (b) Schematic illustration of the fields of view of both sensor systems (radar: blue, video: red).

Figure 1.7 shows the block diagram of the overall collision detection system. The implementation of the radar subsystem (drawn in cyan), the data fusion module (drawn in orange), and the risk assessment module (drawn in magenta) has been carried out at Continental AG (formerly Siemens VDO Automotive AG). The development of the video processing system (drawn in green) has been conducted by the Fraunhofer Institute of Optronics, System Technologies and Image Exploitation (Fraunhofer IOSB, formerly Fraunhofer IITB) in cooperation with Vision and Fusion Lab (Lehrstuhl für Interaktive Echtzeitsysteme) at Karlsruhe Institute of Technology (KIT). It was led by the author of this thesis.

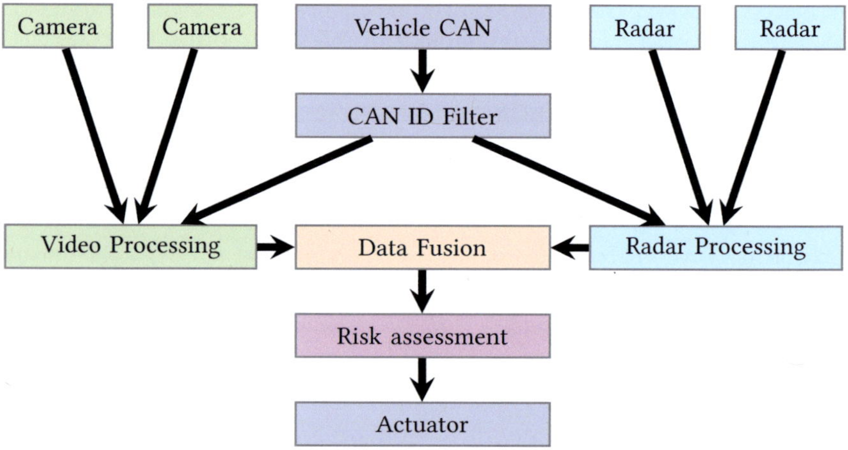

Figure 1.7: Block diagram of the APROSYS SP6 collision detection system. The sensing system consists of four blocks: video subsystem (drawn in green), radar subsystem (drawn in cyan), data fusion module (drawn in orange) and risk assessment module (drawn in magenta).

The following section gives a motivation for the chosen system concept of the video processing system (the green part) and provides basic details about the implemented stereo-video based object detection and tracking framework.

It is worth saying, that the research done within the APROSYS SP6 project has lead to the development of a side pre-crash safety system which can be found in today's cars [Ric15, Dai16]. The contemporary system "PRE-SAFE® Impulse side" available in recent Mercedes-Benz models is, however, based solely on radar sensors. In case of an imminent side collision it undertakes measures to pull the occupant away from the acute danger area. This is done by inflating air chambers in the seat's side bolsters of the backrest. The generated side impulse moves the passenger's head and upper body towards the center of the vehicle.

The growing demand for the 360° vehicle's environment perception, which is needed for highly automated and autonomous driving, in combination with the significant cost reduction of video sensors might lead to reconsideration of using side-looking video sensors in future cars.

1.3 Video processing framework

The goal of the video processing framework is environment perception in terms of robust and reliable real-time detection and tracking of relevant objects (moving vehicles but also stationary objects like trees and poles). To achieve this goal, following subtasks had to be solved:

- detection of relevant signatures in the sensor data,
- extraction of object parameters,
- data association (re-identification),
- dynamic state estimation, and
- track management.

Generally, there exist several possibilities for performing object detection from video images. In the case of a stationary camera (which is mostly the case in surveillance applications) detections are often obtained by means of a simple change detection between consecutive video images (2-frame differencing). Incorporating additional background and motion estimators increase robustness of such approaches. The task becomes much more complicated in case of a moving sensor platform. In this case, additional constraints have to be considered in order to separate foreground objects from the background. A good overview of various image-based object detection methods used in the automotive context is given in

[Sun06, Siv13b]. Figure 1.8 visualizes different possible data processing paths that can be taken for object detection when using video cameras.

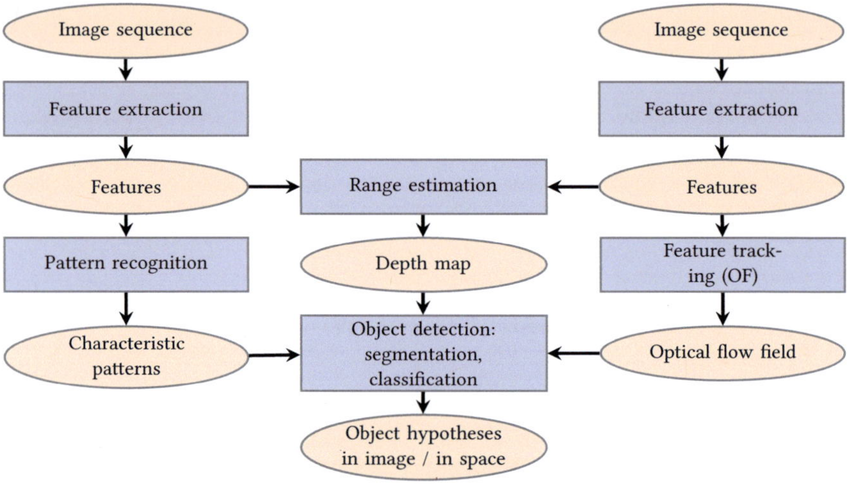

Figure 1.8: Possible data processing paths for object detection from image sequences.

The left path aims at object detection by means of pattern recognition methods [Kal98, Sun02, Ach04b, Siv09, Ryb10, Ohn15] or model-based vehicle detection [Kol97]. The right path makes use of perceived object motion in the image [Mey94, Krü95, Kol96, Lak02, Día03, Dem04, Wan05, Met06]. Multi-ocular arrangements allow for a computation of the range data, which makes it possible to generate object hypotheses directly in the 3D space [Zha98, Fra00, Kae02, Ned05, Cha05, Tou06]. Fusion of range and motion information is also possible both at the lowest level of image pixels and at the high level of object hypotheses [Dan02, Dan05, Fra05a, Gri09, Gri10, Siv11]. Many approaches, especially those developed for front-looking applications, use prior knowledge about the appearance of the vehicles, their relative position and / or motion with respect to the ego vehicle and tracked road markings (lanes) [Büc03, Siv13a]. Often they utilize such properties as symmetry, shadows, expected motion direction and typical appearance features of the vehicles that allow to greatly simplify detection algorithms [Zie92, Tou06, Dic94, Bet96, Han00].

However, in contrast to many forward looking driver assistance systems applications, in case of side-looking cameras, the task of object detection is extremely challenging since there is almost no exploitable a-priori information about the visible environment and the relevant objects. No additional references, such as tracked lanes and position of the road users relative to those lanes can be assumed. As illustrated in Figure 1.9, no restrictions about visibility of the road and objects, their range, appearance angle, orientation, velocity, and motion direction can be made. The same is true for object appearance signatures, such as symmetry, shadows, edge patterns, and texture. Since monochrome cameras have been used, the color information was also not available. This is aggravated by the fact that many different object classes with arbitrary position, orientation, and motion relative to the ego-vehicle have to be taken into consideration.

Figure 1.9: Examples of input images of a side-looking camera.

All this, in conjunction with rapidly changing scene and extensive occlusions (introduced by both restricted sensor field of view and foreground objects) make model-based and appearance-based object detection approaches unsuitable for a real-time application in this context. Thus, for the realization of a robust and reliable video-based object detection and tracking, a generic approach had to be developed [Gri07]. Only very few assumptions could be adopted. One of them is the so called "flat world assumption" meaning that visible world view could be described by means of a ground plane and all objects are situated on this plane. The second assumption is the rigidity of objects of interest. These considerations led to development of the stereo-video based object detection and tracking system described below. A rough schematic diagram of the resulting data processing is shown in Figure 1.10.

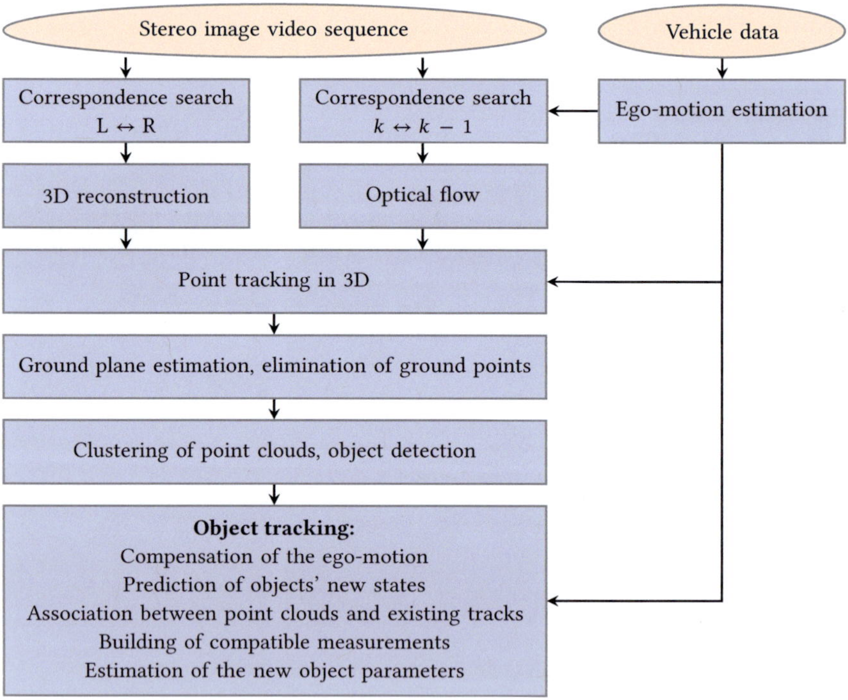

Figure 1.10: Overall framework for visual object detection and tracking.

Finding corresponding pixels between two stereo images allows for estimation of their range as it will be shown in Section 5.5. Known position and orientation of the cameras with respect to the world coordinate system allow for the reconstruction of the corresponding 3D coordinates. Tracking image points between consecutive images of a video sequence (Optical Flow) provides the possibility to determine their 3-dimensional velocity (this approach is known as "6D-Vision" [Fra05a]). After estimation of the ground plane and elimination of the ground points, remaining points may be clustered into point clouds as shown in Figures 1.11 and 1.12. Those point clouds give detections for the subsequent object tracking.

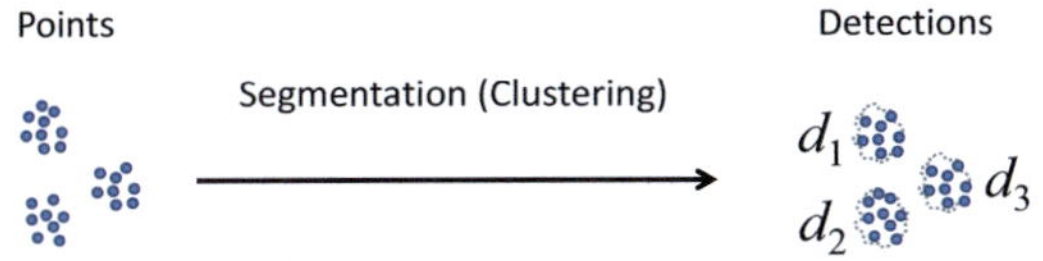

Figure 1.11: Clustering principle

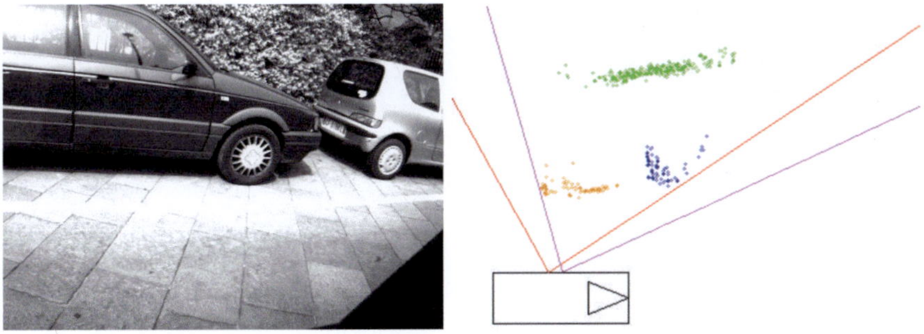

(a) Original camera image.

(b) Clustered point clouds (top view). Red and purple lines visualize the field of view (FoV) of both cameras which are mounted on the left side of the vehicle under test (VUT, visualized by the black rectangle).

Figure 1.12: Object detections obtained by clustering 3d points.

For acceleration of the point clustering, the assumption can be made that one of the dimensions (height of the points above ground) is irrelevant for separation of the point clouds of different objects. Massive object parts that are hanging above ground, such as bridges, tree crowns, etc. are assumed to be taken out of the consideration by preceding preprocessing steps, such as building of regions of interest (ROIs) in the images, removal of too high points, etc. Hence, it is enough to consider the projection of the points onto the ground plane. This reduces the number of dimensions to be considered from three to two. If point velocity is used as an additional clustering parameter, the number of dimensions becomes four.

The next steps comprise building and maintaining object hypotheses as well as estimation of object parameters, such as position, extent, motion direction, velocity, etc. (object tracking). This requires estimation of the new state of tracked objects taking into account the ego-motion between two video frames (dynamic state prediction), extraction of object parameters out of obtained point clouds (measurement generation), association of the obtained point clouds with existing tracks (data association), and parameters update for all tracked objects (dynamic state update).

The output of the resulting video processing for a collision scenario is shown in Figure 1.13. 3-dimensional point clouds that have been obtained by means of stereo processing are visualized by means of colored dots. Their depth is visualized in the camera image by means of vertical lines to the estimated ground (Figure 1.13 (a)). In the top view (Figure 1.13 (b)), the estimated relative object velocity is visualized by a thick red line.

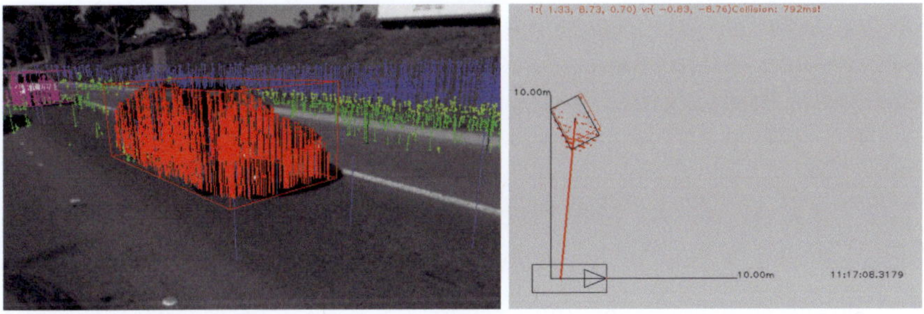

(a) Visualization of video processing results in the original camera image.

(b) Visulaization of video processing results in the top view.

Figure 1.13: Visualization of the video processing results in a side collision scenario.

1.4 Focus: Improvement of object tracking in case of corrupted detections

As mentioned at the beginning of the chapter, the problem of uncertainties, especially of those related to corrupted detections poses a serious challenge to the tracking process. After development of the above-mentioned stereo-video based object detection and implementation of a classical object tracking scheme (which is described in detail in the following chapters), the author had to realize that, although working quite well in crash tests and "clean" scenarios, the tracking had troubles coping with corrupted detections in case of noisy data and occlusions. The well-known weaknesses of the stereo correspondence search algorithms in areas with regular patterns and in homogeneous image areas lead to missing or erroneous range estimation for some image pixels and regions. This resulted in incomplete, falsely augmented, merged, clutter-based, and split detections. Another problem posed incomplete and split detections due to partial occlusions of background objects by both objects in the foreground and by field of view borders of the sensors. Incorporation of measurements obtained from such detections led to biased tracking results, track losses, or instantiation of phantom tracks. This, in turn, could result in failure of the overall system due to missed or false alarms. Thus, the main focus of this work was laid on the development of a robust video-based object tracking system which has the potential to cope with the above-mentioned effects.

1.5 Outline of the thesis

The thesis is structured as follows: Chapter 2 introduces theoretical groundwork of object tracking and provides a formal solution derivation for the state estimation and data association problems. Chapter 3 provides a detailed problem statement regarding corrupted detections and gives an overview of the related work and alternative approaches. A novel solution concept for handling corrupted detections is presented in Chapter 4. Chapter 5 gives details about the video-based object detection and tracking framework which has been introduced in Section 1.3. It provides basic knowledge that is required for understanding each processing step and discusses implementation details of the proposed concept. Chapter 6 deals with evaluation aspects, discusses the achieved results and possible improvements. Finally, a short summary and an outlook is given in Chapter 7.

2 Basics of object tracking

This chapter introduces the basic concepts that will be used in the rest of the thesis. Section 2.1 gives a short introduction to the Multi-Object-Tracking task and its subtasks, Section 2.2 deals with the basics of dynamic state estimation problem, and Section 2.3 provides probabilistic groundwork for solving the data association problem. Subsections 2.2.1, 2.3.3, 2.3.4, and 2.3.6 are key to understanding the formal derivation in Section 4.2.

2.1 Introduction to object tracking

The aim of object tracking is continuous localization of objects (cars, people, airplanes, ships, etc.) in an environment by processing data of sensors such as sonars, radars, lidars, or video cameras. In general, the problem of (automatic) object tracking is divided into four subtasks:

- object detection,
- data association (re-identification),
- dynamic state estimation (filtering), and
- track management.

The first subtask comprises processing of the raw sensor data and building object hypotheses in the sensor data by means of pattern recognition methods such as thresholding, background-foreground segmentation, motion detection, etc. The second subtask is responsible for the correct interpretation of the collected observations, i.e., assignment of sensor measurements to the tracked objects (tracks). The third subtask deals with estimation of the dynamic state of the objects (e.g., kinematics) from a sequence of (noisy) measurements. Finally, the forth subtask is responsible for a consistent internal representation of the tracked objects, which includes instantiation of new and deletion of obsolete tracks. Usually, detections and measurements are used as synonyms. However, in the following we have to make a distinction between those two terms since it will be crucial for the proposed concept. The term ***"detection"*** will be used to describe object representation in the raw sensor data obtained by means of a detection process, i.e., blobs in the image or point clouds in a 3D space obtained by means of background-foreground segmentation, motion analysis, etc. The term ***"measurement"*** will be used to describe the vector of descriptive features such as position and size that can be extracted from the obtained detections. Thus, we will define five instead of four subtasks of object tracking, namely

- object detection,
- generation of measurements,
- data association (re-identification),
- dynamic state estimation (filtering), and
- track management.

An illustration of the resulting object tracking scheme is given in Figure 2.1.

The major focus of this thesis is on the second half of this data processing chain, i.e., on measurement generation, data association and dynamic state estimation (red rectangle). Object detections are considered to be given by a preceding object detection algorithm and to be specified as conglomeration of points in the image or in the 3D space (blobs in the image, 3D point clouds). In most tracking applications, the measurement generation process is implemented by extracting the desired measurement parameters directly from the bounding boxes of the obtained detections. These are fed into the data association and dynamic state estimation algorithms. In this thesis we will question this strategy and propose an alternative approach which will take into account the possibility of getting corrupted detections.

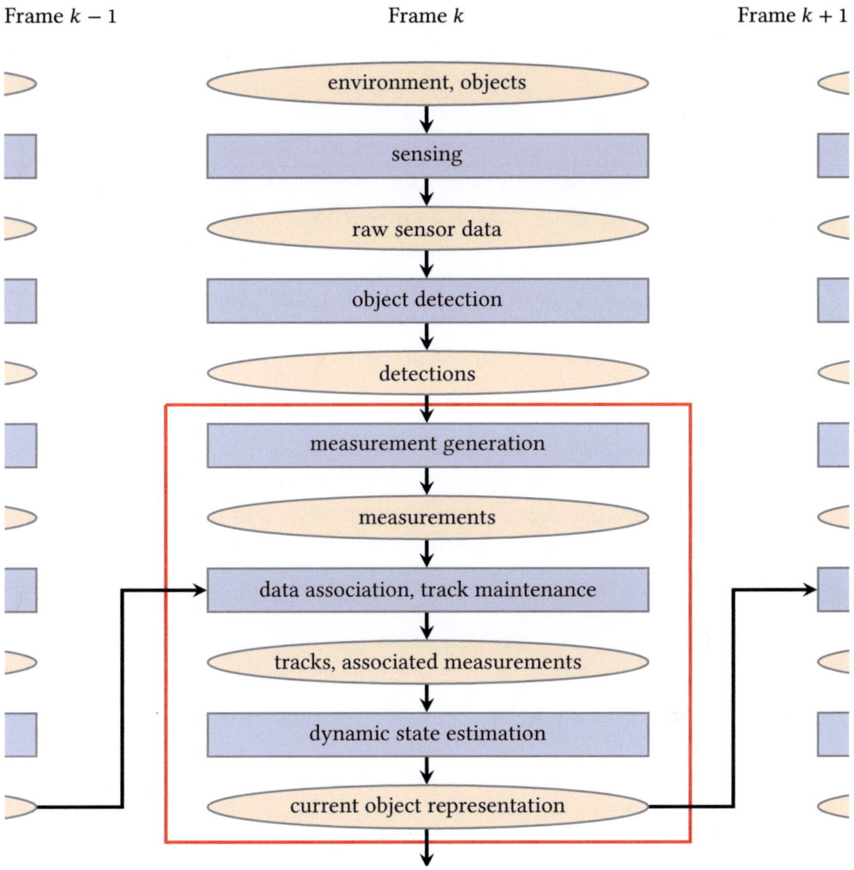

Figure 2.1: Object tracking scheme.

2.2 Dynamic state estimation

Each measurement process contains sources of noise. Thus, obtained measurements may differ from the expected values. The aim of a dynamic state estimator is the determination of the real value of an unknown system state from the obtained (noisy) measurements. This is done by the so-called filtering algorithms that aim at minimization of the noise effects. There exists a variety of such methods. Most of the modern tracking systems use statistical filters that are based on the Bayesian approach. They model the system state and the noise as random variables and estimate their statistics using certain assumptions about their nature.

Applications with real-time requirements often cannot consider the entire measurement history for achieving the best estimation result. Thus, they proceed recursively using only the last estimated system state and the current measurements. The underlying assumption is that all previous measurements are incorporated in the estimated state and are not required to be processed again in each time step.

A system state $\mathbf{x}_k$ at discrete time point k is modeled as a realization of a random variable $\boldsymbol{X}$ in the state space $\mathcal{X}$. A state estimator represents the system state by means of a ***probability density function (pdf)*** $p(\mathbf{x}_k)$ in case of continuous state space and by means of a ***probability mass function (pmf)*** $P(\mathbf{x}_k)$ in case of a discrete state space. The system state between two discrete points in time k and $k+1$ is assumed to behave according to a known system evolution function f (***system model***):

$$\boldsymbol{X}_{k+1} = f(\boldsymbol{X}_k, \mathbf{u}_k, \boldsymbol{W}_k)\,, \tag{2.1}$$

where $\mathbf{u}_k$ represents the (known) system control parameters and $\boldsymbol{W}_k$ represents the stochastic component which cannot be modeled analytically (system noise). The underlying assumption here is that the system is memoryless in the sense that a system state $\mathbf{x}_{k+1}$ at time step $k+1$ depends only on the current state $\mathbf{x}_k$, current control parameters $\mathbf{u}_k$ and noise $\boldsymbol{W}_k$ and does not depend on the previous states

$\mathbf{x}_1, ..., \mathbf{x}_{k-1}$ (Markov property):

$$P(\mathbf{x}_{k+1}|\mathbf{x}_1, ..., \mathbf{x}_k, \mathbf{u}_1, ..., \mathbf{u}_k) = P(\mathbf{x}_{k+1}|\mathbf{x}_k, \mathbf{u}_k) \text{ for the discrete case,} \tag{2.2}$$

$$p(\mathbf{x}_{k+1}|\mathbf{x}_1, ..., \mathbf{x}_k, \mathbf{u}_1, ..., \mathbf{u}_k) = p(\mathbf{x}_{k+1}|\mathbf{x}_k, \mathbf{u}_k) \text{ for the continuous case.} \tag{2.3}$$

This allows to model system evolution as a Markov process and to use recursive formula for state estimation using only the last estimated system state and the current measurements. The probability $P(\mathbf{x}_{k+1}|\mathbf{x}_k, ...)$ in case of discrete state space is called ***transition probability*** and $p(\mathbf{x}_{k+1}|\mathbf{x}_k, ...)$ in case of continuous state space ***transition density***.

The observations $\mathbf{z}_k$ are modeled as a realization of a random variable $\boldsymbol{Z}$ in the measurement space $\mathfrak{Z}$. The measurement process is modeled by means of a ***measurement model*** $h(\boldsymbol{X}_k, \boldsymbol{V}_k)$:

$$\boldsymbol{Z}_k = h(\boldsymbol{X}_k, \boldsymbol{V}_k), \tag{2.4}$$

where $\boldsymbol{V}_k$ represents the stochastic component of the measurement process (measurement noise). The probability $P(\mathbf{z}|\mathbf{x})$ for getting an observation $\mathbf{z}$ given a system state $\mathbf{x}$ is called ***emission probability***. In the case of a continuous observation space it becomes the ***emission density*** $p(\mathbf{z}|\mathbf{x})$.

If the system state can not be observed directly, one speaks of the ***Hidden Markov Model (HMM)***. The relation between system states and observations of a Hidden Markov Model for the case of discrete states is shown in Figure 2.2.

The state estimation is done using the so-called Predictor-Corrector cycle, which consist of two steps:

Prediction of the probability density functions of the new system state and expected measurements based on the latest state estimate by using the system model and the measurement model.

Correction of the estimated system state and adaptation of both models based on the actually obtained measurements. It is also called ***Innovation***, ***Update***, or ***Filtering***.

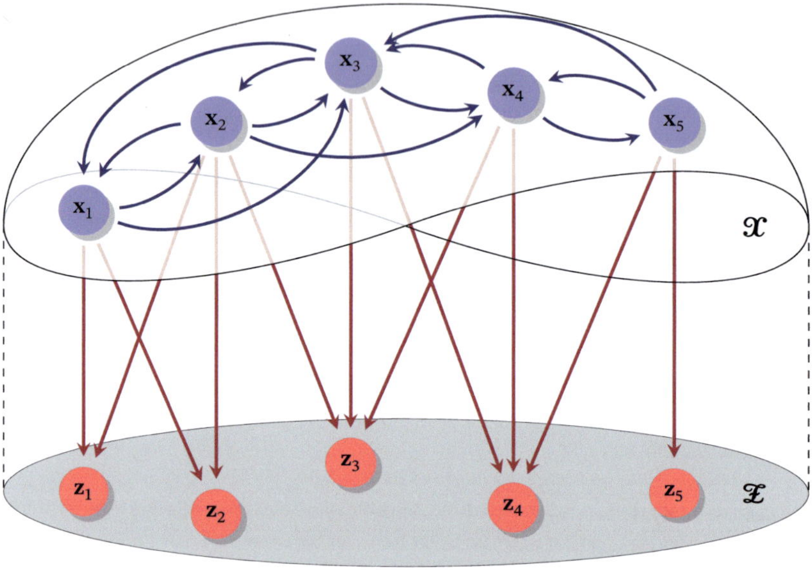

Figure 2.2: Relation between system states and observations in a Hidden Markov Model. Here, the subscripts of the states $\mathbf{x}$ and observations $\mathbf{z}$ are used not for indicating the time index k but serve for enumeration of both sets. Possible state transitions are represented by blue arrows, emission probabilities are indicated as purple arrows. For the sake of simplification, the arrows are not labeled with the respective transition probabilities $P(\mathbf{x}_{k+1,j}|\mathbf{x}_{k,i})$ and the emission probabilities $P(\mathbf{z}_{k,j}|\mathbf{x}_{k,i})$.

The basic principle of a recursive statistical filter is shown in Figure 2.3. The filter works recursively in a predictor-corrector cycle starting with an initial system state estimate $\hat{\mathbf{x}}_1$. Given a state estimation at time step $k-1$ the filter propagates it in the time using the system model $f(\boldsymbol{X}_k, \mathbf{u}_k, \boldsymbol{W}_k)$. In this way, an a-priori estimate of the current system state $\hat{\mathbf{x}}_k^-$ is obtained. Then, the measurement model $h(\boldsymbol{X}_k, \boldsymbol{V}_k)$ is used for estimating the expected measurement $\hat{\mathbf{z}}_k$. After having obtained the actual measurement $\mathbf{z}_k$, a correction step is performed, in which both the current state and the uncertainties of the both models are updated based on the difference (residuals) between the predicted and actually obtained measurements.

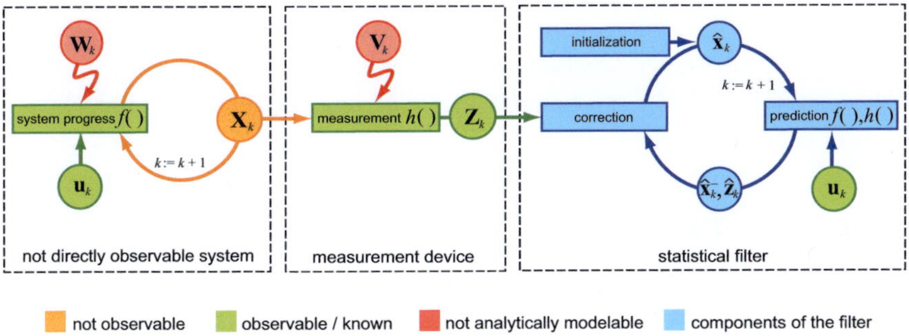

Figure 2.3: Illustration of the dependencies between the observed system and the filtering process of a statistical filter. The filter recursively estimates the unknown system state $\boldsymbol{X}_k$ from the measurement $\boldsymbol{Z}_k$ and estimated state $\hat{\mathbf{x}}_{k-1}$ using the system model $\boldsymbol{X}_{k+1} = f(\boldsymbol{X}_k, \mathbf{u}_k, \boldsymbol{W}_k)$ and the measurement model $\boldsymbol{Z}_k = h(\boldsymbol{X}_k, \boldsymbol{V}_k)$.

One of the simplest statistical dynamic state estimators is the ***Kalman Filter (KF)*** introduced by R. E. Kalman in 1960 [Kal60]. It assumes Gaussian distributions of both the state and the noise variables and provides equations for propagation of those distributions using linear system and measurement models. For the case of $\boldsymbol{W}_k$ and $\boldsymbol{V}_k$ being uncorrelated and having white Gaussian distribution with zero mean, the Kalman Filter is an optimal estimator in the sense of the least square errors and Bayesian filtering.

A Gaussian distribution can be represented by the two first moments (mean and covariance matrix) and is easily propagated through a linear system resulting in another Gaussian distribution. In case of non-linearities in at least one of the both models, this is not the case anymore. For coping with this problem, two different approaches have been proposed. The first one aims at approximation of the non-linear function by using the Taylor series expansion around the mean of the Gaussian distribution (***Extended Kalman Filter (EKF)***, ***Iterative Extended Kalman Filter (IEKF)***). The second approach aims at approximation of the distribution by means of a set of points that can be propagated through the non-linear functions and serve for determination of the new distribution parameters (***Unscented Kalman Filter (UKF)***, ***Central Difference Kalman Filter (CDKF)***, etc.). A generalization of this approach leads to the family of the ***Sequential Monte Carlo Methods (SMCM)***, also known as ***Particle Filters (PF)***.

An overview of different dynamic state estimators can be found in [Bar93, Bro98, Sim06]. The following subsections present the basics of the linear Kalman Filter, Extended Kalman Filter and Iterative Extended Kalman Filter since they will be used in the following chapters.

2.2.1 Linear Kalman Filter

In the case of the linear Kalman Filter, a system model and a measurement model are given as linear equations

$$\boldsymbol{X}_k = \mathbf{F}\boldsymbol{X}_{k-1} + \mathbf{G}\mathbf{u}_k + \boldsymbol{W}_k \qquad \text{(state equation)} \tag{2.5}$$

and

$$\boldsymbol{Z}_k = \mathbf{H}\boldsymbol{X}_k + \boldsymbol{V}_k \qquad \text{(measurement equation)} \tag{2.6}$$

with $\mathbf{F}$, $\mathbf{G}$ and $\mathbf{H}$ being the system matrix, the control matrix, and the measurement matrix, respectively, and

$$\boldsymbol{X}_k \sim \mathcal{N}(\hat{\mathbf{x}}_k, \mathbf{P}_{\mathbf{X}_k\mathbf{X}_k}) \tag{2.7}$$

with

$$\begin{aligned}\mathbf{P}_{\mathbf{X}_k\mathbf{X}_k} := \mathrm{Cov}(\boldsymbol{X}_k, \boldsymbol{X}_k) &= \mathbb{E}\big[(\boldsymbol{X}_k - \mathbb{E}[\boldsymbol{X}_k])(\boldsymbol{X}_k - \mathbb{E}[\boldsymbol{X}_k])^T\big] \\ &= \mathbb{E}\big[(\boldsymbol{X}_k - \hat{\mathbf{x}}_k)(\boldsymbol{X}_k - \hat{\mathbf{x}}_k)^T\big] .\end{aligned} \tag{2.8}$$

The noise components $\boldsymbol{W}$ and $\boldsymbol{V}$ are assumed to be uncorrelated with each other and with the initial state $\mathbf{X}_0$ and to be distributed according to white Gaussian distribution with zero mean and known covariance matrices $\mathbf{Q}_k$ and $\mathbf{R}_k$:

$$\boldsymbol{W}_k \sim \mathcal{N}(\mathbf{0}, \mathbf{Q}_k) , \tag{2.9}$$

$$\boldsymbol{V}_k \sim \mathcal{N}(\mathbf{0}, \mathbf{R}_k) , \tag{2.10}$$

with

$$\mathbf{P}_{\boldsymbol{W}_k\boldsymbol{W}_t} := \mathrm{Cov}(\boldsymbol{W}_k, \boldsymbol{W}_t) = \mathbb{E}\big[\boldsymbol{W}_k\boldsymbol{W}_t^T\big] = \begin{cases} \mathbf{Q}_k & \text{for } t = k \\ \mathbf{0} & \text{for } t \neq k\,, \end{cases} \tag{2.11}$$

$$\mathbf{P}_{\boldsymbol{V}_k\boldsymbol{V}_t} := \mathrm{Cov}(\boldsymbol{V}_k, \boldsymbol{V}_t) = \mathbb{E}\big[\boldsymbol{V}_k\boldsymbol{V}_t^T\big] = \begin{cases} \mathbf{R}_k & \text{for } t = k \\ \mathbf{0} & \text{for } t \neq k\,, \end{cases} \tag{2.12}$$

$$\mathbf{P}_{\boldsymbol{W}_k\boldsymbol{V}_t} := \mathrm{Cov}(\boldsymbol{W}_k, \boldsymbol{V}_t) = \mathbb{E}\big[\boldsymbol{W}_k\boldsymbol{V}_t^T\big] = \mathbf{0} \quad \text{for all } t \text{ and } k\,, \tag{2.13}$$

$$\mathbf{P}_{\boldsymbol{X}_0\boldsymbol{W}_t} := \mathrm{Cov}(\boldsymbol{X}_0, \boldsymbol{W}_t) = \mathbb{E}\big[\boldsymbol{X}_0\boldsymbol{W}_t^T\big] = \mathbf{0} \quad \text{for all } t\,, \tag{2.14}$$

$$\mathbf{P}_{\boldsymbol{X}_0\boldsymbol{V}_t} := \mathrm{Cov}(\boldsymbol{X}_0, \boldsymbol{V}_t) = \mathbb{E}\big[\boldsymbol{X}_0\boldsymbol{V}_t^T\big] = \mathbf{0} \quad \text{for all } t\,. \tag{2.15}$$

There is no possibility to influence the observed system in the considered application. Hence, the control parameter vector $\mathbf{u}$ will be omitted in the following.

As mentioned above, the Kalman Filter gives estimates of the two first moments $\hat{\mathbf{x}}_k$ and $\mathbf{P}_{\boldsymbol{X}_k\boldsymbol{X}_k}$ of the distribution of the true state $\mathbf{x}_k$. The a-priori estimates, which are obtained during the prediction step and do not account for the current measurement are denoted by $\hat{\mathbf{x}}_k^-$ (state prediction) and $\mathbf{P}_{\boldsymbol{X}_k^-\boldsymbol{X}_k^-}$ (state covariance prediction):

$$\hat{\mathbf{x}}_k^- = \mathbb{E}\big[\boldsymbol{X}_k|\mathbf{z}_{1:k-1}\big] \tag{2.16}$$

$$\mathbf{P}_{\boldsymbol{X}_k^-\boldsymbol{X}_k^-} = \mathbb{E}\big[(\boldsymbol{X}_k - \hat{\mathbf{x}}_k^-)(\boldsymbol{X}_k - \hat{\mathbf{x}}_k^-)^T\big]\,. \tag{2.17}$$

Hereby, $\mathbf{z}_{1:k-1}$ denotes the set of all observations obtained up to time step $k-1$.

The correction step incorporates the current measurement into the estimation and obtains the a-posteriori estimates

$$\hat{\mathbf{x}}_k = \mathbb{E}\big[\boldsymbol{X}_k|\mathbf{z}_{1:k}\big] \tag{2.18}$$

$$\mathbf{P}_{\boldsymbol{X}_k\boldsymbol{X}_k} = \mathbb{E}\big[(\boldsymbol{X}_k - \hat{\mathbf{x}}_k)(\boldsymbol{X}_k - \hat{\mathbf{x}}_k)^T\big]\,. \tag{2.19}$$

The Kalman Filter is initialized at time step $k = 1$ with an initial state estimate $\hat{\mathbf{x}}_1$ and a covariance matrix $\mathbf{P}_{\boldsymbol{X}_1\boldsymbol{X}_1}$. The recursive expression for the calculation of the a-priori estimates $\hat{\mathbf{x}}_k^-$ and $\mathbf{P}_{\boldsymbol{X}_k^-\boldsymbol{X}_k^-}$ at time step k from the a-posteriori estimates $\hat{\mathbf{x}}_{k-1}$ and $\mathbf{P}_{\boldsymbol{X}_{k-1}\boldsymbol{X}_{k-1}}$ at the previous time step $k-1$ (***prediction***) is derived by using the state equation (2.5) in the expectation computation:

$$\begin{aligned}
\hat{\mathbf{x}}_k^- &= \mathbb{E}\big[\boldsymbol{X}_k|\mathbf{z}_{1:k-1}\big] \\
&= \mathbb{E}\big[\mathbf{F}\boldsymbol{X}_{k-1} + \boldsymbol{W}_{k-1}|\mathbf{z}_{1:k-1}\big] \\
&= \mathbb{E}\big[\mathbf{F}\boldsymbol{X}_{k-1}|\mathbf{z}_{1:k-1}\big] + \mathbb{E}\big[\boldsymbol{W}_{k-1}|\mathbf{z}_{1:k-1}\big] \\
&= \mathbf{F}\mathbb{E}\big[\boldsymbol{X}_{k-1}|\mathbf{z}_{1:k-1}\big] + \mathbf{0} \\
&= \mathbf{F}\hat{\mathbf{x}}_{k-1}
\end{aligned} \tag{2.20}$$

and

$$\begin{aligned}
\mathbf{P}_{\boldsymbol{X}_k^-\boldsymbol{X}_k^-} =& \mathbb{E}\big[(\boldsymbol{X}_k - \hat{\mathbf{x}}_k^-)(\boldsymbol{X}_k - \hat{\mathbf{x}}_k^-)^T\big] \\
=& \mathbb{E}\big[(\mathbf{F}\boldsymbol{X}_{k-1} + \boldsymbol{W}_{k-1} - \mathbf{F}\hat{\mathbf{x}}_{k-1})(\mathbf{F}\boldsymbol{X}_{k-1} + \boldsymbol{W}_{k-1} - \mathbf{F}\hat{\mathbf{x}}_{k-1})^T\big] \\
=& \mathbb{E}\Big[\big(\mathbf{F}(\boldsymbol{X}_{k-1} - \hat{\mathbf{x}}_{k-1}) + \boldsymbol{W}_{k-1}\big)\big(\mathbf{F}(\boldsymbol{X}_{k-1} - \hat{\mathbf{x}}_{k-1}) + \boldsymbol{W}_{k-1}\big)^T\Big] \\
=& \mathbb{E}\big[\mathbf{F}(\boldsymbol{X}_{k-1} - \hat{\mathbf{x}}_{k-1})(\boldsymbol{X}_{k-1} - \hat{\mathbf{x}}_{k-1})^T\mathbf{F}^T\big] \\
& + \mathbb{E}\big[\mathbf{F}(\boldsymbol{X}_{k-1} - \hat{\mathbf{x}}_{k-1})\boldsymbol{W}_{k-1}^T\big] + \mathbb{E}\big[\boldsymbol{W}_{k-1}(\boldsymbol{X}_{k-1} - \hat{\mathbf{x}}_{k-1})^T\mathbf{F}^T\big] \\
& + \mathbb{E}\big[\boldsymbol{W}_{k-1}\boldsymbol{W}_{k-1}^T\big] \\
=& \mathbf{F}\mathbb{E}\big[(\boldsymbol{X}_{k-1} - \hat{\mathbf{x}}_{k-1})(\boldsymbol{X}_{k-1} - \hat{\mathbf{x}}_{k-1})^T\big]\mathbf{F}^T + \mathbf{0} + \mathbf{0} + \mathbf{Q}_k \\
=& \mathbf{F}\mathbf{P}_{\boldsymbol{X}_{k-1}\boldsymbol{X}_{k-1}}\mathbf{F}^T + \mathbf{Q}_k\,.
\end{aligned} \tag{2.21}$$

In equation (2.21), $\mathbf{Q}_k$ represents the unpredictable noise component. The uncertainty $\mathbf{P}_{\boldsymbol{X}_k^-\boldsymbol{X}_k^-}$ of the state grows in each time step by this expression. The counteraction is achieved by integrating new information about the system state that is contained in the new measurements. This is done in the ***correction*** step (***update***):

$$\begin{aligned}
\hat{\mathbf{x}}_k &= (\mathbf{I} - \mathbf{K}_k\mathbf{H}) \cdot \hat{\mathbf{x}}_k^- + \mathbf{K}_k \cdot \mathbf{z}_k \\
&= \hat{\mathbf{x}}_k^- + \mathbf{K}_k \cdot (\mathbf{z}_k - \mathbf{H}\hat{\mathbf{x}}_k^-) \\
&= \hat{\mathbf{x}}_k^- + \mathbf{K}_k \cdot (\mathbf{z}_k - \hat{\mathbf{z}}_k) \\
&= \hat{\mathbf{x}}_k^- + \mathbf{K}_k \cdot \tilde{\mathbf{z}}_k\,,
\end{aligned} \tag{2.22}$$

and

$$\begin{aligned}\mathbf{P}_{\boldsymbol{X}_k\boldsymbol{X}_k} &= \mathbb{E}\big[(\boldsymbol{X}_k - \hat{\mathbf{x}}_k)(\boldsymbol{X}_k - \hat{\mathbf{x}}_k)^T\big] \\ &= \mathbf{P}_{\boldsymbol{X}_k^-\boldsymbol{X}_k^-} + \mathbf{K}_k\mathbf{P}_{\tilde{\boldsymbol{Z}}_k\tilde{\boldsymbol{Z}}_k}\mathbf{K}_k^T \\ &= \mathbf{P}_{\boldsymbol{X}_k^-\boldsymbol{X}_k^-} + \mathbf{K}_k\mathbf{H}\mathbf{P}_{\boldsymbol{X}_k^-\boldsymbol{X}_k^-}\end{aligned} \tag{2.23}$$

using ***innovation*** $\tilde{\mathbf{z}}_k$ (also called ***residuum***) – a difference between the actually obtained measurement $\mathbf{z}_k$ and the predicted measurement $\hat{\mathbf{z}}_k$

$$\begin{aligned}\tilde{\mathbf{z}}_k &:= \mathbf{z}_k - \hat{\mathbf{z}}_k \\ &= \mathbf{z}_k - \mathbf{H}\hat{\mathbf{x}}_k^-\end{aligned} \tag{2.24}$$

and Kalman gain $\mathbf{K}_k$

$$\begin{aligned}\mathbf{K}_k &= \mathbf{P}_{\boldsymbol{X}_k^-\boldsymbol{X}_k^-}\mathbf{H}^T\mathbf{P}_{\tilde{\boldsymbol{Z}}_k\tilde{\boldsymbol{Z}}_k}^{-1} \\ &= \mathbf{P}_{\boldsymbol{X}_k^-\boldsymbol{X}_k^-}\mathbf{H}^T(\mathbf{H}\mathbf{P}_{\boldsymbol{X}_k^-\boldsymbol{X}_k^-}\mathbf{H}^T + \mathbf{R}_k)^{-1}\end{aligned} \tag{2.25}$$

where the innovation covariance $\mathbf{P}_{\tilde{\boldsymbol{Z}}_k\tilde{\boldsymbol{Z}}_k}$ is derived as follows:

$$\begin{aligned}\mathbf{P}_{\tilde{\boldsymbol{Z}}_k\tilde{\boldsymbol{Z}}_k} =& \mathbb{E}\big[\tilde{\boldsymbol{Z}}_k\tilde{\boldsymbol{Z}}_k^T\big] \\ =& \mathbb{E}\Big[\big((\boldsymbol{Z}_k - \hat{\mathbf{z}}_k) - \mathbf{0}\big)\big((\boldsymbol{Z}_k - \hat{\mathbf{z}}_k) - \mathbf{0}\big)^T\Big] \\ =& \mathbb{E}\big[(\boldsymbol{Z}_k - \hat{\mathbf{z}}_k)(\boldsymbol{Z}_k - \hat{\mathbf{z}}_k)^T\big] \\ & (=\mathbf{P}_{\boldsymbol{Z}_k\boldsymbol{Z}_k}) \\ =& \mathbb{E}\big[(\mathbf{H}\boldsymbol{X}_k + \boldsymbol{V}_k - \mathbf{H}\hat{\mathbf{x}}_k)(\mathbf{H}\boldsymbol{X}_k + \boldsymbol{V}_k - \mathbf{H}\hat{\mathbf{x}}_k)^T\big] \\ =& \mathbb{E}\big[(\mathbf{H}(\boldsymbol{X}_k - \hat{\mathbf{x}}_k) + \boldsymbol{V}_k)(\mathbf{H}(\boldsymbol{X}_k - \hat{\mathbf{x}}_k) + \boldsymbol{V}_k)^T\big] \\ =& \mathbb{E}\big[\mathbf{H}(\boldsymbol{X}_k - \hat{\mathbf{x}}_k)(\boldsymbol{X}_k - \hat{\mathbf{x}}_k)^T\mathbf{H}^T\big] + \mathbb{E}\big[\mathbf{H}(\boldsymbol{X}_k - \hat{\mathbf{x}}_k)\boldsymbol{V}_k^T\big] \\ & + \mathbb{E}\big[\boldsymbol{V}_k(\boldsymbol{X}_k - \hat{\mathbf{x}}_k)^T\mathbf{H}^T\big] + \mathbb{E}\big[\boldsymbol{V}_k\boldsymbol{V}_k^T\big] \\ =& \mathbf{H}\mathbb{E}[(\boldsymbol{X}_k - \hat{\mathbf{x}}_k)(\boldsymbol{X}_k - \hat{\mathbf{x}}_k)^T]\mathbf{H}^T + \mathbf{H}\mathbb{E}[(\boldsymbol{X}_k - \hat{\mathbf{x}}_k)\boldsymbol{V}_k^T] \\ & + \mathbb{E}\big[\boldsymbol{V}_k(\boldsymbol{X}_k - \hat{\mathbf{x}}_k)^T\big]\mathbf{H}^T + \mathbb{E}\big[\boldsymbol{V}_k\boldsymbol{V}_k^T\big] \\ =& \mathbf{H}\mathbf{P}_{\boldsymbol{X}_k\boldsymbol{X}_k}\mathbf{H}^T + \mathbf{R}_k\,.\end{aligned} \tag{2.26}$$

2.2.2 Extended Kalman Filter

In the case of non-linearities in the system and measurement models, the state and measurement equation are given by

$$\boldsymbol{X}_k = f(\boldsymbol{X}_{k-1}, \boldsymbol{W}_k)\,, \tag{2.27}$$

$$\boldsymbol{Z}_k = h(\boldsymbol{X}_k, \boldsymbol{V}_k)\,. \tag{2.28}$$

In most cases an additive noise model is assumed so that

$$\boldsymbol{X}_k = f(\boldsymbol{X}_{k-1}) + \boldsymbol{W}_k \qquad \text{(state equation)}\,, \tag{2.29}$$

$$\boldsymbol{Z}_k = h(\boldsymbol{X}_k) + \boldsymbol{V}_k \qquad \text{(measurement equation)}\,. \tag{2.30}$$

The Extended Kalman Filter approximates the non-linear functions f and h using Taylor series expansion around the current mean estimate. Truncation of the Taylor series to the first order leads to a linear expression, which can be used to propagate the Gaussian distribution as in the linear case. The a-priori estimate for the system state and expected measurement can be obtained directly using both nonlinear functions. When propagating state covariance and computing Kalman gain, Jacobians $\mathbf{F}_{k-1}$, $\mathbf{H}_k$, $\mathbf{W}_k$, and $\mathbf{V}_k$ are used:

Prediction:

$$\hat{\mathbf{x}}_k^- = f(\hat{\mathbf{x}}_k) \tag{2.31}$$

$$\mathbf{P}_{\mathbf{X}_k^-\mathbf{X}_k^-} = \mathbf{F}_{k-1}\mathbf{P}_{\mathbf{X}_{k-1}\mathbf{X}_{k-1}}\mathbf{F}_{k-1}^T + \mathbf{Q}_k \tag{2.32}$$

$$= \mathbf{F}_{k-1}\mathbf{P}_{\mathbf{X}_{k-1}\mathbf{X}_{k-1}}\mathbf{F}_{k-1}^T + \mathbf{W}_k\mathbf{Q}_{k-1}\mathbf{W}_k^T \tag{2.33}$$

Correction:

$$\hat{\mathbf{x}}_k = \hat{\mathbf{x}}_k^- + \mathbf{K}_k \cdot (\mathbf{z}_k - h(\hat{\mathbf{x}}_k^-))$$

$$= \hat{\mathbf{x}}_k^- + \mathbf{K}_k \cdot \tilde{\mathbf{z}}_k \tag{2.34}$$

$$\mathbf{P}_{\mathbf{X}_k\mathbf{X}_k} = (\mathbf{I} - \mathbf{K}_k\mathbf{H}_k)\mathbf{P}_{\mathbf{X}_k^-\mathbf{X}_k^-} \tag{2.35}$$

with innovation $\tilde{\mathbf{z}}_k$ being

$$\tilde{\mathbf{z}}_k = \mathbf{z}_k - \hat{\mathbf{z}}_k = \mathbf{z}_k - h(\hat{\mathbf{x}}_k^-) , \tag{2.36}$$

Kalman gain $\mathbf{K}_k$ being

$$\mathbf{K}_k = \mathbf{P}_{\mathbf{x}_k^-\mathbf{x}_k^-}\mathbf{H}_k^T\mathbf{P}_{\tilde{\mathbf{z}}_k\tilde{\mathbf{z}}_k}^{-1} , \tag{2.37}$$

with innovation covariance

$$\begin{aligned}\mathbf{P}_{\tilde{\mathbf{z}}_k\tilde{\mathbf{z}}_k} &= \mathbf{H}_k\mathbf{P}_{\mathbf{x}_k^-\mathbf{x}_k^-}\mathbf{H}_k^T + \mathbf{R}_k \\ &= \mathbf{H}_k\mathbf{P}_{\mathbf{x}_k^-\mathbf{x}_k^-}\mathbf{H}_k^T + \mathbf{V}_k\mathbf{R}_{k-1}\mathbf{V}_k^T , \end{aligned} \tag{2.38}$$

The Jacobians $\mathbf{F}_{k-1}$, $\mathbf{H}_k$, $\mathbf{W}_k$, and $\mathbf{V}_k$ are computed as

$$\mathbf{F}_{k-1} = \left.\frac{\mathrm{d}f}{\mathrm{d}\mathbf{x}}\right|_{\hat{\mathbf{x}}_{k-1}} , \quad \mathbf{H}_k = \left.\frac{\mathrm{d}h}{\mathrm{d}\mathbf{x}}\right|_{\hat{\mathbf{x}}_k^-} , \quad \mathbf{W}_k = \left.\frac{\mathrm{d}f}{\mathrm{d}\mathbf{w}}\right|_{\hat{\mathbf{x}}_k^-} , \quad \text{and} \quad \mathbf{V}_k = \left.\frac{\mathrm{d}f}{\mathrm{d}\mathbf{v}}\right|_{\hat{\mathbf{x}}_k^-} . \tag{2.39}$$

2.2.3 Iterative Extended Kalman Filter

The Extended Kalman Filter linearizes the measurement function around the a-priori state estimate $\hat{\mathbf{x}}_k^-$, although a better state estimate is given after the integration of the current measurement. Linearization around the a-posteriori state estimate $\hat{\mathbf{x}}_k$ may improve the estimation. This is exploited in the iterative version of the EKF, the Iterative Extended Kalman Filter (IEKF). IEKF iteratively repeats the correction step with the recalculated linearization of the measurement model until a termination constraint is fulfilled. For ensuring non-recurrent integration of the measurement $\mathbf{z}_k$ during the iterations, a correction term $\mathbf{H}_k^{(i)}(\hat{\mathbf{x}}_k^- - \hat{\mathbf{x}}_k^{(i)})$ is used in each iteration i:

$$\hat{\mathbf{x}}_k^{(i+1)} = \hat{\mathbf{x}}_k^- + \mathbf{K}_k^{(i)}(\mathbf{z}_k - h(\hat{\mathbf{x}}_k^{(i)}) - \mathbf{H}_k^{(i)}(\hat{\mathbf{x}}_k^- - \hat{\mathbf{x}}_k^{(i)})) \tag{2.40}$$

$$\mathbf{K}_k^{(i)} = \mathbf{P}_{\mathbf{x}_k^-\mathbf{x}_k^-}(\mathbf{H}_k^{(i)})^T(\mathbf{P}_{\tilde{\mathbf{z}}_k\tilde{\mathbf{z}}_k}^{(i)})^{-1} \tag{2.41}$$

with

$$\mathbf{H}_k^{(i)} = \left.\frac{\mathrm{d}h}{\mathrm{d}\mathbf{x}}\right|_{\hat{\mathbf{x}}_k^{(i)}} \tag{2.42}$$

and start value $\hat{\mathbf{x}}_k^{(1)} = \hat{\mathbf{x}}_k^-$.

2.2.4 Interacting Multiple Models

The ***Interacting Multiple Model (IMM)*** filter allows to simultaneously use different system models. The overall resulting state estimation is obtained from the weighted output of estimators with different underlying models, where the weights depend on how well each model explains the observations. A good overview is provided in [Bla99].

For a car tracking application, several approaches can be imagined: One approach is to combine different motion models (e.g., combination of a constant heading model with a constant yaw rate model). This scenario is helpful for tracking heavily maneuvering targets. In most real world scenarios of side-looking tracking systems, the benefit of such utilization is rather questionable due to a short object observation period.

Another approach is to combine the same underlying motion model with different initialization parameters, e.g., different initial values for object speed and its orientation. This allows for a faster convergence of the filter on a reasonably accurate value.

2.2.5 Sequential Monte Carlo Filter

Sequential Monte Carlo filter (SMC) is another effective implementation of a Bayesian filter that is becoming more and more popular in recent time [Aru02]. It is also known under other names, such as particle filter, sequential sampling-importance resampling filter, bootstrap filter, condensation tracker, interacting particle approximation, or survival of the fittest.

The aim of SMC methods is to estimate the current, but unknown probability density in state space in order to derive statements about the most probable system state. A cloud of so-called particles are generated each consisting of a weight and a point in state space. The cloud in total is supposed to represent the probability density in the initial state (bootstrap). Each of the particles will be assigned one or several solution paths using a stochastic model of system dynamics. Depending on the difference of the solution path and the actual measurements, the particle weights can be adjusted and a better estimation of the evolution of the probability density in the state space is obtained sequentially. Thus, even the initial composition of the cloud can be adjusted to obtain better results (re-bootstrap). the time propagation of the system is influenced by a stochastic process, this is a Monte-Carlo simulation. The translation of a weighted particle cloud to a probability density can be achieved by means of non-parametrized density estimation. The advantages of SMC filters are that:

- They estimate the complete unknown a-posteriori probability density and are applicable also for non-Gaussian densities.
- The distributions obtained can be multi-modal, i.e., they can have more than one maximum.
- System and measurement dynamics are allowed to be non-linear.
- The simulation of the individual particles can be easily adapted for parallel computation.

However, SMC filters require much more computational power than Kalman filters, which dominates over the advantages in time-critical systems. Thus, in the following a Kalman filter based approaches are considered for object state estimation.

2.3 Data association

In order to correctly perform the update step, statistical state estimators such as the Kalman Filter assume a correct assignment of measurements (detections) to tracks. A correct assignment means that in each time step each track is associated with a single measurement that has been originated from the corresponding object. The problem of assigning measurements to the existing tracks is called the data association problem. Data association is not always a trivial process. Given multiple active tracks and multiple detections, there are often several assignment possibilities being more or less probable. Figure 2.4 illustrates the data association ambiguity in case of three objects and four detections.

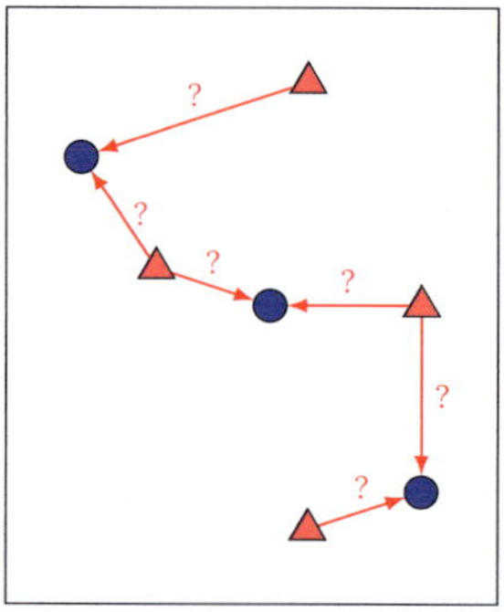

Figure 2.4: Illustration of a possible data association ambiguity in case of three tracks and four detections. The three expected detections are visualized by blue circles, the actually obtained – by red triangles.

Additional uncertainties are introduced due to the fact that a detection may not only be evoked by a real object but may also emerge due to concentration of noise in the data (clutter), or may be missing due to weaknesses of the sensors or of the subsequent data processing algorithms. And finally, in some systems an object may evoke multiple detections and several objects may give a joint detection. This makes unambiguous assignments difficult or even impossible. This is even worse in the case of extended objects since object observability represents another source of uncertainty. Partial and full occlusions result in incomplete and missing detections and make data association even more challenging.

There exists a number of algorithms for solving the data association problem in multi-object tracking applications that can be described as ***single scan algorithms*** (also referred to as ***Single Hypotheses Tracking (SHT)***) and ***multiscan***

algorithms (also referred to as ***Multi-Hypotheses Tracking (MHT)***). While single scan algorithms consider only data of the current frame (scan), multiscan algorithms simultaneously evaluate multiple hypotheses maintaining them throughout several frames in anticipation that the new data will allow to resolve emerging conflicts [Rei79, Cox96]. In practice, single scan algorithms are often preferred due to their simplicity and low computational cost. In the following, algorithms assuming that the number of tracks is known and a detection corresponds to a single track and vice versa will be presented.

2.3.1 Nearest Neighbor algorithms

One of the simplest data association algorithms is the ***Nearest Neighbor algorithm (NN)***. It is a typical single scan algorithm since it considers only measurements belonging to the current data frame (scan). The NN algorithm considers only one data association hypothesis, assigning the closest detection for each track. As illustrated in Figure 2.5 (a), in multi-object tracking scenarios, the NN algorithm is not optimal since it might assign a single detection to multiple tracks despite the presence of other detections. There exists an iterative version of the NN algorithm which prohibits multiple selections. It sequentially chooses track-detection pairs with the closest distance and excludes them from further consideration. This algorithm is suboptimal too, since it minimizes the track-to-detection distances sequentially and thus may miss the global minimum as shown in Figure 2.5 (b). This problem can be solved by the ***Global Nearest Neighbor algorithm (GNN)*** which searches for the globally optimal solution with respect to track-to-detection distances (Figure 2.5 (c)).

Nearest Neighbor algorithms make a ***hard decision*** by minimizing distances between the predicted and actually obtained measurements. This decision might be optimal with respect to the distances in the current frame, however it may be suboptimal with respect to the whole measurement sequence. Especially in applications where missed detections or obtaining clutter-based detections are possible, a hard decision made by the Global Nearest Neighbor algorithm in one frame may lead to severe tracking errors in consecutive frames. This problem was studied thoroughly in the radar tracking literature and led to development of statistical methods based on the idea of the ***Probabilistic Data Association (PDA)*** [Bar75, Bar78]. The next 5 sections discuss the main ideas and give detailed derivations of PDA algorithm and its derivatives IPDA, JPDA, and JIPDA, since they build the basis for the data association and tracking methods proposed in this thesis.

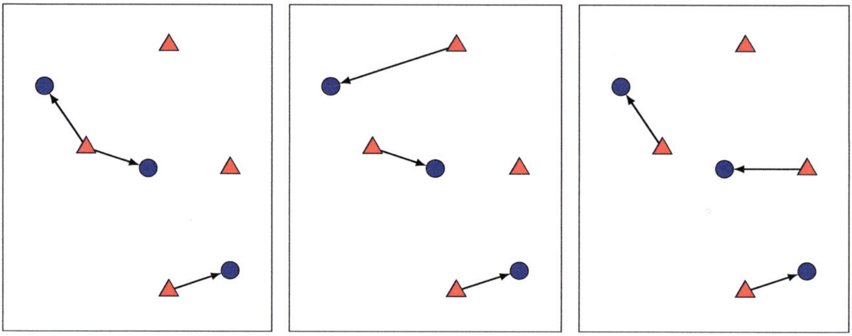

(a) Association produced by the simple Nearest Neighbor algorithm

(b) Association produced by the iterative Nearest Neighbor algorithm

(c) Association produced by the Global Nearest Neighbor algorithm

Figure 2.5: Illustration of Nearest Neighbor data association.

2.3.2 Main idea of PDA-based methods

The main idea of the Probabilistic Data Association algorithm and its derivatives is the minimization of tracking errors introduced through wrong data association in a single frame. This is achieved by using all feasible detections to update a track, by weighting the innovations of different association hypotheses according to their probabilities. Similarly to NN and GNN, PDA-based methods consider at each point in time only currently incoming measurements, i.e., they are single scan algorithms. However, when updating a track, instead of choosing a single measurement with highest association probability, they evaluate multiple association hypotheses and use all neighboring measurements weighting them according to the probabilities of the corresponding hypotheses (***All-Neighbors Data***

Association). Due to this approximation, called ***soft decision*** approach, PDA-based methods suffer less from data association errors and are thus better suited for applications which suffer from clutter-based detections. Although PDA-based methods work with multiple association hypotheses, they are also referred to as single hypotheses tracking algorithms since the hypotheses are combined to a single hypothesis prior to innovation.

2.3.3 Probabilistic Data Association (PDA)

PDA considers each track separately. Let the considered track state be denoted by $\mathbf{x}$ with $\boldsymbol{X}_k \sim \mathcal{N}(\hat{\mathbf{x}}_k, \mathbf{P}_{X_k X_k})$ as in (2.7). Under the Gaussian distribution assumption, the a-priori probability density of the predicted measurement position is given by

$$f_{Z_k^{\mathbf{x}}} := f(\mathbf{z}_k^{\mathbf{x}} | \mathcal{Z}_{1:(k-1)}^{\mathbf{x}}) = \mathcal{N}(\mathbf{z}; \hat{\mathbf{z}}_k^{\mathbf{x}}, \mathbf{P}_{Z_k Z_k}^{\mathbf{x}}), \tag{2.43}$$

with

$$\hat{\mathbf{z}}_k^{\mathbf{x}} = \mathbf{H}\hat{\mathbf{x}}_k^- \quad \text{and} \quad \mathbf{P}_{Z_k Z_k}^{\mathbf{x}} = \mathbf{H}\mathbf{P}_{X_k^- X_k^-}\mathbf{H}^T + \mathbf{R}. \tag{2.44}$$

Similarly to the definition used for the Kalman filter (cf. page 31), $\mathcal{Z}_{1:(k-1)}^{\mathbf{x}}$ denotes all measurements that have been obtained from the beginning of the observation and up to the time step $k-1$, and have been associated with the track $\mathbf{x}$.

2.3.3.1 Measurement validation (gating)

An assignment between a tracked object and a measurement is not always feasible. Too far lying and thus too improbable measurements can be excluded from the consideration right away. This is done by means of the so called gating procedure. Gating helps to reject very unlikely assignments between tracked objects and obtained measurements. For this purpose, a ***gating region*** $\Gamma_k^{\mathbf{x}}$ with volume $V_k^{\mathbf{x}}$ (also referred to as ***validation gate***) is defined around the predicted measurement $\hat{\mathbf{z}}_k^{\mathbf{x}}$ of the track $\mathbf{x}$ at time k. Associations are only performed with measurements falling inside the gating region.

The probability of the correct measurement $\mathbf{z}_k$ to lie inside the gating region (***gating probability***) is given by

$$P_G^{\mathbf{x}_k} = P(\mathbf{z}_k \in \Gamma_k^{\mathbf{x}}) = \int_{\Gamma_k^{\mathbf{x}}} f_{\mathcal{Z}_k^{\mathbf{x}}} \, \mathrm{d}\mathbf{z} \, . \tag{2.45}$$

The a-priori probability density function that accounts for gating is thus defined as:

$$p(\mathbf{z}_k^{\mathbf{x}} | \mathcal{Z}_{1:(k-1)}^{\mathbf{x}}) := \begin{cases} \frac{1}{P_G} f_{\mathcal{Z}_k^{\mathbf{x}}} & \text{for} \quad \mathbf{z}_k^{\mathbf{x}} \in \Gamma_k^{\mathbf{x}} \\ 0 & \text{for} \quad \mathbf{z}_k^{\mathbf{x}} \notin \Gamma_k^{\mathbf{x}} \, . \end{cases} \tag{2.46}$$

Often, validation gates are defined as hyper-ellipsoidal regions around $\hat{\mathbf{z}}_k^{\mathbf{x}}$ such that $P_G^{\mathbf{x}_k} = P_G$ is a constant for all tracks. This is achieved by defining $\Gamma_k^{\mathbf{x}}$ as

$$\Gamma_k^{\mathbf{x}}(\gamma) := \{\mathbf{z} : (\mathbf{z} - \hat{\mathbf{z}}_k^{\mathbf{x}})^T (\mathbf{P}_{Z_k Z_k}^{\mathbf{x}})^{-1} (\mathbf{z} - \hat{\mathbf{z}}_k^{\mathbf{x}}) \leq \gamma\} \tag{2.47}$$

with a constant parameter γ (gating threshold). The term $(\mathbf{z} - \hat{\mathbf{z}}_k^{\mathbf{x}})^T (\mathbf{P}_{Z_k Z_k}^{\mathbf{x}})^{-1} (\mathbf{z} - \hat{\mathbf{z}}_k^{\mathbf{x}})$ is the squared ***Mahalanobis distance*** [Mah36]. Associations for which the Mahalanobis distance exceeds a certain threshold are rejected.

Hereby two assumptions are made. First, a measurement is assumed to depend only on the state of the originating object. Second, the measurements are assumed to be normally distributed, i.e.,

$$(\mathbf{Z} - \hat{\mathbf{z}}_k^{\mathbf{x}})^T (\mathbf{P}_{Z_k Z_k}^{\mathbf{x}})^{-1} (\mathbf{Z} - \hat{\mathbf{z}}_k^{\mathbf{x}}) \sim \chi_{n_z}^2 \, . \tag{2.48}$$

The gating probability is thus given as

$$P_G = P(\mathbf{z}_k \in \Gamma_k^{\mathbf{x}}(\gamma)) = \chi_{n_z}^2(\gamma) \, , \tag{2.49}$$

with n_z being the dimension of the measurement $\mathbf{z}$.

Specification of a constant P_G (e.g., 95%) leads to a certain value of γ, which can be obtained from the quantile tables of the $n_\mathbf{z}$-dimensional chi-square distribution:

$$\gamma = \chi^2_{n_\mathbf{z}, P_G} \,. \tag{2.50}$$

This allows for determination of $\Gamma_k^\mathbf{x} = \Gamma_k^\mathbf{x}(\gamma)$ as well as $V_k^\mathbf{x} = V_k^\mathbf{x}(\gamma)$ which is given as

$$V_k^\mathbf{x}(\gamma) = c_{n_\mathbf{z}} \gamma^{\frac{n_\mathbf{z}}{2}} \left| \mathbf{P}^\mathbf{x}_{\mathbf{z}_k \mathbf{z}_k} \right|^{\frac{1}{2}} , \tag{2.51}$$

where $c_{n_\mathbf{z}}$ is the volume of the $n_\mathbf{z}$-dimensional unit sphere, i.e., $c_1 = 2$, $c_2 = \pi$, $c_3 = \frac{4}{3}\pi$, $c_4 = \frac{1}{2}\pi^2$, etc.

A measurement $\mathbf{z}_{k,j}$ is considered as being possibly originated by track $\mathbf{x}$, if it lies in its gate, i.e., if

$$(\mathbf{z}_{k,j} - \hat{\mathbf{z}}_k^\mathbf{x})^T (\mathbf{P}^\mathbf{x}_{\mathbf{z}_k \mathbf{z}_k})^{-1} (\mathbf{z}_{k,j} - \hat{\mathbf{z}}_k^\mathbf{x}) \leq \gamma \tag{2.52}$$

In the opposite case the measurement is not considered as a feasible observation of the track $\mathbf{x}$.

2.3.3.2 Formation of association hypotheses and computation of the weighting factors

The set of $m_k^\mathbf{x}$ measurements falling into the gating region of a track $\mathbf{x}$ at time step k is denoted by $\mathcal{Z}_k^\mathbf{x}$:

$$\mathcal{Z}_k^\mathbf{x} := \{\mathbf{z}_{k,1}, \dots, \mathbf{z}_{k,m_k^\mathbf{x}}\} \quad \text{with} \quad \mathbf{z}_{k,j} \in \Gamma_k^\mathbf{x} \,. \tag{2.53}$$

For better readability, the superscript $\mathbf{x}$ in $m_k^\mathbf{x}$ will be omitted in the following. For each measurement $\mathbf{z}_{k,j} \in \mathcal{Z}_k^\mathbf{x}$ a hypothesis is formed, where this measurement is assumed to be correct while all other $m_k - 1$ measurements in the gate are assumed to be caused by clutter. This hypothesis is denoted as $\theta_k^{\mathbf{x} \mapsto \mathbf{z}_j}$ with $j \in \{1, \dots, m_k\}$. $\theta_k^{\mathbf{x} \mapsto \mathbf{z}_0}$ denotes the hypothesis of none of the m_k measurements in gate being correct, i.e., that all of them stem from clutter or are false alarms.

In the innovation step of the Bayesian state estimator, estimates produced by each hypothesis are weighted with the weighting factors $\beta_k^{\mathbf{x}\mapsto\mathbf{z}_j}$ (with $j \in \{0, \dots, m_k\}$) that are defined as

$$\beta_k^{\mathbf{x}\mapsto\mathbf{z}_j} := P(\theta_k^{\mathbf{x}\mapsto\mathbf{z}_j} | \mathcal{Z}_{1:k}^{\mathbf{x}}) \tag{2.54}$$

with $\mathcal{Z}_{1:k}^{\mathbf{x}} := \{\mathcal{Z}_1^{\mathbf{x}}, \dots, \mathcal{Z}_k^{\mathbf{x}}\}$ and $\sum_{j=0}^{m_k} \beta_k^{\mathbf{x}\mapsto\mathbf{z}_j} = 1$.

The weighting factors are calculated using Bayes' theorem:

$$\begin{aligned} \beta_k^{\mathbf{x}\mapsto\mathbf{z}_j} &= P(\theta_k^{\mathbf{x}\mapsto\mathbf{z}_j} | \mathcal{Z}_{1:k}^{\mathbf{x}}) = P(\theta_k^{\mathbf{x}\mapsto\mathbf{z}_j} | \mathcal{Z}_k^{\mathbf{x}}, m_k, \mathcal{Z}_{1:(k-1)}^{\mathbf{x}}) \\ &= \frac{1}{c_k} p(\mathcal{Z}_k^{\mathbf{x}} | \theta_k^{\mathbf{x}\mapsto\mathbf{z}_j}, m_k, \mathcal{Z}_{1:(k-1)}^{\mathbf{x}}) P(\theta_k^{\mathbf{x}\mapsto\mathbf{z}_j} | m_k, \mathcal{Z}_{1:(k-1)}^{\mathbf{x}}) \end{aligned} \tag{2.55}$$

with the normalization factor

$$c_k = \sum_{j=0}^{m_k} p(\mathcal{Z}_k^{\mathbf{x}} | \theta_k^{\mathbf{x}\mapsto\mathbf{z}_j}, m_k, \mathcal{Z}_{1:(k-1)}^{\mathbf{x}}) P(\theta_k^{\mathbf{x}\mapsto\mathbf{z}_j} | m_k, \mathcal{Z}_{1:(k-1)}^{\mathbf{x}}) . \tag{2.56}$$

Assuming a Gaussian measurement distribution, the likelihood of the true measurement $\mathbf{z}_{k,j}$ ($j \neq 0$) is given by

$$\begin{aligned} p(\mathbf{z}_{k,j} | \theta_k^{\mathbf{x}\mapsto\mathbf{z}_j}, m_k, \mathcal{Z}_{1:(k-1)}^{\mathbf{x}}) &= \frac{1}{P_G} f_{\mathbf{z}_k^{\mathbf{x}}} = \frac{1}{P_G} \mathcal{N}(\mathbf{z}_{k,j}; \hat{\mathbf{z}}_k^{\mathbf{x}}, \mathbf{P}_{\mathbf{z}_k\mathbf{z}_k}^{\mathbf{x}}) \\ &= \frac{1}{P_G} \mathcal{N}(\mathbf{z}_{k,j} - \hat{\mathbf{z}}_k^{\mathbf{x}}; 0, \mathbf{P}_{\mathbf{z}_k\mathbf{z}_k}^{\mathbf{x}}) \\ &= \frac{1}{P_G} \mathcal{N}(\tilde{\mathbf{z}}_{k,j}^{\mathbf{x}}; 0, \mathbf{P}_{\mathbf{z}_k\mathbf{z}_k}^{\mathbf{x}}) \\ &= \frac{1}{P_G} \cdot |(2\pi)^{n_z} \cdot \mathbf{P}_{\mathbf{z}_k\mathbf{z}_k}^{\mathbf{x}}|^{-\frac{1}{2}} \cdot e^{-\frac{1}{2}(\tilde{\mathbf{z}}_{k,j}^{\mathbf{x}})^T (\mathbf{P}_{\mathbf{z}_k\mathbf{z}_k}^{\mathbf{x}})^{-1} \tilde{\mathbf{z}}_{k,j}^{\mathbf{x}}} \end{aligned} \tag{2.57}$$

with innovation $\tilde{\mathbf{z}}_{k,j}^{\mathbf{x}} = \mathbf{z}_{k,j} - \hat{\mathbf{z}}_k^{\mathbf{x}}$.

Clutter measurements are assumed to be independent from the correct measurement. Their position is assumed to be independent and identically distributed over the whole gating volume $V_k^{\mathbf{x}}$ with uniform distribution on $\Gamma_k^{\mathbf{x}}$. Under these assumptions,

$$p(\mathbf{z}_{k,i}|\theta_k^{\mathbf{x}\mapsto\mathbf{z}_j}, m_k, \mathcal{Z}_{1:(k-1)}^{\mathbf{x}}) = \frac{1}{V_k} \quad j \neq i\,. \tag{2.58}$$

The likelihood of the entire measurement set $\mathcal{Z}_k^{\mathbf{x}}$ falling into the gating region of the track $\mathbf{x}$ at time step k given that all of them are false alarms (i.e., $\theta_k^{\mathbf{x}\mapsto\mathbf{z}_0}$) is given by

$$p(\mathcal{Z}_k^{\mathbf{x}}|\theta_k^{\mathbf{x}\mapsto\mathbf{z}_0}, m_k, \mathcal{Z}_{1:(k-1)}^{\mathbf{x}}) = \prod_{i=1}^{m_k} p(\mathbf{z}_{k,i}|\theta_k^{\mathbf{x}\mapsto\mathbf{z}_0}, m_k, \mathcal{Z}_{1:(k-1)}^{\mathbf{x}}) = \frac{1}{V_k^{m_k}}\,. \tag{2.59}$$

The likelihood of the entire measurement set $\mathcal{Z}_k^{\mathbf{x}}$ falling into the gating region of the track $\mathbf{x}$ at time step k given that the measurement j is the correct measurement and all other measurements are false alarms (i.e., $\theta_k^{\mathbf{x}\mapsto\mathbf{z}_j}$, $z \neq 0$) is given by

$$\begin{aligned} p(\mathcal{Z}_k^{\mathbf{x}}|\theta_k^{\mathbf{x}\mapsto\mathbf{z}_j}, m_k, \mathcal{Z}_{1:(k-1)}^{\mathbf{x}}) &= \prod_{i=1}^{m_k} p(\mathbf{z}_{k,i}|\theta_k^{\mathbf{x}\mapsto\mathbf{z}_j}, m_k, \mathcal{Z}_{1:(k-1)}^{\mathbf{x}}) \\ &= \frac{1}{V_k^{m_k-1}} \frac{1}{P_G} \mathcal{N}(\tilde{\mathbf{z}}_{k,j}^{\mathbf{x}}; 0, \mathbf{P}_{\mathbf{z}_k\mathbf{z}_k}^{\mathbf{x}}), \quad j = 1, \dots, m_k\,. \end{aligned} \tag{2.60}$$

The probability mass function of the hypothesis $\theta_k^{\mathbf{x}\mapsto\mathbf{z}_j}$ conditioned on m_k and $\mathcal{Z}_{1:(k-1)}^{\mathbf{x}}$ is given by

$$\begin{aligned} P(\theta_k^{\mathbf{x}\mapsto\mathbf{z}_j}|m_k, \mathcal{Z}_{1:(k-1)}^{\mathbf{x}}) &= P(\theta_k^{\mathbf{x}\mapsto\mathbf{z}_j}|m_k) \\ &= \frac{P(m_k|\theta_k^{\mathbf{x}\mapsto\mathbf{z}_j})P(\theta_k^{\mathbf{x}\mapsto\mathbf{z}_j})}{\sum_{j=0}^{m_k} P(m_k|\theta_k^{\mathbf{x}\mapsto\mathbf{z}_j})P(\theta_k^{\mathbf{x}\mapsto\mathbf{z}_j})}\,, \end{aligned} \tag{2.61}$$

where $P(\theta_k^{\mathbf{x}\mapsto\mathbf{z}_j})$ (with $j = 1, \dots, m_k$) denotes the a-priori probability that the measurement $\mathbf{z}_j$ originated from track $\mathbf{x}$, $P(\theta_k^{\mathbf{x}\mapsto\mathbf{z}_0})$ denotes the a-priori probability that none of the measurements in the gate has been evoked by track $\mathbf{x}$, and $P(m_k|\theta_k^{\mathbf{x}\mapsto\mathbf{z}_0})$ and $P(m_k|\theta_k^{\mathbf{x}\mapsto\mathbf{z}_j})$ denote the probabilities for receiving m_k measurements given that either none or one of them stems from track $\mathbf{x}$.

$P(\theta_k^{\mathbf{x}\mapsto\mathbf{z}_0})$ is given by

$$P(\theta_k^{\mathbf{x}\mapsto\mathbf{z}_0}) = 1 - P_D P_G \,, \tag{2.62}$$

where P_D is the probability that the track evokes a measurement (detection probability), and P_G is the probability of the measurement to fall into the gating region as defined in (2.45).

Under the assumption that each of the m_k measurements in the gate has equal probability of being evoked by track $\mathbf{x}$, the a-priori association probability $P(\theta_k^{\mathbf{x}\mapsto\mathbf{z}_j})$ for $j = 1, \dots, m_k$ is given by

$$P(\theta_k^{\mathbf{x}\mapsto\mathbf{z}_j}) = \frac{1}{m_k} P_D P_G \quad \forall j = 1, \dots, m_k \,. \tag{2.63}$$

The probability of the number of measurements being m_k given one of the association hypotheses $\theta_k^{\mathbf{x}\mapsto\mathbf{z}_0}$ or $\theta_k^{\mathbf{x}\mapsto\mathbf{z}_j}$ is equivalent to the probability of the number of false measurements being m_k or $m_k - 1$ correspondingly:

$$P(m_k | \theta_k^{\mathbf{x}\mapsto\mathbf{z}_0}) = \mu_F(m_k) \,, \tag{2.64}$$

$$P(m_k | \theta_k^{\mathbf{x}\mapsto\mathbf{z}_j}) = \mu_F(m_k - 1) \,, \tag{2.65}$$

with $\mu_F(m)$ being the probability mass function for the number of clutter-based measurements. $\mu_F(m)$ can be modeled in different ways. The number of the clutter-based measurements can be assumed either to have Poisson distribution (***parametric model***) or to be equally distributed over the set $\{0, \cdots, N-1\}$ with N being the maximal number of clutter-based measurements (***non-parametric model***) [Bar88]:

Parametric model: Poisson distribution

$$\mu_F(m) = e^{-\widehat{m}_k} \frac{\widehat{m}_k^m}{m!} = e^{-\lambda V_k} \frac{(\lambda V_k)^m}{m!} \,, \qquad m \in \mathbb{N}_0 \,, \tag{2.66}$$

where λ is the mean clutter density and $\widehat{m}_k := \lambda V_k$ is the expected number of clutter measurements in the gating region. If λ is a-priori not known, $\widehat{m}_k$ can be estimated by using $\widehat{m}_k = m_k - P_D P_G$.

Non-parametric model: Uniform distribution

$$\mu_F(m) = \frac{1}{N}, \qquad m = 0, 1, \dots, N-1, \tag{2.67}$$

where N can be chosen as a great enough arbitrary number since it will be canceled in the computation of $P(\theta_k^{\mathbf{x} \mapsto \mathbf{z}_j} | m_k, \mathcal{Z}_{1:(k-1)}^{\mathbf{x}})$.

Using (2.62) - (2.65) in (2.61) leads to

$$P(\theta_k^{\mathbf{x} \mapsto \mathbf{z}_j} | m_k, \mathcal{Z}_{1:(k-1)}^{\mathbf{x}}) =$$

$$= \begin{cases} \dfrac{\mu_F(m_k)(1-P_D P_G)}{\mu_F(m_k)(1-P_D P_G)+m_k \cdot \mu_F(m_k-1)\frac{P_D P_G}{m_k}} & j = 0 \\ \\ \dfrac{\mu_F(m_k-1)\frac{P_D P_G}{m_k}}{\mu_F(m_k)(1-P_D P_G)+m_k \cdot \mu_F(m_k-1)\frac{P_D P_G}{m_k}} & j = 1, \dots, m_k \end{cases}$$

$$= \begin{cases} \dfrac{(1-P_D P_G)\frac{\mu_F(m_k)}{\mu_F(m_k-1)}}{P_D P_G+(1-P_D P_G)\frac{\mu_F(m_k)}{\mu_F(m_k-1)}} & j = 0 \\ \\ \dfrac{1}{m_k}\dfrac{P_D P_G}{P_D P_G+(1-P_D P_G)\frac{\mu_F(m_k)}{\mu_F(m_k-1)}} & j = 1, \dots, m_k \end{cases} \tag{2.68}$$

and thus for the *parametric model* to

$$P(\theta_k^{\mathbf{x} \mapsto \mathbf{z}_j} | m_k, \mathcal{Z}_{1:(k-1)}^{\mathbf{x}}) = \begin{cases} \dfrac{(1-P_D P_G)\lambda V_k}{P_D P_G m_k+(1-P_D P_G)\lambda V_k} & j = 0 \\ \\ \dfrac{P_D P_G}{P_D P_G m_k+(1-P_D P_G)\lambda V_k} & j = 1, \dots, m_k \end{cases} \tag{2.69}$$

and for the *non-parametric model* to

$$P(\theta_k^{\mathbf{x} \mapsto \mathbf{z}_j} | m_k, \mathcal{Z}_{1:(k-1)}^{\mathbf{x}}) = \begin{cases} (1 - P_D P_G) & j = 0 \\ \\ \dfrac{1}{m_k} P_D P_G & j = 1, \dots, m_k\,. \end{cases} \tag{2.70}$$

This leads to the following weighting factors $\beta_k^{\mathbf{x}\mapsto\mathbf{z}_j}$:

$$\beta_k^{\mathbf{x}\mapsto\mathbf{z}_j} = \begin{cases} \frac{b}{b+\sum_{i=1}^{m_k} e_i} & j = 0 \\ \\ \frac{e_j}{b+\sum_{i=1}^{m_k} e_i} & j = 1, \dots, m_k \end{cases} \tag{2.71}$$

with

$$e_j = e^{-\frac{1}{2}(\tilde{\mathbf{z}}_{k,j}^{\mathbf{x}})^T (\mathbf{P}_{\mathbf{z}_k\mathbf{z}_k}^{\mathbf{x}})^{-1} \tilde{\mathbf{z}}_{k,j}^{\mathbf{x}}} \tag{2.72}$$

and

$$\begin{aligned} b &= \lambda |2\pi \mathbf{P}_{\mathbf{z}_k\mathbf{z}_k}^{\mathbf{x}}|^{\frac{1}{2}} \frac{(1-P_D P_G)}{P_D} \\ &= \begin{cases} \left(\frac{2\pi}{\gamma}\right)^{\frac{n_z}{2}} \lambda V_k c_{n_z} \frac{(1-P_D P_G)}{P_D}, & \text{parametric model} \\ \\ \left(\frac{2\pi}{\gamma}\right)^{\frac{n_z}{2}} m_k c_{n_z} \frac{(1-P_D P_G)}{P_D}, & \text{non-parametric model.} \end{cases} \end{aligned} \tag{2.73}$$

For each hypothesis, the corresponding state estimate is given by

$$\hat{\mathbf{x}}_k^{\mathbf{z}_j} = \mathbb{E}[\mathbf{X}_k | \theta_k^{\mathbf{x}\mapsto\mathbf{z}_j}, \mathcal{Z}_{1:k}^{\mathbf{x}}] = \begin{cases} \hat{\mathbf{x}}_k^- & j = 0 \\ \hat{\mathbf{x}}_k^- + \mathbf{K}_k(\mathbf{z}_{k,j} - \hat{\mathbf{z}}_k^{\mathbf{x}}) & j = 1, \dots, m_k \, . \end{cases} \tag{2.74}$$

When considering all hypotheses, this leads to the following composite state estimate for the track $\mathbf{x}$:

$$\begin{aligned}
\hat{\mathbf{x}}_k &= \mathbb{E}[\boldsymbol{X}_k|\mathcal{Z}^{\mathbf{x}}_{1:k}] = \sum_{j=0}^{m_k} \mathbb{E}[\boldsymbol{X}_k|\theta_k^{\mathbf{x}\mapsto\mathbf{z}_j}, \mathcal{Z}^{\mathbf{x}}_{1:k}] \cdot P(\theta_k^{\mathbf{x}\mapsto\mathbf{z}_j}|\mathcal{Z}^{\mathbf{x}}_{1:k}) \\
&= \sum_{j=0}^{m_k} \hat{\mathbf{x}}_k^{\mathbf{z}_j} \beta_k^{\mathbf{x}\mapsto\mathbf{z}_j} = \sum_{j=0}^{m_k} \beta_k^{\mathbf{x}\mapsto\mathbf{z}_j} \hat{\mathbf{x}}_k^{\mathbf{z}_j} \\
&= \sum_{j=0}^{m_k} \beta_k^{\mathbf{x}\mapsto\mathbf{z}_j} \hat{\mathbf{x}}_k^- + \mathbf{K}_k \sum_{j=1}^{m_k} \beta_k^{\mathbf{x}\mapsto\mathbf{z}_j} (\mathbf{z}_{k,j} - \hat{\mathbf{z}}_k^{\mathbf{x}}) \\
&= \hat{\mathbf{x}}_k^- + \mathbf{K}_k \sum_{j=1}^{m_k} \beta_k^{\mathbf{x}\mapsto\mathbf{z}_j} \tilde{\mathbf{z}}_{k,j}^{\mathbf{x}} && (2.75) \\
&= \hat{\mathbf{x}}_k^- + \mathbf{K}_k \cdot \tilde{\mathbf{z}}_{k,\text{Comp}}^{\mathbf{x}} && (2.76)
\end{aligned}$$

where

$$\tilde{\mathbf{z}}_{k,j}^{\mathbf{x}} = \mathbf{z}_{k,j} - \hat{\mathbf{z}}_k^{\mathbf{x}} \tag{2.77}$$

is the innovation of the track $\mathbf{x}$ produced by the measurement $\mathbf{z}_j$ at time step k and $\tilde{\mathbf{z}}_{k,\text{Comp}}^{\mathbf{x}}$ the composite innovation for the track $\mathbf{x}$:

$$\tilde{\mathbf{z}}_{k,\text{Comp}}^{\mathbf{x}} := \sum_{j=1}^{m_k} \beta_k^{\mathbf{x}\mapsto\mathbf{z}_j} \tilde{\mathbf{z}}_{k,j}^{\mathbf{x}} \,. \tag{2.78}$$

Although Equation (2.75) seems to be linear, this is not the case as the weighting factors $\beta_k^{\mathbf{x}\mapsto\mathbf{z}_j}$ depend on $\tilde{\mathbf{z}}_{k,j}^{\mathbf{x}}$.

The covariance matrix $\mathbf{P}_{\boldsymbol{X}_k\boldsymbol{X}_k}$ is calculated according to

$$\mathbf{P}_{\boldsymbol{X}_k\boldsymbol{X}_k} = \beta_k^{\mathbf{x}\mapsto\mathbf{z}_0} \mathbf{P}_{\boldsymbol{X}_k^-\boldsymbol{X}_k^-} + (1 - \beta_k^{\mathbf{x}\mapsto\mathbf{z}_0}) \mathbf{P}^c_{\boldsymbol{X}_k\boldsymbol{X}_k} + \widetilde{\mathbf{P}}_k \tag{2.79}$$

with

$$\mathbf{P}^{c}_{\mathbf{x}_k\mathbf{x}_k} = (\mathbf{I} - \mathbf{K}_k\mathbf{H}_k)\mathbf{P}_{\mathbf{x}_k^-\mathbf{x}_k^-} \tag{2.80}$$

and

$$\widetilde{\mathbf{P}}_k = \mathbf{K}_k\Big(\sum_{j=1}^{m_k} \beta_k^{\mathbf{x}\mapsto\mathbf{z}_j}\tilde{\mathbf{z}}^{\mathbf{x}}_{k,j}(\tilde{\mathbf{z}}^{\mathbf{x}}_{k,j})^T - \tilde{\mathbf{z}}^{\mathbf{x}}_{k,\mathrm{Comp}}(\tilde{\mathbf{z}}^{\mathbf{x}}_{k,\mathrm{Comp}})^T\Big)\mathbf{K}_k^T\,. \tag{2.81}$$

The predicted covariance matrix $\mathbf{P}_{\mathbf{x}_k\mathbf{x}_k}$ is weighted with the factor $\beta_k^{\mathbf{x}\mapsto\mathbf{z}_0}$, which is related to the case of none of the obtained measurements being correct. $\mathbf{P}^{c}_{\mathbf{x}_k\mathbf{x}_k}$ is the covariance matrix calculated under the assumption that the innovation is performed with the correct measurement, i.e., , without an association error. It is weighted with the factor $(1 - \beta_k^{\mathbf{x}\mapsto\mathbf{z}_0})$. Since it is not known which of the m_k measurements is the correct one, the state covariance is increased by means of the matrix $\widetilde{\mathbf{P}}_k$ which incorporates the measurement association errors.

2.3.4 Integrated Probabilistic Data Association (IPDA)

The PDA concept implicitly presupposes presence of the tracked object $\mathbf{x}$ and thus needs an additional mechanism for initiation and termination of tracks. In case of possible missing or clutter-based detections, this process is subject to uncertainties. An elegant way of modeling those uncertainties has been proposed by Mušicki et al. [Muš92, Muš94]. The algorithm proposed there is an enhancement of the PDA algorithm. In addition to the expressions for data association probabilities it provides an expression for computing the object existence probability which establishes a basis for track initiations and terminations and allows for a better handling of clutter. Object existence probability is directly accounted for (*integrated*) when computing the association probabilities $\beta_k^{\mathbf{x}\mapsto\mathbf{z}_j}$. This led to the corresponding name of the algorithm: ***Integrated Probability Data Association (IPDA)***.

In the IPDA algorithm the object existence is modeled as a Markov process. Hereby, two models are considered. In the first one (which is preferably taken in the track initiation phase) it is assumed that a tracked object either exists (and may be detected with some detection probability P_D) or does not exist.

The corresponding probabilities are in the following denoted by $P(\exists\mathbf{x})$ and $P(\nexists\mathbf{x}) = 1 - P(\exists\mathbf{x})$.

The second model additionally takes into account the observability aspect. This model accounts for possible occlusions and signal fading and may be used in the track maintenance phase. Here, three possible events are considered: in the current time step the object might be either

- existent and observable with some detection probability P_D (henceforth denoted by $\supset$),
- existent but not observable (i.e., with zero detection probability) (henceforth denoted by $\not\supset$),
- not existent.

This distinction can be also advantageous in multi-object-tracking systems that use sensor types that only deliver evidence about object existence. The probability of the object existence for the second model is given by $P(\exists\mathbf{x}) = P(\supset\mathbf{x}) + P(\not\supset\mathbf{x})$.

Due to the interdependence of the object existence probability $P(\exists\mathbf{x})$ and the dynamic object state $\mathbf{x}_k$, both Markov processes, namely the state estimation and existence probability estimation, are cross-coupled as shown in Figure 2.6.

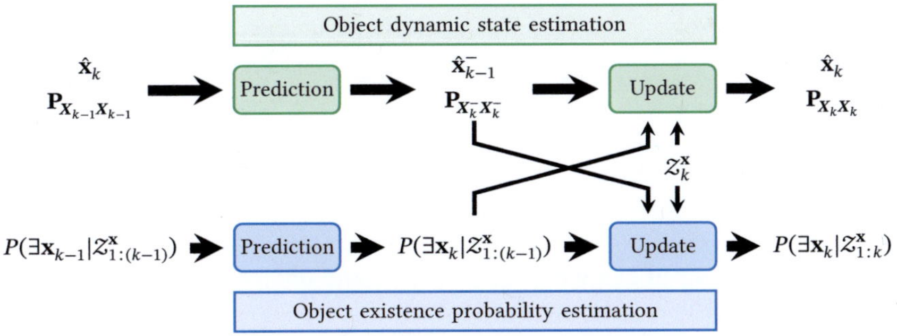

Figure 2.6: Existence and probability modeling in IPDA as two cross-coupled Markov chains. (Adapted from [Mäh08])

Similarly to PDA, the track state estimation in IPDA is given by

$$\begin{aligned}\hat{\mathbf{x}}_k &= \mathbb{E}[\mathbf{X}_k|\exists\mathbf{x}, \mathcal{Z}^{\mathbf{x}}_{1:k}] = \sum_{j=0}^{m_k} \mathbb{E}[\mathbf{X}_k|\theta_k^{\mathbf{x}\mapsto\mathbf{z}_j}, \mathcal{Z}^{\mathbf{x}}_{1:k}] \cdot P(\theta_k^{\mathbf{x}\mapsto\mathbf{z}_j}|\exists\mathbf{x}_k, \mathcal{Z}^{\mathbf{x}}_{1:k}) \\ &= \sum_{j=0}^{m_k} \beta_k^{\mathbf{x}\mapsto\mathbf{z}_j}\hat{\mathbf{x}}_k^- + \mathbf{K}_k \sum_{j=1}^{m_k} \beta_k^{\mathbf{x}\mapsto\mathbf{z}_j}(\mathbf{z}_{k,j} - \hat{\mathbf{z}}_k^{\mathbf{x}}) \\ &= \hat{\mathbf{x}}_k^- + \mathbf{K}_k \sum_{j=1}^{m_k} \beta_k^{\mathbf{x}\mapsto\mathbf{z}_j}\tilde{\mathbf{z}}^{\mathbf{x}}_{k,j} \\ &= \hat{\mathbf{x}}_k^- + \mathbf{K}_k \cdot \tilde{\mathbf{z}}^{\mathbf{x}}_{k,\mathrm{Comp}} \end{aligned} \tag{2.82}$$

with innovation

$$\tilde{\mathbf{z}}^{\mathbf{x}}_{k,j} = \mathbf{z}_{k,j} - \hat{\mathbf{z}}_k^{\mathbf{x}} \tag{2.83}$$

and composite innovation

$$\tilde{\mathbf{z}}^{\mathbf{x}}_{k,\mathrm{Comp}} := \sum_{j=1}^{m_k} \beta_k^{\mathbf{x}\mapsto\mathbf{z}_j}\tilde{\mathbf{z}}^{\mathbf{x}}_{k,j}\,. \tag{2.84}$$

The difference between Equation 2.82 and the state estimation Equation 2.76 in PDA is that the probabilities $P(\theta_k^{\mathbf{x}\mapsto\mathbf{z}_j}|\mathcal{Z}^{\mathbf{x}}_{1:k})$ of the assignment hypotheses $\theta_k^{\mathbf{x}\mapsto\mathbf{z}_j}$ are now conditioned on the object existence, i.e., the weighting factors $\beta_k^{\mathbf{x}\mapsto\mathbf{z}_j}$ are defined as

$$\beta_k^{\mathbf{x}\mapsto\mathbf{z}_j} := P(\theta_k^{\mathbf{x}\mapsto\mathbf{z}_j}|\exists\mathbf{x}_k, \mathcal{Z}^{\mathbf{x}}_{1:k}) = \frac{P(\exists\mathbf{x}_k, \theta_k^{\mathbf{x}\mapsto\mathbf{z}_j}|\mathcal{Z}^{\mathbf{x}}_{1:k})}{P(\exists\mathbf{x}_k|\mathcal{Z}^{\mathbf{x}}_{1:k})}\,. \tag{2.85}$$

2.3.4.1 Derivation of the weighting factors and object existence probability for the first model

In the case of the first model, i.e., when object observability aspect is not accounted for, and in the case that the number of measurements falling into the gate of the track $\mathbf{x}_k$ is $m_k > 0$, the object existence probability $P(\exists\mathbf{x}_k|\mathcal{Z}^{\mathbf{x}}_{1:k})$ is given as the probability of the event assuming that no measurement in the gate originated from the object $\mathbf{x}_k$, although it exists, plus the sum of the probabilities of the mutually exclusive events assuming that each of the m_k measurements falling into the gate of the track $\mathbf{x}_k$ has been evoked by it:

$$P(\exists \mathbf{x}_k | \mathcal{Z}^{\mathbf{x}}_{1:k}) = P(\exists \mathbf{x}_k, \theta_k^{\mathbf{x}\mapsto \mathbf{z}_0} | \mathcal{Z}^{\mathbf{x}}_{1:k}) + \sum_{j=1}^{m_k} P(\exists \mathbf{x}_k, \theta_k^{\mathbf{x}\mapsto \mathbf{z}_j} | \mathcal{Z}^{\mathbf{x}}_{1:k}) \,. \tag{2.86}$$

The probabilities $P(\exists \mathbf{x}_k, \theta_k^{\mathbf{x}\mapsto \mathbf{z}_0} | \mathcal{Z}^{\mathbf{x}}_{1:k})$ and $P(\exists \mathbf{x}_k, \theta_k^{\mathbf{x}\mapsto \mathbf{z}_j} | \mathcal{Z}^{\mathbf{x}}_{1:k})$ are calculated using the Bayes' rule:

$$\begin{aligned}
P(\exists \mathbf{x}_k, \theta_k^{\mathbf{x}\mapsto \mathbf{z}_0} | \mathcal{Z}^{\mathbf{x}}_{1:k}) &= P(\exists \mathbf{x}_k, \theta_k^{\mathbf{x}\mapsto \mathbf{z}_0} | \mathcal{Z}^{\mathbf{x}}_{k}, m_k, \mathcal{Z}^{\mathbf{x}}_{1:(k-1)}) \\
&= \frac{1}{c_k} \cdot p(\mathcal{Z}^{\mathbf{x}}_{k} | \exists \mathbf{x}_k, \theta_k^{\mathbf{x}\mapsto \mathbf{z}_0}, m_k, \mathcal{Z}^{\mathbf{x}}_{1:(k-1)}) P(\exists \mathbf{x}_k, \theta_k^{\mathbf{x}\mapsto \mathbf{z}_0} | m_k, \mathcal{Z}^{\mathbf{x}}_{1:(k-1)}) \\
&= \frac{1}{c'_k} \cdot p(\mathcal{Z}^{\mathbf{x}}_{k} | \exists \mathbf{x}_k, \theta_k^{\mathbf{x}\mapsto \mathbf{z}_0}, m_k, \mathcal{Z}^{\mathbf{x}}_{1:(k-1)}) P(m_k | \exists \mathbf{x}_k, \theta_k^{\mathbf{x}\mapsto \mathbf{z}_0}, \mathcal{Z}^{\mathbf{x}}_{1:(k-1)}) \\
&\quad \cdot P(\exists \mathbf{x}_k, \theta_k^{\mathbf{x}\mapsto \mathbf{z}_0} | \mathcal{Z}^{\mathbf{x}}_{1:(k-1)}) \\
&= \frac{1}{c'_k} \cdot p(\mathcal{Z}^{\mathbf{x}}_{k} | \exists \mathbf{x}_k, \theta_k^{\mathbf{x}\mapsto \mathbf{z}_0}, m_k, \mathcal{Z}^{\mathbf{x}}_{1:(k-1)}) P(m_k | \exists \mathbf{x}_k, \theta_k^{\mathbf{x}\mapsto \mathbf{z}_0}, \mathcal{Z}^{\mathbf{x}}_{1:(k-1)}) \\
&\quad \cdot P(\theta_k^{\mathbf{x}\mapsto \mathbf{z}_0} | \exists \mathbf{x}_k, \mathcal{Z}^{\mathbf{x}}_{1:(k-1)}) P(\exists \mathbf{x}_k | \mathcal{Z}^{\mathbf{x}}_{1:(k-1)})
\end{aligned} \tag{2.87}$$

$$\begin{aligned}
P(\exists \mathbf{x}_k, \theta_k^{\mathbf{x}\mapsto \mathbf{z}_j} | \mathcal{Z}^{\mathbf{x}}_{1:k}) &= P(\exists \mathbf{x}_k, \theta_k^{\mathbf{x}\mapsto \mathbf{z}_j} | \mathcal{Z}^{\mathbf{x}}_{k}, m_k, \mathcal{Z}^{\mathbf{x}}_{1:(k-1)}) \\
&= \frac{1}{c_k} \cdot p(\mathcal{Z}^{\mathbf{x}}_{k} | \exists \mathbf{x}_k, \theta_k^{\mathbf{x}\mapsto \mathbf{z}_j}, m_k, \mathcal{Z}^{\mathbf{x}}_{1:(k-1)}) P(\exists \mathbf{x}_k, \theta_k^{\mathbf{x}\mapsto \mathbf{z}_j} | m_k, \mathcal{Z}^{\mathbf{x}}_{1:(k-1)}) \\
&= \frac{1}{c'_k} \cdot p(\mathcal{Z}^{\mathbf{x}}_{k} | \exists \mathbf{x}_k, \theta_k^{\mathbf{x}\mapsto \mathbf{z}_j}, m_k, \mathcal{Z}^{\mathbf{x}}_{1:(k-1)}) P(m_k | \exists \mathbf{x}_k, \theta_k^{\mathbf{x}\mapsto \mathbf{z}_j}, \mathcal{Z}^{\mathbf{x}}_{1:(k-1)}) \\
&\quad \cdot P(\exists \mathbf{x}_k, \theta_k^{\mathbf{x}\mapsto \mathbf{z}_j} | \mathcal{Z}^{\mathbf{x}}_{1:(k-1)}) \\
&= \frac{1}{c'_k} \cdot p(\mathcal{Z}^{\mathbf{x}}_{k} | \exists \mathbf{x}_k, \theta_k^{\mathbf{x}\mapsto \mathbf{z}_j}, m_k, \mathcal{Z}^{\mathbf{x}}_{1:(k-1)}) P(m_k | \exists \mathbf{x}_k, \theta_k^{\mathbf{x}\mapsto \mathbf{z}_j}, \mathcal{Z}^{\mathbf{x}}_{1:(k-1)}) \\
&\quad \cdot P(\theta_k^{\mathbf{x}\mapsto \mathbf{z}_j} | \exists \mathbf{x}_k, \mathcal{Z}^{\mathbf{x}}_{1:(k-1)}) P(\exists \mathbf{x}_k | \mathcal{Z}^{\mathbf{x}}_{1:(k-1)}) \,,
\end{aligned} \tag{2.88}$$

with

$$c_k = p(\mathcal{Z}^{\mathbf{x}}_{k} | m_k, \mathcal{Z}^{\mathbf{x}}_{1:(k-1)}) \tag{2.89}$$

and

$$
\begin{aligned}
c'_k =& p(\mathcal{Z}_k^{\mathbf{x}} | m_k, \mathcal{Z}_{1:(k-1)}^{\mathbf{x}}) P(m_k | \mathcal{Z}_{1:(k-1)}^{\mathbf{x}}) \\
=& p(\mathcal{Z}_k^{\mathbf{x}} | \nexists \mathbf{x}_k, m_k, \mathcal{Z}_{1:(k-1)}^{\mathbf{x}}) P(m_k | \nexists \mathbf{x}_k, \mathcal{Z}_{1:(k-1)}^{\mathbf{x}}) P(\nexists \mathbf{x}_k | \mathcal{Z}_{1:(k-1)}^{\mathbf{x}}) \\
&+ p(\mathcal{Z}_k^{\mathbf{x}} | \exists \mathbf{x}_k, \theta_k^{\mathbf{x} \mapsto \mathbf{z}_0}, m_k, \mathcal{Z}_{1:(k-1)}^{\mathbf{x}}) P(m_k | \exists \mathbf{x}_k, \theta_k^{\mathbf{x} \mapsto \mathbf{z}_0}, \mathcal{Z}_{1:(k-1)}^{\mathbf{x}}) \\
&\cdot P(\exists \mathbf{x}_k, \theta_k^{\mathbf{x} \mapsto \mathbf{z}_0} | \mathcal{Z}_{1:(k-1)}^{\mathbf{x}}) \\
&+ \sum_{j=1}^{m_k} \Big(p(\mathcal{Z}_k^{\mathbf{x}} | \exists \mathbf{x}_k, \theta_k^{\mathbf{x} \mapsto \mathbf{z}_j}, m_k, \mathcal{Z}_{1:(k-1)}^{\mathbf{x}}) P(m_k | \exists \mathbf{x}_k, \theta_k^{\mathbf{x} \mapsto \mathbf{z}_j}, \mathcal{Z}_{1:(k-1)}^{\mathbf{x}}) \\
&\qquad \cdot P(\exists \mathbf{x}_k, \theta_k^{\mathbf{x} \mapsto \mathbf{z}_j} | \mathcal{Z}_{1:(k-1)}^{\mathbf{x}}) \Big) .
\end{aligned}
\tag{2.90}
$$

As in PDA, the a-priori probability for receiving a relevant measurement given the object existence is given by $P_D \cdot P_G$ with P_D being the detection probability and P_G the probability of the measurement to fall into the gating region. In case of m_k measurements in the gate, the a-priori probability of a measurement to be evoked by the track (given the object existence) is thus given by

$$
P(\theta_k^{\mathbf{x} \mapsto \mathbf{z}_j} | \exists \mathbf{x}_k, m_k, \mathcal{Z}_{1:(k-1)}^{\mathbf{x}}) = \frac{1}{m_k} P_D P_G \quad \forall j = 1, \dots, m_k . \tag{2.91}
$$

The probability that none of the measurements in the gate has been evoked by the track given the object existence is given by

$$
P(\theta_k^{\mathbf{x} \mapsto \mathbf{z}_0} | \exists \mathbf{x}_k, \mathcal{Z}_{1:(k-1)}^{\mathbf{x}}) = 1 - P_D P_G . \tag{2.92}
$$

Further, similar to PDA (compare (2.59) and (2.57)), the a-priori probability density of the measurements in the gating region given that either all of them are false alarms or that the measurement j is the correct measurement and all other measurements are false alarms are given by

$$
p(\mathcal{Z}_k^{\mathbf{x}} | \exists \mathbf{x}_k, \theta_k^{\mathbf{x} \mapsto \mathbf{z}_0}, m_k, \mathcal{Z}_{1:(k-1)}^{\mathbf{x}}) = p(\mathcal{Z}_k^{\mathbf{x}} | \nexists \mathbf{x}_k, m_k, \mathcal{Z}_{1:(k-1)}^{\mathbf{x}}) = \frac{1}{V_k^{m_k}} \tag{2.93}
$$

and

$$p(\mathcal{Z}_k^{\mathbf{x}}|\exists\mathbf{x}_k, \theta_k^{\mathbf{x}\mapsto\mathbf{z}_j}, m_k, \mathcal{Z}_{1:(k-1)}^{\mathbf{x}}) = \frac{1}{V_k^{m_k-1}} p(\mathbf{z}_{k,j}|\exists\mathbf{x}_k, \theta_k^{\mathbf{x}\mapsto\mathbf{z}_j}, \mathcal{Z}_{1:(k-1)}^{\mathbf{x}})$$
$$= \frac{1}{V_k^{m_k-1}} \frac{1}{P_G} f_{\mathcal{Z}_k^{\mathbf{x}}}$$
$$= \frac{1}{V_k^{m_k-1}} \frac{1}{P_G} \mathcal{N}(\tilde{\mathbf{z}}_{k,j}; 0, \mathbf{P}_{\mathbf{z}_k\mathbf{z}_k}^{\mathbf{x}}) \quad j = 1, \cdots, m_k\,. \tag{2.94}$$

The a-priori probability of the number of measurements being m_k is equivalent to the probabilities of the number of false measurements being m_k and $m_k - 1$ correspondingly:

$$P(m_k|\nexists\mathbf{x}_k, \mathcal{Z}_{1:(k-1)}^{\mathbf{x}}) = P(m_k|\nexists\mathbf{x}_k) = \mu_F(m_k)\,, \tag{2.95}$$
$$P(m_k|\exists\mathbf{x}_k, \theta_k^{\mathbf{x}\mapsto\mathbf{z}_0}, \mathcal{Z}_{1:(k-1)}^{\mathbf{x}}) = P(m_k|\exists\mathbf{x}_k, \theta_k^{\mathbf{x}\mapsto\mathbf{z}_0}) = \mu_F(m_k)\,, \tag{2.96}$$
$$P(m_k|\exists\mathbf{x}_k, \theta_k^{\mathbf{x}\mapsto\mathbf{z}_j}, \mathcal{Z}_{1:(k-1)}^{\mathbf{x}}) = P(m_k|\exists\mathbf{x}_k, \theta_k^{\mathbf{x}\mapsto\mathbf{z}_j}) = \mu_F(m_k - 1)\,. \tag{2.97}$$

These probabilities can be calculated using one of both distribution models for the number of clutter measurements described in Section 2.3.3 (s. page 46). For the Poisson distribution model without a-priori known parameter λ, the expected number of measurements $\widehat{m}_k$ can be assumed to be

$$\widehat{m}_k = m_k - P_D P_G P(\exists\mathbf{x}_k|\mathcal{Z}_{1:(k-1)}^{\mathbf{x}})\,. \tag{2.98}$$

Using (2.87) - (2.98) the posterior existence probability from (2.86) is given by

$$P(\exists\mathbf{x}_k|\mathcal{Z}_{1:k}^{\mathbf{x}}) = \frac{1-\delta_k}{1-\delta_k P(\exists\mathbf{x}_k|\mathcal{Z}_{1:(k-1)}^{\mathbf{x}})} P(\exists\mathbf{x}_k|\mathcal{Z}_{1:(k-1)}^{\mathbf{x}}) \tag{2.99}$$

with

$$\delta_k = P_D P_G \cdot \big(1 - \frac{V_k}{\widehat{m}_k} \sum_{j=1}^{m_k} p(\mathbf{z}_{k,j}|\mathcal{Z}_{1:(k-1)}^{\mathbf{x}})\big) \tag{2.100}$$

The association weights are given by

$$\beta_k^{\mathbf{x}\mapsto\mathbf{z}_0} = \frac{1 - P_D P_G}{1 - \delta_k} \tag{2.101}$$

$$\beta_k^{\mathbf{x}\mapsto\mathbf{z}_j} = \frac{P_D P_G}{1 - \delta_k} \frac{V_k}{\widehat{m}_k} p(\mathbf{z}_{k,j} | \mathcal{Z}^{\mathbf{x}}_{1:(k-1)}) , \quad j = 1, \cdots, m_k \tag{2.102}$$

For the special case of no measurements falling into the gating region, $\beta_k^{\mathbf{x}\mapsto\mathbf{z}_0} = 1$. The probability of the object existence in this case can be calculated by using Bayes' rule as follows:

$$\begin{aligned}
P(\exists\mathbf{x}_k | \mathcal{Z}^{\mathbf{x}}_{1:k}) &= P(\exists\mathbf{x}_k | \mathcal{Z}^{\mathbf{x}}_k = \{\emptyset\}, \mathcal{Z}^{\mathbf{x}}_{1:(k-1)}) \\
&= \frac{P(\mathcal{Z}^{\mathbf{x}}_k = \{\emptyset\} | \exists\mathbf{x}_k, \mathcal{Z}^{\mathbf{x}}_{1:(k-1)}) P(\exists\mathbf{x}_k | \mathcal{Z}^{\mathbf{x}}_{1:(k-1)})}{P(\mathcal{Z}^{\mathbf{x}}_k = \{\emptyset\} | \mathcal{Z}^{\mathbf{x}}_{1:(k-1)})} \\
&= \frac{P(\theta_k^{\mathbf{x}\mapsto\mathbf{z}_0} | \exists\mathbf{x}_k, \mathcal{Z}^{\mathbf{x}}_{1:(k-1)}) P(\exists\mathbf{x}_k | \mathcal{Z}^{\mathbf{x}}_{1:(k-1)})}{P(\theta_k^{\mathbf{x}\mapsto\mathbf{z}_0} | \mathcal{Z}^{\mathbf{x}}_{1:(k-1)})} \\
&= \frac{(1 - P_D P_G) P(\exists\mathbf{x}_k | \mathcal{Z}^{\mathbf{x}}_{1:(k-1)})}{1 - P_D P_G P(\exists\mathbf{x}_k | \mathcal{Z}^{\mathbf{x}}_{1:(k-1)})} .
\end{aligned} \tag{2.103}$$

The denominator in (2.103) has been calculated by using (2.92) and taking into account that the a-priori probability for not getting a measurement for the track not conditioned on the object existence probability is given by

$$\begin{aligned}
P(\theta_k^{\mathbf{x}\mapsto\mathbf{z}_0} | \mathcal{Z}^{\mathbf{x}}_{1:(k-1)}) =& P(\theta_k^{\mathbf{x}\mapsto\mathbf{z}_0} | \exists\mathbf{x}_k, \mathcal{Z}^{\mathbf{x}}_{1:(k-1)}) P(\exists\mathbf{x}_k | \mathcal{Z}^{\mathbf{x}}_{1:(k-1)}) \\
&+ P(\theta_k^{\mathbf{x}\mapsto\mathbf{z}_0} | \nexists\mathbf{x}_k, \mathcal{Z}^{\mathbf{x}}_{1:(k-1)}) P(\nexists\mathbf{x}_k | \mathcal{Z}^{\mathbf{x}}_{1:(k-1)}) \\
=& P(\theta_k^{\mathbf{x}\mapsto\mathbf{z}_0} | \exists\mathbf{x}_k, \mathcal{Z}^{\mathbf{x}}_{1:(k-1)}) P(\exists\mathbf{x}_k | \mathcal{Z}^{\mathbf{x}}_{1:(k-1)}) \\
&+ P(\theta_k^{\mathbf{x}\mapsto\mathbf{z}_0} | \nexists\mathbf{x}_k, \mathcal{Z}^{\mathbf{x}}_{1:(k-1)}) (1 - P(\exists\mathbf{x}_k | \mathcal{Z}^{\mathbf{x}}_{1:(k-1)})) \\
=& (1 - P_D P_G) P(\exists\mathbf{x}_k | \mathcal{Z}^{\mathbf{x}}_{1:(k-1)}) \\
&+ 1 \cdot (1 - P(\exists\mathbf{x}_k | \mathcal{Z}^{\mathbf{x}}_{1:(k-1)})) \\
=& 1 - P_D P_G P(\exists\mathbf{x}_k | \mathcal{Z}^{\mathbf{x}}_{1:(k-1)}) .
\end{aligned} \tag{2.104}$$

The calculation of the a-priori object existence probability $P(\exists\mathbf{x}_k | \mathcal{Z}^{\mathbf{x}}_{1:(k-1)})$ from the posterior object existence probability $P(\exists\mathbf{x}_{k-1} | \mathcal{Z}^{\mathbf{x}}_{1:(k-1)})$ from the last frame is done using the Markov chain equations with transition probabilities $P^{\exists\to\exists}$, $P^{\nexists\to\exists}$, $P^{\exists\to\nexists}$, and $P^{\nexists\to\nexists}$:

$$P(\exists\mathbf{x}_k|\mathcal{Z}^{\mathbf{x}}_{1:(k-1)}) = P^{\exists\to\exists}P(\exists\mathbf{x}_{k-1}) + P^{\nexists\to\exists}P(\nexists\mathbf{x}_{k-1}) \tag{2.105}$$

$$P(\nexists\mathbf{x}_k|\mathcal{Z}^{\mathbf{x}}_{1:(k-1)}) = P^{\exists\to\nexists}P(\exists\mathbf{x}_{k-1}) + P^{\nexists\to\nexists}P(\nexists\mathbf{x}_{k-1})\,. \tag{2.106}$$

The coefficients $P^{\exists\to\exists}$, $P^{\nexists\to\exists}$, $P^{\exists\to\nexists}$, and $P^{\nexists\to\nexists}$ may be interpreted as object persistence probability, object appearance probability, object disappearance probability and object absence probability, respectively. It is obvious that

$$P^{\exists\to\nexists} = 1 - P^{\exists\to\exists} \quad \text{and} \quad P^{\nexists\to\nexists} = 1 - P^{\nexists\to\exists}\,. \tag{2.107}$$

Figure 2.7 illustrates states and state transitions of the existence estimation Markov chain in case of the first model.

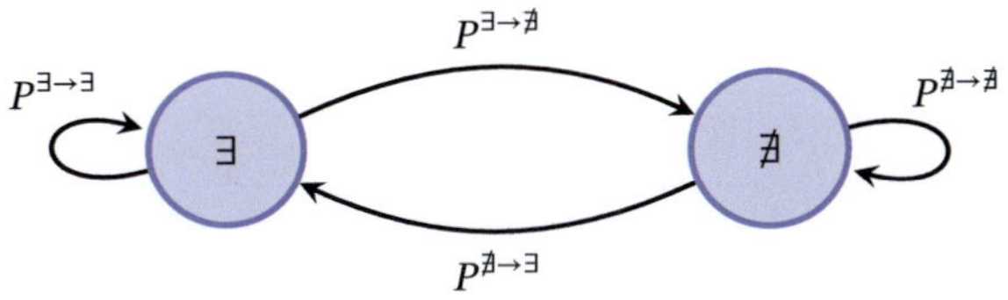

Figure 2.7: Object existence modeling in IPDA as a Markov chain with two states (first model): object exists ($\exists$) and object does not exist (i.e., it is a phantom track) ($\nexists$).

2.3.4.2 Derivation of the weighting factors and object existence probability for the second model

If observability aspect is accounted for, the association weights $\beta_k^{\mathbf{x}\mapsto\mathbf{z}_j}$ are derived analogously using

$$P(\exists\mathbf{x}_k|\mathcal{Z}^{\mathbf{x}}_{1:k}) = P(\supset\mathbf{x}_k|\mathcal{Z}^{\mathbf{x}}_{1:k}) + P(\not\supset\mathbf{x}_k|\mathcal{Z}^{\mathbf{x}}_{1:k})\,. \tag{2.108}$$

They are given by

$$\begin{aligned}\beta_k^{\mathbf{x}\mapsto\mathbf{z}_0} &:= P(\theta_k^{\mathbf{x}\mapsto\mathbf{z}_0}|\exists\mathbf{x},\mathcal{Z}_{1:k}^{\mathbf{x}}) = \frac{P(\exists\mathbf{x}_k,\theta_k^{\mathbf{x}\mapsto\mathbf{z}_0}|\mathcal{Z}_{1:k}^{\mathbf{x}})}{P(\exists\mathbf{x}_k|\mathcal{Z}_{1:k}^{\mathbf{x}})}\\ &= \frac{P(\supset\mathbf{x}_k,\theta_k^{\mathbf{x}\mapsto\mathbf{z}_0}|\mathcal{Z}_{1:k}^{\mathbf{x}}) + P(\not\supset\mathbf{x}_k,\theta_k^{\mathbf{x}\mapsto\mathbf{z}_0}|\mathcal{Z}_{1:k}^{\mathbf{x}})}{P(\supset\mathbf{x}_k|\mathcal{Z}_{1:k}^{\mathbf{x}}) + P(\not\supset\mathbf{x}_k|\mathcal{Z}_{1:k}^{\mathbf{x}})}\end{aligned} \tag{2.109}$$

and

$$\begin{aligned}\beta_k^{\mathbf{x}\mapsto\mathbf{z}_j} &:= P(\theta_k^{\mathbf{x}\mapsto\mathbf{z}_j}|\exists\mathbf{x},\mathcal{Z}_{1:k}^{\mathbf{x}}) = \frac{P(\exists\mathbf{x}_k,\theta_k^{\mathbf{x}\mapsto\mathbf{z}_j}|\mathcal{Z}_{1:k}^{\mathbf{x}})}{P(\exists\mathbf{x}_k|\mathcal{Z}_{1:k}^{\mathbf{x}})}\\ &= \frac{P(\supset\mathbf{x}_k,\theta_k^{\mathbf{x}\mapsto\mathbf{z}_j}|\mathcal{Z}_{1:k}^{\mathbf{x}})}{P(\supset\mathbf{x}_k|\mathcal{Z}_{1:k}^{\mathbf{x}}) + P(\not\supset\mathbf{x}_k|\mathcal{Z}_{1:k}^{\mathbf{x}})}, \quad j = 1,\cdots,m_k\,,\end{aligned} \tag{2.110}$$

which leads to

$$\beta_k^{\mathbf{x}\mapsto\mathbf{z}_0} = \frac{(1 - P_D P_G)P(\supset\mathbf{x}_k|\mathcal{Z}_{1:(k-1)}^{\mathbf{x}}) + P(\not\supset\mathbf{x}_k|\mathcal{Z}_{1:(k-1)}^{\mathbf{x}})}{(1-\delta_k)P(\supset\mathbf{x}_k|\mathcal{Z}_{1:(k-1)}^{\mathbf{x}}) + P(\not\supset\mathbf{x}_k|\mathcal{Z}_{1:(k-1)}^{\mathbf{x}})}, \tag{2.111}$$

$$\beta_k^{\mathbf{x}\mapsto\mathbf{z}_j} = \frac{P_D P_G P(\supset\mathbf{x}_k|\mathcal{Z}_{1:(k-1)}^{\mathbf{x}})\frac{V_k}{\hat{m}_k}p(\mathbf{z}_{k,j}|\mathcal{Z}_{1:(k-1)}^{\mathbf{x}})}{(1-\delta_k)P(\supset\mathbf{x}_k|\mathcal{Z}_{1:(k-1)}^{\mathbf{x}}) + P(\not\supset\mathbf{x}_k|\mathcal{Z}_{1:(k-1)}^{\mathbf{x}})}, \quad j = 1,\dots,m_k \tag{2.112}$$

with δ_k being defined as in equation 2.100.

The posterior probabilities are given by

$$P(\supset\mathbf{x}_k|\mathcal{Z}_{1:k}^{\mathbf{x}}) = \frac{(1-\delta_k)P(\supset\mathbf{x}_k|\mathcal{Z}_{1:(k-1)}^{\mathbf{x}})}{1-\delta_k P(\supset\mathbf{x}_k|\mathcal{Z}_{1:(k-1)}^{\mathbf{x}})} \tag{2.113}$$

$$P(\not\supset\mathbf{x}_k|\mathcal{Z}_{1:k}^{\mathbf{x}}) = \frac{P(\not\supset\mathbf{x}_k|\mathcal{Z}_{1:(k-1)}^{\mathbf{x}})}{1-\delta_k P(\supset\mathbf{x}_k|\mathcal{Z}_{1:(k-1)}^{\mathbf{x}})} \tag{2.114}$$

$$P(\exists\mathbf{x}_k|\mathcal{Z}_{1:k}^{\mathbf{x}}) = P(\supset\mathbf{x}_k|\mathcal{Z}_{1:k}^{\mathbf{x}}) + P(\not\supset\mathbf{x}_k|\mathcal{Z}_{1:k}^{\mathbf{x}})\,. \tag{2.115}$$

The Markov chain equations for computation of the prior probabilities from the posterior probabilities from the last frame are given by

$$P(\supset\mathbf{x}_k|\mathcal{Z}^{\mathbf{x}}_{1:(k-1)}) = P^{\supset\to\supset}P(\supset\mathbf{x}_{k-1}) + P^{\not\supset\to\supset}P(\not\supset\mathbf{x}_{k-1}) + P^{\nexists\to\supset}P(\nexists\mathbf{x}_{k-1}) \tag{2.116}$$

$$P(\not\supset\mathbf{x}_k|\mathcal{Z}^{\mathbf{x}}_{1:(k-1)}) = P^{\supset\to\not\supset}P(\supset\mathbf{x}_{k-1}) + P^{\not\supset\to\not\supset}P(\not\supset\mathbf{x}_{k-1}) + P^{\nexists\to\not\supset}P(\nexists\mathbf{x}_{k-1}) \tag{2.117}$$

$$P(\nexists\mathbf{x}_k|\mathcal{Z}^{\mathbf{x}}_{1:(k-1)}) = P^{\supset\to\nexists}P(\supset\mathbf{x}_{k-1}) + P^{\not\supset\to\nexists}P(\not\supset\mathbf{x}_{k-1}) + P^{\nexists\to\nexists}P(\nexists\mathbf{x}_{k-1}) \tag{2.118}$$

with nine coefficients $p^{\supset\to\supset}$, $p^{\not\supset\to\supset}$, $p^{\nexists\to\supset}$, $p^{\supset\to\not\supset}$, $p^{\not\supset\to\not\supset}$, $p^{\nexists\to\not\supset}$, $p^{\supset\to\nexists}$, $p^{\not\supset\to\nexists}$, and $p^{\nexists\to\nexists}$.

It must hold that

$$p^{\supset\to\supset} + p^{\supset\to\not\supset} + p^{\supset\to\nexists} = 1 \tag{2.119}$$

$$p^{\not\supset\to\supset} + p^{\not\supset\to\not\supset} + p^{\not\supset\to\nexists} = 1 \tag{2.120}$$

$$p^{\nexists\to\supset} + p^{\nexists\to\not\supset} + p^{\nexists\to\nexists} = 1\,. \tag{2.121}$$

A graphical visualization of the Markov chain states and transitions for the second model is given in Figure 2.8.

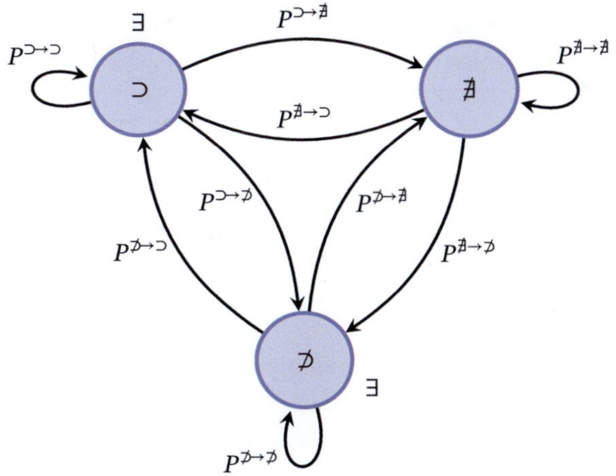

Figure 2.8: Object existence modeling in IPDA as a Markov chain with three states (second model): object exists and is observable (⊃), object exists but is not observable (⊅), and object does not exist (i.e., it is a phantom track) (∄).

2.3.5 Joint Probabilistic Data Association (JPDA)

In PDA, each tracked object is considered separately. This justifies the assumption that either all or all but one measurements falling into the gating region of a track are due to clutter. In the presence of multiple closely spaced objects this assumption may be invalid since true measurements of one object may fall into the gating region of another object causing permanent non-random interference. This issue is accounted for in an extension of the PDA called ***Joint Probabilistic Data Association (JPDA)*** proposed by Bar Shalom et al. [For83]. Instead of considering each tracked object separately, JPDA considers association configurations, the so-called ***joint association events*** or, in short, ***joint events***. A joint event $\Theta_k(\mathcal{T})$ is defined as a conjunction of associations $\theta_k^{\mathbf{x}_{t_j} \mapsto \mathbf{z}_j}$ between measurements $\mathbf{z}_j$ and possible causes $\mathbf{x}_{t_j}$ that can be given either by a tracked object ($t_j \neq 0$) or by clutter ($t_j = 0$):

$$\Theta_k(\mathcal{T}) = \bigcup_{j=1}^{m_k} \theta_k^{\mathbf{x}_{t_j} \mapsto \mathbf{z}_j}, \quad \mathcal{T} = (t_1, \ldots, t_{m_k}), \quad t_j \in \{0, \ldots, n_k\}, \tag{2.122}$$

with n_k being number of currently tracked objects. $\mathcal{T}$ are ordered sets of m_k (possibly repeating) track numbers t_j including 0, which represents the clutter source.

For reduction of complexity, tracked objects are partitioned into independent clusters and joint events are built for each cluster separately. A cluster is defined as a set of tracks which share no measurements with tracks that do not belong to the cluster.

For easier clutter handling, clutter measurements are considered to be identically distributed over the whole cluster volume V independently of the gating regions of the tracks. This implies that each measurement should be able to be associated with each track in the cluster and hence $P_G = 1$. However, this would also imply usage of too far lying measurements for update of a track. In order to avoid this, a binary ***validation matrix*** Ω_k is defined:

$$\Omega_k = [\omega_{ji}]_k, \quad j = 1, \cdots, m_k; \quad i = 0, 1, \cdots, n_k \tag{2.123}$$

with

$$\omega_{ji} := \begin{cases} 0 & \text{if} \quad \mathbf{z}_j \notin \Gamma_k^{\mathbf{x}_i}(\gamma) \\ 1 & \text{if} \quad \mathbf{z}_j \in \Gamma_k^{\mathbf{x}_i}(\gamma), \end{cases} \tag{2.124}$$

and gating regions $\Gamma_k^{\mathbf{x}_i}(\gamma)$ as defined in (2.47). The first column ($i = 0$) of Ω_k stands for association with no track, i.e., indicates that a measurement j stems from clutter. As mentioned above, this can be applicable to each measurement in cluster, hence $\forall j : \omega_{j0} = 1$.

Each joint event $\Theta_k(\mathcal{T})$ can be represented through a binary matrix $\widehat{\Omega}(\Theta_k(\mathcal{T}))$ with

$$\widehat{\Omega}(\Theta_k(\mathcal{T})) = [\widehat{\omega}_{ji}(\Theta_k(\mathcal{T}))], \quad j = 1, \cdots, m_k; \quad i = 0, 1, \cdots, n_k \tag{2.125}$$

and

$$\widehat{\omega}_{ji}(\Theta_k(\mathcal{T})) = \begin{cases} 1 & \text{if} \quad \theta_k^{\mathbf{x}_i \mapsto \mathbf{z}_j} \subset \Theta_k(\mathcal{T}) \\ 0 & \text{else}\,. \end{cases} \tag{2.126}$$

In JPDA, a joint event $\Theta_k(\mathcal{T})$ is considered to be ***"feasible"*** under the following conditions:

- A measurement may have only one origin:

$$\sum_{i=0}^{n_k} \widehat{\omega}_{ji}(\Theta_k(\mathcal{T})) = 1, \quad j = 1, \cdots, m_k \tag{2.127}$$

- A track may evoke at most one measurement:

$$\sum_{j=1}^{m_k} \widehat{\omega}_{ji}(\Theta_k(\mathcal{T})) \leq 1, \quad i = 1, \cdots, n_k\,. \tag{2.128}$$

A matrix $\widehat{\Omega}$ defining a feasible event $\Theta_k(\mathcal{T})$ can be built from the validation matrix Ω_k by picking out elements in a way such that each row and each column contains at most one "1". The only exception is made for the first column which may contain multiple non-zero entries since more than one measurement may be due to clutter. The set of all feasible joint events in the following is denoted by $\boldsymbol{\Theta}_k$ with

$$\sum_{\Theta_k(\mathcal{T})\in\boldsymbol{\Theta}_k} P(\Theta_k(\mathcal{T})) = 1\,. \tag{2.129}$$

For better readability, in the following three auxiliary entities $\vartheta_i(\Theta_k(\mathcal{T}))$, $\tau_j(\Theta_k(\mathcal{T}))$ and $\phi(\Theta_k(\mathcal{T}))$ are defined for a joint event $\Theta_k(\mathcal{T})$:

$$\vartheta_i(\Theta_k(\mathcal{T})) := \sum_{j=1}^{m_k} \widehat{\omega}_{ji}(\Theta_k(\mathcal{T})), \quad i = 1,\cdots,n_k \tag{2.130}$$

$$\tau_j(\Theta_k(\mathcal{T})) := \sum_{i=1}^{n_k} \widehat{\omega}_{ji}(\Theta_k(\mathcal{T})), \quad j = 1,\cdots,m_k \tag{2.131}$$

$$\phi(\Theta_k(\mathcal{T})) := \sum_{j=1}^{m_k}(1-\tau_j(\Theta_k(\mathcal{T}))) \tag{2.132}$$

$\vartheta_i(\Theta_k(\mathcal{T}))$ indicates whether in $\Theta_k(\mathcal{T})$ the ith track has been assigned a measurement. $\tau_j(\Theta_k(\mathcal{T}))$ indicates whether in $\Theta_k(\mathcal{T})$ the jth measurement has been assigned to a track. Finally, $\phi(\Theta_k(\mathcal{T}))$ specifies the number of the clutter based measurements in $\Theta_k(\mathcal{T})$.

The weighting factors $\beta_k^{\mathbf{x}_i\mapsto\mathbf{z}_j}$ $(i = 1,\cdots,n_k;\quad j = 0,\cdots,m_k)$ can be calculated as follows:

$$\beta_k^{\mathbf{x}_i\mapsto\mathbf{z}_j} := P(\theta_k^{\mathbf{x}_i\mapsto\mathbf{z}_j}|\mathcal{Z}_{1:k}) = \sum_{\Theta_k(\mathcal{T})\in\boldsymbol{\Theta}_k} P(\Theta_k(\mathcal{T})|\mathcal{Z}_{1:k})\cdot\widehat{\omega}_{ji}(\Theta_k(\mathcal{T}))\,. \tag{2.133}$$

The a-posteriori probability of a joint event $\Theta_k(\mathcal{T})$ conditioned on all received measurements including the current measurement set can be calculated using the Bayes' rule:

$$\begin{aligned} P(\Theta_k(\mathcal{T})|\mathcal{Z}_{1:k}) &= P(\Theta_k(\mathcal{T})|\mathcal{Z}_k, m_k, \mathcal{Z}_{1:(k-1)}) \\ &= \frac{1}{c_k} p(\mathcal{Z}_k|\Theta_k(\mathcal{T}), m_k, \mathcal{Z}_{1:(k-1)}) P(\Theta_k(\mathcal{T})|m_k, \mathcal{Z}_{1:(k-1)}) \end{aligned} \tag{2.134}$$

with

$$c_k = \sum_{\Theta_k(\mathcal{T}) \in \boldsymbol{\Theta}_k} p(\mathcal{Z}_k | \Theta_k(\mathcal{T}), m_k, \mathcal{Z}_{1:(k-1)}) P(\Theta_k(\mathcal{T}) | m_k, \mathcal{Z}_{1:(k-1)}) \,. \tag{2.135}$$

Similar to the calculations in the PDA, the likelihood of a measurement $\mathbf{z}_{k,j}$ given that it stems from a track $\mathbf{x}_{t_j}$ with $t_j \neq 0$ is given by

$$p(\mathbf{z}_{k,j} | \theta_k^{\mathbf{x}_{t_j} \mapsto \mathbf{z}_j}, \mathcal{Z}_{1:(k-1)}) = \mathcal{N}(\mathbf{z}_{k,j}; \hat{\mathbf{z}}_k^{\mathbf{x}_{t_j}}, \mathbf{P}_{\mathbf{z}_k \mathbf{z}_k}^{\mathbf{x}_{t_j}}) \quad \text{for } t_j \neq 0 \,. \tag{2.136}$$

and the likelihood of a clutter-based measurement is given by

$$p(\mathbf{z}_{k,j} | \theta_k^{\mathbf{x}_{t_j} \mapsto \mathbf{z}_j}, \mathcal{Z}_{1:(k-1)}) = \frac{1}{V} \quad \text{for } t_j = 0 \,. \tag{2.137}$$

Under the previously mentioned independence assumption of the clutter-based measurements and the true measurements, this leads to the following expression for the likelihood of the current measurement set $\mathcal{Z}_k$ conditioned on a joint event $\Theta_k(\mathcal{T})$ and number of measurements being m_k in (2.134) and (2.135):

$$\begin{aligned} p(\mathcal{Z}_k | \Theta_k(\mathcal{T}), m_k, \mathcal{Z}_{1:(k-1)}) &= \prod_{j=1}^{m_k} p(\mathbf{z}_{k,j} | \theta_k^{\mathbf{x}_{t_j} \mapsto \mathbf{z}_j}, \mathcal{Z}_{1:(k-1)}) \\ &= \frac{1}{V^{\phi(\Theta_k(\mathcal{T}))}} \prod_{j=1}^{m_k} \left(\mathcal{N}(\mathbf{z}_{k,j}; \hat{\mathbf{z}}_k^{\mathbf{x}_{t_j}}, \mathbf{P}_{\mathbf{z}_k \mathbf{z}_k}^{\mathbf{x}_{t_j}}) \right)^{\tau_j(\Theta_k(\mathcal{T}))} \,, \end{aligned} \tag{2.138}$$

where $\phi(\Theta_k(\mathcal{T}))$ is the number of the clutter-based measurements in the joint event $\Theta_k(\mathcal{T})$ and $\tau_j(\Theta_k(\mathcal{T}))$ serves for picking out the likelihoods of the measurements, that in $\Theta_k(\mathcal{T})$ have been declared as being non-clutter.

The a-priori probability $P(\Theta_k(\mathcal{T}) | m_k, \mathcal{Z}_{1:(k-1)})$ of a joint event $\Theta_k(\mathcal{T}) \in \boldsymbol{\Theta}_k$ in (2.134), conditioned on the number of received measurements is equivalent to the probability of assigning the tracks according to $\vartheta_i(\Theta_k(\mathcal{T}))$ and getting additionally

$\phi(\Theta_k(\mathcal{T}))$ clutter-based measurements:

$$
\begin{aligned}
P(\Theta_k(\mathcal{T})|m_k, \mathcal{Z}_{1:(k-1)}) = \\
&= P\big(\Theta_k(\mathcal{T}),\ \vartheta_1(\Theta_k(\mathcal{T})), \dots, \vartheta_{n_k}(\Theta_k(\mathcal{T})),\ \phi(\Theta_k(\mathcal{T}))|\mathcal{Z}_{1:(k-1)}\big) \\
&= P\big(\Theta_k(\mathcal{T})\,|\,\vartheta_1(\Theta_k(\mathcal{T})), \dots, \vartheta_{n_k}(\Theta_k(\mathcal{T})),\ \phi(\Theta_k(\mathcal{T}))\big) \\
&\quad \cdot P\big(\vartheta_1(\Theta_k(\mathcal{T})), \dots, \vartheta_{n_k}(\Theta_k(\mathcal{T})),\ \phi(\Theta_k(\mathcal{T}))|\mathcal{Z}_{1:(k-1)}\big)\,.
\end{aligned} \tag{2.139}
$$

An expression for the computation of the first factor follows from combinatorics with an assumption that each of the joint events $\Theta_k(\mathcal{T})$ has equal a-priori probability. It is given as a reciprocal of the number of all events that assign measurements to the tracks as defined by $\vartheta_i(\Theta_k(\mathcal{T}))$ for $i = 1, \dots, n_k$ and have $\phi(\Theta_k(\mathcal{T}))$ clutter measurements:

$$
\begin{aligned}
P(\Theta_k(\mathcal{T})|\vartheta_1(\Theta_k(\mathcal{T})), \dots, \vartheta_{n_k}(\Theta_k(\mathcal{T})), \phi(\Theta_k(\mathcal{T}))) &= \left(\frac{m_k!}{\phi(\Theta_k(\mathcal{T}))!}\right)^{-1} \\
&= \frac{\phi(\Theta_k(\mathcal{T}))!}{m_k!}
\end{aligned} \tag{2.140}
$$

The second factor is given by

$$
\begin{aligned}
&P(\vartheta_1(\Theta_k(\mathcal{T})), \dots, \vartheta_{n_k}(\Theta_k(\mathcal{T})), \phi(\Theta_k(\mathcal{T}))|\mathcal{Z}_{1:(k-1)}) \\
&\quad = \prod_{i=1}^{n_k} \left(\left(P_D^{\mathbf{x}_i}\right)^{\vartheta_i(\Theta_k(\mathcal{T}))} \cdot \left(1 - P_D^{\mathbf{x}_i}\right)^{1-\vartheta_i(\Theta_k(\mathcal{T}))} \right) \cdot \mu_F(\phi(\Theta_k(\mathcal{T})))
\end{aligned} \tag{2.141}
$$

with $P_D^{\mathbf{x}_i}$ being the probability for the tracked object $\mathbf{x}_i$ to be detected and $\mu_F(\phi(\Theta_k(\mathcal{T})))$ being the probability mass function for the number of clutter-based measurements that can be modeled as described in Section 2.3.3 (see page 46).

This leads to

$$P(\Theta_k(\mathcal{T})|\mathcal{Z}_{1:k}) = \frac{1}{c_k} \cdot \frac{\phi(\Theta_k(\mathcal{T}))!}{m_k!} \frac{\mu_F(\phi(\Theta_k(\mathcal{T})))}{V^{\phi(\Theta_k(\mathcal{T}))}} \tag{2.142}$$

$$\cdot \prod_{j=1}^{m_k} \left(\mathcal{N}(\mathbf{z}_{k,j}; \hat{\mathbf{z}}_k^{\mathbf{x}_{t_j}}, \mathbf{P}_{\mathbf{Z}_k \mathbf{Z}_k}^{\mathbf{x}_{t_j}}) \right)^{\tau_j(\Theta_k(\mathcal{T}))} \tag{2.143}$$

$$\cdot \prod_{i=1}^{n_k} \left((P_D^{\mathbf{x}_i})^{\vartheta_i(\Theta_k(\mathcal{T}))} (1 - P_D^{\mathbf{x}_i})^{1-\vartheta_i(\Theta_k(\mathcal{T}))} \right) \tag{2.144}$$

and hence to

$$P(\Theta_k(\mathcal{T})|\mathcal{Z}_{1:k}) = \lambda^{\phi(\Theta_k(\mathcal{T}))} \frac{e^{-\lambda V}}{c_k \cdot m_k!} \cdot \prod_{j=1}^{m_k} \left(\mathcal{N}(\mathbf{z}_{k,j}; \hat{\mathbf{z}}_k^{\mathbf{x}_{t_j}}, \mathbf{P}_{\mathbf{Z}_k \mathbf{Z}_k}^{\mathbf{x}_{t_j}}) \right)^{\tau_j(\Theta_k(\mathcal{T}))}$$
$$\cdot \prod_{i=1}^{n_k} \left((P_D^{\mathbf{x}_i})^{\vartheta_i(\Theta_k(\mathcal{T}))} (1 - P_D^{\mathbf{x}_i})^{1-\vartheta_i(\Theta_k(\mathcal{T}))} \right) \tag{2.145}$$

for the *parametric model* of clutter distribution and to

$$P(\Theta_k(\mathcal{T})|\mathcal{Z}_{1:k}) = \frac{1}{\tilde{c}_k} \frac{\phi(\Theta_k(\mathcal{T}))!}{V^{\phi(\Theta_k(\mathcal{T}))}} \prod_{j=1}^{m_k} \left(\mathcal{N}(\mathbf{z}_{k,j}; \hat{\mathbf{z}}_k^{\mathbf{x}_{t_j}}, \mathbf{P}_{\mathbf{Z}_k \mathbf{Z}_k}^{\mathbf{x}_{t_j}}) \right)^{\tau_j(\Theta_k(\mathcal{T}))}$$
$$\cdot \prod_{i=1}^{n_k} \left((P_D^{\mathbf{x}_i})^{\vartheta_i(\Theta_k(\mathcal{T}))} (1 - P_D^{\mathbf{x}_i})^{1-\vartheta_i(\Theta_k(\mathcal{T}))} \right) \tag{2.146}$$

for the *nonparametric model* of clutter distribution.

The state estimation of the JPDA is done analogously to that of the PDA by

$$
\begin{aligned}
\hat{\mathbf{x}}_{k,i} &= \mathbb{E}[\mathbf{X}_{k,i}|\mathcal{Z}_{1:k}] = \sum_{j=0}^{m_k} \mathbb{E}[\mathbf{X}_k|\theta_k^{\mathbf{x}_i \mapsto \mathbf{z}_j}, \mathcal{Z}_{1:k}] \cdot P(\theta_k^{\mathbf{x}_i \mapsto \mathbf{z}_j}|\mathcal{Z}_{1:k}) \\
&= \sum_{j=0}^{m_k} \hat{\mathbf{x}}_{k,i}^{\mathbf{z}_j} \beta_k^{\mathbf{x}_i \mapsto \mathbf{z}_j} = \sum_{j=0}^{m_k} \beta_k^{\mathbf{x}_i \mapsto \mathbf{z}_j} \hat{\mathbf{x}}_{k,i}^{\mathbf{z}_j} \\
&= \sum_{j=0}^{m_k} \beta_k^{\mathbf{x}_i \mapsto \mathbf{z}_j} \hat{\mathbf{x}}_{k,i}^{-} + \mathbf{K}_k \sum_{j=1}^{m_k} \beta_k^{\mathbf{x}_i \mapsto \mathbf{z}_j} (\mathbf{z}_{k,j} - \hat{\mathbf{z}}_k^{\mathbf{x}_i}) \\
&= \hat{\mathbf{x}}_{k,i}^{-} + \mathbf{K}_k \sum_{j=1}^{m_k} \beta_k^{\mathbf{x}_i \mapsto \mathbf{z}_j} \tilde{\mathbf{z}}_{k,j}^{\mathbf{x}_i} \\
&= \hat{\mathbf{x}}_{k,i}^{-} + \mathbf{K}_k \cdot \tilde{\mathbf{z}}_{k,\mathrm{Comp}}^{\mathbf{x}_i}
\end{aligned}
\tag{2.147}
$$

with innovation

$$
\tilde{\mathbf{z}}_{k,j}^{\mathbf{x}_i} = \mathbf{z}_{k,j} - \hat{\mathbf{z}}_k^{\mathbf{x}_i}
\tag{2.148}
$$

and composite innovation

$$
\tilde{\mathbf{z}}_{k,\mathrm{Comp}}^{\mathbf{x}_i} := \sum_{j=1}^{m_k} \beta_k^{\mathbf{x}_i \mapsto \mathbf{z}_j} \tilde{\mathbf{z}}_{k,j}^{\mathbf{x}_i} \,.
\tag{2.149}
$$

2.3.6 Joint Integrated Probabilistic Data Association (JIPDA)

The combination of JPDA and IPDA resulted in the ***Joint Integrated Probabilistic Data Association (JIPDA)*** algorithm [Muš02].

The state estimation in JIPDA is done similarly to that of IPDA and JPDA by

$$\begin{aligned}\hat{\mathbf{x}}_{k,i} &= \mathbb{E}[\mathbf{X}_{k,i}|\exists\mathbf{x}_{k,i}, \mathcal{Z}_{1:k}] = \sum_{j=0}^{m_k} \mathbb{E}[\mathbf{X}_k|\theta_k^{\mathbf{x}_i\mapsto\mathbf{z}_j}, \mathcal{Z}_{1:k}] \cdot P(\theta_k^{\mathbf{x}_i\mapsto\mathbf{z}_j}|\exists\mathbf{x}_{k,i}, \mathcal{Z}_{1:k}) \\ &= \sum_{j=0}^{m_k} \beta_k^{\mathbf{x}_i\mapsto\mathbf{z}_j} \hat{\mathbf{x}}_k^- + \mathbf{K}_k \sum_{j=1}^{m_k} \beta_k^{\mathbf{x}_i\mapsto\mathbf{z}_j} (\mathbf{z}_{k,j} - \hat{\mathbf{z}}_k^{\mathbf{x}_i}) \\ &= \hat{\mathbf{x}}_k^- + \mathbf{K}_k \sum_{j=1}^{m_k} \beta_k^{\mathbf{x}_i\mapsto\mathbf{z}_j} \tilde{\mathbf{z}}_{k,j}^{\mathbf{x}_i} \\ &= \hat{\mathbf{x}}_k^- + \mathbf{K}_k \cdot \tilde{\mathbf{z}}_{k,\mathrm{Comp}}^{\mathbf{x}_i}\end{aligned} \tag{2.150}$$

with composite innovation for the track $\mathbf{x}_{k,i}$ being

$$\tilde{\mathbf{z}}_{k,\mathrm{Comp}}^{\mathbf{x}_i} := \sum_{j=1}^{m_k} \beta_k^{\mathbf{x}_i\mapsto\mathbf{z}_j} \tilde{\mathbf{z}}_{k,j}^{\mathbf{x}_i} . \tag{2.151}$$

For a given track $\mathbf{x}_i$ the weighting factors $\beta_k^{\mathbf{x}_i\mapsto\mathbf{z}_j}$ $(i = 1, \cdots, n_k; \quad j = 0, \cdots, m_k)$ are calculated as follows:

$$\beta_k^{\mathbf{x}_i\mapsto\mathbf{z}_j} := P(\theta_k^{\mathbf{x}_i\mapsto\mathbf{z}_j}|\exists\mathbf{x}_{k,i}, \mathcal{Z}_{1:k}) = \frac{P(\exists\mathbf{x}_{k,i}, \theta_k^{\mathbf{x}_i\mapsto\mathbf{z}_j}|\mathcal{Z}_{1:k})}{P(\exists\mathbf{x}_{k,i}|\mathcal{Z}_{1:k})} . \tag{2.152}$$

In [Muš02], the derivation of the posterior object existence probability $P(\exists\mathbf{x}_k|\mathcal{Z}_{1:k}^{\mathbf{x}})$ is given only for the Markov process model of the first type (which does not take into account the observability aspect). In this case it is computed as

$$P(\exists\mathbf{x}_{k,i}|\mathcal{Z}_{1:k}) = P(\exists\mathbf{x}_{k,i}, \theta_k^{\mathbf{x}_i\mapsto\mathbf{z}_0}|\mathcal{Z}_{1:k}) + \sum_{j=1}^{m_k} P(\exists\mathbf{x}_{k,i},\theta_k^{\mathbf{x}_i\mapsto\mathbf{z}_j}|\mathcal{Z}_{1:k}) \cdot \omega_{ji} , \tag{2.153}$$

with ω_{ji} being the indicator function indicating whether the measurement $\mathbf{z}_j$ falls into the gate of the track $\mathbf{x}_i$ as defined in (2.124).

For better readability, we denote the set of joint events that assume that at time k the measurement $\mathbf{z}_j$ stems from the track $\mathbf{x}_i$ as $\boldsymbol{\Theta}_k^{\mathbf{x}_i \mapsto \mathbf{z}_j}$. The set of joint events that assume that the track $\mathbf{x}_i$ does not evoke any measurement at time k is denoted as $\boldsymbol{\Theta}_k^{\mathbf{x}_i \mapsto \mathbf{z}_0}$:

$$\boldsymbol{\Theta}_k^{\mathbf{x}_i \mapsto \mathbf{z}_j} = \{\Theta_k(\mathcal{T}) | \theta_k^{\mathbf{x}_i \mapsto \mathbf{z}_j} \in \Theta_k(\mathcal{T})\} \tag{2.154}$$

and

$$\boldsymbol{\Theta}_k^{\mathbf{x}_i \mapsto \mathbf{z}_0} = \{\Theta_k(\mathcal{T}) | \theta_k^{\mathbf{x}_i \mapsto \mathbf{z}_0} \in \Theta_k(\mathcal{T})\} . \tag{2.155}$$

The probability of an association $P(\exists \mathbf{x}_{k,i}, \theta_k^{\mathbf{x}_i \mapsto \mathbf{z}_j} | \mathcal{Z}_{1:k})$ can be represented as a sum of the probabilities of the joint events $\Theta_k(\mathcal{T}) \in \boldsymbol{\Theta}_k^{\mathbf{x}_i \mapsto \mathbf{z}_j}$ containing this association:

$$\begin{aligned} P(\exists \mathbf{x}_{k,i}, \theta_k^{\mathbf{x}_i \mapsto \mathbf{z}_j} | \mathcal{Z}_{1:k}) &= \sum_{\Theta_k(\mathcal{T}) \in \boldsymbol{\Theta}_k^{\mathbf{x}_i \mapsto \mathbf{z}_j}} P(\exists \mathbf{x}_{k,i}, \Theta_k(\mathcal{T}) | \mathcal{Z}_{1:k}) \\ &= \sum_{\Theta_k(\mathcal{T}) \in \boldsymbol{\Theta}_k} P(\exists \mathbf{x}_{k,i}, \Theta_k(\mathcal{T}) | \mathcal{Z}_{1:k}) \cdot \widehat{\omega}_{ji}(\Theta_k(\mathcal{T})) . \end{aligned} \tag{2.156}$$

The factor $\widehat{\omega}_{ji}(\Theta_k(\mathcal{T}))$ which has been defined in (2.126) serves for selection of the feasible joint events that contain the association $\theta_k^{\mathbf{x}_i \mapsto \mathbf{z}_j}$ since it evaluates the addend only for those joint events.

The probability $P(\exists \mathbf{x}_{k,i}, \theta_k^{\mathbf{x}_i \mapsto \mathbf{z}_0} | \mathcal{Z}_{1:k})$ that the tracked object $\mathbf{x}_i$ exists and does not evoke a measurement is obtained by applying the Bayes rule and taking into account that, similar to IPDA, the a-priori probability of an existing object to not evoke a measurement is given by

$$P(\theta_k^{\mathbf{x}_i \mapsto \mathbf{z}_0} | \exists \mathbf{x}_{k,i}, \mathcal{Z}_{1:(k-1)}) = 1 - P_D P_G \tag{2.157}$$

and that the a-priori probability for not getting a measurement for a track not conditioned on the object existence probability is given by

$$\begin{aligned}
P(\theta_k^{\mathbf{x}_i \mapsto \mathbf{z}_0} | \mathcal{Z}_{1:(k-1)}) =& P(\theta_k^{\mathbf{x}_i \mapsto \mathbf{z}_0} | \exists \mathbf{x}_{k,i}, \mathcal{Z}_{1:(k-1)}) \cdot P(\exists \mathbf{x}_{k,i} | \mathcal{Z}_{1:(k-1)}) \\
&+ P(\theta_k^{\mathbf{x}_i \mapsto \mathbf{z}_0} | \nexists \mathbf{x}_{k,i}, \mathcal{Z}_{1:(k-1)}) \cdot (1 - P(\exists \mathbf{x}_{k,i} | \mathcal{Z}_{1:(k-1)})) \\
=& (1 - P_D P_G) \cdot P(\exists \mathbf{x}_{k,i} | \mathcal{Z}_{1:(k-1)}) \\
&+ 1 \cdot (1 - P(\exists \mathbf{x}_{k,i} | \mathcal{Z}_{1:(k-1)})) \\
=& P(\exists \mathbf{x}_{k,i} | \mathcal{Z}_{1:(k-1)}) - P_D P_G \cdot P(\exists \mathbf{x}_{k,i} | \mathcal{Z}_{1:(k-1)}) \\
&+ 1 - P(\exists \mathbf{x}_{k,i} | \mathcal{Z}_{1:(k-1)}) \\
=& 1 - P_D P_G \cdot P(\exists \mathbf{x}_{k,i} | \mathcal{Z}_{1:(k-1)})
\end{aligned} \tag{2.158}$$

(compare equations (2.92) and (2.104) in the IPDA description). Contrary to the original JPDA derivation, in [Muš02] gating probability P_G is explicitly accounted for. Proceeding as described above leads to

$$\begin{aligned}
&P(\exists \mathbf{x}_{k,i}, \theta_k^{\mathbf{x}_i \mapsto \mathbf{z}_0} | \mathcal{Z}_{1:k}) \\
&= \sum_{\Theta_k(\mathcal{T}) \in \mathbf{\Theta}_k^{\mathbf{x}_i \mapsto \mathbf{z}_0}} P(\exists \mathbf{x}_{k,i}, \Theta_k(\mathcal{T}) | \mathcal{Z}_{1:k}) \\
&= \sum_{\Theta_k(\mathcal{T}) \in \mathbf{\Theta}_k^{\mathbf{x}_i \mapsto \mathbf{z}_0}} P(\exists \mathbf{x}_{k,i} | \Theta_k(\mathcal{T}), \mathcal{Z}_{1:k}) \cdot P(\Theta_k(\mathcal{T}) | \mathcal{Z}_{1:k}) \\
&= \sum_{\Theta_k(\mathcal{T}) \in \mathbf{\Theta}_k^{\mathbf{x}_i \mapsto \mathbf{z}_0}} P(\exists \mathbf{x}_{k,i} | \theta_k^{\mathbf{x}_i \mapsto \mathbf{z}_0}, \mathcal{Z}_{1:(k-1)}) \cdot P(\Theta_k(\mathcal{T}) | \mathcal{Z}_{1:k}) \\
&= \sum_{\Theta_k(\mathcal{T}) \in \mathbf{\Theta}_k^{\mathbf{x}_i \mapsto \mathbf{z}_0}} \Big(\frac{P(\theta_k^{\mathbf{x}_i \mapsto \mathbf{z}_0} | \exists \mathbf{x}_{k,i}, \mathcal{Z}_{1:(k-1)}) \cdot P(\exists \mathbf{x}_{k,i} | \mathcal{Z}_{1:(k-1)})}{P(\theta_k^{\mathbf{x}_i \mapsto \mathbf{z}_0} | \mathcal{Z}_{1:(k-1)})} \\
&\quad \cdot P(\Theta_k(\mathcal{T}) | \mathcal{Z}_{1:k}) \Big) \\
&= \sum_{\Theta_k(\mathcal{T}) \in \mathbf{\Theta}_k^{\mathbf{x}_i \mapsto \mathbf{z}_0}} \frac{(1 - P_D P_G) \cdot P(\exists \mathbf{x}_{k,i} | \mathcal{Z}_{1:(k-1)})}{1 - P_D P_G \cdot P(\exists \mathbf{x}_{k,i} | \mathcal{Z}_{1:(k-1)})} \cdot P(\Theta_k(\mathcal{T}) | \mathcal{Z}_{1:k}) \\
&= \frac{(1 - P_D P_G) \cdot P(\exists \mathbf{x}_{k,i} | \mathcal{Z}_{1:(k-1)})}{1 - P_D P_G \cdot P(\exists \mathbf{x}_{k,i} | \mathcal{Z}_{1:(k-1)})} \\
&\quad \cdot \sum_{\Theta_k(\mathcal{T}) \in \mathbf{\Theta}_k(\mathcal{T})} P(\Theta_k(\mathcal{T}) | \mathcal{Z}_{1:k}) \cdot \widehat{\omega}_{0i}(\Theta_k(\mathcal{T})) .
\end{aligned} \tag{2.159}$$

The probability $P(\exists \mathbf{x}_{k,i}, \theta_k^{\mathbf{x}_i \mapsto \mathbf{z}_j} | \mathcal{Z}_{1:k})$ that the tracked object $\mathbf{x}_i$ exists and evokes a measurement $\mathbf{z}_j$ with $j \neq 0$ is given by

$$\begin{aligned} P(\exists \mathbf{x}_{k,i}, \theta_k^{\mathbf{x}_i \mapsto \mathbf{z}_j} | \mathcal{Z}_{1:k}) &= \sum_{\Theta_k(\mathcal{T}) \in \boldsymbol{\Theta}_k^{\mathbf{x}_i \mapsto \mathbf{z}_j}} P(\Theta_k(\mathcal{T}) | \mathcal{Z}_{1:k}) \\ &= \sum_{\Theta_k(\mathcal{T}) \in \boldsymbol{\Theta}_k(\mathcal{T})} P(\Theta_k(\mathcal{T}) | \mathcal{Z}_{1:k}) \cdot \widehat{\omega}_{ji}(\Theta_k(\mathcal{T})) \,. \end{aligned} \tag{2.160}$$

In (2.159) and (2.160), the expression for the a-posteriori probability of the joint event $\Theta_k(\mathcal{T})$ can be calculated analogously to JPDA (cf. equation (2.134)):

$$\begin{aligned} P(\Theta_k(\mathcal{T}) | \mathcal{Z}_{1:k}) &= P(\Theta_k(\mathcal{T}) | \mathcal{Z}_k, m_k, \mathcal{Z}_{1:(k-1)}) \\ &= \frac{1}{c_k} \cdot p(\mathcal{Z}_k | \Theta_k(\mathcal{T}), m_k, \mathcal{Z}_{1:(k-1)}) \\ &\cdot P(\Theta_k(\mathcal{T}) | m_k, \mathcal{Z}_{1:(k-1)}) \end{aligned} \tag{2.161}$$

with

$$c_k = \sum_{\Theta_k(\mathcal{T}) \in \boldsymbol{\Theta}_k} p(\mathcal{Z}_k | \Theta_k(\mathcal{T}), m_k, \mathcal{Z}_{1:(k-1)}) \cdot P(\Theta_k(\mathcal{T}) | m_k, \mathcal{Z}_{1:(k-1)}) \tag{2.162}$$

Like in Equations (2.136) and (2.137) in JPDA (but with accounting for $P_G < 1$), the likelihood of the measurement $\mathbf{z}_j$ given that it originated from a track $\mathbf{x}_{t_j}$ with $t_j \neq 0$ is given by

$$p(\mathbf{z}_{k,j} | \theta_k^{\mathbf{x}_{t_j} \mapsto \mathbf{z}_j}, \mathcal{Z}_{1:(k-1)}) = \frac{1}{P_G} \mathcal{N}(\mathbf{z}_{k,j}; \hat{\mathbf{z}}_k^{\mathbf{x}_{t_j}}, \mathbf{P}_{\mathbf{z}_k \mathbf{z}_k}^{\mathbf{x}_{t_j}}) \quad \text{for } t_j \neq 0 \,. \tag{2.163}$$

and the likelihood of a clutter-based measurement is given by

$$p(\mathbf{z}_{k,j} | \theta_k^{\mathbf{x}_{t_j} \mapsto \mathbf{z}_j}, \mathcal{Z}_{1:(k-1)}) = \frac{1}{V_k} \quad \text{for } t_j = 0 \,. \tag{2.164}$$

This leads to the following expression for the likelihood of the current measurement set $\mathcal{Z}_k$ conditioned on the joint event $\Theta_k(\mathcal{T})$ in (2.161) and (2.162):

$$
\begin{aligned}
p(\mathcal{Z}_k|\Theta_k(\mathcal{T}), m_k, \mathcal{Z}_{1:(k-1)}) &= \prod_{j=1}^{m_k} p(\mathbf{z}_{k,j}|\theta_k^{\mathbf{x}_{t_j} \mapsto \mathbf{z}_j}, \mathcal{Z}_{1:(k-1)}) \\
&= \frac{1}{V^{\phi(\Theta_k(\mathcal{T}))}} \prod_{j=1}^{m_k} \left(\frac{1}{P_G} \mathcal{N}(\mathbf{z}_{k,j}; \hat{\mathbf{z}}_k^{\mathbf{x}_{t_j}}, \mathbf{P}_{\mathbf{z}_k\mathbf{z}_k}^{\mathbf{x}_{t_j}}) \right)^{\tau_j(\Theta_k(\mathcal{T}))} .
\end{aligned}
\tag{2.165}
$$

As in JPDA, $\phi(\Theta_k(\mathcal{T}))$ is the number of the clutter-based measurements in the joint event $\Theta_k(\mathcal{T})$ and $\tau_j(\Theta_k(\mathcal{T}))$ serves for picking out the likelihoods of the measurements, that in $\Theta_k(\mathcal{T})$ have been declared as being non-clutter. Similarly, in the following $\vartheta_i(\Theta_k(\mathcal{T}))$ will serve for picking out tracks that have been associated a measurement.

The a-priori probability $P(\Theta_k(\mathcal{T})|m_k, \mathcal{Z}_{1:(k-1)})$ of a joint event $\Theta_k(\mathcal{T})$ in (2.161) conditioned on the number of received measurements is, as in JPDA, equivalent to the probability of assigning the tracks according to $\vartheta_i(\Theta_k(\mathcal{T}))$ and getting additionally $\phi(\Theta_k(\mathcal{T}))$ clutter-based measurements:

$$
\begin{aligned}
&P(\Theta_k(\mathcal{T})|m_k, \mathcal{Z}_{1:(k-1)}) = \\
&\quad = P\big(\Theta_k(\mathcal{T}), \vartheta_1(\Theta_k(\mathcal{T})), \dots, \vartheta_{n_k}(\Theta_k(\mathcal{T})), \phi(\Theta_k(\mathcal{T}))|\mathcal{Z}_{1:(k-1)}\big) \\
&\quad = P\big(\Theta_k(\mathcal{T}) \,|\, \vartheta_1(\Theta_k(\mathcal{T})), \dots, \vartheta_{n_k}(\Theta_k(\mathcal{T})), \phi(\Theta_k(\mathcal{T}))\big) \\
&\qquad \cdot P\big(\vartheta_1(\Theta_k(\mathcal{T})), \dots, \vartheta_{n_k}(\Theta_k(\mathcal{T})), \phi(\Theta_k(\mathcal{T}))|\mathcal{Z}_{1:(k-1)}\big) .
\end{aligned}
\tag{2.166}
$$

The first factor in (2.166) is calculated in the same way as in (2.140) from combinatorics:

$$
\begin{aligned}
P(\Theta_k(\mathcal{T})|\vartheta_1(\Theta_k(\mathcal{T})), \dots, \vartheta_{n_k}(\Theta_k(\mathcal{T})), \phi(\Theta_k(\mathcal{T}))) &= \left(\frac{m_k!}{\phi(\Theta_k(\mathcal{T}))!} \right)^{-1} \\
&= \frac{\phi(\Theta_k(\mathcal{T}))!}{m_k!} .
\end{aligned}
\tag{2.167}
$$

The second factor is given by

$$\begin{aligned}
&P(\vartheta_1(\Theta_k(\mathcal{T})), \dots, \vartheta_{n_k}(\Theta_k(\mathcal{T})), \phi(\Theta_k(\mathcal{T}))|\mathcal{Z}_{1:(k-1)})\\
&=P(\vartheta_1(\Theta_k(\mathcal{T})), \dots, \vartheta_{n_k}(\Theta_k(\mathcal{T})), |\mathcal{Z}_{1:(k-1)})P(\phi(\Theta_k(\mathcal{T}))|\mathcal{Z}_{1:(k-1)})\\
&=\prod_{i=1}^{n_k}\Big(\big(1 - P(\theta_k^{\mathbf{x}_i\mapsto\mathbf{z}_0}|\mathcal{Z}_{1:(k-1)})\big)^{\vartheta_i(\Theta_k(\mathcal{T}))}\\
&\qquad\cdot \big(P(\theta_k^{\mathbf{x}_i\mapsto\mathbf{z}_0}|\exists\mathbf{x}_{k,i}, \mathcal{Z}_{1:(k-1)})\big)^{1-\vartheta_i(\Theta_k(\mathcal{T}))}\Big)\\
&\quad\cdot \mu_F\big(\phi(\Theta_k(\mathcal{T}))\big)\\
&=\prod_{i=1}^{n_k}\Big(\big(P_D P_G P(\exists\mathbf{x}_{k,i}|\mathcal{Z}_{1:(k-1)})\big)^{\vartheta_i(\Theta_k(\mathcal{T}))}\\
&\qquad\cdot \big(1 - P_D P_G P(\exists\mathbf{x}_{k,i}|\mathcal{Z}_{1:(k-1)})\big)^{1-\vartheta_i(\Theta_k(\mathcal{T}))}\Big)\\
&\quad\cdot \mu_F\big(\phi(\Theta_k(\mathcal{T}))\big)
\end{aligned} \tag{2.168}$$

with $\mu_F(m_c)$ being the probability mass function of the number of clutter based measurements. As described in Section 2.3.3 (s. page 46), $\mu_F(m_c)$ might be modeled either as a uniform distribution over the set {0, ..., N} with N being the maximal possible number of clutter-based measurements in the cluster volume (*non-parametric model*) with

$$\mu_F(m_c) = \frac{1}{N} \tag{2.169}$$

or by means of a Poisson distribution (*parametric model*) with

$$\begin{aligned}
\mu_F(m_c) &= e^{-\widehat{m}_k}\frac{\widehat{m}_k^{m_c}}{m_c!} = e^{-\widehat{m}_k}\frac{\widehat{m}_k^{m_c}\,\widehat{m}_k^{m_k-m_c}\,m_k!}{m_c!\,\widehat{m}_k^{m_k-m_c}\,m_k!}\\
&= e^{-\widehat{m}_k}\frac{\widehat{m}_k^{m_k}}{m_k!}\frac{m_k!}{m_c!\,\widehat{m}_k^{m_k-m_c}} = \mu_F(m_k)\frac{m_k!}{m_c!\,\widehat{m}_k^{m_k-m_c}}\,.
\end{aligned} \tag{2.170}$$

With $m_c = \phi(\Theta_k(\mathcal{T}))$ one gets

$$\mu_F(\phi(\Theta_k(\mathcal{T}))) = \mu_F(m_k)\frac{m_k!}{\phi(\Theta_k(\mathcal{T}))!\,\widehat{m}_k^{m_k-\phi(\Theta_k(\mathcal{T}))}}\,. \tag{2.171}$$

The estimation of the number of expected clutter measurements $\hat{m}_k$ now takes into account the existence probability of the tracked objects:

$$\hat{m}_k = \sum_{j=1}^{m_k} \Big(\prod_{i=1}^{n_k} (1 - \frac{1}{m_k^{\mathbf{x}_i}} P_D P_G P(\exists \mathbf{x}_{k,i} | \mathcal{Z}_{1:(k-1)}))^{\omega_{ji}} \Big) , \tag{2.172}$$

with $m_k^{\mathbf{x}_i}$ being the number of measurements in the gate of the track $\mathbf{x}_i$. The a-priori probability $P(\Theta_k(\mathcal{T}) | m_k, \mathcal{Z}_{1:(k-1)})$ of a joint event when assuming Poisson distribution of the number of clutter measurements is thus given by

$$\begin{aligned} P(\Theta_k(\mathcal{T}) | m_k, \mathcal{Z}_{1:(k-1)}) = {} & \frac{\phi(\Theta_k(\mathcal{T}))!}{m_k!} \cdot \prod_{i=1}^{n_k} \Big((P_D P_G P(\exists \mathbf{x}_{k,i} | \mathcal{Z}_{1:(k-1)}))^{\vartheta_i(\Theta_k(\mathcal{T}))} \\ & \cdot (1 - P_D P_G P(\exists \mathbf{x}_{k,i} | \mathcal{Z}_{1:(k-1)}))^{1-\vartheta_i(\Theta_k(\mathcal{T}))} \Big) \\ & \cdot \mu_F(m_k) \frac{m_k!}{\phi(\Theta_k(\mathcal{T}))! \, \hat{m}_k^{m_k - \phi(\Theta_k(\mathcal{T}))}} \\ = {} & \prod_{i=1}^{n_k} \Big((\frac{1}{\hat{m}_k} P_D P_G P(\exists \mathbf{x}_{k,i} | \mathcal{Z}_{1:(k-1)}))^{\vartheta_i(\Theta_k(\mathcal{T}))} \\ & \cdot (1 - P_D P_G P(\exists \mathbf{x}_{k,i} | \mathcal{Z}_{1:(k-1)}))^{1-\vartheta_i(\Theta_k(\mathcal{T}))} \Big) \\ & \cdot \mu_F(m_k) \, . \end{aligned} \tag{2.173}$$

This leads to the following expression for the a-posteriori probability $P(\Theta_k(\mathcal{T})|\mathcal{Z}_{1:k})$ of a joint event:

$$\begin{aligned}
P(\Theta_k(\mathcal{T})|\mathcal{Z}_{1:k}) &= P(\Theta_k(\mathcal{T})|\mathcal{Z}_k, m_k, \mathcal{Z}_{1:(k-1)}) \\
&= \frac{1}{c_k} p(\mathcal{Z}_k|\Theta_k(\mathcal{T}), m_k, \mathcal{Z}_{1:(k-1)}) P(\Theta_k(\mathcal{T})|m_k, \mathcal{Z}_{1:(k-1)}) \\
&= \frac{1}{c_k} \frac{1}{V^{\phi(\Theta_k(\mathcal{T}))}} \prod_{j=1}^{m_k} \left(\frac{1}{P_G} \mathcal{N}(\mathbf{z}_{k,j}; \hat{\mathbf{z}}_k^{\mathbf{x}_{t_j}}, \mathbf{P}_{\mathbf{Z}_k\mathbf{Z}_k}^{\mathbf{x}_{t_j}}) \right)^{\tau_j(\Theta_k(\mathcal{T}))} \cdot \mu_F(m_k) \\
&\quad \cdot \prod_{i=1}^{n_k} \Bigg(\left(\frac{1}{\hat{m}_k} P_D^{\mathbf{x}_i} P_G \cdot P(\exists \mathbf{x}_{k,i}|\mathcal{Z}_{1:(k-1)}) \right)^{\vartheta_i(\Theta_k(\mathcal{T}))} \\
&\quad \cdot \left(1 - P_D^{\mathbf{x}_i} P_G \cdot P(\exists \mathbf{x}_{k,i}|\mathcal{Z}_{1:(k-1)})\right)^{1-\vartheta_i(\Theta_k(\mathcal{T}))} \Bigg) \\
&= \frac{1}{c_k} \frac{\mu_F(m_k)}{V_k^{m_k}} \prod_{j=1}^{m_k} \left(\frac{1}{P_G} \mathcal{N}(\mathbf{z}_{k,j}; \hat{\mathbf{z}}_k^{\mathbf{x}_{t_j}}, \mathbf{P}_{\mathbf{Z}_k\mathbf{Z}_k}^{\mathbf{x}_{t_j}}) \right)^{\tau_j(\Theta_k(\mathcal{T}))} \\
&\quad \cdot \prod_{i=1}^{n_k} \Bigg(\left(\frac{V_k}{\hat{m}_k} P_D^{\mathbf{x}_i} P_G \cdot P(\exists \mathbf{x}_{k,i}|\mathcal{Z}_{1:(k-1)}) \right)^{\vartheta_i(\Theta_k(\mathcal{T}))} \\
&\quad \cdot \left(1 - P_D^{\mathbf{x}_i} P_G \cdot P(\exists \mathbf{x}_{k,i}|\mathcal{Z}_{1:(k-1)})\right)^{1-\vartheta_i(\Theta_k(\mathcal{T}))} \Bigg) \\
&= \frac{1}{c_k''} \cdot \prod_{j=1}^{m_k} \left(\frac{1}{P_G} \mathcal{N}(\mathbf{z}_{k,j}; \hat{\mathbf{z}}_k^{\mathbf{x}_{t_j}}, \mathbf{P}_{\mathbf{Z}_k\mathbf{Z}_k}^{\mathbf{x}_{t_j}}) \right)^{\tau_j(\Theta_k(\mathcal{T}))} \\
&\quad \cdot \prod_{i=1}^{n_k} \Bigg(\left(\frac{V_k}{\hat{m}_k} P_D^{\mathbf{x}_i} P_G \cdot P(\exists \mathbf{x}_{k,i}|\mathcal{Z}_{1:(k-1)}) \right)^{\vartheta_i(\Theta_k(\mathcal{T}))} \\
&\quad \cdot \left(1 - P_D^{\mathbf{x}_i} P_G \cdot P(\exists \mathbf{x}_{k,i}|\mathcal{Z}_{1:(k-1)})\right)^{1-\vartheta_i(\Theta_k(\mathcal{T}))} \Bigg)
\end{aligned} \tag{2.174}$$

with

$$c_k'' = \frac{\mu_F(m_k)}{V_k^{m_k}} c_k \, . \tag{2.175}$$

The cluster area V_k can be approximated as follows:

$$V_k = \max(V_{k,max}, V_{k,ap}) \tag{2.176}$$

where

$$V_{k,ap} = \frac{m_k}{\sum_{i=1}^{n_k} m_k^{\mathbf{x}_i}} \sum_{i=1}^{n_k} V_i \tag{2.177}$$

and

$$V_{k,max} = \max_{i=1,\cdots,n_k} V_i \tag{2.178}$$

with V_i being volume of the gating region of the track $\mathbf{x}_i$.

2.3.7 Multi-Hypotheses Tracking (MHT)

The idea of the Multi-Hypotheses Tracking algorithms is to retard the final decision about the assignment of measurements to tracks until an unambiguous solution is possible. It allows multiple association hypotheses and maintains them throughout several frames, scoring them according to some matching criteria. This leads to an exponentially growing tree-like structure. After N frames, a retrospective decision can be made; Branches with low scores are deleted. The original approach, which in [Bla04] is classified as the Hypothesis Oriented MHT (HOMHT), has been described in [Rei79]. The Track Oriented MHT (TOMHT) has been described in [Kur90]. It is similar to the HOMHT, however, a decision tree is generated separately for each track. A global hypothesis has to be extracted from all trees. Cox & Hingorani presented a functional implementation of TOMHT in [Cox96]. An overview of different MHT algorithms is given in [Bla04]. A conventional MHT algorithms assumes a 1:1 assignment between tracks and measurements, i.e., it requires an extension in order to handle split and merged detections [Ma09, Mak14]. This aggravates the main problem of the MHT algorithm, namely its complexity, even more.

3 Problem statement and related work

3.1 Problem of corrupted detections

Estimation of the object existence probability as proposed in IPDA and JIPDA offers a solid basis for track initiations and terminations and allows for better handling of clutter and missed detections. However, as mentioned previously, these approaches (as well as many other state-of-the-art state estimation algorithms) start with the assumptions that an object may evoke at most one detection, that a detection may stem from at most one tracked object, and that an obtained measurement represents the entire object. These assumptions may work perfectly fine for tracking distant objects that give point-shaped detections (e.g., in radar tracking applications). In certain special cases of video-based object tracking one may use knowledge about the appearance of the objects that are to be tracked and derive a correct measurement from a partial detection. This is particularly the case when using model-based and appearance-based object detection methods, such as those in [Kol96, Kol97, Fle02, Ott08] and [Lei08]. In general, however, the aforementioned assumptions may be violated. In many cases generic approaches have to be used which are based on detecting and tracking moving point clouds in 3D space or moving 2D blobs in video images. Centroids and dimensions of the detections are computed and used as measurements for data association and dynamic state estimation algorithms.

As an example let us consider several possible video-based object tracking applications. The first one is an automotive collision detection system based on 3D data of a stereo video camera [Gri07]. The second one is an indoor people tracking application based on a moving blob detection algorithm [Mon09, Ste12]. Additional examples are a ship tracking application within a maritime surveillance system

[Teu10, Teu11] and vehicle tracking in Wide Area Motion Imagery (WAMI) data [Teu16].

Due to the limited field of view of the cameras, occlusions, and lacking texture in homogeneous object regions, the obtained detections may be incomplete, i.e., represent only a part of the object (***"partial detection"***, narrowed detection). In certain cases, such as when there is a large homogeneous region in the middle of an object or there are occlusions of the middle part of an object, one may obtain two or more such partial detections for a single object (***"split detection"***). Another problem is often given by an unintended detection augmentation by clutter or (in case of the moving blob segmentation) by shadows, reflections, etc. (***"falsely augmented detections"***, bloated detections). Finally, proximate objects may produce a single detection (***"merged detection"***). In the case of object tracking by means of moving blob detection in the images of a monocular camera this may also happen when the corresponding 2D image projections become too close without objects themselves coming too close – as illustrated in Figure 3.1.

(a) **(b)** **(c)**

Figure 3.1: Merged detection in a surveillance application: (a): Original image. (b): Detected moving blob. (d): Detection bounding box.

Figure 3.2 illustrates some reasons and consequences of such ***"corrupted detections"*** using the example of a car-mounted side-looking stereo camera developed for a side pre-crash detection system [Gri07, Mel09]. 3-dimensional point clouds that have been obtained by means of stereo processing are visualized by means of colored vertical lines to the estimated ground.

Figure 3.2: (a): Phantom object due to clutter.
(b): Merged detection of closely spaced objects.
(c) and (d): Data association problem in case of split detections (truck in the background). In case of an object entering the field of view (car in the foreground) its visible extent grows causing wrong position and velocity estimation.

In Figure 3.2 (a), a regular pattern of the palisade fence in the background causes lots of clutter which leads to a clutter-based detection and creation of a phantom track (visualized in blue). In Figure 3.2 (b), two closely spaced cars produce a single detection (orange lines). Figure 3.2 (c) and (d) illustrate effects of partial occlusions. In the frame corresponding to Figure 3.2 (c), clustering of the 3-dimensional point clouds yielded three detections that were correctly associated to the three visible objects. In the course of the sequence, lack of feature points in the homogeneous area on the door and on the occluded rear part of the truck prevented the remaining points from being clustered together resulting in three independent detections. Only one of these detections (the middle one) could be associated with the track (green box), for the other two detections new tracks had to be initiated (magenta and cyan boxes in Figure 3.2 (d)). In general, such "splits" (as well as "merges") lead to erroneous estimation of the track position and velocity and to track losses. A similar effect can be expected in the case of the white car in the foreground. In the course of the sequence it is entering the field of view (FoV) and thus "growing" in the image. It is obvious that a centroid-based tracking of such a "growing" object leads to erroneous position and velocity estimation.

All these effects, which will henceforth be referred to as corrupted detections lead to the generation of incorrect measurements. This leads to problems with both data association and dynamic state estimation. Such problems may emerge in all tracking applications that have to deal with extended nearby objects and rely on the obtained detections without using any prior knowledge about object appearance. However, unlike radar tracking applications, video-based tracking applications offer a great potential for re-identification of objects and their parts. This thesis aims at developing a novel feature-based probabilistic data association and object tracking concept based on re-identification and tracking of image points (feature points) which can correctly resolve the aforementioned problems.

3.2 Related work

Along with the fundamental work in the field of radar-based target tracking, where object tracking research was initiated, there has been a lot of research work on object tracking done in the fields of surveillance, robotics, and ADAS in the 90s and 2000s. A considerable cost reduction of video sensors over the past few decades lead to a rapid growth of video-based surveillance and ADAS applications. A broad overview of existing object detection, data association, and state estimation approaches would go beyond the constraints of this thesis. Therefore we will restrict this section to a short overview of multi-object tracking approaches that introduce similar ideas to those proposed in this thesis. This is done in Subsection

3.2.1. In addition, we would like to refer the reader to the fundamental books on object tracking and data association, such as [Bar92, Bar93, Bla99, Bar00, Cha11, Koc14], the book of Thrun et al. on probabilistic robotics [Thr05], the book on vision-based environment perception and motion control by Dickmanns [Dic07], the book on video tracking by Maggio & Cavallaro [Mag11], as well as to the book "Statistical multisource-multitarget information fusion" by Mahler [Mah07].

An overview of results of various state-of-the-art multi-object tracking approaches for a *front-looking application* can be found at the website of the KITTI Vision Benchmark Suite [Gei12]. As one can see there, the state-of-the-art approaches are still far from being perfect, even though many of them incorporate appearance-based object recognition methods. As pointed out in [Jan17], a reliable tracking-by-detection can only be achieved using reasonable object detections. Corrupted detections remain a great problem for most of the state-of-the-art approaches. The comparison of the tracking results using a real object detector with those using ground truth detections [Jan17] is quite impressive. Many state-of-the-art approaches show much better performance when using ground truth detection data, i.e., there is a lot room for improvement, if one could properly handle corrupted detections, which are an inevitable curse of observing dynamic scenes with unknown objects from a restricted perspective.

Regarding object *detection* in the automotive context, we would like to refer the reader to the short summary given in Section 1.3 and particularly to the surveys by Sun et al. [Sun04], Sivaraman & Trivedi [Siv13b], Mukhtar et al. [Muk15] and Janai et al. [Jan17].

3.2.1 Related and alternative approaches

As mentioned in Section 1.3, this thesis is based on the idea of combining stereo and motion information for tracking individual pixels in 3D space as proposed in [Fra05b]. The major motivation there was to detect relevant objects (i.e., objects with certain speed and motion direction) directly in the image. An extension to this approach has been reported in [Rab07], where vision-based computation of the ego-motion has been added for increasing accuracy and robustness of position and velocity estimation of the individual 3D points. Initial object hypotheses were created by applying connected component analysis to the 3D points in a top view map.

A different approach for fusing depth and motion information has been proposed by Dang et al. in [Dan02]. Optical flow and disparity of individual feature points were used as measurements in a single Extended Kalman Filter, which assumes a purely translational motion of a rigid point cloud with respect to the camera coordinates. The method for building initial object hypotheses for this approach has been described in [Dan05]. First, a general obstacle detection is performed based on a disparity map. Then, a segmentation of the detected obstacles based on the estimated motion of equidistantly sampled image points is done.

In [Bar08], Barth & Franke proposed a method for estimating the yaw rate of the detected objects based on [Rab07]. Initial object hypotheses are derived by segmenting 3-dimensional point tracks, which are generated as described in [Rab07]. From now on, the points belonging to an object are assumed to be known. Disparity and 2D displacement of the tracked points are utilized as measurements for an Extended Kalman Filter, which is used to track a reference point of the object. The rotational object motion is modeled by means of a yaw around a rotation point, position of which is estimated separately. Point positions relative to the estimated object reference point are updated in the course of time. Points that could not be tracked in the image and points with missing disparity measurements are removed from the object's point list straight away. New points can be added to the list, if they comply to specific constraints. The approach has been shown to be effective for tracking oncoming and leading vehicles. However, the proposed point management scheme is not sufficient for handling complex scenarios with long-term occlusions and track splits and merges.

Utilization of dense depth maps for detecting and tracking vehicles has been proposed in [Dan07]. All objects – moving vehicles as well as stationary objects – are modeled as cuboids aligned parallel to the camera viewing direction. Object detection is done by eliminating the road points, projecting the remaining points onto the ground plain, and grouping the resulting 2D points in a compressed top view space, which is produced by transforming the trapezoidal field of view into a rectangular 2-dimensional image. The resulting cuboids are tracked using a Kalman Filter.

The authors tackled the problem of associating split detections and partial detections due to the field of view restrictions. They proposed a data association approach consisting of two steps: a "coarse" association of predicted and detected 3D cuboids and a "fine" 2D matching of projections of predicted and detected objects in the image domain. The "coarse" association is performed by evaluating intersections of the top view projection of the predicted cuboids with the rectangles obtained by detection. The "fine" image-based matching evaluates observable object corners, allowing to determine the object boundaries as soon as they become observable. The authors do not allow association of a measurement to multiple objects, i.e., there is no proper handling of merged detections. However, an association of a single predicted object to multiple detections is allowed. Split detections are handled by creating "meta-measurements", which are defined as envelopes of the individual rectangles in the camera image. Detections which touch the image boundaries are assumed to possibly be only partly observable. No new tracks are instantiated from such detections. However, if the detection is associated to an existing track, it is used for an update. The position measurement is inferred from the position of the visible object corners and the predicted cuboid size. Obviously, the described procedure assumes frontally approaching objects, i.e., it is limited to a front-looking application and is not capable of instantly tracking overtaking and crossing vehicles.

In [Bar09a], the approach proposed in [Bar08] has been extended. The authors use an Extended Kalman Filter to estimate the yaw rate of the oncoming vehicles. Initial object hypotheses are derived from segmented 3-dimensional point tracks. In [Bar09b] the approach proposed in [Bar08] has been extended to using dense depth maps as an input for stereo data. Cuboids were used as a geometric object model additionally to the tracked point clouds. In [Bar10] the authors used an IMM-based approach for increasing the overall robustness of the tracking for maneuvering (turning) vehicles.

In [Bad09], the idea of a compact representation of the obstacle information, the stixels, has been presented. This memory-efficient medium-level representation of the 3D world can abstract from the 3D points but still allows a more fine-granular representation of obstacles and moving objects than a simple cuboid. It offers an intuitive representation of the scene information in conjunction with a drastic compression of the data amount to be processed. Initially the stixels were limited to the closest obstacle along each viewing angle. In [Pfe11], the approach has been extended in order to model several obstacles for each image column.

A 3D extension to dense optical flow called "scene flow" has been proposed by Vedula et al. in [Ved99]. With the increasing processing power, the computation of the scene flow found its way into the automotive applications [Rab10]. Current approaches consider the scene flow as a labeling problem [Bac10, Vog13]. Vogel et al. proposed to model the scene as consisting of multiple rigidly moving piecewise planar surfaces, which correspond to superpixels in the image domain [Vog13]. Menze & Geiger proposed to model the motion of the surface patches by further clustering them to independently moving objects [Men15]. In general, scene flow computation yields much better results than a simple combination of stereo of optical flow computation [Vog15]. The computation is, however, very time-consuming (currently in the range of multiple seconds up to minutes per frame, i.e., it is not yet real-time capable).

In [Oše17], Ošep et al. propose a combined 2D-3D tracker based on a fusion of 2D detections, depth information and scene flow. They use a Conditional Random Field (CRF) model for selecting suitable observations and for solving the data association problem. The tracking is done using Kalman Filters with a joint 2D-3D state. Far-away objects are tracked in the image domain, while close-range objects are tracked using a combined 2D-3D observations consisting of a 2D detection and a 3D point cluster. The authors do not estimate the orientation of the tracked objects, i.e., all objects are modeled as cuboids coplanar to the image space. Also, they assume a 1:1 matching between a 2D detection and 3D point cluster when generating observations, which in reality is not always the case. They do not utilize the information from the scene flow for associating existing tracks with observations, which could greatly simplify and at the same time enhance the data association. While merged 3D detections can be resolved using the 2D detections, no handling for partial or split 3D detections is described. In cases of partial or split 3D detections, the algorithm has to rely solely on 2D detections or, if they are unavailable, on predictions. In conjunction with the missing estimation of the orientation, the yaw, and the acceleration of the tracked objects, this might pose a serious problem in complex road scenarios.

Although presenting quite impressive results, most of the aforementioned papers, however, do not provide a consistent approach for a comprehensive handling of corrupted detections with an appropriate track management.

The topic of the track management has been tackled in [Lim11]. They use a front-looking stereo camera to detect obstacles and classify them by means of the cascaded AdaBoost algorithm. The GNN data association is used to assign multiple detections to multiple tracks by a one-to-one mapping. Instead of relying on object existence probabilities as proposed in JIPDA, FBPDA [Gri09], and this work, the authors propose to use an explicit track scoring which is calculated by the associated detection reliability, associated recognition reliability, and associated detection-by-tracking reliability. The authors do not perform any explicit handling of split and merged detections since a 1:1 correspondence between a tracked object and an obtained detection is assumed due to the nature of the appearance-based object detection approach.

In [Mäh07], Mählisch et al. proposed to use IPDA for sensor data fusion. In the following work [Mäh08] they extend their approach to JIPDA by using weighted filter innovations with multiple ambiguous association pairs. Both schemes are based on the assumption that a measurement may by evoked by at most one object and vice versa. Finally, in [Mun09], they allow possibility of assignment between several measurements and one track for handling splits.

Genovesio et al. proposed to create ***virtual measurements*** that always allow for an appropriate update [Gen04] in case of merged measurements. Thereby the most probable association is used. For splitting of joint measurements evoked by several tracks, they proposed to use the k-means algorithm, which may become problematic when merged objects have unequal dimensions. Furthermore, if the centroid of the joint measurement does not lie within the gate of one or more corresponding tracks, the merge cannot be recognized and handled at all. Partial occlusions represent another still open issue.

Kumar et al. proposed a method which copes with split and merge effects in a surveillance application by evaluating the associations between the combined detections and tracks, and choosing the ones of maximal probability based on distance between contours of the resulting image blobs [Kum06]. However, even with identified split or merge events it is not possible to perform an appropriate update step. Instead, prediction is used for further processing until a resolution can be made.

Another approach for coping with incomplete, split and merged detections in a surveillance application was proposed in [Ma09]. The authors use data from a stationary video camera. Object detection is done by a foreground-background segmentation and the data association problem is formulated as the maximum a-posteriori graph traversing problem. The data association approach is based on the MHT paradigm, i.e., it is based on a retrospective consideration of image sequences. The authors analyze the overlap of the predicted tracks and obtained detections in order to recognize corrupted detections and generate virtual measurements in case of split, merged and missed detections. Virtual measurements are build by applying the Mean Shift algorithm [Che95] to the appearance histogram of the corresponding tracks.

An approach for solving the problem of split and merged detections by means of a particle filter was proposed by Khan et al. in [Kha05]. The authors applied their algorithm for tracking ants that were detected by means of a color segmentation algorithm. The data association is performed using the Markov Chain Monte Carlo (MCMC) method. They allow assignments between a track and multiple measurements (split detection) and between a measurement and multiple tracks (merged detection). Simultaneous splits and merges, however, are not allowed. The results of two runs have been presented showing a correct performance in one case and track loss in the case of three interacting ants. Besides, no statements about the real-time capability of the algorithm have been made.

Currently (as of June 2017), the best ranking object tracking approach according to the KITTY benchmark dataset [Gei12, Gei] is the Multi-Class Multi-Object Tracking (MCMOT) approach by Lee et al. [Lee16]. It is based on MCMC as well. The authors use an ensemble of object detectors, namely deep feature based global object detector, deep feature based local object detector, color detector, and motion detector and apply the deep learning based object detection technology Faster R-CNN [Ren15]. Besides, the algorithm uses a forward-backward error validation for recognizing track drifts that are due to changing appearance and occlusions, and is thus not suited for a real-time application.

The currently best online-capable approach according to the KITTY benchmark dataset is the approach by Xiang et al. [Xia15]. They model the data association as a Markov Decision Process (MDP) and propose to use a reinforcement learning algorithm for learning the similarity function for the data association task from training data. However, they use a sophisticated appearance-based object detector [Xia17] for the initial object detection and for validation of the tracking results in the consecutive images. Starting from the initial object detector they learn an initial object template and track it throughout the image sequence using optical flow. Multiple object templates are learned in the course of the tracking process in order to compensate for appearance changes. The data association and the track management are performed on a per-track basis using the MDP. Similarly to the approach in [Lim11], the authors do not perform any explicit handling of split and merged detections, since a 1:1 correspondence between a tracked object and an obtained detection is assumed due to the nature of the appearance-based object detection approach.

Another family of object detection and tracking approaches aim at learning and re-identifying object parts [Sch13]. Wu & Nevatia proposed an approach for detecting and tracking multiple possibly partially occluded humans by using edgelet based part detectors [Wu07]. A human body is represented as an assembly of body parts. In [Lei04] and [Lei08], Leibe et al. proposed an iterative algorithm for learning an Implicit Shape Model (ISM) of an object, which in [And08] and [Lei07a] was used for detecting and tracking pedestrians undergoing severe occlusions. The original approach in [Lei04] is based on matching image patches which are extracted around interest points with a learned "codebook of local appearance". The codebook contains not only the appearance of object parts but also their position with respect to the object center. Each detected object part votes for a certain object location in the image and scale. Object hypotheses are generated by clustering points in the 3dimesional voting space (where object scale s is the third dimension along with the image coordinates x and y. In [Lei07b] the authors proposed the idea of coupling detection and tracking in a surveillance application by imposing object detection at certain locations based on estimated object trajectories. They make a distinction between static and moving objects, which are handled differently. The locations of static objects are computed by building a weighted mean of inliers to the existing hypotheses. The moving objects are tracked using an EKF.

In 2009, in parallel with our first publication of the feature-based data association and tracking [Gri09], Jüngling & Arens published a paper where they also propose to use tracked feature points for object tracking [Jün09]. The described target application is a surveillance application with a stationary camera. The initial object detection is done based on a pre-learned codebook of object parts as suggested in [Lei08]. Instead of Local Shape Descriptors used by Leibe et al., the authors use SURF features [Bay06] to learn an ISM of the appearance of the object classes that are to be detected and tracked. Object detection is done by means of a voting procedure similar to those in [Lei08], the authors, however, use a slightly different method for estimating object center. In the tracking phase, the extracted SURF features that have been assigned to an object are cached and tracked using a Kalman Filter and an object motion model of a constant acceleration. In the consecutive frames the cached features are matched with the newly extracted SURF features using the revised Hungarian method [Mun57]. Newly detected features that vote for the same object center location as the successfully matched features are integrated into the object representation and contribute to the estimation process of the new object location. After removing the features that are recognized to belong to already tracked objects, the remaining features are used to detect and instantiate new tracks. The approach is reported to show good performance for detecting people, re-identifying them in case of overlapping appearances in the image, and tracking them throughout occlusion phases. In contrast to that work, the approach proposed in this thesis does not rely on any pre-learned object appearance features. Object detection is done based solely on extracted range and motion information. Nevertheless, the good performance of the approach described in [Jün09] witnesses the general applicability of the feature-based object tracking proposed in this thesis.

Along with classification approaches based on 2D object recognition, there exist methods based on recognition of 3D structures from point clouds [Hac17]. Weinmann et al. propose a method for labeling pixels directly from 3D point clouds using multiscale features and discriminative learning [Wei15]. They perform an object classification based on 2D and 3D features, including verticality, absolute height, height difference, standard deviation of the height values, local point density, radius of the k-NN, and eigenvalues-dependent features, such as linearity, planarity, scattering, omnivariance, anisotropy, eigenentropy, sum of eigenvalues, and local surface variation. Altogether the authors evaluate 21 2D and 3D features. A classification framework based on this work has been presented in [Wei16] and [Wei17].

The topic of high-level object management and object-oriented environment perception and world modeling has been tackled by my colleagues Gheţa et al. at the Vision and Fusion Lab (IES) of the Karlsruhe Institute of Technology (KIT) [Ghe08, Ghe10]. The Object-Oriented World Model presented there has found its application not only in the domain of humanoid robots but also in the domains of indoor and maritime surveillance applications [Bau10, Bel12, Fis12].

An alternative representation of object presence is given by a family of approaches which use a global grid-based scene representation [Sav17]. Global occupancy grids have been used for sensor fusion and navigation of mobile robots since 80s [Mor88, Elf89]. With the falling costs of high-resolution 3D sensors, they found a wide entry into the automotive application area both for solving the Simultaneous Localization And Mapping (SLAM) tasks [Thr98, Thr05, Wan07], as well as for model-free object tracking and collision avoidance tasks for mobile robots [Cou03, Tay08]. A big advantage of grid-based approaches is that they allow to perform sensor data association on a very low level. This helps to avoid many problems that arise when trying to solve data association problem on the object level. The disadvantage of a global grid is the necessity to maintain and update occupancy information (and possibly additional information) for the entire field of view, which results in high computational costs.

4 Feature-Based Probabilistic Data Association and Tracking Algorithm (FBPDATA)

This chapter is structured as follows: Section 4.1 describes the basic ideas of the proposed FBPDATA approach including a detailed description of the data association. Section 4.2 gives a formal derivation of the FBPDATA formulas. The computation of the a-priori joint event probabilities and the detection likelihoods is addressed in Section 4.2.3 and Section 4.2.4 correspondingly. The computation of the point-to-track affiliation probabilities is described in Section 4.2.5.

4.1 Basic concepts

4.1.1 Distinction between measurements and detections

First, we must make a distinction between a detection and a measurement. In the following, the term ***"detection"*** describes a 3D point cloud (or an image blob in the case of a 2D tracking application). In contrast, the term ***"measurement"*** describes the characteristic features of a detection such as its centroid and extent which can be used in the filtering process. The process of detection and measurement generation is depicted in Figure 4.1.

Measurements are denoted by $\mathbf{z}$, whereas detections (i.e point clouds or blobs) are denoted by d. Similarly, the jth detection at time step k is denoted by $d_{k,j}$, the entire set of detections at time step k is denoted by $\mathcal{D}_k$, and the set of detection sets since the beginning of the observation and up to time step k is denoted by

$\mathcal{D}_{1:k}$. The proposed data association is performed using raw detections d, (e.g., point clouds or image blobs) instead of measurements $\mathbf{z}$.

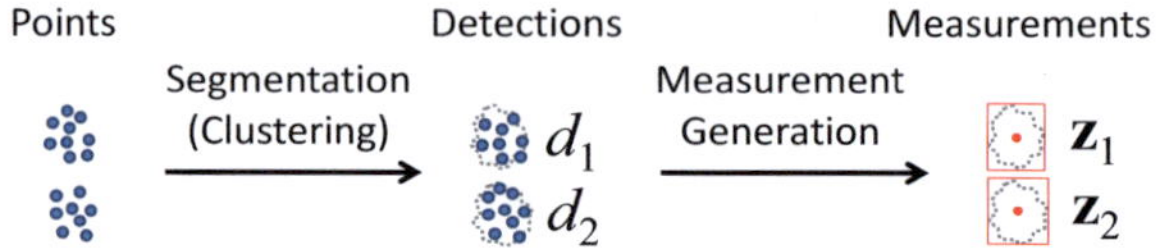

Figure 4.1: Visualization of detection and measurement generation process.

4.1.2 Detection-by-Tracking instead of Tracking-by-Detection paradigm

The principle of the classical ***Tracking-by-Detection*** paradigm is shown in Figure 4.2 (a) and (b). Data association is done between track states $\mathbf{x}_i$ and measurements $\mathbf{z}_j$, which are directly obtained from detections d_j. Since one-to-one assignments only are allowed, this leads for both merged detection scenario (a) and split detection scenario (b) to three possible assignment paths, none of which is correct.

In case of a merged detection (a), the left assignment path leads to an erroneous track state estimation for the first track ($\mathbf{x}_1$) and to using the prediction due to the missed detection for the second tracked object. The middle assignment path leads to an erroneous track state estimation for the second tracked object ($\mathbf{x}_2$) and to using the prediction due to the missed detection for the first tracked object. The right assignment path leads to instantiation of a spurious track ($\mathbf{x}_3$) and to using the prediction due to the missed detections for both existing tracks.

In case of a split detection (b), the left assignment path leads to an erroneous track state estimation for the tracked object ($\mathbf{x}_1$) and to instantiation of a spurious track ($\mathbf{x}_2$). The middle assignment path leads to another erroneous track state estimation for the tracked object and to instantiation of another spurious track ($\mathbf{x}_3$). The right assignment path leads to instantiation of two spurious tracks (**x**2 and $\mathbf{x}_3$) and to using the prediction due to the missed detections for the existing track.

FBPDATA replaces the classical ***Tracking-by-Detection*** scheme by the ***Detection-by-Tracking*** paradigm. Its basic idea is illustrated in Figure 4.2 (c) and (d).

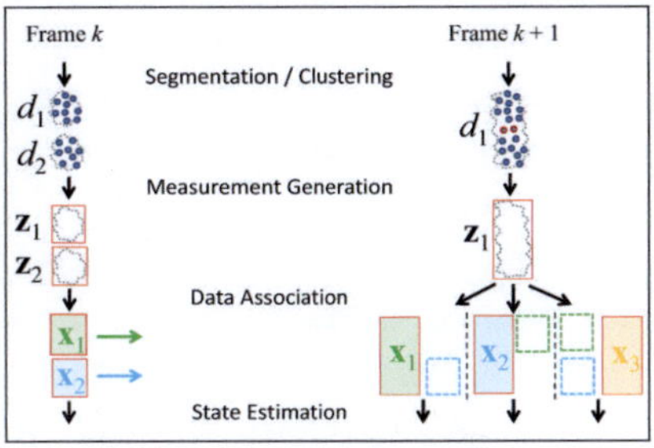

(a) Data association in the case of a merged detection: classical Tracking-By-Detection approach.

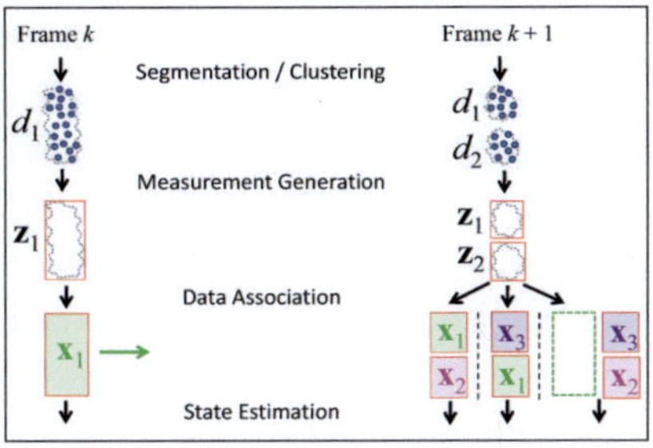

(b) Data association in the case of a split detection: classical Tracking-By-Detection approach.

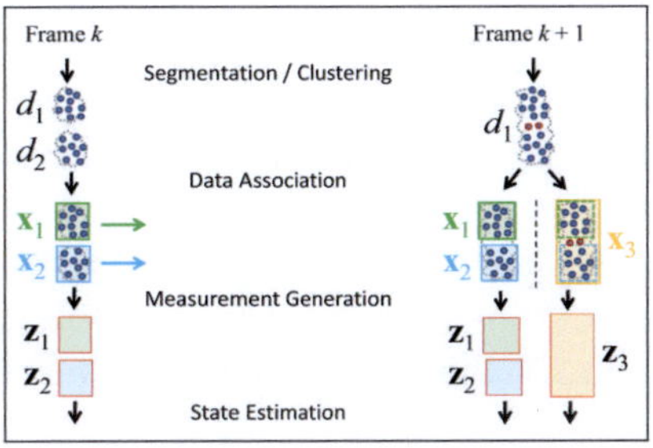

(c) Data association in the case of a merged detection: FBPDATA (Detection-by-Tracking).

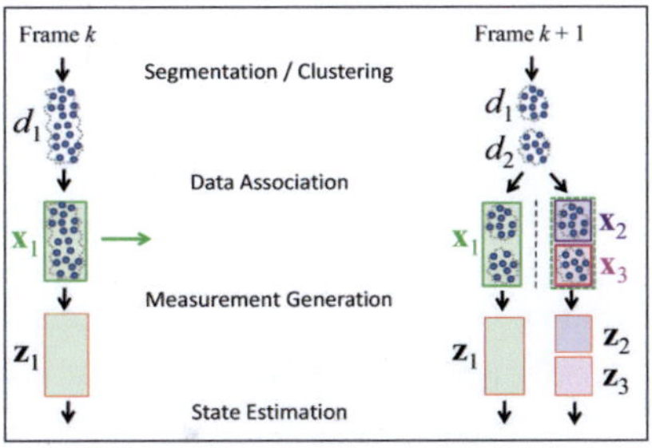

(d) Data association in the case of a split detection: FBPDATA (Detection-by-Tracking).

Figure 4.2: Comparison of a data association approach with the classical Tracking-by-Detection paradigm with that of FBPDATA for the cases of merged detection ((a) and (c)) and split detection ((b) and (d)).
The principle of the classical Tracking-by-Detection approach is shown in (a) and (b). Data association is done between track states $\mathbf{x}_i$ and measurements $\mathbf{z}_j$, which are directly obtained from detections d_j. Since one-to-one assignments only are allowed, this leads for both merged (a) and split (b) detection scenario to three possible assignment possibilities, none of which is correct.
The basic idea of FBPDATA is illustrated in (c) and (d). Measurement generation ("reconstruction") is done not before, but rather after the data association between tracked objects and obtained detections ("Detection-by-Tracking" paradigm). Both data association and measurement reconstruction are based on the affiliations of the individual feature points to the tracked objects.

Generation of track measurements from the obtained detections for the object tracking process in FBPDATA is done not before, but rather after the data association step. Data association is performed between tracked objects and raw detections and is based on the affiliation of the individual feature points within the detection to the tracked objects. Instead of a "blind" conversion of detections d_j into measurements $\mathbf{z}_j$, the appropriate measurements $\mathbf{z}_i$ are "reconstructed" from the obtained point clouds using knowledge about the previous affiliation of individual feature points to the detected objects $\mathbf{x}_i$ from previous frames. This leads for both merged detection scenario (c) and split detection scenario (d) to two different assignment possibilities, both of which are theoretically feasible. A distinction between a merged detection (MD) and track merge (TM) (left and right assignment possibilities in (c)) as well as a distinction between a split detection (SD) and a track split (TS) (left and right assignment possibilities in (d)) needs to be done. This issue is addressed in Section 4.1.6.

The feature-based ***measurement reconstruction*** offers a solution to the problem of split, merged, and partial detections, as well as to the problem of detections which are bloated due to clutter. Occlusion handling is facilitated by maintaining a ***grid-based object extent representation*** in 3D. A more detailed description of both concepts is given in the following sections.

4.1.3 Feature-based reconstruction of object dynamics

The feature-based measurement reconstruction method is based on the idea illustrated in Figure 4.3. Knowing the spatial relationship between a group of tracked feature points belonging to an object and a reference point $\mathbf{p}_O$ on this object at time $k-1$ it is possible to reconstruct the position of the reference point at time k.

The reconstructed position of the reference point may be used as measurement for the data association and track state update. Using such "virtual" measurements instead of e.g., detection centroids allows to obtain much more accurate estimates of object position and velocity, especially in cases of partial detections due to occlusions and in cases of bloated or narrowed detections due to wrong segmentation.

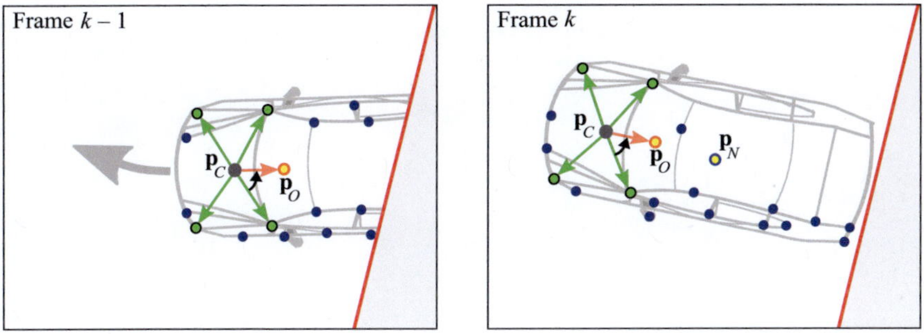

(a) Frame $k-1$ **(b)** Frame k

Figure 4.3: Feature-based reconstruction of reference point position (top view). A reference point $\mathbf{p}_O$ on a car, which enters the field of view of the sensor (visualized by a red line), can be reconstructed using its spatial relationship to the center of gravity $\mathbf{p}_C$ of the tracked object points (green).

4.1.4 Grid-based reconstruction of object dimensions

After having obtained a correct position of a reference point for each tracked object we can proceed with estimating object dimensions. Internally we represent object extent not only by means of a cuboid but also by means of a spatial occupancy function, modeled as a local grid with occupancy and occlusion estimation for each cell. This ***grid-based object extent representation*** offers a compromise between a coarse and a fine-granular modeling of the objects' extent and allows for both detection and a proper handling of occlusion situations. Figure 4.4 shows an sample visualization of a grid-based object representation with occupied cells.

During state prediction we use the grid-based object representation to generate ***appearance masks*** $M_{\mathrm{A}}^{\mathbf{x}_i}(u,v) \in \{0,1\}$ for each object $\mathbf{x}_i$ by projecting the occupied grid cells into the camera image. By weighting the appearance masks with the corresponding object existence probabilities and an additional probability factor for being non-transparent, we get the ***appearance probability masks*** $M_{\mathrm{P}}^{\mathbf{x}_i}(u,v)$. Image inversion of the appearance probability masks leads to the ***transparency probability masks*** $M_{\mathrm{T}}^{\mathbf{x}_i}(u,v) = 1 - M_{\mathrm{P}}^{\mathbf{x}_i}(u,v)$.

Figure 4.4: Grid-based object representation.

The multiplication of the transparency probability masks of foreground objects and image inversion of the results yield the ***observability probability masks*** $M_{\supset}^{\mathbf{x}_i}(u,v)$ and the ***occlusion probability masks*** $M_{\not\supset}^{\mathbf{x}_i}(u,v) = 1 - M_{\supset}^{\mathbf{x}_i}(u,v)$ for background objects. This allows to make an occlusion reasoning for their grid cells, as shown in Figure 4.5. Occupied grid cells can thus be preserved in case of occlusions, which allows to maintain the occluded object portions, to "reconstruct" the corresponding extent measurement, and to correctly update the track dimensions.

During the update step we create one composite object extent measurement from all point clouds associated to the track. This is done by sorting points of each associated point cloud into the grid, which is aligned according to the updated dynamic track parameters. Points of each point cloud contribute to the occupancy value of the respective grid cell according to their affiliation probability to the track and the association probability of the point cloud. Occupation of occluded grid cells is preserved too, as shown in Figure 4.6.

The resulting updated occupancy grid is used as a basis for generation of the track extent measurement. We treat each occupied cell as a data point and fit a cuboid into the point cloud obtained in this way. The length, width, and height of the obtained cuboid are used as the "reconstructed" measurements for the track dimensions.

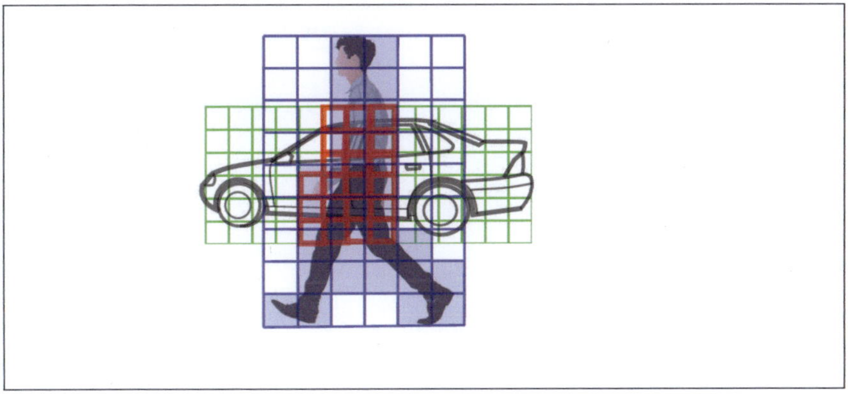

(a)

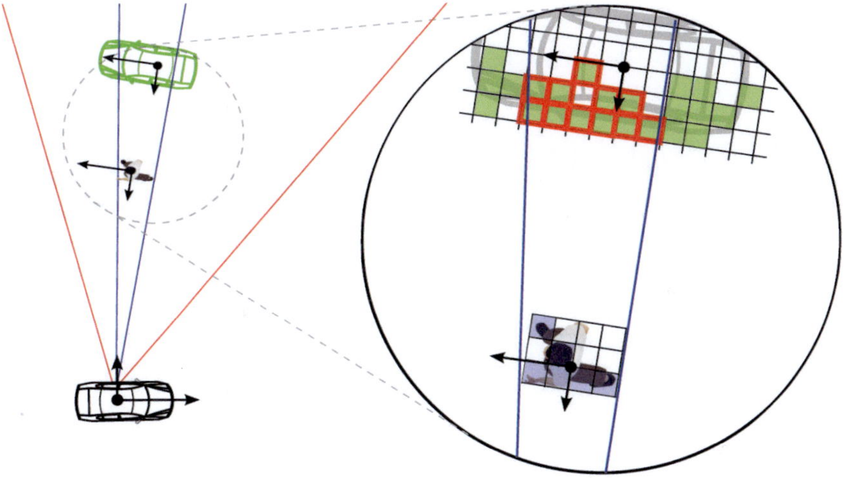

(b)

Figure 4.5: Grid-based object representation and procedure of estimating occlusion probabilities of occupied object cells (camera image (a) and top view (b)). Estimation of occlusion probabilities for individual grid cells of tracked objects is achieved by means of appearance masks (blue) and occlusion mask (red).

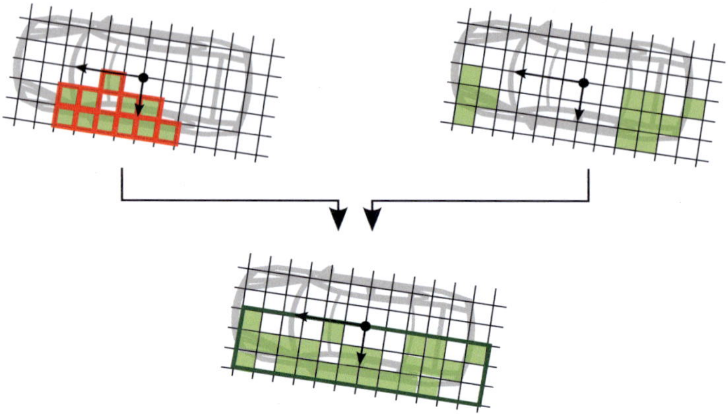

Figure 4.6: Grid-based reconstruction of object dimensions measurement.

4.1.5 Reference point filtering

At the track instantiation we use the center of the fitted cuboid as the reference point that is to be tracked. In the consecutive frames, the center of the cuboid, which is obtained by means of the grid-based extent reconstruction, does not necessarily coincide with this tracked reference point. Ignoring this fact leads to an erroneous relocation of the estimated object shape to the old reference point $\mathbf{p}_O$. Especially in the cases of objects entering the FoV of the sensors, the estimated object shape is systematically placed around the wrong reference point as shown in Figure 4.7.

Shifting the reference point to the center $\mathbf{p}_N$ of the fitted cuboid leads to incorrect results as well, as shown in Figure 4.8. This is due to the fact that the object dimensions are filtered, i.e., a weighted sum of prediction and measurement is used as the a-posteriori state estimation of the object extent.

In order to cope with this problem, we propose to shift the reference point to a filtered position $\mathbf{p}_F$, i.e., to weight coordinates of both the originally estimated reference point and the measured cuboid center with factors that are computed from the ratio of the corresponding predicted and filtered object dimensions.

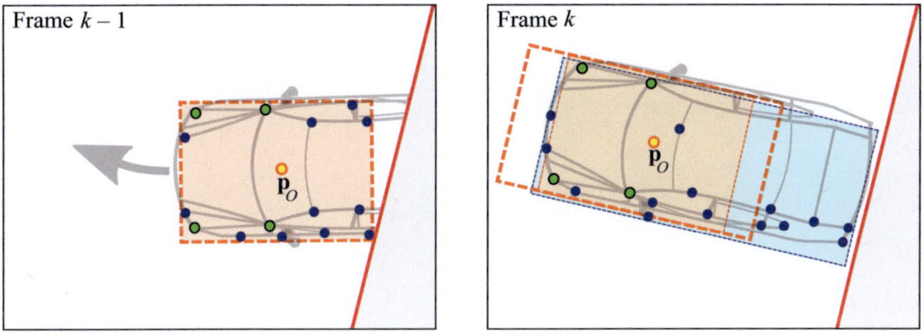

(a) Frame k (b) Frame $k-1$

Figure 4.7: Wrong placement of the estimated object shape in the case of ignoring relocation of the reference point. The estimated (i.e., filtered) object shape (thick orange box) protrudes from the real object extend, if placed around the tracked reference point. Thin orange box: predicted measurement of the object extent; thin blue box: measured object extent.

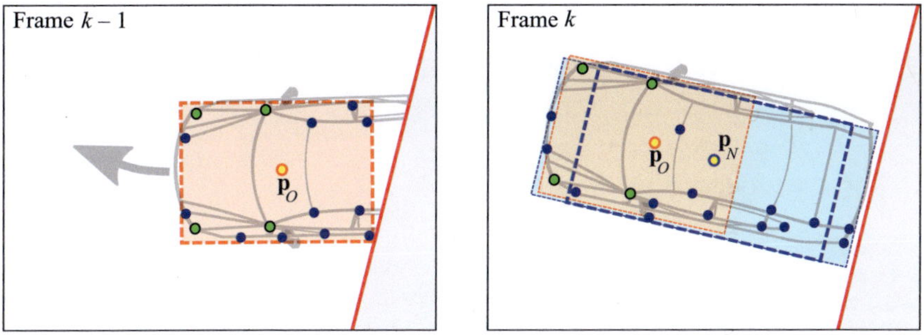

(a) Frame $k-1$ (b) Frame k

Figure 4.8: Wrong placement of the estimated object shape in the case of explicitly setting the reference point to the new cuboid center. The estimated (i.e., filtered) object shape (thick blue box) lags behind (especially with regard to the car front), if shifted to the center of the fitted cuboid. Thin orange box: predicted measurement of the object extent; thin blue box: measured object extent; thick blue box: filtered object shape placed around the measured cuboid center.

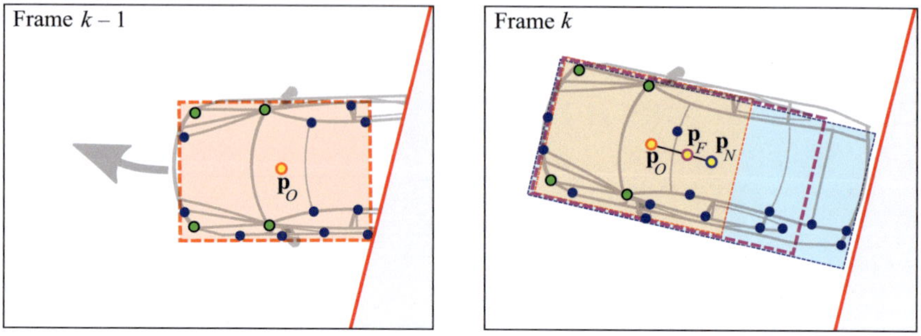

(a) Frame $k-1$ **(b)** Frame k

Figure 4.9: Correct placement of the estimated object shape in the case of filtering reference point position. The car front is correctly tracked, if the estimated (i.e., filtered) object shape is placed around the filtered reference point position. Thin orange box: predicted measurement of the object extent; thin blue box: measured object extent; thick magenta box: filtered object shape placed around the filtered reference point position.

The filtered position is computed as follows:

$$x_F = x_O + (x_N - x_O) \cdot \rho_x \,, \tag{4.1}$$

$$y_F = y_O + (y_N - y_O) \cdot \rho_y \,, \tag{4.2}$$

$$z_F = 1/2 \cdot h_U \,, \tag{4.3}$$

with weighting factors

$$\rho_x = \frac{|\Delta x_P - \Delta x_U|}{|\Delta x_P - \Delta x_U| + |\Delta x_P - \Delta x_M|} \tag{4.4}$$

and

$$\rho_y = \frac{|\Delta y_P - \Delta y_U|}{|\Delta y_P - \Delta y_U| + |\Delta y_P - \Delta y_M|} \,, \tag{4.5}$$

where x_F, y_F, and z_F are the coordinates of the filtered reference point position $\mathbf{p}_F$; x_O and y_O are the coordinates of the old reference point $\mathbf{p}_O$ in Frame k; x_N and y_N are the coordinates of the center $\mathbf{p}_N$ of the fitted cuboid; Δx_P and Δy_P are the predicted lateral and longitudinal object extent; Δx_M and Δy_M are the measured (reconstructed) lateral and longitudinal object extent; and Δx_U, Δy_U, and h_U are the updated lateral and longitudinal object extent as well as updated object height after the Kalman Filter correction step.

The result of the proposed ***reference point filtering*** procedure is shown in Figure 4.9.

4.1.6 Distinction between four split & merge data association events

The next important issue is the introduction of a classification scheme of data association events incorporating assignments between a track and multiple detections and vice versa. In order to correctly handle such multiple assignments, one has to make a distinction between different possible reasons for such situations. In addition to the regular data association events, such as correct detection (true positive), correct non-detection (true negative), phantom detection (false positive), and missing detection (false negative), we introduce four basic split & merge data association events:

- ***Merged detection*** (MD)
- ***Track merge*** (TM)
- ***Split Detection*** (SD)
- ***Track split*** (TS)

They are illustrated in Figure 4.10.

When two tracks result in a single detection, there are two scenarios that could have led to this situation. The first one is when two objects evoke a single detection due to an incorrect segmentation, as shown in Figures 3.1 and 3.2 (b). In this case (we will speak here of a ***"Merged Detection" (MD)***) both tracks have to be maintained and the (corrupted) detection has to be appropriately handled in order to enable a correct update of both tracks. But there is also another scenario that one can think of. The existing tracks may correspond to parts of a real object that has not been detected correctly in previous time steps due to over-segmentation.

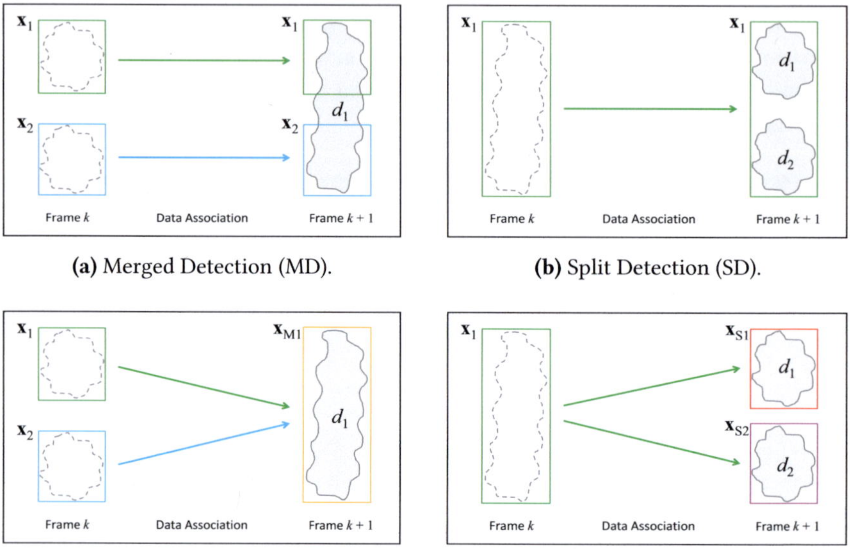

(a) Merged Detection (MD).

(b) Split Detection (SD).

(c) Track Merge (TM).

(d) Track Split (TS).

Figure 4.10: Classification of data association events that incorporate splits and merges.

In this case (which will be referred to as a ***"Track Merge" (TM)***) a new track has to be created and the existing tracks have to be deleted.

A similar ambiguity arises when a single track is assigned to two or more detections. Each detection may correspond either to a part of the previously correctly tracked object (***"Split Detection" (SD)***), as shown in Figure 3.2 (d) or to an actually existing small object that in the past has been detected together with other objects due to an under-segmentation (***"Track Split" (TS)***).

An appropriate distinction between the MD and the TM scenarios, as well as between the SD and the TS scenarios is only possible, if a dedicated appearance-based or model-based object recognition method is available. If such possibility is not given, the only assumption one can make in order to resolve these ambiguities is that the segmentation errors occur sporadically and most of the time a correct segmentation is given.

The disambiguation can be made only in the course of time. Until then both hypotheses have to be established and maintained in parallel. Adoption of this strategy would lead to implementation of a computationally intensive multiscan approach (Multi-Hypotheses-Tracking), which propagates multiple mutually exclusive object representations throughout multiple frames. FBPDATA offers a suboptimal but significantly less computationally expensive alternative.

4.1.7 Distinction between different causes for missed and unassociated detections

In addition to the distinction between a non-existence and non-observability of an object in case of a missed detection, which is made in [Muš02], we make an additional distinction between a non-detection due to deficiencies of the sensors or a failure of the object detection algorithm (in the following denoted as $\varnothing$) and a non-detection due to an – in many cases predictable – occlusion situation (denoted as $\not\varnothing$). Furthermore, for detections that cannot be associated to any of the existing tracks, two possible causes are taken into consideration: high clutter density and appearance of new, previously not known objects. The two sources are denoted as Ⓒ (the ***clutter source***) and Ⓑ (the ***birth source***). Often there exist some criteria that allow for a distinction between clutter-based detections and true object detections. Examples of such criteria are density of the feature points, homogeneity of their velocities, texture characteristics of the relevant image region etc. The FBPDATA approach allows to integrate this information by taking it into account when computing the corresponding likelihoods. The same is valid for the spatial distribution of the detections. Emergence of new objects is usually justified only at the borders of the sensor's field of view or occlusions. This can be also taken into account by integrating this information into the a-priori probability computation.

4.1.8 Definition of stochastic joint data association events

Similar to JIPDA, we estimate object existence probabilities and use them for track instantiation, confirmation, and termination, as well as for computation of the association weights β that are used during the track state update. The respective equations are derived from the state estimation problem formulation similarly to the derivation in JIPDA. FBPDATA also considers mutually exclusive joint data association events, which are conjunctions of assignments between tracks and observed detections. A joint data association event Θ is defined in a way that allows to make the following statements:

- for each obtained detection whether it is due to
  - an already tracked object
  - merge of two (or more) detections of already tracked objects
  - a new previously not known object
  - clutter
- for each maintained track:
  - whether it exists
  - whether it is occluded
  - whether it gives a split detection
  - whether a corresponding detection is absent due to a sensor or detection failure.

As an illustration, joint events may be visualized by means of bipartite graphs connecting current detections with their causes, as shown in Figure 4.11 (a). On the left side of the bipartite graph we put tracks $\mathbf{x}_1, \dots, \mathbf{x}_{n_k}$ that are currently known to the system. On the right side we put the currently obtained detections $d_1, \dots, d_{m_k}$. Additionally, on the track side we put two special elements: the clutter source Ⓒ, which is responsible for emerging of the clutter-based detections, and the birth source Ⓑ, which is responsible for appearance of the new, previously not known objects. On the detection side we additionally put three possible causes for a missed detection, namely $\varnothing$, which indicates a missed detection due to a failure of the sensor or detection algorithms, $\not\supset$, which indicates a missed detection due to non-observability (i.e., occlusion), and $\nexists$, which indicates that the corresponding object does not exist, which obviously also implies absence of a detection.

Joint events are considered to be feasible when each regular element (track or measurement) is interconnected either with a special element or with one or more regular elements on the other side of the graph. Associations between two special elements are prohibited.

A feasible joint data association event Θ may thus contain six types of edges θ_k between observations and their sources:

- $\theta_k^{\mathbf{x}_i \mapsto d_j}$: assumption that detection d_j has been caused by the tracked object $\mathbf{x}_i$
- $\theta_k^{Ⓑ \mapsto d_j}$: detection d_j has been caused by a so far not known object
- $\theta_k^{Ⓒ \mapsto d_j}$: assumption that detection d_j has been caused by clutter
- $\theta_k^{\mathbf{x}_i \mapsto \not\supset}$: track $\mathbf{x}_i$ did not evoke a detection because it is occluded
- $\theta_k^{\mathbf{x}_i \mapsto \varnothing}$: track $\mathbf{x}_i$ did not evoke a detection because of a sensing error
- $\theta_k^{\mathbf{x}_i \mapsto \nexists}$: track $\mathbf{x}_i$ did not evoke a detection because the it does not exist

Joint events can also be visualized by means of a matrix, as shown in Figure 4.11 (b). Both representations are equivalent.

(a) Modeling of data association by means of a bipartite graph

(b) Representation of a joint event by means of a matrix

Figure 4.11: A possible joint data association event for the case of three tracks and two detections represented as a graph and as a matrix.

The fact of not receiving a measurement for a known track will be in the following denoted by d_0, which is an aggregation of the two special elements $\varnothing$ and $\not\supset$. Similarly, the aggregation of the clutter source and the birth source will be denoted by $\mathbf{x}_0$.

In order to represent the dependencies within the joint events Θ we introduce the following elementary events:

Event of existence of the target $\mathbf{x}_i$ at time step k:

$$\exists \mathbf{x}_{k,i} : \quad \theta^{\mathbf{x}_{k,i} \mapsto \nexists} \notin \Theta . \tag{4.6}$$

Event of non-existence of the target $\mathbf{x}_i$ at time step k:

$$\nexists \mathbf{x}_{k,i} : \quad \theta^{\mathbf{x}_{k,i} \mapsto \nexists} \in \Theta . \tag{4.7}$$

Missed detection event for the object $\mathbf{x}_i$ at time step k:

$$\varnothing \mathbf{x}_{k,i} : \quad \theta^{\mathbf{x}_{k,i} \mapsto \varnothing} \in \Theta . \tag{4.8}$$

Event of a clutter-based d_j detection event at time step k:

$$\copyright_j : \quad \theta^{\copyright \mapsto d_{k,j}} \in \Theta . \tag{4.9}$$

Event of the track birth from the detection d_j at time step k:

$$Ⓑ_j : \quad \theta^{Ⓑ \mapsto d_{k,j}} \in \Theta . \tag{4.10}$$

Non-observability event for the object $\mathbf{x}_i$ at time step k due to occlusion (occlusion event):

$$\not\supset \mathbf{x}_{k,i} : \quad \theta^{\mathbf{x}_{k,i} \mapsto \not\supset} \in \Theta . \tag{4.11}$$

Non-occlusion event for the object $\mathbf{x}_i$ at time step k:

$$\supset \mathbf{x}_{k,i} : \quad \theta^{\mathbf{x}_{k,i} \mapsto \nexists} \notin \Theta \wedge \theta^{\mathbf{x}_{k,i} \mapsto \not\supset} \notin \Theta . \tag{4.12}$$

Split detection event for the track $\mathbf{x}_i$ at time step k:

$$i \prec \{j\} : \quad \forall r \in \{1, \dots, m_k\} : r \in \{j\} \Leftrightarrow \theta^{\mathbf{x}_{k,i} \mapsto d_{k,r}} \in \Theta . \tag{4.13}$$

Merged detection event for the tracks $\{\mathbf{x}_i\}$ at time step k:

$$\{i\} \succ j : \quad \forall r \in \{1, \dots, n_k\} : r \in \{i\} \Leftrightarrow \theta^{\mathbf{x}_{k,r} \mapsto d_{k,j}} \in \Theta \,. \tag{4.14}$$

The occurrence of the elementary events within a joint association event is modeled by means of multi-dimensional random variables $\boldsymbol{E}_k(\Theta)$, $\boldsymbol{B}_k(\Theta)$, $\boldsymbol{O}_k(\Theta)$, $\boldsymbol{S}_k(\Theta)$, $\boldsymbol{M}_k(\Theta)$, $\boldsymbol{N}_k(\Theta)$, and $\boldsymbol{C}_k(\Theta)$, that give statements about object existence, births and occlusions, as well as about splits, merges, missed, and clutter-based detections respectively, and are defined as

$$\boldsymbol{E}_k(\Theta) = \begin{bmatrix} E_{k,1}(\Theta) \\ \vdots \\ E_{k,i}(\Theta) \\ \vdots \\ E_{k,n_k}(\Theta) \end{bmatrix}, \; \boldsymbol{B}_k(\Theta) = \begin{bmatrix} B_{k,1}(\Theta) \\ \vdots \\ B_{k,j}(\Theta) \\ \vdots \\ B_{k,m_k}(\Theta) \end{bmatrix}, \text{ etc.} \tag{4.15}$$

with formative random variables

$$E_{k,i}(\Theta) = \begin{cases} 1 & \text{if } \; \exists \mathbf{x}_{k,i} \\ 0 & \text{if } \; \nexists \mathbf{x}_{k,i} \end{cases} \tag{4.16}$$

$$B_{k,j}(\Theta) = \begin{cases} 1 & \text{if } \; \text{Ⓑ}_j \\ 0 & \text{else} \end{cases} \tag{4.17}$$

$$O_{k,i}(\Theta) = \begin{cases} 1 & \text{if } \; \not\supset \mathbf{x}_{k,i} \\ 0 & \text{if } \; \supset \mathbf{x}_{k,i} \end{cases} \tag{4.18}$$

$$S_{k,i \mapsto \{j\}}(\Theta) = \begin{cases} 1 & \text{if } \; i \prec \{j\} \\ 0 & \text{else} \end{cases} \tag{4.19}$$

$$M_{k,\{i\}\mapsto j}(\Theta) = \begin{cases} 1 & \text{if} \quad \{i\} \succ j \\ 0 & \text{else} \end{cases} \tag{4.20}$$

$$N_{k,i}(\Theta) = \begin{cases} 1 & \text{if} \quad \varnothing \mathbf{x}_{k,i} \\ 0 & \text{else} \end{cases} \tag{4.21}$$

$$C_{k,j}(\Theta) = \begin{cases} 1 & \text{if} \quad \copyright_j \\ 0 & \text{else} . \end{cases} \tag{4.22}$$

4.1.9 Track clustering

For computation of the a-posteriori association probabilities between tracks and point clouds (association weights), all possible assignment hypotheses (joint events) have to be considered. The number of joint events that have to be evaluated grows exponentially with the number of tracks and point clouds. As shown in [Col92], this is an NP hard problem. In order to reduce the computational complexity, we use a track clustering scheme similar to the one described in [Muš02]. Prior to the actual data association, tracks are divided into disjoint groups with no common point clouds, that are then considered separately. Joint events are built and evaluated separately for each cluster. This allows to drastically reduce the number of considered joint data association events and significantly reduces the algorithm complexity.

4.1.10 Gating based on feature point affiliations

In most Multi-Object Tracking applications, a position-based gating is done, i.e., a detection is rejected, if its centroid does not lie within the gate of the tracked object [Kum06, Mäh08]. In PDA and JPDA, gating is done based on the Mahalanobis distance between the predicted and the real measurement (s. Section 2.3.3.1, page 41). Specification of a gating probability leads to definition of a hyperelliptical gating region around the predicted measurement $\hat{\mathbf{z}}_k$. This makes sense for point-shaped targets and under assumption that a track may evoke only one detection and vice versa. In case of extended objects with possibly incomplete or merged detections, this may lead to erroneous rejections as shown in Fig. 4.12.

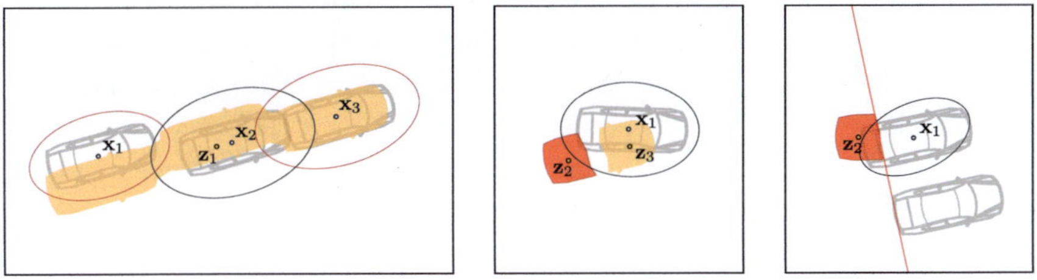

(a) Merged detection **(b)** Split detection **(c)** Partial occlusion

Figure 4.12: Erroneous measurement rejection caused by a position-based gating in cases of corrupted detections.

In the case of a video-based application with feature point tracking, rejection of detections may be done based on the affiliation of the appertaining points to tracks. Associations are considered infeasible and are rejected straight away, if a detection does not contain any tracked points that are affiliated to the considered track.

The only case that has to be considered separately is the case of objects that reappear after an occlusion phase. Identification of such cases is done using the feature-based approach too. The detection may be assumed to be a re-emerging object part, if most of the appertaining feature points are not yet affiliated to any tracked object. The association to the track is considered feasible, if the detected point cloud lies within the predicted object extent or not far from it and if the measurement reconstruction procedure produces a feasible measurement for the reference point of the track. Incorporation of the reconstructed reference point position instead of the detection centroid allows to efficiently avoid gating errors that are due to bias between predicted measurements and real measurements obtained from bloated or partial detections.

4.1.11 Feature point management

Noise, blurring effects, correspondence confusion errors, and short-term occlusions cause temporary dropouts in feature point tracking. In the case of a front-looking automotive application, there might be additional causes for dropouts, such as rain drops, spray clouds raised by preceding vehicles, or windshield wipers. This problem is solved by means of an efficient feature point management scheme which allows to maintain point tracking in spite of measurement dropouts of both spatial and temporal correspondence search algorithms.

In case of dropouts in depth estimation, points can be tracked further using predicted depth values until the regular depth estimation is possible again. In case of ambiguous or missing correspondences between two consecutive frames (optical flow dropouts), points can be propagated using predicted point motion in the hope that at some point an unambiguous correspondence will be found. Re-identification trials are made in each frame using optical flow computation between the current frame and the latest frame in which the point has been seen.

4.1.12 Track management

Track management in FBPDATA follows the ***Track-Before-Detect (TBD)*** paradigm, i.e., tracking of hypotheses before confirming them as valid tracks. Track instantiation is done, if a detection lies outside of the gates of existing tracks or if the probability of representing a new track is higher than the sum of association probabilities to existing tracks. Initialization of track position and extent are done using position and extent of the cuboid fitted into the point cloud. Since detections consist of already tracked points, their mean velocity is used for initialization of the object velocity. This leads to a much better convergence of the state estimator. Yaw rate and acceleration are initialized with zero. A track is confirmed, if the object existence probability exceeds a pre-defined threshold $T_{\exists}$. It should be chosen high enough to allow confirmation of tracks whose existence have been unambiguously confirmed through a sequence of measurements. Absence of measurements for erroneously initiated clutter-based tracks, as well as high death probability for tracks that leave the field of view of the sensors, lead to decreasing existence probability of such tracks. If existence probability falls below a certain (small) threshold $T_{\nexists}$, tracks are terminated. Obviously, for correct track management according to this scheme, track birth probability should lie above $T_{\nexists}$ but below $T_{\exists}$. An example of track management according to this scheme is shown in Figure 4.13.

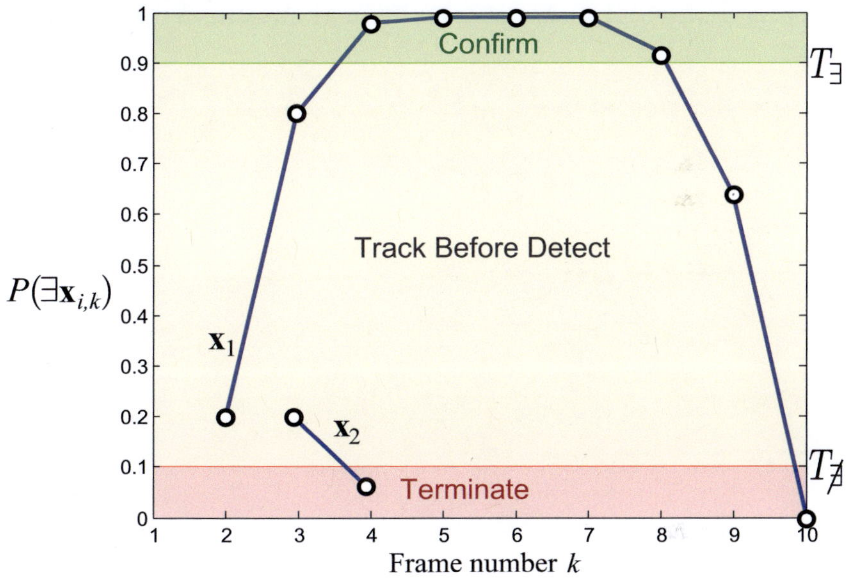

Figure 4.13: Existence based confirmation and termination of tracks according to Track-Before-Detect scheme. A track $\mathbf{x}_1$, which has been initialized for a real object, is confirmed through further observations. At the end of the sequence, it leaves the field of view of the sensors, which leads to a decreasing existence probability and fast track termination. The second track $\mathbf{x}_2$ is falsely initialized due to clutter. Absence of further detections leads to termination of this track.

4.2 Formal derivation

4.2.1 State estimation problem formulation

Before we derive the FBPDATA formulas, let us consider the object state estimation problem as it has been formulated in JIPDA (cf. Equation (2.150) on Page 67):

$$\begin{aligned}
\hat{\mathbf{x}}_{k,i} &= \mathbb{E}[\boldsymbol{X}_{k,i}|\exists \mathbf{x}_{k,i}, \mathcal{Z}_{1:k}] = \sum_{j=0}^{m_k} \mathbb{E}[\boldsymbol{X}_k|\theta_k^{\mathbf{x}_i \mapsto \mathbf{z}_j}, \mathcal{Z}_{1:k}] \cdot P(\theta_k^{\mathbf{x}_i \mapsto \mathbf{z}_j}|\exists \mathbf{x}_{k,i}, \mathcal{Z}_{1:k}) \\
&= \sum_{j=0}^{m_k} \beta_k^{\mathbf{x}_i \mapsto \mathbf{z}_j} \hat{\mathbf{x}}_k^- + \mathbf{K}_k \sum_{j=1}^{m_k} \beta_k^{\mathbf{x}_i \mapsto \mathbf{z}_j} (\mathbf{z}_{k,j} - \hat{\mathbf{z}}_k^{\mathbf{x}_i}) \\
&= \hat{\mathbf{x}}_k^- + \mathbf{K}_k \sum_{j=1}^{m_k} \beta_k^{\mathbf{x}_i \mapsto \mathbf{z}_j} \tilde{\mathbf{z}}_{k,j}^{\mathbf{x}_i} \\
&= \hat{\mathbf{x}}_k^- + \mathbf{K}_k \cdot \tilde{\mathbf{z}}_{k,\mathrm{Comp}}^{\mathbf{x}_i}
\end{aligned} \tag{4.23}$$

with innovation

$$\tilde{\mathbf{z}}_{k,j}^{\mathbf{x}_i} = \mathbf{z}_{k,j} - \hat{\mathbf{z}}_k^{\mathbf{x}_i} \tag{4.24}$$

being the innovation of the track $\mathbf{x}_i$ produced by the measurement $\mathbf{z}_j$ at time step k and

$$\tilde{\mathbf{z}}_{k,\mathrm{Comp}}^{\mathbf{x}_i} := \sum_{j=1}^{m_k} \beta_k^{\mathbf{x}_i \mapsto \mathbf{z}_j} \tilde{\mathbf{z}}_{k,j}^{\mathbf{x}_i} \tag{4.25}$$

being the composite innovation for the track $\mathbf{x}_{k,i}$. One of the assumptions made by JPDA and JIPDA at this point is that a detection (and the corresponding measurement) are evoked by at most one track or by clutter (cf. Section 2.3.5, Page 61). This assumption does not hold in case of merged detections. Additionally, all PDA derivates including JPDA and JIPDA assume that measurements depend only on the state of the originating object and that measurement errors have a Gaussian distribution (cf. Section 2.3.3.1, Page 42). These assumptions are systematically violated in occlusion situations as well as in cases of measurements obtained from split, merged and bloated detections.

Measurements that are built from corrupted detections in general have a non-Gaussian error distribution and are furthermore not independent on the constellation of objects with respect to the sensor. Both the existence and appearance of the individual measurements depend on the constellation of the scene, i.e., tracks may not be considered independently from each other.

In case of a corrupted detection $d_{k,j}$, the obtained measurement $\mathbf{z}_{k,j}$ will be biased. The innovation $\tilde{\mathbf{z}}^{\mathbf{x}_i}_{k,j}$, computed from the predicted "ideal" measurement $\hat{\mathbf{z}}^{\mathbf{x}_i}_k$ and the actually obtained biased measurement $\mathbf{z}_{k,j}$, will be biased as well. A state estimation based on it does not make much sense. A more reasonable approach would be to consider different possible joint data association events Θ and to build a weighted sum

$$\begin{aligned}\hat{\mathbf{x}}_{k,i} &= \mathbb{E}[\mathbf{X}_{k,i}|\exists\mathbf{x}_{k,i}, \mathcal{D}_{1:k}] \\ &= \sum_{\Theta\in\mathbf{\Theta}_k^{\mathbf{x}_i\mapsto\exists}} \mathbb{E}[\mathbf{X}_{k,i}|\Theta, \exists\mathbf{x}_{k,i}, \mathcal{D}_{1:k}] \cdot P(\Theta|\exists\mathbf{x}_{k,i}, \mathcal{D}_{1:k})\end{aligned} \tag{4.26}$$

of the joint event dependent conditional expectations

$$\hat{\mathbf{x}}^{\Theta}_{k,i} := \mathbb{E}[\mathbf{X}_{k,i}|\Theta, \exists\mathbf{x}_{k,i}, \mathcal{D}_{1:k}]\,, \tag{4.27}$$

where

$$\mathbf{\Theta}_k^{\mathbf{x}_i\mapsto\exists} := \{\Theta|\theta^{\mathbf{x}_{k,i}\mapsto\nexists} \notin \Theta\} \tag{4.28}$$

is the set of joint events Θ that assume existence of the track $\mathbf{x}_i$ at time k.

The joint event dependent conditional expectation from 4.27 can be computed using the joint event dependent innovation $\tilde{\mathbf{z}}^{\mathbf{x}_i,\Theta}_{k,\mathrm{Corr}} := \mathbf{z}^{\mathbf{x}_i,\Theta}_{k,\mathrm{Corr}} - \hat{\mathbf{z}}^{\mathbf{x}_i,\Theta}_k$

$$\begin{aligned}\mathbb{E}[\mathbf{X}_{k,i}|\Theta, \exists\mathbf{x}_{k,i}, \mathcal{D}_{1:k}] &= \hat{\mathbf{x}}^-_{k,i} + \mathbf{K}_k(\Theta)\cdot(\mathbf{z}^{\mathbf{x}_i,\Theta}_{k,\mathrm{Corr}} - \hat{\mathbf{z}}^{\mathbf{x}_i,\Theta}_k) \\ &= \hat{\mathbf{x}}^-_{k,i} + \mathbf{K}_k(\Theta)\cdot\tilde{\mathbf{z}}^{\mathbf{x}_i,\Theta}_{k,\mathrm{Corr}}\,.\end{aligned} \tag{4.29}$$

where $\hat{\mathbf{z}}^{\mathbf{x}_i,\Theta}_k$ is the joint event dependent measurement prediction for track $\mathbf{x}_i$ (i.e., measurement prediction under the assumption of detection corruption due to occlusions, splits and merges as they are defined in the joint event Θ), and $\mathbf{z}^{\mathbf{x}_i,\Theta}_{k,\mathrm{Corr}}$ is the measurement obtained from the corresponding real detection $d_{k,\mathrm{Corr}}^{\mathbf{x}_i,\Theta}$. $\mathbf{K}_k(\Theta)$ is the joint event dependent Kalman gain.

In principle, this means that for each track $\mathbf{x}_{k,i}$, one has to predict corresponding detections $\hat{d}_k^{\mathbf{x}_i,\Theta}$ for all conceivable joint events Θ, i.e., detections that would be obtained according to occlusions, splits and merges defined by the respective joint event Θ. For distant tracking of point-shaped targets this approach might be reasonable, as shown in [Cha84]. The reason is a rather simple measurement model that allows for an independence assumption of the single measurements and leads to a great simplification. In our case this approach is not applicable. It would imply prediction of all steps of the detection process, which is a quite complex problem since it requires modeling of the complete data acquisition and measurement formation process including emerging uncertainties at all process stages such as feature extraction, stereo correspondence search, computation of optical flow, point clustering, fitting etc. Note also the dependence of the Kalman gain $\mathbf{K}_k(\Theta)$ on the joint event Θ. Different joint events may imply different measurement formation models (e.g., in cases of incomplete detections, merges and splits), which in turn lead to different Kalman gains. In most cases it will even not be possible to obtain a linear measurement model, which would lead to the failure of the entire approach.

FBPDATA proposes an alternative solution to this problem. The idea of predicting expected observations $\hat{d}_k^{\mathbf{x}_i,\Theta}$ for each conceivable joint event and comparing them with the actually obtained detections is abandoned. Instead, the "ideal" prediction $\hat{\mathbf{z}}_k^{\mathbf{x}_i}$ is computed for each track (i.e., the measurement that would be obtained in the ideal case, if no effects such as (partial) occlusions, splits and merges influenced the measurement process). For each joint event Θ, this "ideal" prediction is set into relation with the artificially generated "ideal" measurement $\mathbf{z}_{k,\mathrm{Reco}(\Theta)}^{\mathbf{x}_i}$. The index "Reco" stands for "Reconstructed" and means that the measurement is artificially reconstructed from detections $d_{k,j}$ that according to the currently considered joint event Θ are associated to the track $\mathbf{x}_i$.

In this case Equation (4.29) transforms to

$$\begin{aligned}\mathbb{E}[\boldsymbol{X}_{k,i}|\Theta, \exists \mathbf{x}_{k,i}, \mathcal{D}_{1:k}] &= \hat{\mathbf{x}}_{k,i}^{-} + \mathbf{K}_k(\Theta) \cdot (\mathbf{z}_{k,\text{Reco}(\Theta)}^{\mathbf{x}_i} - \hat{\mathbf{z}}_k^{\mathbf{x}_i}) \\ &= \hat{\mathbf{x}}_{k,i}^{-} + \mathbf{K}_k(\Theta) \cdot \tilde{\mathbf{z}}_{k,\text{Reco}(\Theta)}^{\mathbf{x}_i} \,.\end{aligned} \tag{4.30}$$

Here, $\tilde{\mathbf{z}}_{k,\text{Reco}(\Theta)}^{\mathbf{x}_i}$ is the joint event dependent innovation obtained from the "ideal" prediction and the reconstructed "ideal" measurement.

Equation (4.26) becomes then

$$\begin{aligned}\hat{\mathbf{x}}_{k,i} &= \mathbb{E}[\boldsymbol{X}_{k,i}|\exists \mathbf{x}_{k,i}, \mathcal{D}_{1:k}] \\ &= \sum_{\Theta \in \boldsymbol{\Theta}_k^{\mathbf{x}_i \mapsto \exists}} \mathbb{E}[\boldsymbol{X}_{k,i}|\Theta, \exists \mathbf{x}_{k,i}, \mathcal{D}_{1:k}] \cdot P(\Theta|\exists \mathbf{x}_{k,i}, \mathcal{D}_{1:k}) \\ &= \sum_{\Theta \in \boldsymbol{\Theta}_k^{\mathbf{x}_i \mapsto \exists}} \hat{\mathbf{x}}_{k,i}^{\Theta} \cdot P(\Theta|\exists \mathbf{x}_{k,i}, \mathcal{D}_{1:k}) \\ &= \sum_{\Theta \in \boldsymbol{\Theta}_k^{\mathbf{x}_i \mapsto \exists}} \hat{\mathbf{x}}_{k,i}^{-} \cdot P(\Theta|\exists \mathbf{x}_{k,i}, \mathcal{D}_{1:k}) \\ &\quad + \sum_{\Theta \in \boldsymbol{\Theta}_k^{\mathbf{x}_i \mapsto \supset}} \mathbf{K}_k(\Theta) \cdot (\mathbf{z}_{k,\text{Reco}(\Theta)}^{\mathbf{x}_i} - \hat{\mathbf{z}}_k^{\mathbf{x}_i}) \cdot P(\Theta|\exists \mathbf{x}_{k,i}, \mathcal{D}_{1:k}) \\ &= \hat{\mathbf{x}}_{k,i}^{-} + \sum_{\Theta \in \boldsymbol{\Theta}_k^{\mathbf{x}_i \mapsto \supset}} \mathbf{K}_k(\Theta) \cdot \tilde{\mathbf{z}}_{k,\text{Reco}(\Theta)}^{\mathbf{x}_i} \cdot P(\Theta|\exists \mathbf{x}_{k,i}, \mathcal{D}_{1:k}) \,,\end{aligned} \tag{4.31}$$

where $\boldsymbol{\Theta}_k^{\mathbf{x}_i \mapsto \supset}$ denotes the set of joint events that assume the track $\mathbf{x}_i$ being visible at time k. A great simplification can be achieved when assuming that the reconstruction rules with respect to a track are the same for each actually obtained detection independently on the joint event Θ. This means that a detection should contribute to the track reconstruction in the same manner regardless of whether it is considered as being a 1:1 correspondence of the track, a part of it, or a conglomeration of several tracks. Such approach can be realized by means of a feature-based measurement reconstruction. Doing so allows to use a unified (and much simpler) measurement model and a joint event-independent Kalman gain $\mathbf{K}_k(\Theta) = \mathbf{K}_k$.

In case of a joint event assuming a split detection for a track, the reconstructed measurement $\mathbf{z}^{\mathbf{x}_i}_{k,\mathrm{Reco}(\Theta)}$ is composed from several detections. Here, the reconstructions $\mathbf{z}^{\mathbf{x}_i}_{k,\mathrm{Reco}(j)}$ obtained from the single detections have to be weighted according to their importance factors $\varpi^{\mathbf{x}_{k,i} \mapsto d_{k,j}}(\Theta)$ within the joint event:

$$\mathbf{z}^{\mathbf{x}_i}_{k,\mathrm{Reco}(\Theta)} = \sum_{j=1}^{m_k} \varpi^{\mathbf{x}_{k,i} \mapsto d_{k,j}}(\Theta) \cdot \mathbf{z}^{\mathbf{x}_i}_{k,\mathrm{Reco}(j)} \,. \tag{4.32}$$

These weighting factors $\varpi^{\mathbf{x}_{k,i} \mapsto d_{k,j}}(\Theta)$ reflect how much detection $d_{k,j}$ contributes to the state estimation of track $\mathbf{x}_{k,i}$ within joint event Θ. One may think of different approaches for defining this detection importance factor. Along with the feature-based computation of a similarity measure one may incorporate the number of contributing feature points and their affiliation probabilities to the track. Another, much simpler approximation can be done by assuming that all associated detections within a joint event have the same importance, i.e., to use the uniform weight distribution function:

$$\varpi^{\mathbf{x}_{k,i} \mapsto d_{k,j}}(\Theta) := \begin{cases} 0\,, & \text{if} \quad \theta^{\mathbf{x}_{k,i} \mapsto d_{k,j}} \notin \Theta\,, \\ \frac{1}{|\{j | \theta^{\mathbf{x}_{k,i} \mapsto d_{k,j}} \in \Theta\}|}\,, & \text{otherwise}\,. \end{cases} \tag{4.33}$$

This leads to

$$
\begin{aligned}
\hat{\mathbf{x}}_{k,i} &= \mathbb{E}[\boldsymbol{X}_{k,i} | \exists \mathbf{x}_{k,i}, \mathcal{D}_{1:k}] \\
&= \sum_{\Theta \in \boldsymbol{\Theta}_k^{\mathbf{x}_i \mapsto \exists}} \mathbb{E}[\boldsymbol{X}_{k,i} | \Theta, \exists \mathbf{x}_{k,i}, \mathcal{D}_{1:k}] \cdot P(\Theta | \exists \mathbf{x}_{k,i}, \mathcal{D}_{1:k}) \\
&= \hat{\mathbf{x}}_{k,i}^{-} + \sum_{\Theta \in \boldsymbol{\Theta}_k^{\mathbf{x}_i \mapsto \supset}} \mathbf{K}_k(\Theta) \cdot (\mathbf{z}_{k,\mathrm{Reco}(\Theta)}^{\mathbf{x}_i} - \hat{\mathbf{z}}_k^{\mathbf{x}_i}) \cdot P(\Theta | \exists \mathbf{x}_{k,i}, \mathcal{D}_{1:k}) \\
&= \hat{\mathbf{x}}_{k,i}^{-} + \mathbf{K}_k \cdot \sum_{\Theta \in \boldsymbol{\Theta}_k^{\mathbf{x}_i \mapsto \supset}} \Bigg(\left(\sum_{j=1}^{m_k} \varpi^{\mathbf{x}_{k,i} \mapsto d_{k,j}}(\Theta) \cdot \mathbf{z}_{k,\mathrm{Reco}(j)}^{\mathbf{x}_i} - \hat{\mathbf{z}}_k^{\mathbf{x}_i} \right) \\
&\qquad \cdot P(\Theta | \exists \mathbf{x}_{k,i}, \mathcal{D}_{1:k}) \Bigg) && (4.34) \\
&= \hat{\mathbf{x}}_{k,i}^{-} + \mathbf{K}_k \cdot \sum_{\Theta \in \boldsymbol{\Theta}_k^{\mathbf{x}_i \mapsto \supset}} \Bigg(\sum_{j=1}^{m_k} \varpi^{\mathbf{x}_{k,i} \mapsto d_{k,j}}(\Theta) \cdot \left(\mathbf{z}_{k,\mathrm{Reco}(j)}^{\mathbf{x}_i} - \hat{\mathbf{z}}_k^{\mathbf{x}_i} \right) \\
&\qquad \cdot P(\Theta | \exists \mathbf{x}_{k,i}, \mathcal{D}_{1:k}) \Bigg) && (4.35) \\
&= \hat{\mathbf{x}}_{k,i}^{-} + \mathbf{K}_k \cdot \sum_{j=1}^{m_k} (\mathbf{z}_{k,\mathrm{Reco}(j)}^{\mathbf{x}_i} - \hat{\mathbf{z}}_k^{\mathbf{x}_i}) \cdot \Bigg(\sum_{\Theta \in \boldsymbol{\Theta}_k^{\mathbf{x}_i \mapsto \supset}} \varpi^{\mathbf{x}_{k,i} \mapsto d_{k,j}}(\Theta) \\
&\qquad \cdot P(\Theta | \exists \mathbf{x}_{k,i}, \mathcal{D}_{1:k}) \Bigg) && (4.36) \\
&= \hat{\mathbf{x}}_{k,i}^{-} + \mathbf{K}_k \cdot \sum_{j=1}^{m_k} \tilde{\mathbf{z}}_{k,\mathrm{Reco}(j)}^{\mathbf{x}_i} \cdot \sum_{\Theta \in \boldsymbol{\Theta}_k^{\mathbf{x}_i \mapsto d_j}} \varpi^{\mathbf{x}_{k,i} \mapsto d_{k,j}}(\Theta) \cdot P(\Theta | \exists \mathbf{x}_{k,i}, \mathcal{D}_{1:k}) && (4.37) \\
&= \hat{\mathbf{x}}_{k,i}^{-} + \mathbf{K}_k \cdot \sum_{j=1}^{m_k} \left(\tilde{\mathbf{z}}_{k,\mathrm{Reco}(j)}^{trki} \cdot \beta^{\mathbf{x}_{k,i} \mapsto d_{k,j}} \right), && (4.38)
\end{aligned}
$$

where

$$
\beta^{\mathbf{x}_{k,i} \mapsto d_{k,j}} = \sum_{\Theta \in \boldsymbol{\Theta}_k^{\mathbf{x}_i \mapsto d_j}} \varpi^{\mathbf{x}_{k,i} \mapsto d_{k,j}}(\Theta) \cdot P(\Theta | \exists \mathbf{x}_{k,i}, \mathcal{D}_{1:k}) \tag{4.39}
$$

are the association weights similar to those in JPDA and JIPDA and

$$
\boldsymbol{\Theta}_k^{\mathbf{x}_i \mapsto d_j} := \{\Theta | \theta^{\mathbf{x}_{k,i} \mapsto d_{k,j}} \in \Theta\}. \tag{4.40}
$$

Note that the step between (4.34) and (4.35) is possible due to the fact that

$$\sum_{j=1}^{m_k} \varpi^{\mathbf{x}_{k,i} \mapsto d_{k,j}}(\Theta) = 1\,, \tag{4.41}$$

and the step between (4.35) and (4.36) is possible due to the fact that the measurement reconstruction $\mathbf{z}^{\mathbf{x}_i}_{k,\mathrm{Reco}(j)}$ for individual detections and thus also the corresponding innovations $\tilde{\mathbf{z}}^{\mathbf{x}_i}_{k,\mathrm{Reco}(j)} = (\mathbf{z}^{\mathbf{x}_i}_{k,\mathrm{Reco}(j)} - \hat{\mathbf{z}}^{\mathbf{x}_i}_{k})$ are independent on the considered joint event Θ.

Restricting the sum to joint events containing the association $\theta^{\mathbf{x}_{k,i} \mapsto d_{k,j}}$ in (4.37) may be done due to the fact that according to the definition in (4.33)

$$\varpi^{\mathbf{x}_{k,i} \mapsto d_{k,j}}(\Theta) := 0 \quad \text{if} \quad \theta^{\mathbf{x}_{k,i} \mapsto d_{k,j}} \notin \Theta\,. \tag{4.42}$$

4.2.2 Computation of the association weights $\beta^{\mathbf{x}_{k,i} \mapsto d_{k,j}}$

In (4.39), the a-posteriori joint event probability conditioned on the existence of an object $\mathbf{x}_{k,i}$ is given by

$$P(\Theta|\, \exists \mathbf{x}_{k,i}, \mathcal{D}_{1:k}) = \frac{P(\exists \mathbf{x}_{k,i}|\, \Theta, \mathcal{D}_{1:k}) \cdot P(\Theta|\, \mathcal{D}_{1:k})}{P(\exists \mathbf{x}_{k,i}|\, \mathcal{D}_{1:k})}\,, \tag{4.43}$$

where

$$P(\exists \mathbf{x}_{k,i}|\, \Theta, \mathcal{D}_{1:k}) = \begin{cases} 1 & \text{for} \quad \theta^{\mathbf{x}_{k,i} \mapsto \nexists} \notin \Theta \\ 0 & \text{otherwise} \end{cases} \tag{4.44}$$

and

$$\begin{aligned} P(\exists \mathbf{x}_{k,i}|\, \mathcal{D}_{1:k}) &= \sum_{\Theta \in \boldsymbol{\Theta}_k} P(\exists \mathbf{x}_{k,i}|\, \Theta, \mathcal{D}_{1:k}) \cdot P(\Theta|\mathcal{D}_{1:k}) \\ &= \sum_{\Theta \in \boldsymbol{\Theta}_k^{\mathbf{x}_i \mapsto \exists}} P(\Theta|\, \mathcal{D}_{1:k}) \end{aligned} \tag{4.45}$$

similar to JIPDA. However, the a-posteriori probability $P(\Theta|\mathcal{D}_{1:k})$ of a joint event is computed differently. It is done using the Bayesian approach:

$$\begin{aligned} P(\Theta|\ \mathcal{D}_{1:k}) &= P(\Theta|\ \mathcal{D}_k, \mathcal{D}_{1:k-1}) \\ &= \frac{1}{C_k^{\text{FBPDA}}} \cdot p(\mathcal{D}_k|\ \Theta, \mathcal{D}_{1:k-1}) \cdot P(\Theta|\ \mathcal{D}_{1:k-1}), \end{aligned} \tag{4.46}$$

where $P(\Theta|\mathcal{D}_{1:k-1})$ is the a-priori probability of a joint event Θ and $p(\mathcal{D}_k|\Theta, \mathcal{D}_{1:k-1})$ is the likelihood of the obtained detection set conditioned on this joint event. C_k^{FBPDA} is the normalization constant. Equations for computation of the a-priori joint event probability $P(\Theta|\mathcal{D}_{1:k-1})$ and the likelihood $p(\mathcal{D}_k|\Theta, \mathcal{D}_{1:k-1})$ of a detection set conditioned on this joint event are presented in Sections 4.2.3 and 4.2.4.

4.2.3 Computation of the a-priori joint event probabilities

When computing the a-priori joint event probabilities one has to take into account dependencies between the individual random variables. The observability of a track depends on the existence of other tracks in the scene, splits and merges are only possible, if a track is assumed to be detectable, and so on. Hence, $P(\Theta|\ \mathcal{D}_{1:k-1})$ is computed as follows:

$$\begin{aligned} &P(\Theta|\ \mathcal{D}_{1:k-1}) = \\ &\quad = P\left(\boldsymbol{C}_k(\Theta), \boldsymbol{M}_k(\Theta), \boldsymbol{S}_k(\Theta), \boldsymbol{N}_k(\Theta), \boldsymbol{O}_k(\Theta), \boldsymbol{B}_k(\Theta), \boldsymbol{E}_k(\Theta)|\ \mathcal{D}_{1:k-1}\right) \\ &\quad = P\left(\boldsymbol{C}_k(\Theta)|\ \boldsymbol{M}_k(\Theta), \boldsymbol{S}_k(\Theta), \boldsymbol{N}_k(\Theta), \boldsymbol{O}_k(\Theta), \boldsymbol{B}_k(\Theta), \boldsymbol{E}_k(\Theta), \mathcal{D}_{1:k-1}\right) \\ &\qquad\quad \cdot P\left(\boldsymbol{M}_k(\Theta)|\ \boldsymbol{S}_k(\Theta), \boldsymbol{N}_k(\Theta), \boldsymbol{O}_k(\Theta), \boldsymbol{B}_k(\Theta), \boldsymbol{E}_k(\Theta), \mathcal{D}_{1:k-1}\right) \\ &\qquad\quad \cdot P\left(\boldsymbol{S}_k(\Theta)|\ \boldsymbol{N}_k(\Theta), \boldsymbol{O}_k(\Theta), \boldsymbol{B}_k(\Theta), \boldsymbol{E}_k(\Theta), \mathcal{D}_{1:k-1}\right) \\ &\qquad\quad \cdot P\left(\boldsymbol{N}_k(\Theta)|\ \boldsymbol{O}_k(\Theta), \boldsymbol{B}_k(\Theta), \boldsymbol{E}_k(\Theta), \mathcal{D}_{1:k-1}\right) \\ &\qquad\quad \cdot P\left(\boldsymbol{O}_k(\Theta)|\ \boldsymbol{B}_k(\Theta), \boldsymbol{E}_k(\Theta), \mathcal{D}_{1:k-1}\right) \\ &\qquad\quad \cdot P\left(\boldsymbol{B}_k(\Theta)|\ \boldsymbol{E}_k(\Theta), \mathcal{D}_{1:k-1}\right) \\ &\qquad\quad \cdot P\left(\boldsymbol{E}_k(\Theta)|\ \mathcal{D}_{1:k-1}\right) . \end{aligned} \tag{4.47}$$

The computation of the probabilities in (4.47) is addressed in the remainder of this section.

4.2.3.1 A-priori joint existence probability

The a-priori joint existence probability $P_{k|k-1}(\boldsymbol{E}(\Theta))$ is computed as the product of the individual a-priori existence probabilities of the tracked objects in the joint association event:

$$P_{k|k-1}(\boldsymbol{E}(\Theta)) := P\left(\boldsymbol{E}_k(\Theta)|\mathcal{D}_{1:(k-1)}\right) = \prod_{i=1}^{n_k} P\left(E_{k,i}(\Theta)|\ \mathcal{D}_{1:(k-1)}\right) \tag{4.48}$$

with

$$\begin{aligned}
P\left(E_{k,i}(\Theta) = 1|\ \mathcal{D}_{1:(k-1)}\right) &= P\left(\exists \mathbf{x}_{k,i}|\ \mathcal{D}_{1:(k-1)}\right) \\
&= P\left(\exists \mathbf{x}_{k,i}|\ \exists \mathbf{x}_{k-1,i}\right) \cdot P\left(\exists \mathbf{x}_{k-1,i}|\ \mathcal{D}_{1:(k-1)}\right) \\
&\quad + P\left(\exists \mathbf{x}_{k,i}|\ \nexists \mathbf{x}_{k-1,i}\right) \cdot P\left(\nexists \mathbf{x}_{k-1,i}|\ \mathcal{D}_{1:(k-1)}\right) \\
&= P^{\exists\to\exists}(\mathbf{x}_{k,i}) \cdot P\left(\exists \mathbf{x}_{k-1,i}|\ \mathcal{D}_{1:(k-1)}\right) \\
&\quad + P^{\nexists\to\exists}(\mathbf{x}_{k,i}) \cdot P\left(\nexists \mathbf{x}_{k-1,i}|\ \mathcal{D}_{1:(k-1)}\right)
\end{aligned} \tag{4.49}$$

and

$$\begin{aligned}
P\left(E_{k,i}(\Theta) = 0|\ \mathcal{D}_{1:(k-1)}\right) &= P\left(\nexists \mathbf{x}_{k,i}|\ \mathcal{D}_{1:(k-1)}\right) \\
&= 1 - P\left(\exists \mathbf{x}_{k,i}|\ \mathcal{D}_{1:(k-1)}\right),
\end{aligned} \tag{4.50}$$

where $P^{\exists\to\exists}(\mathbf{x}_{k,i})$ is the persistence probability and $P^{\nexists\to\exists}(\mathbf{x}_{k,i})$ the birth probability for the track $\mathbf{x}_i$ at time point k. The a-posteriori existence and non-existence probabilities $P\left(\exists \mathbf{x}_{k-1,i}|\ \mathcal{D}_{1:(k-1)}\right)$ and $P\left(\nexists \mathbf{x}_{k-1,i}|\ \mathcal{D}_{1:(k-1)}\right)$ from the last time step are assumed to be known. This corresponds to the Markov chain approach used in IPDA.

4.2.3.2 A-priori joint birth probability

To enable track initiation, each detection may be also considered as being evoked by a new, previously not known track. For preventing creation of multiple equivalent representations for the same object, the a-priori probability $P\left(B_{k,j}(\Theta)|\boldsymbol{E}_k(\Theta), \mathcal{D}_{1:k-1}\right)$ of track birth from a detection j is conditioned on the existence of other tracks around this detection. If the track that is going to be created from a detection seems to correspond to one of the already existing tracks, the a-priori joint birth probability has to be drastically reduced. This may be realized using Mahalanobis distance as a measure for track similarity. In our approach we utilize the point-to-track affiliations instead. If a point cloud mainly consists of tracked points that are affiliated to existing objects, its a-priori birth probability is set to zero. If a point cloud mainly consists of tracked points that are not affiliated to any existing objects, and it can not be associated to a re-emerging object part, its a-priori birth probability is set to $(1 - P_c^{FP})$ where P_c^{FP} is the cardinal probability of a false negative detection due to clutter.

The a-priori joint birth probability $P\left(\boldsymbol{B}_k(\Theta)|\, \boldsymbol{E}_k(\Theta), \mathcal{D}_{1:k-1}\right)$ is computed as the product of the individual a-priori probabilities:

$$\begin{aligned} P_{k|k-1}\left(\boldsymbol{B}(\Theta)\right) \,:&= P\left(\boldsymbol{B}_k(\Theta)|\, \boldsymbol{E}_k(\Theta), \mathcal{D}_{1:k-1}\right) \\ &= \prod_{\{j|B_{k,j}(\Theta)=1\}} P\left(B_{k,j}(\Theta)|\, \boldsymbol{E}_k(\Theta), \mathcal{D}_{1:k-1}\right) . \end{aligned} \tag{4.51}$$

4.2.3.3 A-priori joint occlusion probability

The probability for the tracked objects to be occluded depends on the probability of the existence of the other objects in the foreground. Furthermore, it depends on the size of the visible object surface and opacity of the occluding objects. For computation of the occlusion probability we first determine which objects lie in foreground of other objects and can be occluded at all. Then we compute the so-called appearance masks for both foreground and background objects. This is done by projecting the occupied cells of an object into the camera image. Evaluating those appearance masks for each joint event as described in Section 4.1.4 we can predict occluded and visible areas of the background objects. In order to get a detection, the visible area in the image (i.e., number of visible pixels) has to exceed some pre-defined threshold. Another possibility to estimate the a-priori occlusion probability is given due to the grid-based object representation approach. The probability of occlusion may be computed from the number of the object cells that are predicted as being visible. If their number exceeds some threshold, the occlusion probability will be set to zero. This kind of occlusion reasoning automatically excludes physically impossible occlusion configurations (e.g., an occluded object without an occluder) from further consideration by setting their probability to zero.

The functional dependency between the visible object area and occlusion probability may be modeled by means of the function shown in Figure 4.14. Here, A is (dependent on the model) either the number of visible object pixels or the number of visible object grid cells and ϵ is the residual probability to see the object through the occluders.

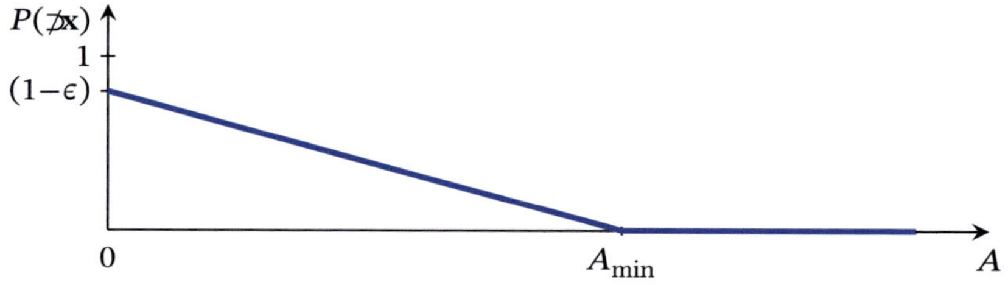

Figure 4.14: Estimation of the a-priori occlusion probability from the number of visible pixels

The a-priori joint occlusion probability is computed as the product of the individual a-priori probabilities:

$$
\begin{aligned}
P_{k|k-1}(\boldsymbol{O}(\Theta)) :=& P\big(\boldsymbol{O}_k(\Theta)|\ \boldsymbol{E}_k(\Theta), \boldsymbol{B}_k(\Theta), \mathcal{D}_{1:k-1}\big) \\
=& \prod_{\{i|E_{k,i}(\Theta)=1\}} P\big(O_{k,i}(\Theta)|\ \boldsymbol{E}_k(\Theta), \boldsymbol{B}_k(\Theta), \mathcal{D}_{1:k-1}\big)\,. \qquad (4.52)
\end{aligned}
$$

4.2.3.4 A-priori joint probability for missing detections

The a-priori probability for a tracked object to be not detected due to low resolution of the sensor or failure of the detection algorithm depends on the size and texture of the visible object surface in the image and on the parameters of the detection algorithms. An approximation of this dependency can be made by taking into consideration the predicted size of the visible object parts and comparing them with the size of the area sufficient for making a detection:

$$\begin{aligned} P(\varnothing \mathbf{x}_{k,i} | \exists \mathbf{x}_{k,i}, \supset \mathbf{x}_{k,i}, \boldsymbol{O}_k(\Theta), \boldsymbol{B}_k(\Theta), \boldsymbol{E}_k(\Theta), \mathcal{D}_{1:k-1}) = \\ &= P(N_{k,i}(\Theta) = 1 | \exists \mathbf{x}_{k,i}, \supset \mathbf{x}_{k,i}, \boldsymbol{O}_k(\Theta), \boldsymbol{B}_k(\Theta), \boldsymbol{E}_k(\Theta), \mathcal{D}_{1:k-1}) \\ &= \max\left(1 - \frac{A}{A_{\min}}, 0\right) \end{aligned} \tag{4.53}$$

and

$$\begin{aligned} P(N_{k,i}(\Theta) = 0 | \exists \mathbf{x}_{k,i}, \supset \mathbf{x}_{k,i}, \boldsymbol{O}_k(\Theta), \boldsymbol{B}_k(\Theta), \boldsymbol{E}_k(\Theta), \mathcal{D}_{1:k-1}) = \\ &= \min\left(\frac{A}{A_{\min}}, 1\right), \end{aligned} \tag{4.54}$$

with A being the area of the predicted visible object surface (disregarding occlusions) and $A_{\min}$ being minimal visible area which is sufficient for making a detection. This dependency is depicted in Figure 4.15.

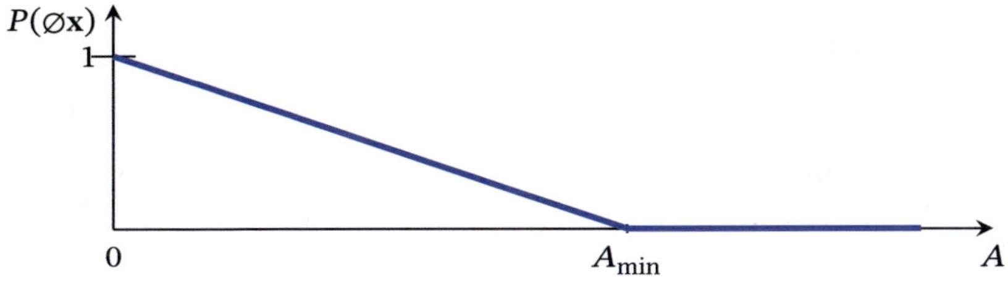

Figure 4.15: Estimation of the a-priori probability of a missed detection from the number of visible pixels

The individual misses are considered to be mutually independent, thus the a-priori joint probability is computed as the product of the individual probabilities:

$$\begin{aligned} P_{k|k-1}(\boldsymbol{N}(\Theta)) &:= P(\boldsymbol{N}_k(\Theta) | \boldsymbol{O}_k(\Theta), \boldsymbol{B}_k(\Theta), \boldsymbol{E}_k(\Theta), \mathcal{D}_{1:k-1}) \\ &= \prod_{\{i | O_{k,i}(\Theta) = 0\}} P(N_{k,i}(\Theta) | \boldsymbol{O}_k(\Theta), \boldsymbol{B}_k(\Theta), \boldsymbol{E}_k(\Theta), \mathcal{D}_{1:k-1}) \,. \end{aligned} \tag{4.55}$$

4.2.3.5 A-priori joint probability for split detections

A split detection may occur in the following cases: If there is a homogeneous area or an occlusion in the middle of an object. This is rather difficult to model. However, the probability of an object to evoke a split detection grows with the object size. One may approximate this dependency by means of the function depicted in Figure 4.16 where w is the visible object width in pixels, which is determined from the object appearance mask, w_{min} is the minimal visible object width for making a detection, w_{max} is the image width, and λ is the maximal a-priori probability of a split detection.

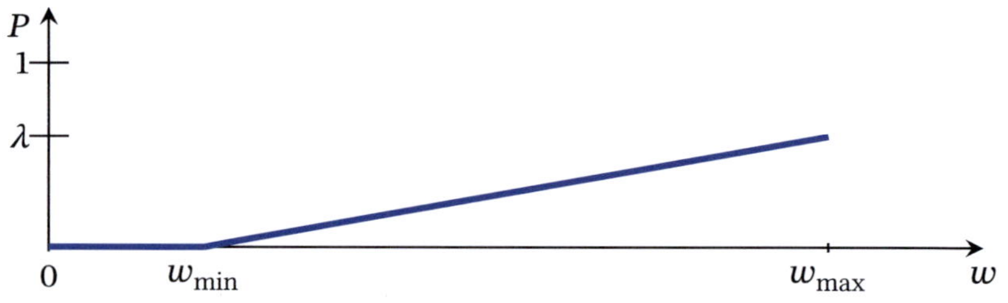

Figure 4.16: Estimation of the a-priori probability for getting a split detection

The feature-based approach allows to considerably simplify the computation. Due to the fact that we have the possibility to robustly detect split detections based on the point-to-track affiliations, the probabilistic handling may be dropped. We set the a-priori probability of an object to evoke a split detection to one, if points affiliated to the corresponding track are found in more than one detection. In the opposite case the probability is set to zero.

Since the individual split events are mutually independent, the corresponding a-priori joint probability can be computed as the product of the individual probabilities for each track:

$$P(\boldsymbol{S}_k(\Theta)|\, \boldsymbol{N}_k(\Theta), \boldsymbol{O}_k(\Theta), \boldsymbol{B}_k(\Theta), \boldsymbol{E}_k(\Theta), \mathcal{D}_{1:k-1}) = \\ = \prod_{\{i|\ S_{k,i\prec\{j\}}(\Theta)=1\}} P(S_{k,i\prec\{j\}}(\Theta)|\ \dots) \,. \quad (4.56)$$

4.2.3.6 A-priori joint probability for merged detections

A merged detection may occur in cases when two objects are sufficiently close to each other and there is a lot of clutter in between. This is also an issue which is very hard to model exactly.

Approximation of the merge probability between two tracks i and l may be modeled using the function depicted in Figure 4.17. Here, $\Delta_p(\mathbf{x}_{k,i}, \mathbf{x}_{k,\ell})$ represents the distance between the two closest points of the tracks $\mathbf{x}_{k,i}$ and $\mathbf{x}_{k,\ell}$. $\Delta_{\max}$ denotes the maximal possible distance that still allows for a merge.

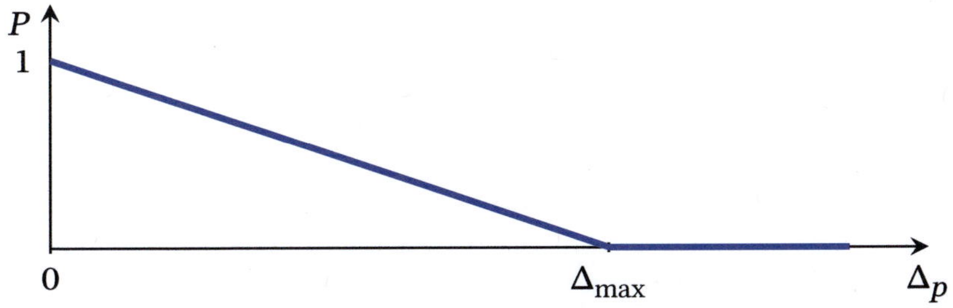

Figure 4.17: Estimation of the a-priori probability for getting a merged detection

Due to the fact that we have the possibility to robustly detect merged detections based on the point-to-track affiliations, the probabilistic handling may be considerably simplified here too. We set the a-priori probability of a detection to be a merged detection of two tracks to one, if its points are affiliated to both tracks. In the opposite case the probability is set to zero.

The joint merge probability is computed analogous to other probabilities as the product of the probabilities of the individual merges.

4.2.3.7 A-priori joint probability for clutter-based detections

The a-priori probability for getting clutter-based detections as specified by $\boldsymbol{C}_k(\Theta)$ may be modeled similarly to the JPDA approach [For80] using a Poisson distribution. However, we model it differently, using the feature-based approach instead.

This is done analogously to the procedure described in Section 4.2.3.2. Similarly to the procedure used for the birth probability computation we utilize the point-to-track affiliations. If a point cloud mainly consists of tracked points that are affiliated to existing objects, its a-priori probability of being a clutter-based detection is set to zero. If a point cloud d_j mainly consists of tracked points that are not affiliated to any tracked objects, and it can not be associated to a re-emerging object part, the a-priori probability

$$P\big(C_{k,j}(\Theta) = 1 |\, \boldsymbol{M}_k(\Theta), \boldsymbol{S}_k(\Theta), \boldsymbol{N}_k(\Theta), \boldsymbol{O}_k(\Theta), \boldsymbol{B}_k(\Theta), \boldsymbol{E}_k(\Theta), \mathcal{D}_{1:k-1}\big)$$

is set to P_c^{FP}.

The a-priori joint clutter probability

$$P\big(\boldsymbol{C}_k(\Theta) |\, \boldsymbol{M}_k(\Theta), \boldsymbol{S}_k(\Theta), \boldsymbol{N}_k(\Theta), \boldsymbol{O}_k(\Theta), \boldsymbol{B}_k(\Theta), \boldsymbol{E}_k(\Theta), \mathcal{D}_{1:k-1}\big)$$

is computed as the product of the individual a-priori probabilities:

$$\begin{aligned} P_{k|k-1}\left(\boldsymbol{C}(\Theta)\right) :=& P\big(\boldsymbol{C}_k(\Theta) |\, \boldsymbol{M}_k(\Theta), \dots, \mathcal{D}_{1:k-1}\big) \\ =& \prod_{\{j|C_{k,j}(\Theta)=1\}} P\big(C_{k,j}(\Theta) |\, \boldsymbol{M}_k(\Theta), \dots, \mathcal{D}_{1:k-1}\big) \,. \end{aligned} \tag{4.57}$$

4.2.4 Likelihood computation of an observation set

The conditional likelihood $p(\mathcal{D}_k |\, \Theta, \mathcal{D}_{1:k-1})$ of the complete detection set $\mathcal{D}_k$ is given as the product of the individual conditional detection likelihoods $p(d_{k,j} |\, \Theta, \mathcal{D}_{1:k-1})$:

$$p(\mathcal{D}_k |\, \Theta, \mathcal{D}_{1:k-1}) = \prod_{j=1}^{m_k} p(d_{k,j} |\, \Theta, \mathcal{D}_{1:k-1}) \,. \tag{4.58}$$

The likelihoods $p(d_{k,j} |\, \Theta, \mathcal{D}_{1:k-1})$ of detections that in the joint event Θ are assumed to be evoked by a regular track are computed using the Mahalanobis distance between the predicted and the reconstructed measurements. As mentioned in Section 4.1.7, in the case of detections that are assumed to be evoked by clutter or by a new not yet tracked object, the likelihood computation may introduce a distinction between the two origins. Parameters for the distinction might be e.g., the density of the feature points, the homogeneity of their velocities, or the texture characteristics of the relevant image region.

4.2.5 Computation of the point-to-track affiliations

Each tracked point $\mathbf{p}_q$ is considered to have an affiliation either to one or more objects in the scene or to clutter. The corresponding affiliation probability is denoted as $P(\mathbf{x}_i \mapsto \mathbf{p}_q)$ and $P(\copyright \mapsto \mathbf{p}_q)$ correspondingly. The affiliation probabilities can be determined based on the association weights $\beta_k^{\mathbf{x}_i \mapsto d_j}$ of the association between the detection $d_{k,j}$ containing the considered point $\mathbf{p}_q$ and the track $\mathbf{x}_{k,i}$.

This can be derived from the following equation:

$$\begin{aligned} P(\mathbf{x}_{k,i} \mapsto \mathbf{p}_q | \mathcal{D}_{1:k}) &= \sum_{j=1}^{m_k} P(\theta^{\mathbf{x}_{k,i} \mapsto d_{k,j}}, \mathbf{p}_q \in d_{k,j} | \mathcal{D}_{1:k}) \\ &= \sum_{j=1}^{m_k} P(\theta^{\mathbf{x}_{k,i} \mapsto d_{k,j}}, | \mathcal{D}_{1:k}) \cdot P(\mathbf{p}_q \in d_{k,j} | \mathcal{D}_{1:k}) \\ &= \sum_{j=1}^{m_k} \beta^{\mathbf{x}_{k,i} \mapsto d_{k,j}} \cdot P(\mathbf{p}_q \in d_{k,j} | \mathcal{D}_{1:k}) \,, \end{aligned} \tag{4.59}$$

with

$$P(\mathbf{p}_q \in d_{k,j} | \mathcal{D}_{1:k}) = \begin{cases} 1 & \text{if} \quad \mathbf{p}_q \in d_{k,j} \,, \\ 0 & \text{else} \,. \end{cases} \tag{4.60}$$

In order to overcome sporadically occurring corrupted detections, we introduce a memory effect by implementing a recursive filter with a gain factor $g \in [0; 1]$:

$$P(\mathbf{x}_{k,i} \mapsto \mathbf{p}_q | \mathcal{D}_{1:k}) = g \cdot \beta_k^{\mathbf{x}_i \mapsto d_j} + (1 - g) \cdot P(\mathbf{x}_{k,i} \mapsto \mathbf{p}_q | \mathcal{D}_{1:k-1}) \,. \tag{4.61}$$

The underlying assumption is that corrupted detections are exceptions and that most of the time detections reflect the correct picture and can be used as the representatives of objects (or their parts). The new point affiliation to each track is hence computed as a weighted sum of the old (predicted) affiliation probability to the track $P(\mathbf{x}_{k-1,i} \mapsto \mathbf{p}_q | \mathcal{D}_{1:k-1})$ and the current association weight $\beta_k^{\mathbf{x}_i \mapsto d_j}$ of the edge between the track and the the point cloud containing the point.

5 Stereo-video based object tracking system for side collision detection

5.1 Overview

In Section 1.3, an overview flowchart of the video data processing pipeline was presented. A more detailed flowchart is depicted in Figure 5.1.

The video processing framework consists of 5 main modules:

- Stereo Processing Module
- Point Tracking Module
- Ego-Motion Estimation Module
- Object Detection Module
- Object Tracking Module

The Stereo Processing Module is responsible for processing the corresponding binocular image pairs and obtaining depth data. It consists of submodules for feature extraction, correspondence analysis and depth reconstruction. For facilitation of feature point tracking, the Stereo Correspondence Module incorporates a sophisticated feature extraction procedure that re-uses already tracked features.

The Point Tracking Module fuses depth values of the feature points that are obtained from the Stereo Processing Module with the 2D displacements that are obtained by establishing correspondences in consecutive monocular images. This allows tracking of object points in the 3-dimensional space.

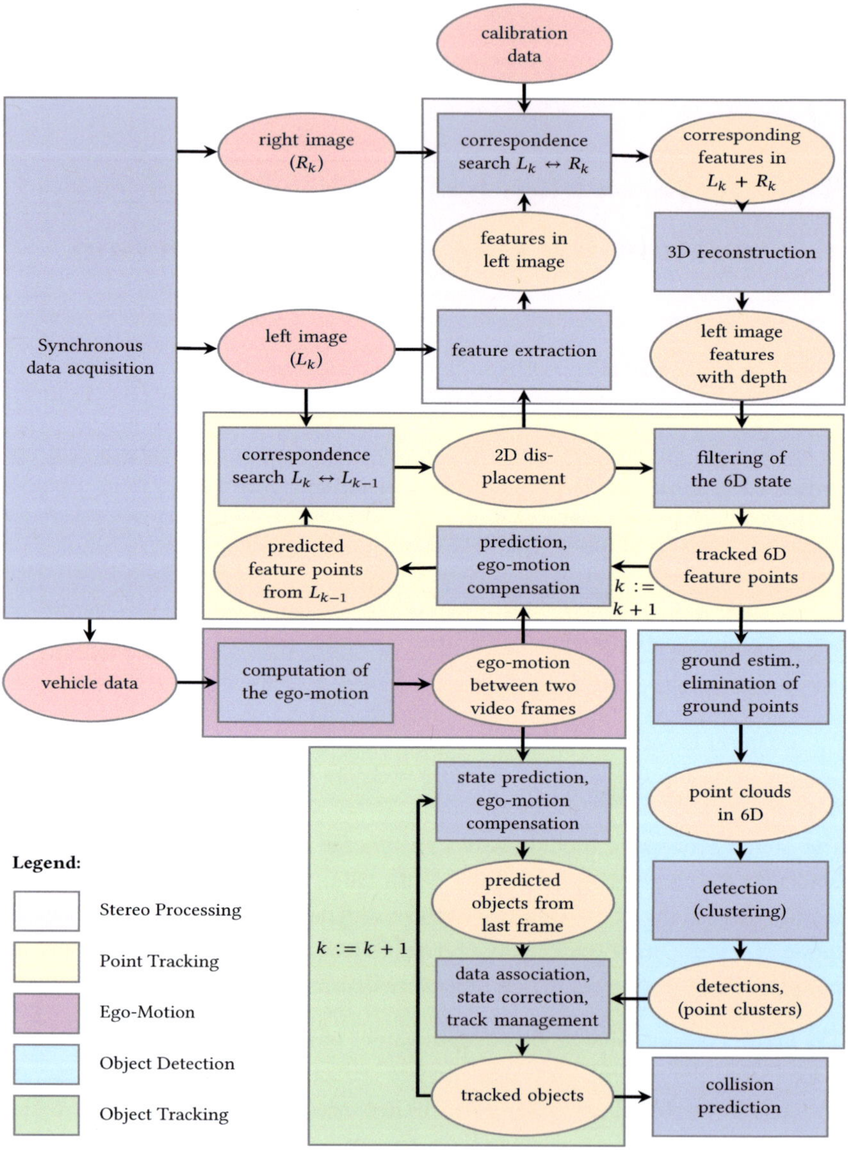

Figure 5.1: Flowchart of the video processing.

In order to obtain an initial search region for correspondence establishment, a projection of the predicted 3D position into the image is used. For this purpose, the camera motion between two consecutive frames has to be estimated and compensated. This is done by means of the vehicle data within the Ego-Motion Estimation Module.

The Object Detection Module uses clustering methods in order to obtain detections from the sets of 6-dimensional feature points. As a preprocessing step, points belonging to the ground have to be eliminated. Remaining points are clustered and give detections for the subsequent tracking.

The next step is generation of more elaborate object hypotheses, i.e., estimation of object properties such as position, extent and motion parameters. This is done within the Object Tracking Module, which performs data association, dynamic state estimation, and track management. At this step, a natural assumption of classical tracking-by-detection algorithms is that each detection corresponds to a single object (true positive) or to clutter (false positive) and that a measurement obtained from a true positive detection represents the entire object. Thus, data association and track state estimation are performed using measurements, which, in our case, can be generated by fitting cuboids into the obtained point clouds. In FBPDATA we revise this assumption, i.e., we assume that a detection does not necessarily correspond to a single object and vice versa. As pointed out in Section 4.1, data association in FBPDATA is performed using raw detections instead of measurements. Dedicated object hypotheses are built after the data association step using a feature-based approach for reconstructing object dynamics and a grid-based approach for reconstructing object dimensions and location.

In order to enable usage of the most simple object motion models and risk assessment constraints, the system uses absolute coordinates and velocities of the tracked points and objects. However, in order to avoid numerical problems and errors through dead reckoning, in each frame the absolute coordinate system (world coordinate system) is re-attached to the new vehicle position i.e., moved according to the the motion of the ego-vehicle. This requires an appropriate compensation procedure for all absolute coordinates and velocities. This compensation is done using the ego-motion parameters (rotation and translation) that are estimated within the Ego-Motion Estimation Module.

The following sections give background knowledge and describe implementation of the framework and its modules. Section 5.2 gives details about motion modeling for the ego-vehicle. Section 5.3 deals with camera modeling and calibration. Section 5.4 introduces the concept of optical flow. In Section 5.5, basics of stereo vision are presented. Section 5.6 describes the principle and the implementation of the 3D point tracking and discusses the issue of image feature selection. Section 5.7 describes the object detection process. Finally, Section 5.8 deals with the aspects of the implemented object tracking cycle.

5.2 Ego-motion computation

In this work, ego-vehicle motion is modeled by means of the so called ***"bicycle model"*** which gives a very good approximation of the real vehicle motion and is often used for modeling vehicle dynamics [Zom91, Mit04]. The model is motivated by the actual kinematics of a wheeled vehicle with a front wheel steering. It assumes that the normals of both front wheels coincide which makes it possible to model them by means of a rigid steerable front axis with a single virtual wheel in the middle of the axis. The same is done for the rear wheels. This reduces the vehicle to a two-wheeler, from which the model derives its name. Bicycle model neglects drift angle and slip, the velocity is attached to the rear axis and is oriented along the wheelbase.

In case of constant steering angle, the bicycle model describes a circular motion around the ***instantaneous center of rotation (ICR)*** which is defined by the intersection point of both normals. The angle between the normals of both virtual wheels corresponds to the steering angle as shown in Figure 5.2.

The radius r of the circle can be calculated from the wheelbase l_{WB} and the angle between the two wheel normals (which corresponds to the steering angle α):

$$r = \frac{l_{\mathrm{WB}}}{\tan(\alpha)} . \tag{5.1}$$

Knowing the current vehicle velocity, steering angle and the video frame rate allows to compute the translation and the rotation of the vehicle between two video frames.

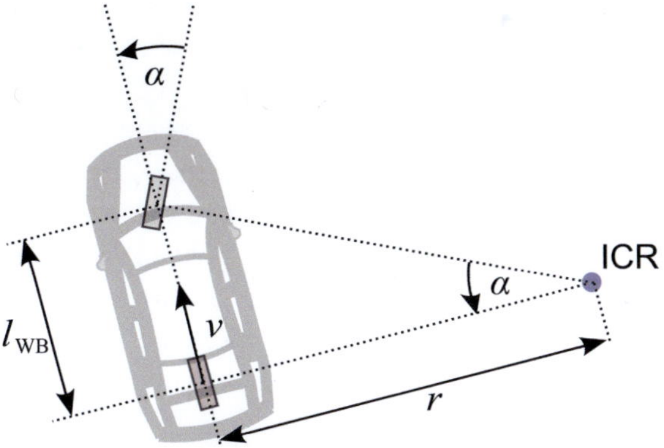

Figure 5.2: Bicycle model.

5.3 Camera modeling

For making statements about the scene observed by a video camera one requires a geometric camera model, i.e., a transformation model that describes the relationship between the scene structure and the captured image. A camera model allows to derive the rules for transforming a world point $\mathbf{p}_W = (x_W, y_W, z_W)$ into the image (pixel) coordinates $\mathbf{p} = (u, v)$. The inverse problem of determining a world point from its image coordinates is called ***back projection*** or ***reconstruction***. The inverse problem is under-determined since a third parameter, the ***depth*** is missing. It can only be solved using additional constraints such as e.g., stereopsis which is described in Section 5.5.

5.3.1 Idealized camera modeling

The simplest, idealized camera model is the so called ***pinhole camera model***. It is shown in Figure 5.3. It assumes that the world is observed through an infinitely small aperture $\mathbf{o}_C$, referred to as the optical center of the camera or the camera projection center. The image plane I is situated behind the optical center at the distance f (focal length). Each point on the image plane I defines a viewing ray that goes through the optical center. The optical center is the origin of the pinhole camera coordinate system. Its z axis is perpendicular to the image plane and defines the viewing direction of the camera. z is called ***optical axis*** of the camera. The x and y axes are perpendicular to the z axis and are spanning the focal plane $FocalPlane$. The focal plane is thus parallel to the image plane.

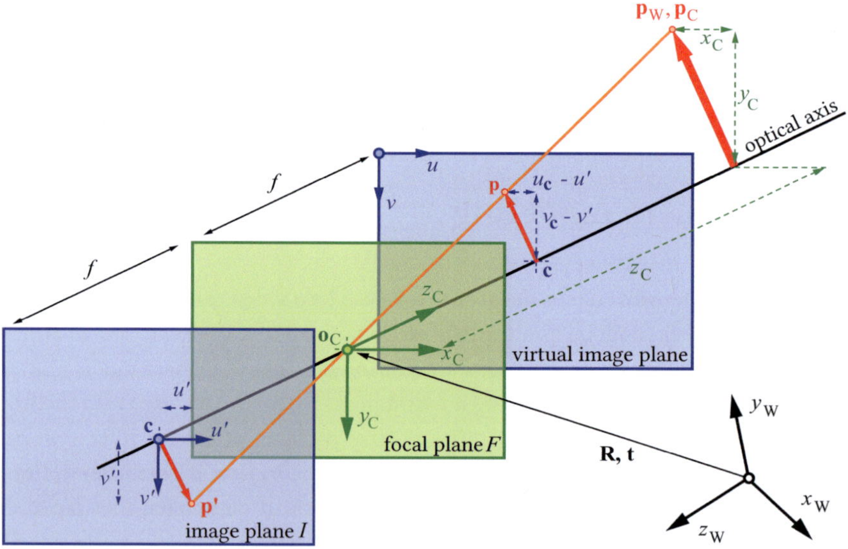

Figure 5.3: Pinhole camera model.

The pinhole camera model provides upside down images. This can be avoided by introduction of a virtual image in front of the optical center as shown in Figure 5.3. The z axis intersects the (virtual) image plane in a point $\mathbf{c}$ called ***principal point***.

For the image coordinates with the origin in the principal point and u' and v' axes parallel to the x and y axes of the camera coordinate system, this leads to the following projection rules:

For a world point $\mathbf{p}_W = (x_W, y_W, z_W)$ with camera coordinates $\mathbf{p}_C = (x_C, y_C, z_C)$, the corresponding point $\mathbf{p}' = (u', v')$ in image coordinates is derived by means of the intercept theorem:

$$u' = f \cdot \frac{x_C}{z_C}\,, \tag{5.2}$$

$$v' = f \cdot \frac{y_C}{z_C}\,. \tag{5.3}$$

Since image processing algorithms work with pixels, there are additional necessary steps. First of all, the origin of the image coordinate system is set not to the principal point but to an image corner, usually the upper left one. Furthermore, two scaling factors s_u and s_v are introduced for conversion of the image coordinates u and v from meters to pixels. They also allow to model non-quadratic pixels (when $s_u \neq s_v$). And, finally, an optional skew factor s can also be modeled for the case of non-rectangular pixels. In most cases however, the $s_u = s_v$ and the skew factor is zero.

Using $f_u := s_u \cdot f$ and $f_v := s_v \cdot f$, the new projection rules are thus given by

$$u = f_u \cdot \frac{x_C + s \cdot y_C}{z_C} + u_\mathbf{c}\,, \tag{5.4}$$

$$v = f_v \cdot \frac{y_C}{z_C} + v_\mathbf{c}\,, \tag{5.5}$$

with $(u_\mathbf{c}, v_\mathbf{c})$ being the coordinates of the principal point in pixels. The overall transformation from camera coordinates into normalized image coordinates can be formulated as a matrix multiplication:

$$\underbrace{\begin{pmatrix} u \\ v \\ 1 \end{pmatrix}}_{\check{\mathbf{p}}} = \frac{1}{z_C} \cdot \underbrace{\begin{pmatrix} f_u & s & u_\mathbf{c} \\ 0 & f_v & v_\mathbf{c} \\ 0 & 0 & 1 \end{pmatrix}}_{\mathbf{C}} \cdot \underbrace{\begin{pmatrix} x_C \\ y_C \\ z_C \end{pmatrix}}_{\mathbf{p}_C}\,. \tag{5.6}$$

Division by z_C executes the projection $u' = \frac{x_\mathrm{C}}{z_\mathrm{C}}$ and $v' = \frac{y_\mathrm{C}}{z_\mathrm{C}}$ thus performing a normalization of the vector $\mathbf{p}_\mathrm{C} = (x_\mathrm{C}, y_\mathrm{C}, z_\mathrm{C})^T$ so that the last (third) coordinate becomes 1. This yields the vector $\check{\mathbf{p}}_\mathrm{C} = (u', v', 1)^T$ in normalized image coordinates. The camera matrix $\mathbf{C}$ contains the so called ***intrinsic camera parameters***, i.e., parameters responsible for the imaging process and not related to the observed world. It transforms the normalized camera coordinates $(u', v', 1)$ into image coordinates $(u, v, 1)$, with unit focal length as the applicate.

The camera coordinates $(x_\mathrm{C}, y_\mathrm{C}, z_\mathrm{C})$ of a world point are, on their part, obtained from the world coordinates $(x_\mathrm{W}, y_\mathrm{W}, z_\mathrm{W})$ by an affine transformation consisting of a rotation $\mathbf{R}$ and a translation vector $\mathbf{t}$:

$$\mathbf{p}_\mathrm{C} = \mathbf{R} \cdot \mathbf{p}_\mathrm{W} + \mathbf{t}\,. \tag{5.7}$$

The overall transformation can be represented in a compact way using homogeneous coordinates:

$$\underbrace{\begin{pmatrix} u \\ v \\ 1 \end{pmatrix}}_{\check{\mathbf{p}}} \simeq \underbrace{\underbrace{\begin{pmatrix} f_u & s & u_\mathrm{c} \\ 0 & f_v & v_\mathrm{c} \\ 0 & 0 & 1 \end{pmatrix}}_{\mathbf{C}} \cdot \underbrace{\begin{pmatrix} r_{11} & r_{12} & r_{13} & t_x \\ r_{21} & r_{22} & r_{23} & t_y \\ r_{31} & r_{32} & r_{33} & t_z \end{pmatrix}}_{\mathbf{E}=(\mathbf{R}|\mathbf{t})} \cdot \underbrace{\begin{pmatrix} x_\mathrm{W} \\ y_\mathrm{W} \\ z_\mathrm{W} \\ 1 \end{pmatrix}}_{\check{\mathbf{p}}_\mathrm{W}}}_{\check{\mathbf{p}}_\mathrm{C}}\,. \tag{5.8}$$

The matrix $\mathbf{E}$ contains the ***extrinsic parameters*** of the camera that are independent from the actually used camera and describe its position and orientation with respect to the scene. Note that the projection-related normalization is performed implicitly in homogeneous coordinates.

5.3.2 Distortions

In contrast to the pinhole model, real cameras use lenses for gathering the incoming light and focusing it on the imager. This leads to several side effects, such as limited depth of field and distortions. Distortions can be modeled by means of a nonlinear function $d(\cdot) : \check{\mathbf{p}}_\mathrm{C} \mapsto \check{\mathbf{p}}_\mathrm{D}$ which is applied to the undistorted normalized image coordinates $\check{\mathbf{p}}_\mathrm{C}$ that are obtained before applying the camera matrix $\mathbf{C}$:

$$\check{\mathbf{p}}_\mathrm{D} = d(\check{\mathbf{p}}_\mathrm{C})\,. \tag{5.9}$$

According to the distortion model of Brown [Bro71], the distorted image coordinates $\check{\mathbf{p}}_\mathrm{D} = (u'', v'')$ may be approximated by

$$u'' = u'(1 + \kappa_1 r^2 + \kappa_2 r^4) + 2\rho_1 u'v' + \rho_2(r^2 + u'^2)\,, \tag{5.10}$$

$$v'' = v'(1 + \kappa_1 r^2 + \kappa_2 r^4) + 2\rho_2 u'v' + \rho_1(r^2 + v'^2)\,. \tag{5.11}$$

The radial distortion parameters κ_1 and κ_2 unfold their effect depending on the radius $r = \sqrt{u'^2 + v'^2}$ from the principal point $\mathbf{c} = (u_\mathbf{c}, v_\mathbf{c})$ and play the most dominant role. The tangential distortion parameters ρ_1 and ρ_2 play a minor part and are often neglected by setting them to zero as done in [Zha00]. The overall transformation $\check{\mathbf{p}}_\mathrm{W} \mapsto \check{\mathbf{p}}$ for the pinhole model with distortions is given by

$$\check{\mathbf{p}} = \mathbf{C} \cdot \check{\mathbf{p}}_\mathrm{D} = \mathbf{C} \cdot d(\check{\mathbf{p}}_\mathrm{C}) = \mathbf{C} \cdot d(\mathbf{E} \cdot \check{\mathbf{p}}_\mathrm{W})\,. \tag{5.12}$$

Since distortion parameters are independent from the scene they also belong to intrinsic parameters of a camera. Both intrinsic and extrinsic parameters are obtained by means of a calibration process which is described in Section 5.3.3.

5.3.3 Camera calibration

The parameters of the pinhole camera model are obtained in a process called calibration. In this work the intrinsic camera calibration method proposed by Zhengyou Zhang in [Zha00] is used. It uses a planar chess board pattern with known number and size of the squares. The pattern does not need to be placed in a certain position, it is sufficient to capture several images while either the pattern or the camera is moved around so that different views of the pattern are obtained.

In order to obtain the extrinsic camera parameters, an image of a scene with several marked points with known image coordinates has to be taken. Then camera rotation and translation with respect to the world coordinate system are obtained by marking those points in the image and performing robust estimation of the 6 degrees of freedom of the transformation. Figure 5.4 shows examples of images taken for intrinsic and extrinsic camera calibration.

(a) Chess board pattern used for intrinsic camera calibration.

(b) Image taken for extrinsic calibration. Position of the black and white tiles are known in the world coordinates.

Figure 5.4: Example of images taken for intrinsic and extrinsic camera calibration.

5.4 Optical flow

If an image sequence is captured while there is a relative motion between the camera and the observed scene, i.e., either the camera or the observed objects are moving, the same scene points are projected to different image coordinates. The perceived displacement in the image is called ***optical flow (OF)***[1]. A vector $\mathbf{d} = (\Delta u, \Delta v)$ describing displacement between two corresponding image points $\mathbf{p}_k = (u_1, v_1)$ and $\mathbf{p}_{k+1} = (u_2, v_2)$ (i.e., image points belonging to the same scene point $\mathbf{p}_\mathrm{W} = (x_\mathrm{W}, y_\mathrm{W}, z_\mathrm{W})$) in two consecutive images is called ***optical flow vector***. The entirety of the OF vectors in an image is called ***optical flow field***. An example of an optical flow field is shown in Figure 5.5.

A distinction is made between ***dense*** and ***sparse*** optical flow fields. Dense flow fields assign an optical flow vector to each image pixel, in sparse flow fields flow vectors are defined only for a set of selected image points.

[1] sometimes also ***optic flow***

(a) Image from a video sequence taken from a moving vehicle by a side-looking camera.

(b) Corresponding optical flow field (visualized by means of black lines).

Figure 5.5: Example of a sparse optical flow field (black lines in the right image) for a set of selected image points (green points in the left image).

For calculation of the optical flow there have to be established correspondences between the consecutive images. The problem of finding corresponding points in two images is referred to as the ***correspondence problem***. The correspondence problem may have an ambiguous or even no solution. The reasons for this issue are explained in the following.

5.4.1 Challenges of the correspondence problem

Solution to the corresponding problem is based on the assumption that scene points look similar in all consecutive images, i.e., that they have specific characteristic properties that do not change significantly throughout the sequence. However, in addition to the thermal measurement noise of the image pixels and quantization errors that occur during the image acquisition process there are four additional cases that may make an unambiguous determination of the correct correspondences impossible. These problems are illustrated in Figure 5.6

Aperture problem

Figure 5.6 (a) illustrates the classical aperture problem. For pixels on an edge, both ends of which are outside of the considered image region, only a displacement perpendicular to this edge can be measured. Any motion along the edge cannot be perceived. As shown in Figure 5.6 (b) there are additional types of image elements and corresponding motion patterns that do not allow unambiguous displacement determination. They are also referred to as the aperture problem.

Assignment problem

If several image points have the same characteristic properties, the correct assignment of the corresponding points in the consecutive frames might be ambiguous as well. This problem is referred to as assignment problem. It is illustrated in Figure 5.6 (c). This problem is particularly severe when optical flow is calculated for each point separately.

Occlusions

Another major problem emerges when the world point corresponding to an image point $\mathbf{p}_k$ gets out of the field of view of the camera or gets occluded in the course of the image sequence as shown in Figure 5.6 (d). In this case there exists no image point $\mathbf{p}_{k+1}$ that would correspond to the point $\mathbf{p}_k$.

Unequal capturing conditions

Characteristic properties of points may change in case of strong changes of illumination, shutter interval of the camera or viewing perspective. Additional errors may be introduced through pseudo-motion caused by shadows or reflections.

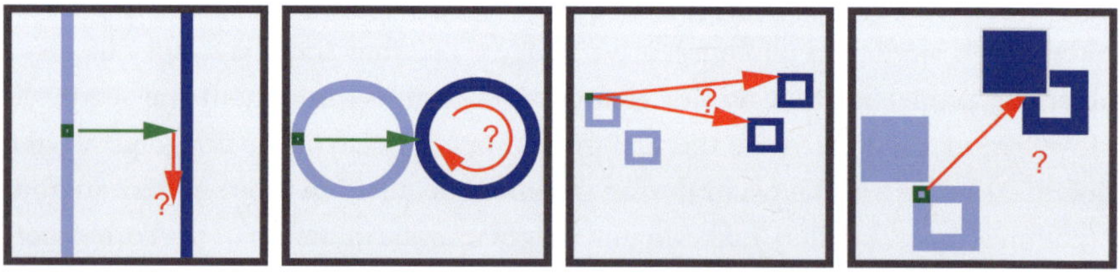

(a) Aperture problem **(b)** Modified aperture problem **(c)** Assignment problem **(d)** Occlusion

Figure 5.6: Ambiguities of the OF correspondence problem. Light blue and dark blue colors represent objects in the image k and $k+1$ respectively.

There is a number of methods for optical flow estimation that aim at solving the correspondence problem in one way or another. They can be classified into ***global*** and ***local approaches***.

Local approaches consider for each individual image point a small environment around it and try to find an appropriate match with similar environment in the consecutive image. They use correlation based techniques and are mostly limited to points with discriminative characteristics (***feature points***) [Har88, Shi94, Rod06, Low04, Bay06]. The resulting optical flow fields are sparse. In contrast, global approaches consider matches for all points in the entire image simultaneously. There are frequency based and gradient based approaches. The holistic view of the global approaches allows for better solving the assignment and aperture problem.

Since most of the global approaches use smoothing techniques, they can produce approximate solutions even for those image regions where there is no possibility to directly find the correspondences. This allows to estimate dense optical flow fields, i.e., optical flow fields that assign optical flow vectors for each pixel. However, depending on the smoothing technique, the approximations might cause undesirable side effects, especially at object boundaries. An overview of different approaches and their performance is given in [Sin91], [Bar94], and [Sun14].

In this work, implementations of the pyramidal Lucas-Kanade algorithm [Luc81], Horn-Schunck algorithm [Hor81], Farneback algorithm [Far00] and Brox et al. algorithm [Bro04] that are available in the OpenCV library [Wil] have been adopted for the estimation of the optical flow. Since this work aims at tracking a set of individual feature points as accurately as possible, local approaches are preferable. However, one has to take into account the fact that optical flow and stereo processing have to draw on the same feature points in order to facilitate their tracking in 3D space. Thus, when using sensors that directly provide depth maps (e.g., [Woo06]), one might want to use algorithms that produce dense flow fields in order to get more tracked points.

5.5 Depth perception through stereo vision

The imaging process is a projection from 3D to 2D space. The third dimension – the depth – gets lost during this process. Without any additional constraints it is impossible to determine the range of an observed image point since each image point corresponds to a line in the 3D world and each point on this line would be projected onto the same image point. However, if a point is observed through at least two cameras, the intersection constraint of the corresponding lines allows for the reconstruction of its 3D coordinates as shown in Figure 5.7 (a). Stereo vision, or stereopsis, is the capability of a system to perceive depth of a scene from two or more 2-dimensional images that are taken from different points of view. In order to do this, two problems have to be solved: the correspondence problem and the 3D reconstruction problem.

5.5.1 The correspondence problem

The correspondence problem of stereo vision is similar to that of the optical flow. The difference is that in stereo vision images are taken simultaneously by different cameras, whereas in optical flow both images are taken by the same camera at different times. If the mutual positions and orientations of the cameras are known, the correspondence problem can be significantly simplified, since the search of a corresponding point in the second image does not have to be performed in the whole image but may be restricted to a curve that corresponds to the viewing ray of the first camera (***epipolar curve***). This condition is called the ***epipolar constraint***. In the case of undistorted images the epipolar curve becomes a straight line as shown in Figure 5.7 (a). Restriction of the correspondence search to the epipolar curve eliminates some of the ambiguities mentioned in Section 5.4.1. The aperture problem may occur only for image regions that are homogeneous in direction of the epipolar curve. The same applies to the assignment problem.

Another simplification can be achieved through ***rectification*** of the images, i.e., transformation into a common image plane. As a result, the epipolar lines coincide and corresponding image points of the both rectified images turn out to lie in the same image line, as shown in Figure 5.7 (b).

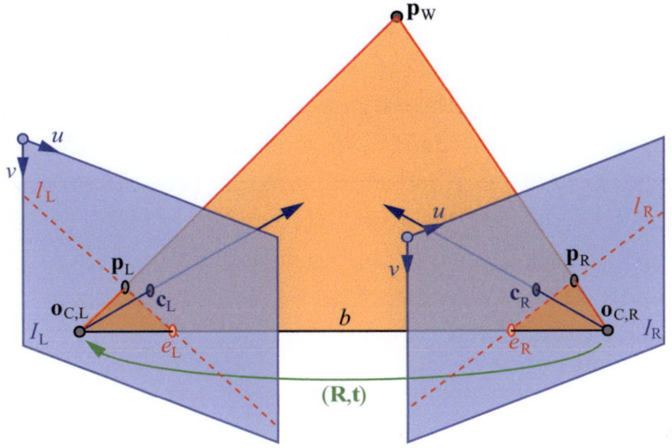

(a) Visualization of the epipolar geometry for an arbitrary camera alignment.

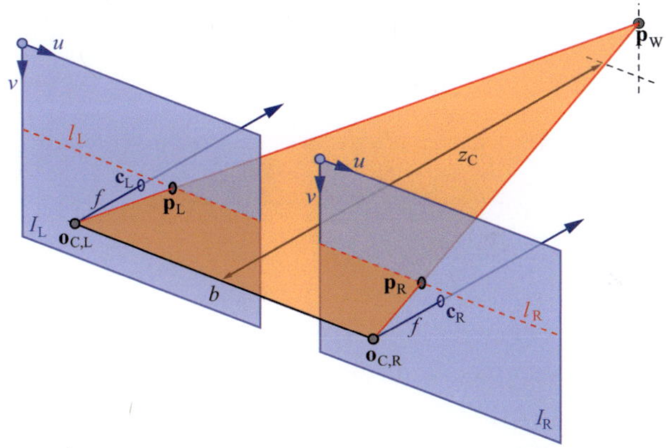

(b) Simplified search for correspondences in rectified images.

Figure 5.7: Principle of the stereo vision.
(a): Finding corresponding image points $\mathbf{p}_L$ and $\mathbf{p}_R$ in the left and right camera images I_R and I_L allows to reconstruct 3D coordinates of the world point $\mathbf{p}_W$. To achieve this, one needs to know mutual orientation and distance of both cameras (given e.g., as a rotation matrix $\mathbf{R}$ and translation vector $\mathbf{t}$). Corresponding image points come to lie on the epipolar lines l_L and l_R.
(b): The search for correspondences may be simplified by rectifying the images, i.e., projecting them into a common plane. This leads to coincidence of the epipolar lines and a simple formula for the range (depth) z_C.

The horizontal coordinate offset of the corresponding points $\mathbf{p}_L$ and $\mathbf{p}_R$ in rectified images is called ***disparity***. In analogy to the optical flow fields one speaks about ***disparity fields*** when describing the entirety of disparities of image points. Similarly to methods for estimation of dense and sparse optical flow fields, there exist methods for computation of dense and sparse disparity fields. In general, the latter need less computation time. Disparity fields may be visualized by assigning a pseudo-color value for each disparity value, as shown in Figure 5.8 (b). Blue corresponds to small disparities and red corresponds to large disparities. Resulting images are called ***disparity maps***.

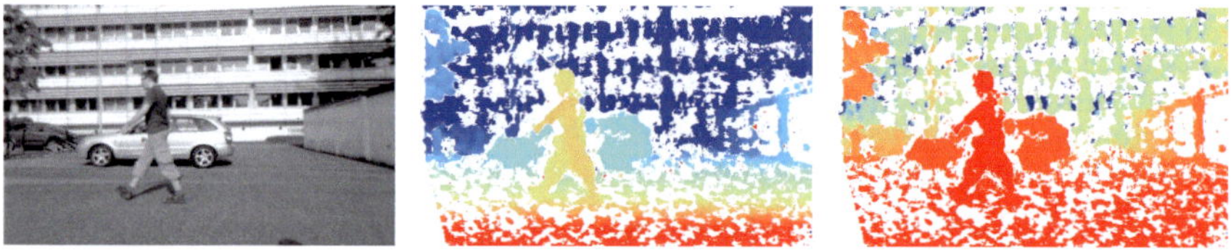

(a) Original Image. **(b)** Disparity map. **(c)** Depth map.

Figure 5.8: Example of a disparity map and a depth map.

5.5.2 3D reconstruction

Having obtained pairs of corresponding points, their depth can be reconstructed by means of triangulation, i.e., calculation of the point of intersection of the viewing rays of the cameras. In practice, due to noise and calculation inaccuracies, both lines might not intersect. A geometrically motivated solution to this problem is choosing e.g., the center of the perpendicular to both lines as an approximation of the real 3D point. An algebraical solution is based on solving the corresponding system of linear equations by means of the least squares method.

In the case of rectified cameras, there exists a simple formula for obtaining depth from disparity which is derived from the intercept theorem:

$$z_C = f \cdot \frac{b}{\Delta u}\,, \tag{5.13}$$

where b stands for the base of the two cameras i.e., distance between the two optical centers, $\Delta u = (u_R - u_L)$ stands for the disparity, and f stands for the focal length after rectification which is equal for both cameras. With knowledge of z_C, the 3D coordinates of the point can be obtained by means of the inverse pinhole camera model.

Using (5.13), a disparity map can be transformed into a ***depth map***. An example of a depth map is shown in Figure 5.8 (c). Similar to disparities depth values are visualized with pseudo-colors: red means near and blue means far.

5.5.3 Synchronous image acquisition

In the case of dynamic scenes and especially in the case of a moving camera platform, a proper synchronization of the image acquisition of both cameras of a stereo system has to be ensured. In the opposite case, i.e., if there is a delay between the acquisition of the images, both the correspondence search and 3D reconstruction may fail completely or deliver wrong results due to the intermediate motion of the observed scene points in one of the images. In APROSYS SP6, the synchronization of the image acquisition was achieved through a hardware-based triggering of the cameras. The overview of the required architecture, which also allows for synchronization between the video and radar subsystems, is depicted in Figure 5.9.

When the video processing system is ready for image acquisition, it generates a special trigger message that is sent over the CAN bus interconnecting the collision detection system components. A dedicated piece of hardware that in Figure 5.9 is referred to as the "CAN ID Filter" [1] transforms this message with negligible delay into a synchronous hardware trigger signal for both video cameras. The trigger CAN message is received by the radar (fusion) system as well. Since the message contains the current system time of the video PC ("image acquisition time stamp"), this allows to refer the acquired images and the latter track data to the corresponding acquisition time and in this way to to synchronize both sensor systems.

[1] The working principle and the architecture of the CAN ID Filter is described in detail in the APROSYS deliverable report AP-SP62-0035-D624 [Tan08a].

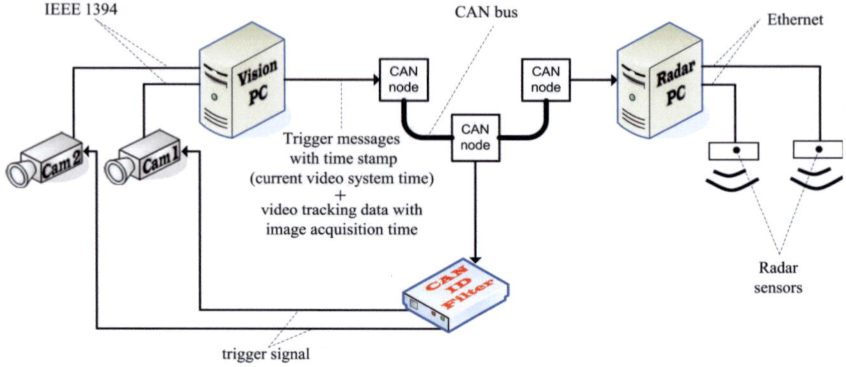

Figure 5.9: Hardware architecture of the APROSYS sensing system.

5.6 Point tracking

Finding correspondences between pixels of two stereo images allows for an estimation of their range as shown in Section 5.5. Knowing the position and orientation of the cameras with respect to the world coordinate system allows to reconstruct the corresponding 3D coordinates. Optical flow techniques described in Section 5.4 allow to track feature points in consecutive images of a video sequence. Combination of both stereo vision and optical flow techniques allows for determination of not only 3D coordinates of the world points but also of their 3D velocities. This idea, which is known as ***"6D-Vision"*** [Fra05a] is used in this work to enable a robust object detection and tracking.

In our framework, up to 3000 feature points are tracked simultaneously in 3D space using Extended Kalman Filters. Point motion in space is modeled as a straight-line steady motion. The six-dimensional state vectors $[x, y, z, v_x, v_y, v_z]^T$ of the points are estimated from the stereo depth measurements as well as from their displacement in the image between consecutive frames (optical flow measurements). The measurement vector for the point state estimation is given by $[u, v, z_C]^T$ with image coordinates (u, v) and feature depth z_C. The measurement model for the image coordinates (u, v) which has to be used in the Kalman filter is given in Equation (5.12). The measurement model for the feature depth z_C is given in Equation (5.13).

The system model for point tracking which describes the propagation of the point coordinates between two consecutive frames has to account for the vehicle ego-motion which is estimated from the vehicle data as discussed in Section 5.2. The incorporation of the ego-motion is done after the application of the regular linear motion model by transforming the point coordinates and velocities from the old into the new vehicle coordinate system. The uncertainties of the ego-motion estimation are incorporated by adapting the corresponding noise terms appropriately.

5.6.1 Handling of ambiguous and missing correspondences

As mentioned above, in certain cases the correspondence problem may have an ambiguous or even no solution. Sometimes ambiguous or ill-posed solution to the correspondence problem is a permanent issue but in some cases this is only a temporary issue which lasts only for a couple of frames and can be overcome, if handled properly. This is true for both optical flow and stereo depth estimation techniques.

In the case of dropouts in depth estimation, points can be tracked further using predicted depth values. In the case of ambiguous or missing correspondences between two consecutive frames (optical flow dropouts), points can be propagated using predicted point motion in the hope that at some point an unambiguous correspondence will be found. Re-identification trials are made in each frame using optical flow computation between the current frame and the frame in which the point has been seen for the last time.

In order to to enable maximal exploitation of the available information despite measurement dropouts in both optical flow or stereo depth estimation, each point is provided with an additional 3-dimensional state vector $[\hat{u}, \hat{v}, \hat{z}_C]^T$ for the measurement space and the respective covariance matrices in addition to the estimated 6-dimensional state vector $[\hat{x}, \hat{y}, \hat{z}, \hat{v}_x, \hat{v}_y, \hat{v}_z]^T$. In the case of successful optical flow estimation but missing depth measurements, the predicted depth value is used together with the new image coordinates allowing thus to track point with a higher accuracy than if pure prediction by means of the system model was taken.

Along with the measurement dropouts, one of the biggest problems is point state corruption due to wrong correspondences (confusion errors) of both algorithms. If such confusion errors remain undiscovered, the respective points become ***outliers*** and might disturb subsequent algorithms leading to errors in object detection and tracking. In order to remove measurement outliers caused by the correspondence errors in both algorithms, a plausibility check is applied before performing further processing steps. Points not falling into the sigma ellipsoid around the predicted position are marked as outliers and ignored when processing the current frame.

Sharp camera movements due to e.g., potholes that are not sufficiently covered by the system model may cause the aforementioned outlier detection method to fail. In such cases all points may be classified as outliers. In order to prevent this effect, an alternative outlier detection method based on a modified version of the RANSAC algorithm was developed by the author of this thesis [Sch12], [Gri12]. In contrast to the standard RANSAC algorithm [Fis81], the best consensus set is chosen not as the set having maximal number of inlier points, but depending on the weighted sum of these. The weighting takes into account both the error value e and a quality measure regarding repeated point re-identification. The total weight ϖ of an inlier is calculated as the product of the model error weight ϖ_m and the tracking quality weight ϖ_t with $\varpi_m = (e_{max} - e)/e_{max}$ and $\varpi_t = t_m/t_o$ where e_{max} is the error threshold, i.e., the error value from which on a point is considered an outlier. The tracking quality weight ϖ_t is computed as the ratio of the number t_m of successfully matched frames (i.e., frames, in which the point has been successfully re-identified) to the total object tracking duration t_o (measured in frames).

5.6.2 Point management

In order to enable handling of outliers and measurement dropouts and to facilitate efficient memory management, a special point management scheme with memory recycling has been designed.

The memory allocation for the points is done in advance. In addition to the vectors and matrices for physical state description of the feature points, each point is provided with a flag that allows to mark its current tracking status. Additionally, there are counters for successfully established correspondences and measurement dropouts. Deletion of bad feature points is done by marking them as idle. This allows to reuse the corresponding array elements without unnecessarily releasing and allocating memory. A fast iteration through array elements with a certain tracking status is facilitated by using linked pointer lists.

Points can be marked as *"free"*, *"new"*, *"tracked"*, *"ignored"*, and *"ignoreZ"*. At the beginning of the processing all points are marked as *"free"*. This means that the corresponding elements are currently idle and are available for filling with newly extracted feature points.

The status *"new"* is assigned to the feature points that are seen for the first time. This is done in the Feature Extraction Submodule of the Stereo Processing Module. If there could be established no stereo correspondence or the depth reconstruction delivers implausible results, such points are immediately deleted. In the opposite case they are successfully forwarded to other modules. *"New"* points have to be treated specially by the Point Tracking Module, since they do not yet have a valid prediction. Despite lacking velocity estimation, *"new"* points may be utilized in the Ground Estimation and Clustering submodules of the Object Detection Module. Filter initialization of the *"new"* points is done under assumption of their stationarity, i.e., by using $[v_x, v_y, v_z]^T = [0, 0, 0]^T$. For a faster filter convergence one may use the Interacting Multiple Models approach with several different initializations as described in Section 2.2.4, however, this is not currently implemented.

In each frame (except the first one) the optical flow between $\ell >= 1$ previous frames and the current frame is computed prior to the feature extraction and the stereo depth estimation. Feature points from last frames that could be re-identified in the current frame are marked as *"tracked"*. In order to prevent multiple tracking of the same feature point, extraction of new features is suppressed in close proximity to the *"tracked"* feature points.

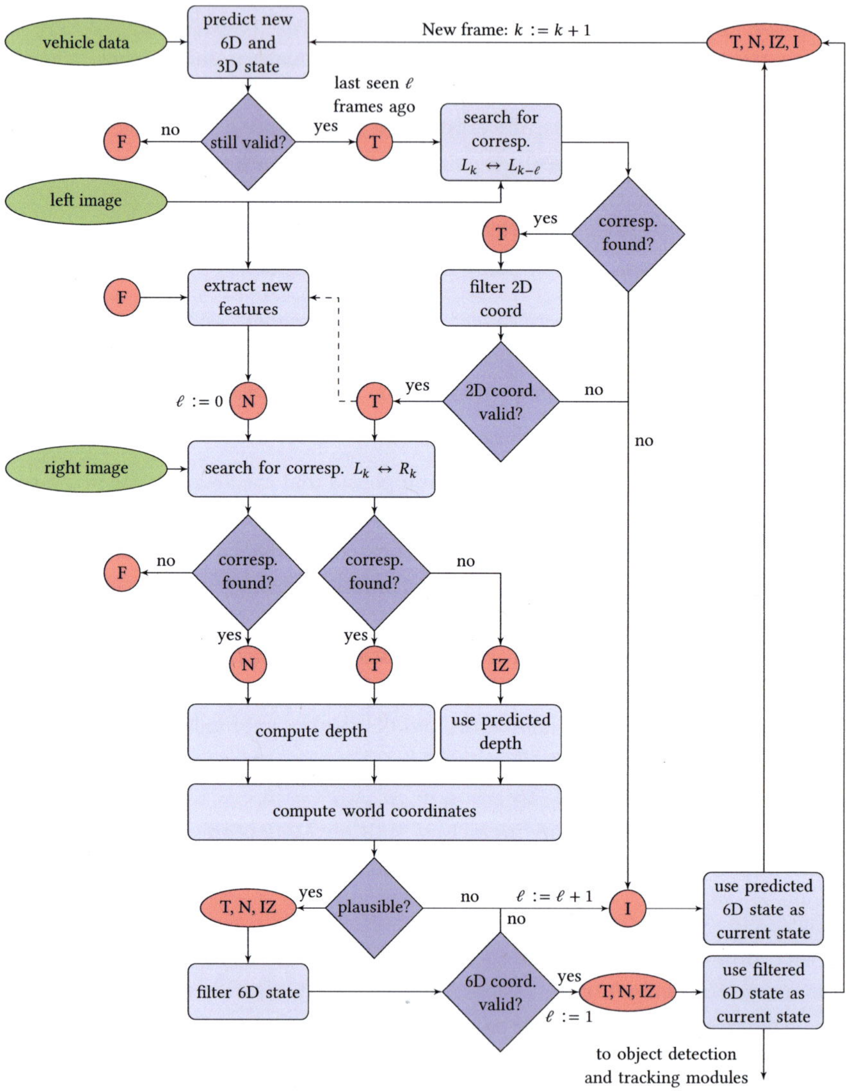

Figure 5.10: Detailed flowchart of the point tracking with tracking status transitions. The possible status flags are *"free"* (F), *"new"* (N), *"tracked"* (T), *"ignoreZ"* (IZ), and *"ignored"* (I).

"Tracked" feature points for which no stereo correspondence can be established are marked as *"ingoreZ"*. As mentioned above, their 6-dimensional state vector is updated using their new image coordinates and the predicted depth value. Due to the resulting uncertainty, points with the status *"ignoreZ"* should not be incorporated into the object detection and tracking process. In our implementation they are ignored by the Object Detection and Object Tracking Modules.

Points that could not be unambiguously re-identified in the current frame are marked as *"ignored"*. Point management stores their old image coordinates and the ID of the frame in which they have been seen at last in order to retry the re-identification in one of the subsequent frames. Their new image coordinates are predicted from the previous 6D state by combining the system model and the measurement model. Similarly to the points with the status *"ignoreZ"*, points with the status *"ignored"* are not incorporated into the object detection and tracking process due to their uncertainty. If the uncertainty becomes too large, the points are deleted. An additional reason for point deletion is posed by repeated measurement dropouts.

The entire flowchart of the point management cycle is shown in Figure 5.10.

5.7 Initial object detection through clustering of 6D point clouds

Generation of object hypotheses (object detection) from resulting 6D point clouds is done by means of clustering. We use the flat world assumption mentioned in Section 1.3 which allows to estimate the ground plane and eliminate points that belong to the ground. The remaining points are assumed either to belong to the scene objects or to be outliers caused by data processing errors (clutter). The second assumption is that 6D points that belong to the same object are compact in the sense that they may be separated from point clouds belonging to other objects by means of an appropriate clustering algorithm in 6D space. Clustering is a term for unsupervised classification methods that build groups of data objects in such a way that data objects of the same group are as similar as possible and differ as much as possible from the data objects of other groups. An overview of different clustering methods is given in [Gan07a]. There are hierarchical, center-based, search-based, density-based, graph-based, model-based, grid-based and fuzzy clustering algorithms.

Since neither the number, extent, nor shape of the clusters is known a-priori, only density-based and grid-based clustering methods can be taken into consideration. Density-based clustering methods are based on the assumption that the local point density inside a cluster is higher than between two clusters. The local point density is defined by means of the number of neighboring points in the immediate surroundings of the point. Thresholding allows to find connected regions of high point density. The resulting clusters may have an arbitrary shape. Points that do not belong to any cluster are interpreted as outliers (noise).

Grid-based clustering methods divide the space into cells. Instead of considering individual points they analyze and cluster cells based on their occupancy.

In this work, two clustering algorithms have been implemented: ***Reduced Bucket Clustering*** and ***GDBSCAN*** [Est96]. Reduced Bucket Clustering is a representative of grid-based clustering methods whereas GDBSCAN is a representative of density-based clustering.

A great simplification can be achieved, if one assumes that objects may not hang over each other, i.e., that points that have the same horizontal coordinates belong to the same object. Massive object parts that are hanging above ground, such as bridges, tree crowns, etc. are assumed to be taken out of consideration by preceding preprocessing steps, such as building of regions of interest (ROIs) in the images, removal of points which are too high, etc. This allows to meet the assumption that one of the dimensions (height of the points above ground) is irrelevant for separation of point clouds of different objects. Hence, it is enough to consider the projection of the points onto the ground plane. Also one may assume that objects move parallel to the ground. This reduces the number of dimensions to be considered from six to four. In our application we assume that objects with very different ground velocities do not come close together, i.e., it is sufficient to perform spacial clustering for separating such objects. This allows to drop the ground velocity components as the clustering parameters. The number of clustering dimensions becomes two.

5.7.1 GDBSCAN

The principle of GDBSCAN algorithm is shown in Figure 5.11 (a). For each point an environment with radius ϵ (***ϵ-environment***) is defined. Then for each unvisited point, points within its ϵ-environment are counted. If there are too few neighboring points, the considered point is marked as noise. However, if the number of points within the ϵ-environment exceeds a certain threshold, the considered point is defined as a ***"cluster seed point"*** and a new cluster containing this point is created. Then the following recursion is performed: All points within the ϵ-environment of the cluster seed point are added to this cluster and marked as classified. Points that have enough neighbors within their ϵ-environment are defined as cluster seed points. If one of the points within the ϵ-environment of a cluster seed point belongs to another cluster, both clusters are merged.

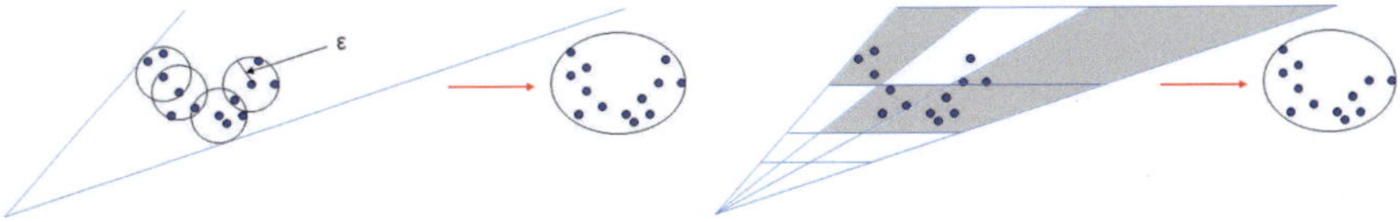

(a) Density-based clustering procedure. **(b)** Grid-based clustering procedure.

Figure 5.11: Working principles of density-based and grid-based clustering algorithms.

5.7.2 Reduced Bucket Clustering

In order to perform the Reduced Bucket Clustering algorithm, points are sorted into a grid structure. Camera projection properties are accounted for by using a log-polar coordinate system. A considerable acceleration of the algorithm can be achieved, if cameras are aligned parallel to the ground plane so that there is no tilt and roll. Then, image columns can serve as the angular coordinates and depth obtained by means of stereo processing can be used as the radial coordinate. Quantization of both coordinates allows to sort the points into a grid structure as shown in Figure 5.12. Points of neighboring non-empty cells (buckets) are merged into clusters as illustrated in Figure 5.11 (b). In order to reduce the influence of noise points (outliers), a threshold regarding the minimal number of the points in a cell is used for cell occupancy classification.

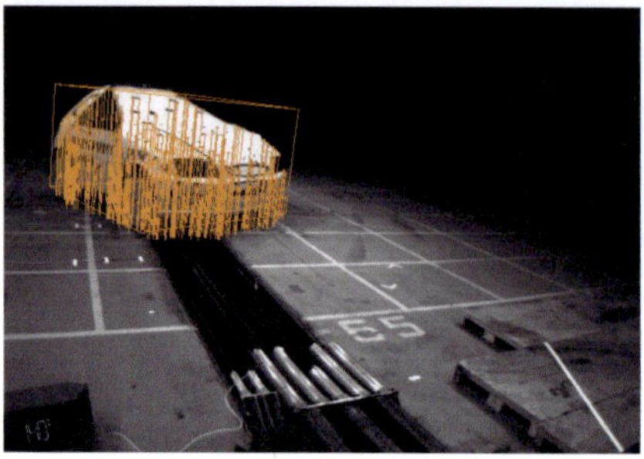

(a) Original image with visualized object points. Point depth is visualized by means of vertical lines to the ground.

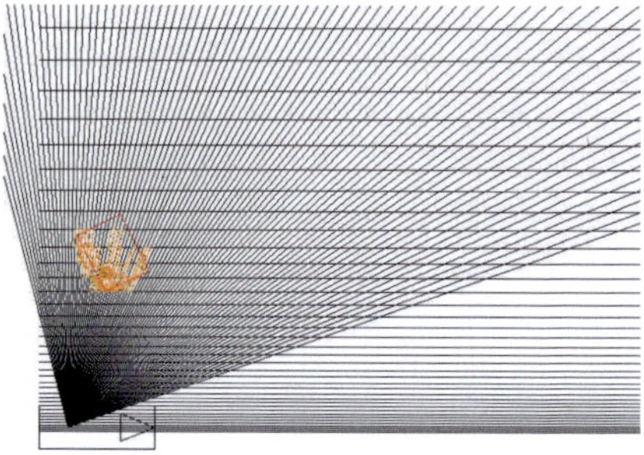

(b) Results of clustering and rectangle fitting (top view). Occupied grid cells are highlighted in orange. Fitted rectangle is drawn in red.

Figure 5.12: Principle of the Reduced Bucket Clustering.

5.7.3 Comparison

A great advantage of the Bucket Clustering algorithm is its high speed since it has the complexity of $O(n + m)$ with n being the number of points and m being the number of non-empty buckets (with $m \ll n$) compared to $O(n \cdot \log n)$ of the GDBSCAN algorithm. Another advantage is the automatic incorporation of the physical properties of the camera projection. However, use of a non-Cartesian coordinate system also carries disadvantages. The resulting fine quantization for small ranges and coarse quantization for large ranges may lead to split detections in the area close to the camera and merged detections at large ranges.

5.8 Object Tracking

5.8.1 Tracking cycle overview

Clustering algorithms generate detections in the form of 6-dimensional point clouds. The next step is generation of more elaborate object hypotheses, i.e., estimation of object properties such as position, extent and motion parameters. The process flow differs for the classical data association and tracking approach and for FBPDATA. The overall tracking cycles of the classical approach and of FBPDATA are depicted in Figure 5.13.

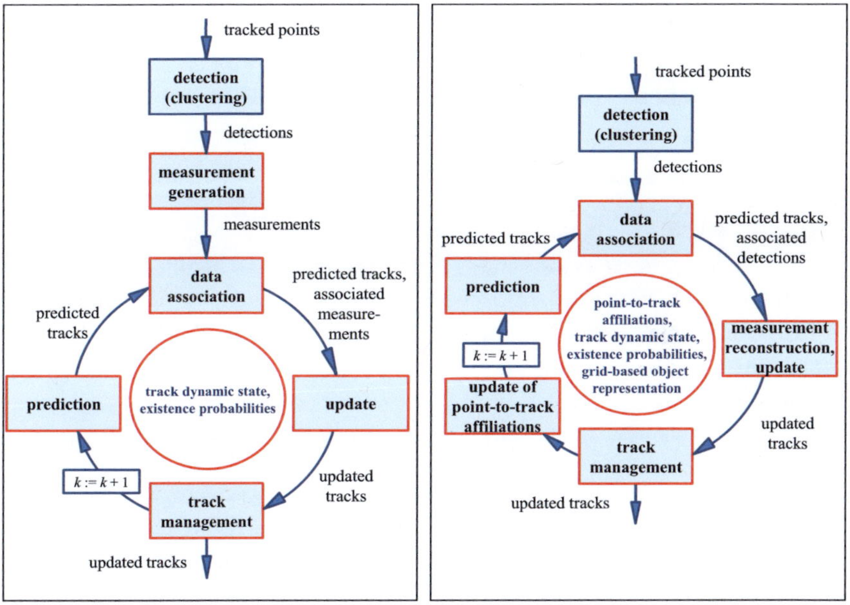

(a) Implementation of the classical tracking-by-detection approach.

(b) Tracking cycle in FBPDATA.

Figure 5.13: Implementation of the tracking cycle: classical tracking-by-detection approach (a) and FBPDATA (b).

The tracking cycles consist of the following steps:

- Prediction
- Measurement generation (only classical approach)
- Data association, including
  - occlusion reasoning (only FBPDATA),
  - specification of joint events,
  - computation of association weights
- Measurement reconstruction (only FBPDATA), consisting of
  - feature-based reconstruction of a reference point,
  - realigning occupancy grid according to the updated object location
  - grid-based reconstruction of object dimensions
  - filtering of the reference point position
- Track state update
- Track management
- Update of point-to-track affiliations (only FBPDATA)

At the beginning of the processing of a new frame k, state prediction is done for each track. Along with the conventional prediction of the dynamic track state, in FBPDATA we additionally compute the a-priori object existence and observability probability. This is done based on the predicted observability probability masks of the tracked objects, which, in turn, are computed from the appearance masks of all tracked objects in the camera image as described in Section 4.1.4.

As mentioned in Section 5.1, measurements for the implemented classical data association and tracking approach can be generated by fitting cuboids into the obtained 3-dimensional point clouds. We simplify this problem by projecting all object points into the ground plane and by fitting rectangles into the resulting 2-dimensional point clouds. This procedure is described in Section 5.8.3. The height of the highest point is used as the object height measurement. Due to the fact that often only a part of an object is visible to the sensors, the orientation of the obtained cuboid may differ from the estimated object motion orientation. Hence, the geometrical orientation ϕ is modeled separately. Internally, objects are modeled as cuboids with a centroid (x, y, z), dimensions (l, w, h), geometrical orientation ϕ, motion orientation φ, speed v, acceleration a and yaw rate $\dot{\varphi}$. This corresponds to the Constant Yaw Rate Model with Acceleration, which has proved to deliver the best performance in the case of a side-looking system [Rüh08]. Details about this and alternative motion models are given in Section 5.8.2.

Next we specify candidate association hypotheses (the set $\boldsymbol{\Theta}_k$ of feasible joint data association events Θ) based on the set $\mathcal{D}_k$ of detections $d_{k,j}$ obtained at time step k. For the reduction of computational complexity, tracks are first divided into clusters that can be considered independently from each other. In FBPDATA we use the feature-based gating scheme that is described in Section 4.1.10 for track clustering and joint event definition. Then, association likelihoods for assignments between detections and tracks and association weights are computed. This is done in four steps. First the individual detection-to-track assignment likelihoods $P(\theta^{\mathbf{x}_{k,i} \mapsto d_{k,j}} |\ \mathcal{D}_{1:k-1})$ are computed. They are saved into lookup tables. Then, for each joint event Θ the likelihood $p(\mathcal{D}_k |\ \Theta, \mathcal{D}_{1:k-1})$ of the obtained detection set is computed by multiplying the corresponding edge probabilities. The overall a-posteriori joint event probabilities $P(\Theta|\mathcal{D}_{1:k})$ are computed by multiplying those likelihoods with the a-priori joint event probabilities $P(\Theta|\mathcal{D}_{1:k-1})$ and normalizing them with a normalization constant. Then, for each possible detection-to-track assignment the probabilities of the joint events containing this assignment are summed up. The resulting association weights β are saved into separate lookup tables for further use in the correction step.

The a-posteriori object existence probability for a track $\mathbf{x}_i$ is calculated as the sum of the probabilities of all assignment hypotheses assuming existence of the corresponding object divided by the sum of the probabilities of all possible hypotheses:

$$P(\exists \mathbf{x}_{k,i} |\ \mathcal{D}_{1:k}) = \frac{\sum_{\Theta \in \boldsymbol{\Theta}_k^{\mathbf{x}_i \mapsto \exists}} P(\Theta |\ \mathcal{D}_{1:k})}{\sum_{\Theta \in \boldsymbol{\Theta}_k} P(\Theta |\ \mathcal{D}_{1:k})} . \tag{5.14}$$

Similarly:

$$P(\nexists \mathbf{x}_{k,i} |\ \mathcal{D}_{1:k}) = \frac{\sum_{\Theta \in \boldsymbol{\Theta}_k^{\mathbf{x}_i \mapsto \nexists}} P(\Theta |\ \mathcal{D}_{1:k})}{\sum_{\Theta \in \boldsymbol{\Theta}_k} P(\Theta |\ \mathcal{D}_{1:k})} , \tag{5.15}$$

and

$$P(\varnothing \mathbf{x}_{k,i} | \mathcal{D}_{1:k}) = \frac{\sum_{\Theta \in \boldsymbol{\Theta}_k^{\mathbf{x}_i \mapsto \varnothing}} P(\Theta | \mathcal{D}_{1:k})}{\sum_{\Theta \in \boldsymbol{\Theta}_k} P(\Theta | \mathcal{D}_{1:k})} . \tag{5.16}$$

In FBPDATA, measurements are generated after and not before the data association and may be composed of multiple (split) detections or "reconstructed" out of partial, bloated, and merged detections. Measurement reconstruction is done both for the object dynamic parameters and for its extent. First, we reconstruct the objects' reference point in the new frame using the information about stably tracked points and their spatial relationship to the corresponding point in the old frame. Each associated point cloud contributes according to its association weight β. This is described in Section 5.8.4. The reconstructed reference point is used for performing the innovation of the dynamic object state. Then we update the location and the orientation of the grid-based object extent representation. After aligning it according to the updated dynamics we recompute appearance masks, appearance probability masks and transparency masks for all objects. This allows to compute observability probability mask, occlusion probability mask, and occlusion probabilities for the occupied cells of each tracked object. Grid occupancy of all tracked objects is updated using associated point clouds. In occluded object areas, predicted occupancy is preserved. Details about this procedure are given in Section 5.8.5. Extracting object dimensions measurements out of the composed grid-based object representation is done analogously to the procedure in the classical approach, which is described in Section 5.8.3 – by treating each occupied cell as a data point and fitting a cuboid into the resulting point cloud. After updating the object dimensions, the reference point is shifted to a filtered position as described in Section 4.1.5.

Finally, the probabilities $P(\mathbf{x}_{k,i} \mapsto \mathbf{p}_q)$ for points $\mathbf{p}_q$ to belong to individual objects $\mathbf{x}_{k,i}$ are updated.

5.8.2 Object motion modeling

The task of a collision detection system is not only to detect all relevant objects, but to estimate their size and motion parameters (referred to as "dynamic state") and to predict whether a collision with the ego-vehicle will take place (and if yes, when and where exactly). As mentioned in Section 2.2, for a dynamic state prediction, a system model has to be defined.

This model makes assumptions about object motion of the observed objects. In many applications very simplified assumptions are made, e.g., each velocity coordinate is considered independently. Also, object orientation can often be assumed constant, which simplifies object hypothesis generation and object tracking considerably. If sensors are monitoring a narrow area in front of a road vehicle, such assumptions might be sufficient. However, for stable object tracking and prediction of complex scenarios these assumptions are insufficient.

In the following, six different motion models with correlated velocity components are introduced. In the course of this work all six models have been implemented and evaluated. Results of this evaluation have been presented at the International Workshop on Intelligent Transportation (WIT) in 2008 and can be found in [Rüh08].

5.8.2.1 Constant heading models

The simplest model considers vehicle as a mass particle with constant velocity (***constant heading model with constant velocity***). It is described by two parameters: motion direction (orientation angle φ) and speed v. Vehicle state vector $\mathbf{x}$ in Cartesian coordinates has thus 4 dimensions:

$$\mathbf{x} = (x, y, \varphi, v)^T. \tag{5.17}$$

Taking into account possible acceleration a leads to the ***constant heading model with constant acceleration*** with the state vector

$$\mathbf{x} = (x, y, \varphi, v, a)^T. \tag{5.18}$$

5.8.2.2 Constant yaw rate models

Both previous models assume straight ahead motion. A simple way of modeling turning maneuvers can be done by introducing another state variable, the yaw rate $\dot{\varphi}$ which changes the orientation of the motion. In the case of constant velocity this yields in the ***constant yaw rate model with constant velocity***. Its state vector is given by $\mathbf{x} = (x, y, \varphi, v, \dot{\varphi})^T$. Additionally modeling acceleration yields in the ***constant yaw rate model with constant acceleration*** with the state vector $\mathbf{x} = (x, y, \varphi, v, \dot{\varphi}, a)^T$.

5.8.2.3 Bicycle model

A better approximation of the real vehicle motion can be achieved through the bicycle model which is described in Section 5.2.

Although the wheelbase l_{WB} is a constant, it has to be included into the state vector of the model since it is a-priori unknown and has to be estimated along with other object state variables. The state vector of the ***bicycle model with constant velocity*** is thus given by $\mathbf{x} = (x, y, \varphi, \alpha, l_{\mathrm{WB}}, v)^T$.

In the case of a straight-line motion ($\alpha = 0$), radius r is infinite. Because of this and due to the fact that neither l_{WB} nor α can be measured directly, the inverse of r, ρ with $\rho = \frac{1}{r} = \frac{\tan(\alpha)}{l_{\mathrm{WB}}}$ can be used as a representative state variable instead [Rüh08]. This leads to the state vector $\mathbf{x} = (x, y, \varphi, \rho, v)^T$.

The bicycle model can be easily extended by the acceleration, leading to the ***bicycle model with constant acceleration***.

5.8.2.4 Suitability of the models for the side collision detection application

The six models described above were evaluated with data taken both in a controlled environment and in regular traffic scenes. Hereby, the focus was laid on the correct position and velocity estimation of the detected objects as well as on the fast filter convergence and proper collision prediction results.

In Appendix A, an evaluation of two sequences is presented, one taken in a crash hall and one outdoors in a round-about situation. The experiments have shown that the constant heading models are not sufficient for prediction of complex object trajectories in the regular traffic observed from a side-looking stereo camera. The big disadvantage of the bicycle model in our application is that the steering angle cannot be directly observed and so the filter tends to oscillate. The best results have been achieved when using the constant yaw rate model. Explicitly modeling acceleration lead to oscillations at the beginning of the estimation and slower filter convergence.

In the above considerations the steering angle (and hence the yaw rate) of the observed vehicles as well as its acceleration (if any) were assumed to be nearly constant. In a side-looking video-based pre-crash system with relatively short expected object observation time, these assumptions seem to be feasible. Instead of modeling $\dot{\alpha}$ or $\ddot{\varphi}$ and $\dot{a}$, which may additionally slow down the filter convergence, it is more feasible to use the Interacting Multiple Models (IMM) approach [Bla99] for coping with severe steering, acceleration and deceleration maneuvers, as done in e.g., [Kae05] and [Bar10].

5.8.3 Fitting rectangles into point clouds

Although stereo data processing provides point clouds in 3-dimensional space, this data is not true 3D object data. Only points on the visible object surfaces are obtained. One speaks of $2\frac{1}{2}$D information. Since most of the vehicles have a rectangular ground shape, in the bird's-eye view the visible vehicle sides are reduced to line segments. The majority of the obtained points which are situated on the visible vehicle sides thus form in the bird's-eye view "L", "I" or "U" shapes as shown in Fig. 5.14 (a). However, due to quantization and mismatches of the stereo processing these shapes are extremely noisy as shown in Fig. 5.14 (b). Another problem is posed by the fact that although the majority of the points is situated on the mostly vertical surfaces, there might be also some inclined surfaces that would lead to an additional spread out. Thus, the task of estimation of the correct object position, spatial orientation and size is not trivial.

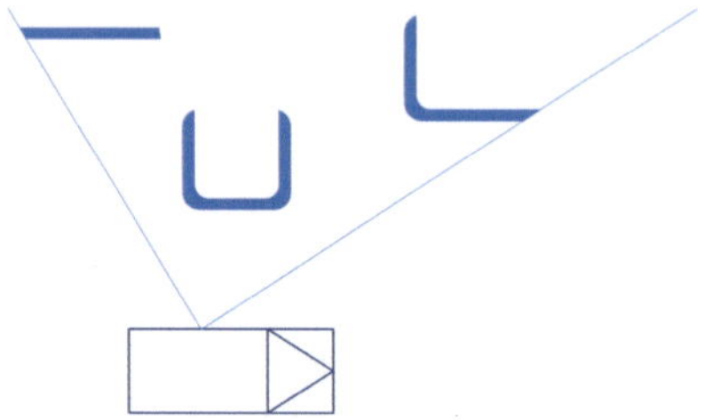

(a) Visible object sides as "I", "L" and "U" shapes in the bird's-eye view.

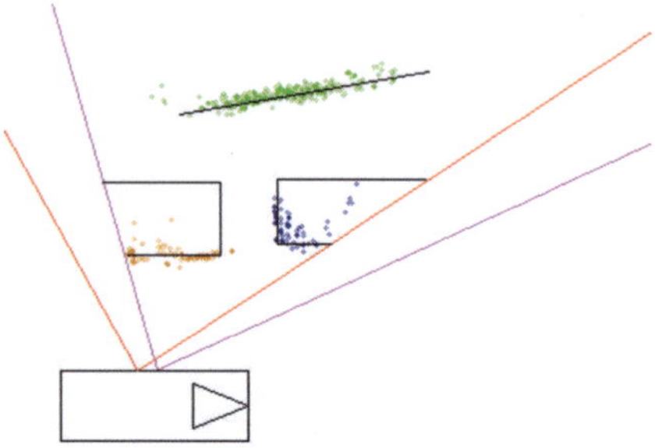

(b) Real data: point spread due to inclinations, quantization and mismatches.

Figure 5.14: Possible visible object shapes in the bird's-eye view.

In the course of this work several algorithms that are conceivable for fitting rectangles into such data have been considered. The simplest one computes the minimal area bounding box, others aim at estimation of the object sides by identifying the main extent direction of the cluster or by fitting one or two major line segments into the ground projection of the cluster points. In order to do so, algorithms based on ***Principle Component Analysis (PCA)*** [Pea01] and the ***RANSAC*** algorithm [Fis81] have been implemented and tested.

PCA also known as the ***Karhunen-Loève Transform*** is a method for structuring complex data sets in order to reduce their dimensionality or in order to obtain a better visualization. It aims at finding the principal components of the data, i.e., linearly uncorrelated variables for which the data have the largest possible variance. In our case it is enough to find the first principle component, which is the major extent direction of the cluster as illustrated in Figure 5.15 (a).

The RANSAC algorithm chooses two arbitrary cluster points in each iteration. The line going through those points is hypothesized to contain the edge that corresponds to the ground projection of the major visible object side. All other cluster points are considered to belong to this edge, if their distance to the line does not exceed a pre-defined threshold, i.e., if they lie within a scatter tolerance corridor. The aim is to identify a line for which most of the points can be considered as edge points (s. Figure 5.15 (b)). After having done this, an adjustment is done for the best matching line. The new line parameters are computed from the corresponding edge points using the Least Squares method. Then the object extent along this line and perpendicular to the line are computed. An extension to the algorithm that identifies a second line perpendicular to the first one after removal of the identified edge points has been implemented. It did not yield any improvement when applied to the real data sets and was thus discarded.

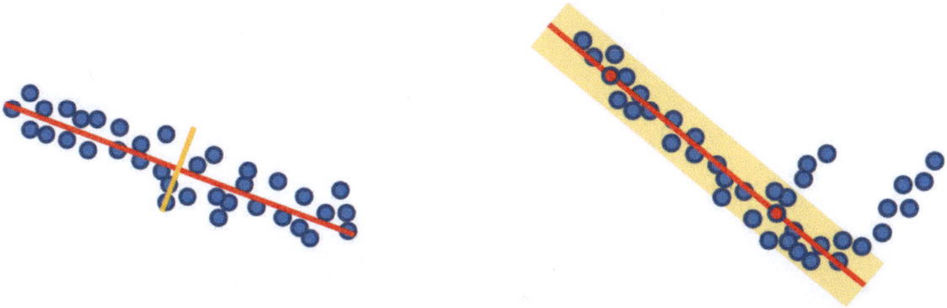

(a) Principle Component Analysis. The object extent in the direction of the first principal component (red line) is maximal.

(b) RANSAC. The tolerance corridor (yellow) around a line through two cluster points (red) should contain as many points as possible.

Figure 5.15: Functional principle of the PCA and RANSAC algorithms.

Experiments have shown, that both the computation of the minimal area rectangle and the PCA based algorithm have some disadvantages when applied to $2\frac{1}{2}$D data.

As shown in Figure 5.16 (a), rectangle of minimal area is not necessarily aligned parallel to the actual object sides. The main extent direction of a cluster found by the PCA algorithm may also differ from the longest visible object side as illustrated in Figure 5.16 (b). Optimal results for noisy real world data have been achieved when using the RANSAC based algorithm. Thus it has been adopted for the system use.

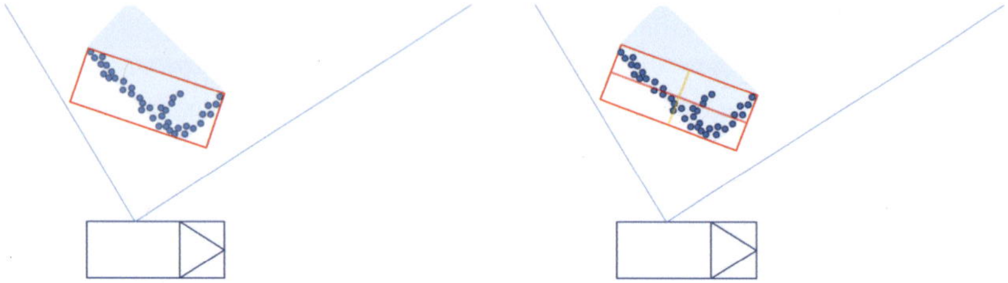

(a) Minimal area rectangle might be not parallel to the real object sides.

(b) The first principal component might not correspond to the largest visible object side.

Figure 5.16: Failure cases of the fitting algorithms.

5.8.4 Feature-point based reconstruction of track's position and orientation

For the reconstruction of the track reference point $\mathbf{p}_O$ from an associated point cloud, we first calculate the centroid $\mathbf{p}_C$ of the stably tracked points $\mathbf{p}_q$ of this point cloud both in the current and previous frame. Hereby we are weighting the points' 3-D positions with their track affiliation probability (known from the previous frame). Having computed $\mathbf{p}_C$ in both current and previous frames, we can for each tracked point $\mathbf{p}_q$ reconstruct the vector $(\overrightarrow{\mathbf{p}_C\mathbf{p}_O})_q$ pointing from the $\mathbf{p}_C$ to the object reference point $\mathbf{p}_O$ in the current frame using knowledge about the relative orientation of this vector regarding the vector $\overrightarrow{\mathbf{p}_C\mathbf{p}_q}$ in the previous frame (cf. Fig. 5.17).

Building a weighted mean of the resulting vectors $(\overrightarrow{\mathbf{p}_C\mathbf{p}_O})_q$ according to the affiliation probability of the respective points $\mathbf{p}_q$ we get the new position of the track's reference point with respect to the considered point cloud and the yaw between two frames. If more than one point cloud is associated to a track, the corresponding reference point position and yaw measurements are weighted according to the association probabilities of the point clouds to the track. The composed measurement is then used for the innovation of the Kalman Filter responsible for the track's dynamics.

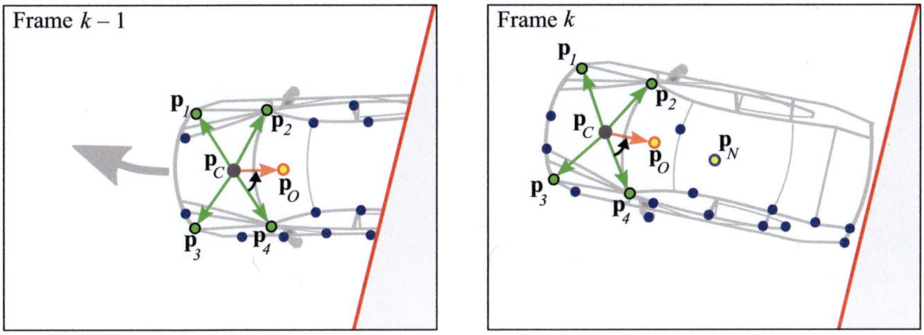

(a) Frame $k-1$ **(b)** Frame k

Figure 5.17: Object position reconstruction based on spatial relationship of a reference point to stably tracked points.

5.8.5 Grid-based reconstruction of the object extent

The object extent in FBPDATA is obtained as follows. After aligning the predicted occupancy grid of the tracked objects according to the updated object dynamic state, we recompute appearance masks, appearance probability masks and transparency masks for all objects. This allows to compute observability probability mask, occlusion probability mask, and occlusion probabilities for the occupied cells of each tracked object.

Next, points of each associated point cloud are sorted into the grid and grid occupancy values are computed. To avoid an update of the occupancy value of an occluded cell with 0, we filter the occupancy values of the cells using their occlusion probability. Additionally, the probability of not receiving a detection due to a sensor failure is accounted for. This process is visualized in Fig. 5.18.

A rth cell $c_{k,r}^{\mathbf{x}_i}$ of the track $\mathbf{x}_i$ is marked as being occupied, if at least one point belonging to one of the associated point clouds is affiliated to this track to more than 50%. Its observability probability $P(\supset c_{k,r}^{\mathbf{x}_i})$ is set to 1, the occlusion probability $P(\not\supset c_{k,r}^{\mathbf{x}_i})$ and the non-detectability probability $P(\varnothing c_{k,r}^{\mathbf{x}_i})$ are set to 0. In all other cases the non-visibility probability of a cell due to sensor failure $P(\varnothing c_{k,r}^{\mathbf{x}_i})$ is set from the object non-detectability probability $P(\varnothing \mathbf{x}_{k,i} | \, \exists \mathbf{x}_{k,i} \mathcal{D}_{1:k})$ conditioned on the object existence:

$$P(\varnothing c_{k,r}^{\mathbf{x}_i}) = P(\varnothing \mathbf{x}_{k,i} | \, \exists \mathbf{x}_{k,i} \mathcal{D}_{1:k}) \,. \tag{5.19}$$

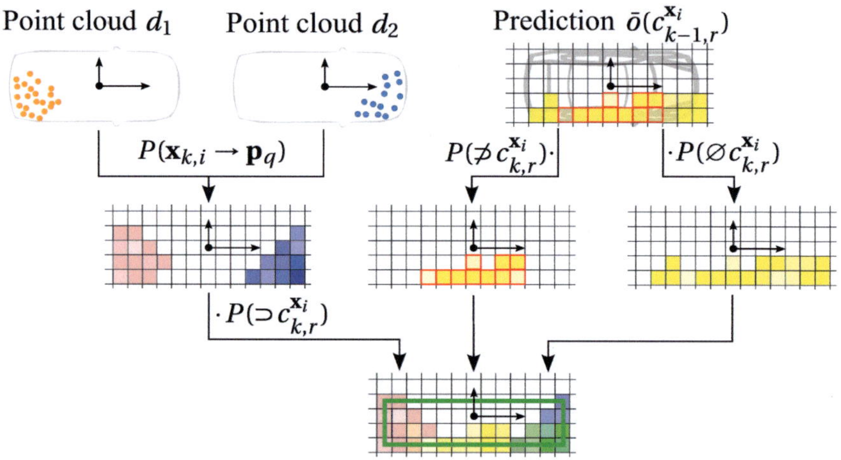

Figure 5.18: Process of the grid-based measurement composition for the track extent. Grid cell occupancies of the track $\mathbf{x}_{k,i}$ are computed as a composition of the measured cell occupancies from the associated point clouds d_1 and d_2 (orange and blue points) and the predicted cell occupancies (yellow). Occluded cells are highlighted in red. Fitting a rectangle into the ground projection of the occupied grid cells yields a measurement for the track extent (green rectangle).

The cell visibility probability $P(\supset c_{k,r}^{\mathbf{x}_i})$ is computed as follows:

$$P(\supset c_{k,r}^{\mathbf{x}_i}) = M_{\supset}^{\mathbf{x}_i}(u_{c_{k,r}}, v_{c_{k,r}}) \cdot (1 - P(\varnothing \mathbf{x}_{k,i} | \, \exists \mathbf{x}_{k,i} \mathcal{D}_{1:k})) \,. \tag{5.20}$$

The non-visibility probability of a cell due to occlusion $P(\not\supset c_{k,r}^{\mathbf{x}_i})$ is computed as follows:

$$P(\not\supset c_{k,r}^{\mathbf{x}_i}) = M_{\not\supset}^{\mathbf{x}_i}(u_{c_{k,r}}, v_{c_{k,r}}) \cdot (1 - P(\varnothing \mathbf{x}_{k,i} | \, \exists \mathbf{x}_{k,i} \mathcal{D}_{1:k})) \,. \tag{5.21}$$

For each cell $c_{k,r}^{\mathbf{x}_i}$ its filtered occupancy value $\bar{o}(c_{k,r}^{\mathbf{x}_i})$ at time step k is given by

$$\bar{o}(c_{k,r}^{\mathbf{x}_i}) = P(\supset c_{k,r}^{\mathbf{x}_i}) \cdot o(c_{k,r}^{\mathbf{x}_i}) + (P(\not\supset c_{k,r}^{\mathbf{x}_i}) + P(\varnothing c_{k,r}^{\mathbf{x}_i})) \cdot \bar{o}(c_{k-1,r}^{\mathbf{x}_i}) \,. \tag{5.22}$$

Object's geometric orientation and dimensions are obtained using a RANSAC based estimation of the main visible object surface in the top view and fitting a rectangle with this orientation into the ground projection of the occupied grid cells. Together, these parameters form the resulting composite measurement which is then used for the innovation of the track's geometric orientation and its dimensions.

6 Evaluation

6.1 Introduction

In this chapter we provide a sound evaluation of the concept presented in this thesis. FBPDATA has been evaluated on several typical scenarios that are known to bear problems for the classical data association and tracking approach. In the following, the term "classical approach" will be used as the synonym for the Tracking-by-Detection approach as described in Section 5.8.1 and illustrated in Figures 5.13a and 4.2. Both FBPDATA and the classical approach use clustered 6D point clouds as the input (we use GDBSCAN (see Section 5.7.1) for clustering and the Iterative Extended Kalman Filter (see Section 2.2.3) for point tracking in 6D). In contrast to the classical approach, in which measurements are generated by fitting rectangles to the resulting point clouds (we use RANSAC-based algorithm described in Section 5.8.3) and are then associated to the existing tracks using the GNN algorithm (see Section 2.3.1), FBPDATA uses the raw detections (clustered point clouds) as the input to the data association and performs measurement reconstruction of the track position and extent as described in Sections 5.8.4 and 5.8.5. Both algorithms use the Extended Kalman Filter (see Section 2.2.2) for the object state estimation.

Both simulated and real data have been used in the experiments. In our evaluation, we started by selecting known failure modes of the classical data association and object tracking approach and running a multitude of simulations of relatively easy as well as challenging scenarios. We then compared our approach to the classical approach on a real-world sequence that combines several of the challenges. Sections 6.2 to 6.7 describe evaluations performed on simulated data, whereas Section 6.8 deals with a real-world scenario evaluation.

6.2 Simulation tool

In order to perform a basic evaluation of the proposed data association and object tracking methods a point cloud generation tool has been developed. This simulation tool allows to model tracked objects as sets of points with fixed relative positions. Modeled object properties include dimensions, starting position, velocity, acceleration, and yaw rate. In each simulated time frame, a tracked object is modeled as being either invisible or visible by means of one or multiple detections (fragments), which consist of clustered 6D points. This allows to simulate different scenarios such as partial occlusions, splitting and merging point clouds, or objects entering and leaving the FoV of the sensors.

For each simulated frame, the tool generates lists of labeled 3D points, pre-clustered 6D points (raw detections), rectangular detections (fragments), and labeled objects. It also allows to add noise to positions and velocities of the (otherwise fixed) 3D points. In principle, the output of the tool may be used as input data for Point Tracking, Clustering, Object Detection, and Object Tracking modules, i.e., as the input at different stages of the object tracking. In our evaluation, however, we used only pre-clustered point clouds, which served as simulated (partial or whole) object detections for both FBPDATA and the classical approach.

Pre-clustering the point clouds and setting part of them to invisible mode allowed us to relatively easily generate some typical scenarios such as partial occlusions, split and merged detections, and missing point correspondences. In order to evaluate the system and the proposed approach we used several simulated scenarios, four of which are described in detail in Sections 6.3 to 6.6. Additionally, we have performed a robustness evaluation by adding white Gaussian noise to the point positions and by deleting individual points. This is described in Section 6.7.

Figures 6.1 and 6.2 show the main GUIs of the simulation tool. Figure 6.1 shows the tool dialog for configuring detection fragments and corresponding 3D points. The fragments may be framewise set to invisible mode in order to model splits or partial occlusions. Figure 6.2 shows the dialog for configuring detection visibility for each track.

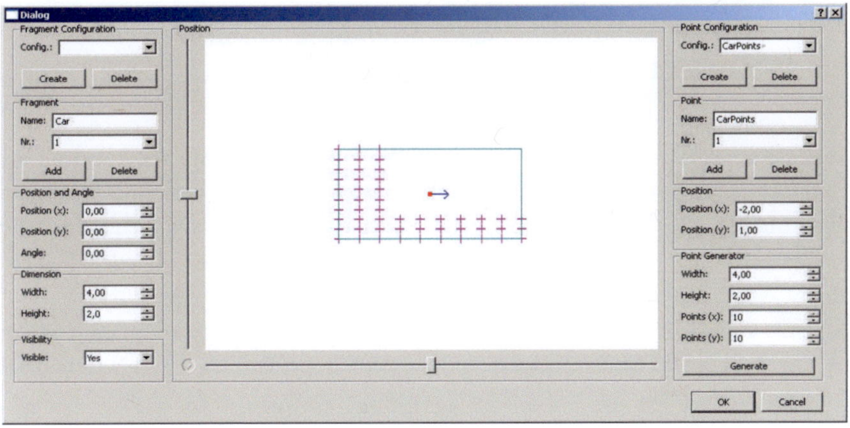

Figure 6.1: GUI of the simulation tool: point cloud configuration.

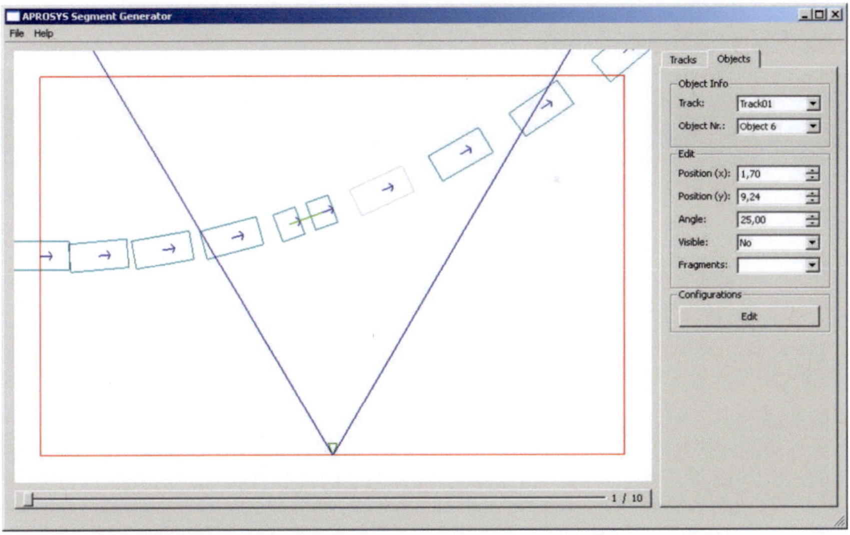

Figure 6.2: GUI of the simulation tool: framewise track configuration.

6.3 Simulated scenario 1: Object crossing the field of view

In the first scenario, an object crosses the field of view (FoV) of the sensors from left to right while the sensor-carrying vehicle remains stationary. Figure 6.3 illustrates this scenario. The sensor-carrying vehicle is visualized by a black rectangle at the image bottom. The borders of the FoV of the stereo camera are visualized as red lines. The observed object (visualized as a blue rectangle) is modeled by means of a point cloud which is depicted by black dots. The points are colored green as soon as they become visible and are being clustered. The cluster centroid is visualized by a thick green dot.

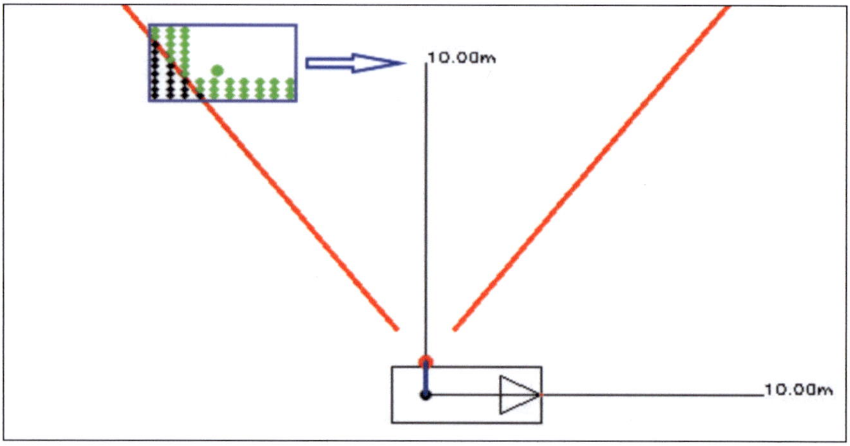

Figure 6.3: Top view of a simple scenario with an object crossing the FoV of the sensors (red lines). The ego vehicle remains stationary. The observed object is modeled by a point cloud. The points are clustered and build a detection as soon as they enter the FoV (green dots). Thick green dot visualizes the centroid of the cluster. Points beyond the FoV are depicted in black. They are not "seen" by the tracking system.

Figure 6.4 shows simulated clusters (a) and results of the object detection, data association, and tracking achieved by the classical approach (b) and FBPDATA (c).

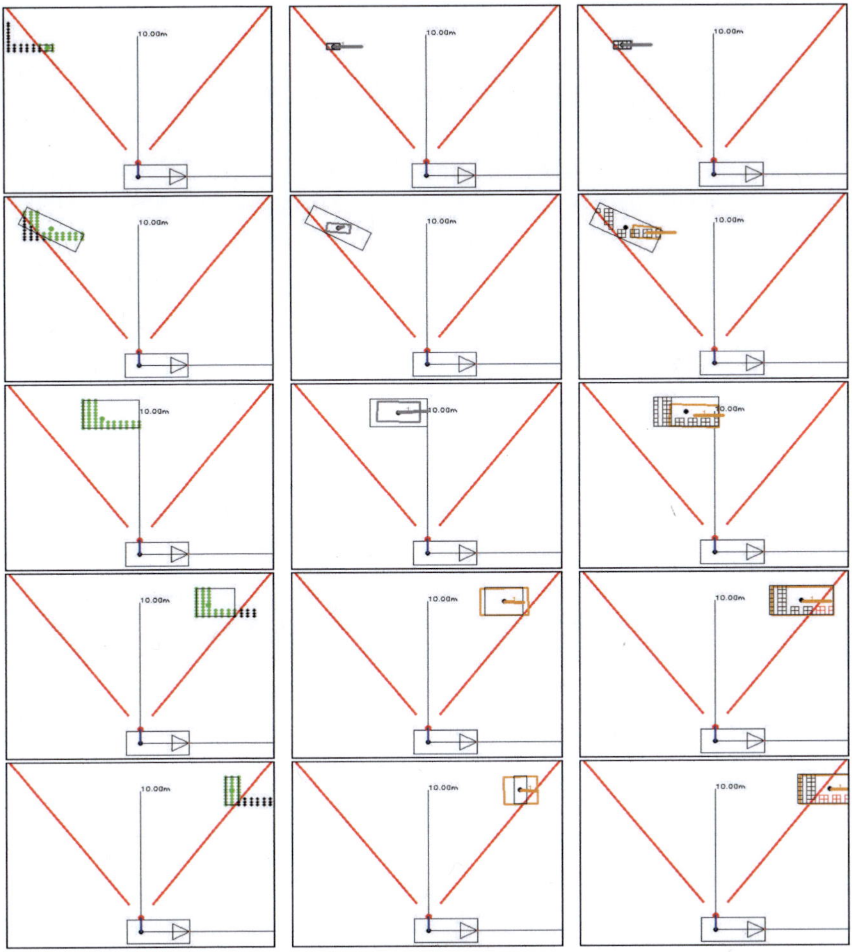

(a) Simulated clusters

(b) Tracking results: classical approach

(c) Tracking results: FBPDATA

Figure 6.4: Tracking results for a simple simulated scenario with an object crossing the FoV of the sensors (top view; Frames 2, 3, 4, 8, 10).

The left column shows the simulated clusters. At the beginning, when the object enters the FoV of the sensors, only a small set of points is visible. When the visible portion of the object becomes larger, the point cluster seems to "grow". Its centroid moves towards the real object centroid and remains there for a couple of frames. Towards the end of the sequence, when the object is leaving the FoV borders, the visible part becomes smaller again. The cluster seems to "shrink". Its centroid moves further towards the rear part of the object.

The second column shows the results of the object tracking using the classical data association and object tracking approach. Fitting a rectangular into the clustered points results in an object detection. This is plotted as a black rectangle. The instantiated but not yet confirmed object is depicted in gray. The orange rectangle visualizes the results of filtering (the tracked and confirmed object). The thick orange line visualizes the estimated object velocity.

At first, when the object enters the FoV, its initial velocity estimation is derived from the velocities of the clustered points. Thus, it matches the ground truth value. However, the cluster centroid "jumps" in the course of the next frames, resulting in a reduced velocity estimation. The object seems to decelerate. Furthermore, the direction of the motion is estimated incorrectly. This is due to the fact that the detection seems to have rotated between the frames, which is interpreted as a yaw. As soon as the entire object becomes visible and the cluster centroid adheres to the real object centroid, the object seems to accelerate. After a short transient process, the velocity estimation finally approaches the ground truth and the yaw rate becomes zero. However, this lasts only for a few frames. As soon as the object starts leaving the FoV, it seems to "stick" to the FoV border, decelerating again.

The third column shows the results of the object tracking using FBPDATA. Object detections are shown as black rectangles as well. Occlusion handling is done by means of the grid-based object representation. Occupied cells of the grid are visualized by small black rectangles. Occupied cells that are estimated as being occluded are colored red. As one can see, the orange line, which visualizes the estimated object velocity, matches the real object velocity pretty well through the whole sequence despite "jumps" of the cluster centroid. The object position is also estimated pretty well throughout the whole sequence starting with Frame 3 (second row).

The relevant parameters of the estimated object state are plotted in Figure 6.5.

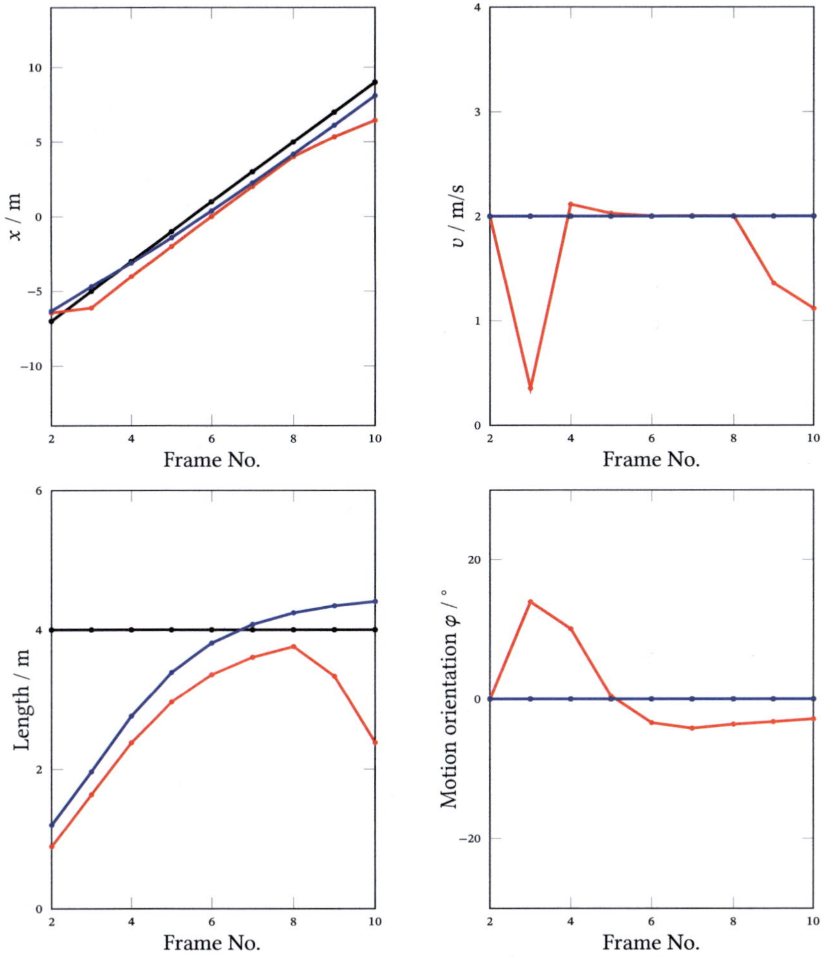

Figure 6.5: Simple simulated scenario with an object crossing the FoV of the sensors: plots of the lateral position x, speed v, length l, and motion orientation angle φ: classical approach (red), FBPDATA (blue) and ground truth (black).

As expected, tracking based on the estimated point cloud centroid suffers from the effects of partial occlusion. It causes an erroneous underestimation of the object's velocity followed by an acceleration as soon as the entire object becomes visible. At the end of the sequence, while the object leaves the FoV of the cameras, the centroid of the visible points becomes slower again causing the track to decelerate and to partially remain in the FoV. In contrast to that behavior, FBPDATA manages to correctly estimate the object parameters and even to correctly track the object when it's almost completely outside of the field of view of the sensors.

6.4 Simulated scenario 2: Split detection due to a clustering error

The second experiment is based on the first one but additionally simulates a split detection due to a clustering error in Frame 7. This is shown in Figure 6.6.

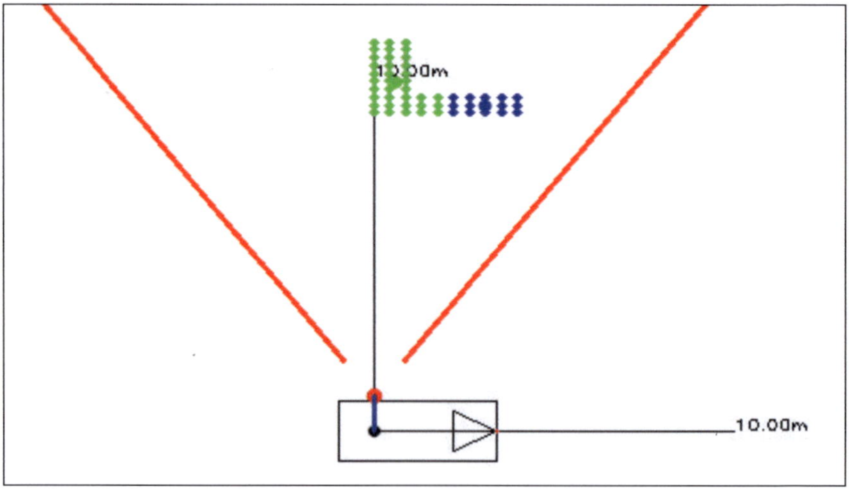

Figure 6.6: Frame 7 of the second scenario: Object is modeled by two distinct point clusters (depicted in green and blue). Thick blue and green dots visualize cluster centroids.

Figure 6.7 shows simulated clusters and results of the object detection, data association, and tracking achieved by the classical approach and FBPDATA. The second column shows tracking results of the classical approach. The points are recognized as a single cloud when the object enters the FoV. Later, the point cloud is split into two parts. This causes instantiation of a new track from the smaller point cloud. The bigger one is associated to the already tracked object. This seems to decelerate rapidly due to the "jump" of the centroid of the associated point cloud. In the following frames the entire object is detected as a whole again. As soon as this happens, the track seems to accelerate. In contrast to that behavior, FBPDATA manages to correctly estimate the object parameters in spite of the split as shown in the third column. Even though the cloud split produces two partial detections, the overall state estimation is not affected. The relevant parameters of the estimated object state are plotted in Figure 6.8.

(a) Simulated clusters

(b) Tracking results: classical approach

(c) Tracking results: FBPDATA

Figure 6.7: Tracking results for a simple simulated scenario with a split detection (top view; frames 2, 3, 7, 8, 10).

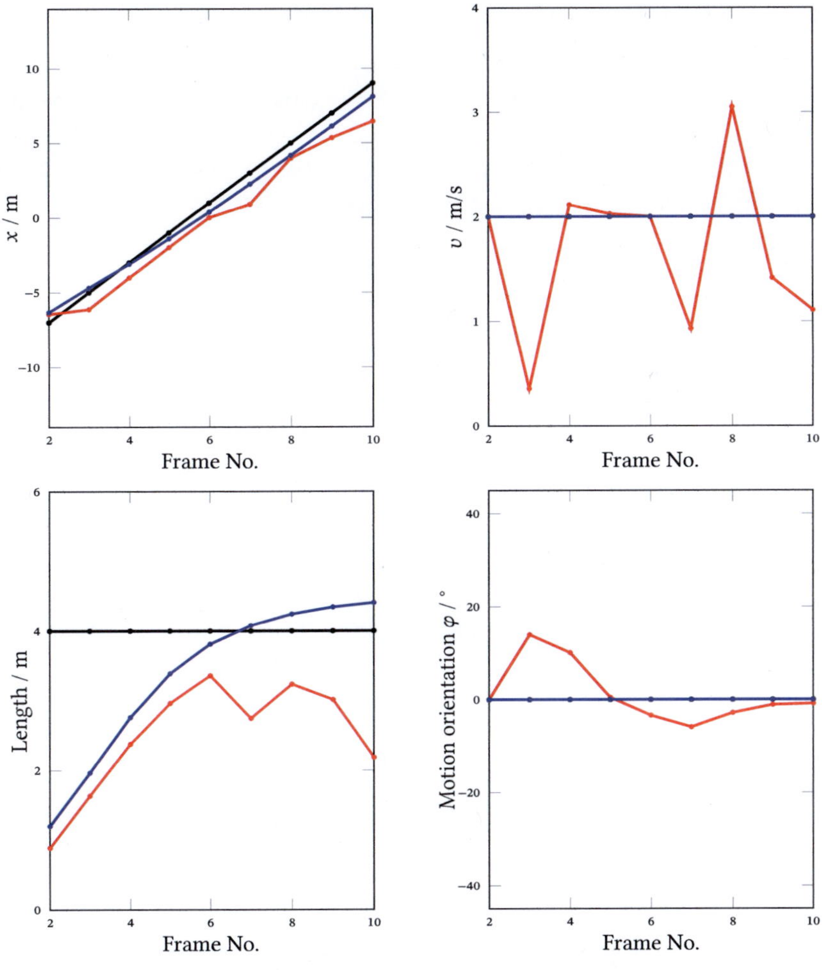

Figure 6.8: Simulated scenario with a split detection: plots of the lateral position x, speed v, length l, and motion orientation angle φ: classical approach (red), FBPDATA (blue) and ground truth (black).

6.5 Simulated scenario 3: Occlusion

Figure 6.9 shows a simple occlusion scenarios with two objects. In this scenario an object, which is depicted in orange, is driving through the field of view being occluded both by the FoV borders (visualized as red lines) and by another stationary object in the foreground (depicted in magenta).

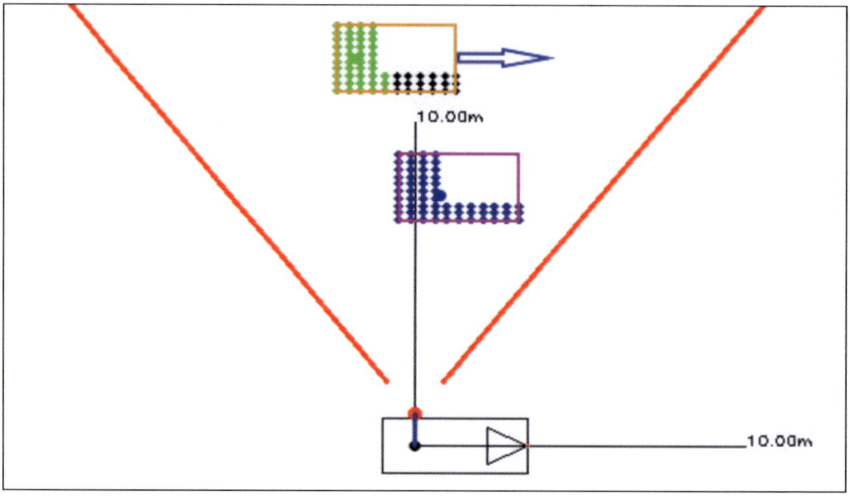

Figure 6.9: Simulated occlusion scene (top view): Partial occlusion of the background object (orange) due to a foreground object (magenta).

Figure 6.10 and Figure 6.11 show a comparison of the results achieved by the classical data association and tracking approach and FBPDATA. The classical association and tracking approach suffers from the occlusion effects. They lead to considerable corruption of the position and velocity estimation of the background object and even to termination of the corresponding track and re-instantiation of a new one as shown in Figure 6.10b and Figure 6.11. Due to the occlusion, results of the classical approach differ considerably from the ground truth beginning with Frame 11. The object seems to decelerate and to shrink. Missing detections finally lead to track termination in Frame 17. In Frame 19 a new track has to be instantiated.

Unlike the classical approach, FBPDATA manages to maintain both tracks and to correctly update tracks' parameters through the occlusion phases. Figure 6.10c visualizes tracking results of FBPDATA together with the underlying grid-based object representation. The occupied grid cells are depicted as black rectangles. Occluded but still tracked grid cells are colored red.

Figure 6.11 shows plots of some of the estimated object parameters delivered by both approaches in comparison to the ground truth.

(a) Simulated clusters

(b) Tracking results: classical approach

(c) Tracking results: FBPDATA

Figure 6.10: Tracking results for a simple simulated occlusion scenario (top view; frames 10, 14, 18, 20, 23, 25).

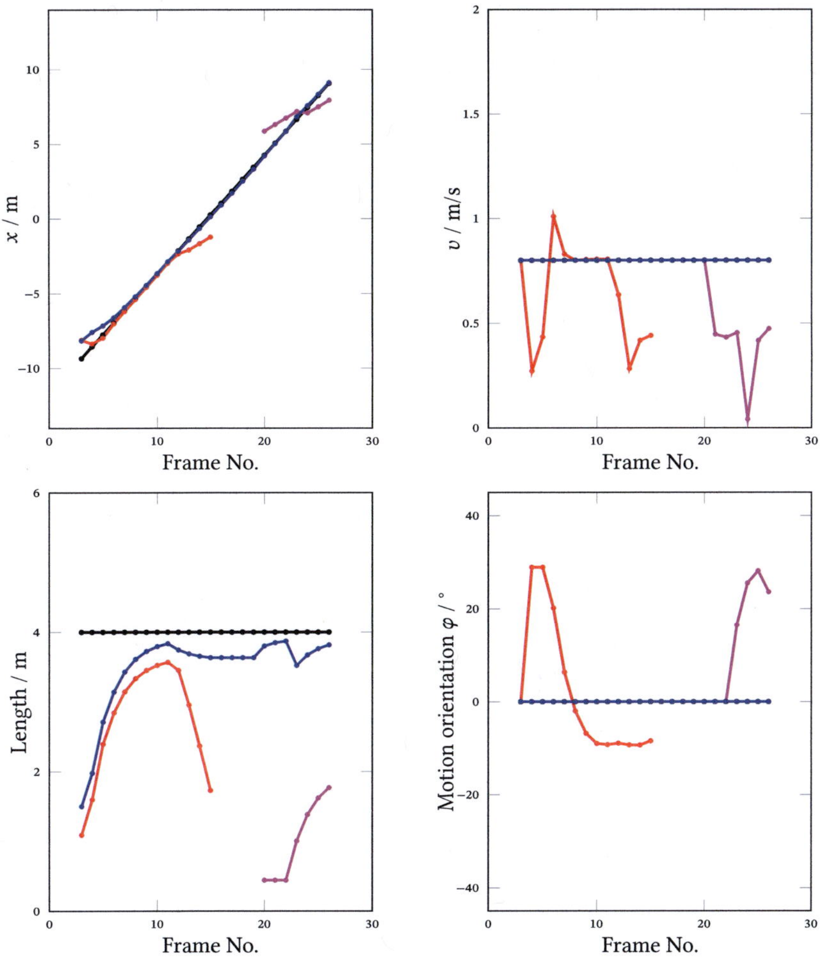

Figure 6.11: Simulated occlusion scenario: plots of the lateral position x, speed v, length l, and motion orientation angle φ of the upper object: classical approach (red and magenta), FBPDATA (blue) and ground truth (black).

6.6 Simulated scenario 4: Splitting and merging point clouds

Figure 6.12 shows another scenario with two objects. In this scenario, one object approaches the sensor-carrying vehicle and turns back while another object is crossing the FoV. In the middle of the sequence (Frame 9) there is a simultaneous merge and split of the corresponding point clouds followed by a merge in the next frame. The respective point clusters are depicted in Figures 6.13 and 6.14.

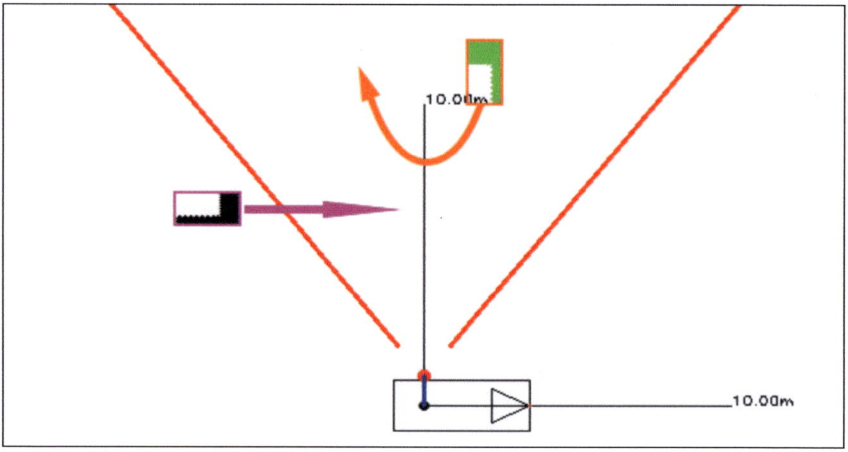

Figure 6.12: Simulated Split & Merge scene (top view): simulated points and corresponding ground truth objects.

The output of both data association and tracking algorithms for these and three further frames of the "Split and Merge" sequence are shown in Figure 6.15. In Frame 9, the lower track (colored magenta) is associated with the small partial detection which results from a split of the lower point cloud. The centroid of the magenta point cloud moves to the rear part of the object causing a deceleration of the track. The large merged detection is associated with the upper track (colored orange), causing this to grow and to slightly accelerate towards the sensor-carrying vehicle instead of moving to the left.

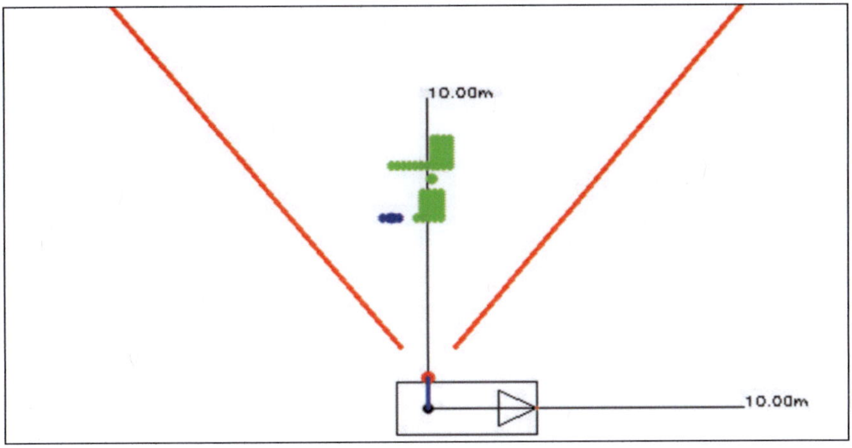

Figure 6.13: Simulated Split & Merge scene (top view, Frame 9): merge. The simulated point cluster is depicted in green. Thick green dot visualizes the centroid of the cluster.

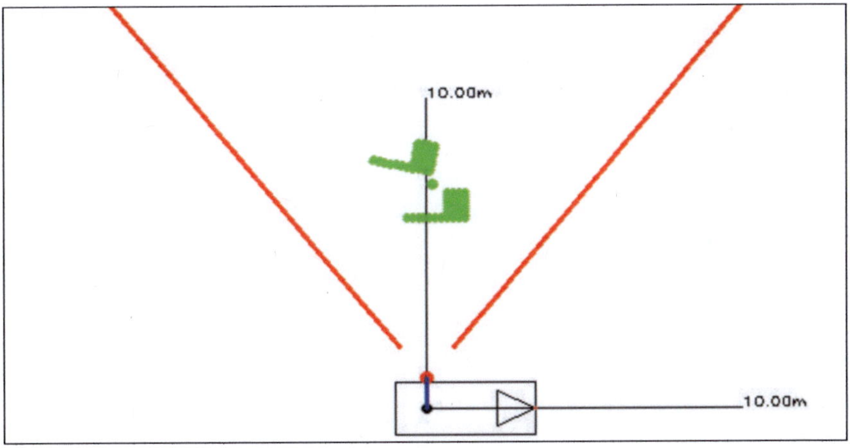

Figure 6.14: Simulated Split & Merge scene (top view, Frame 10): simultaneous split and merge. The simulated point clusters are depicted in green and blue. Thick green dot visualizes the centroid of the green cluster.

In the next frame, the small point cloud is merged with the large one as shown in Figure 6.14. The lower track does not get any associated detection and remains almost on the same spot adopting the predicted low speed value. The upper track is associated with the merged detection. The centroid of this large point cluster also happens to remain on the same spot, causing the upper track to abruptly decelerate. The track continues growing. The impact of these two effects show through in the next couple of frames. In Frame 11 and in the following frames non-corrupted detections are obtained again. However, upper detection cannot be associated with the correct track anymore since it is outside of the track's gate. A new track has to be instantiated for this detection (depicted in gray). Detection corruption leaves its mark on the lower track too. It has to strongly accelerate in order to compensate for the previous deceleration phase and needs several frames to recover from the induced acceleration oscillation.

In contrast to such behavior, FBPDATA manages to maintain both tracks and to reasonably update tracks' parameters.

Figure 6.16 and Figure 6.17 show a comparison of the relevant track parameter of the upper and the lower object for both approaches in comparison.

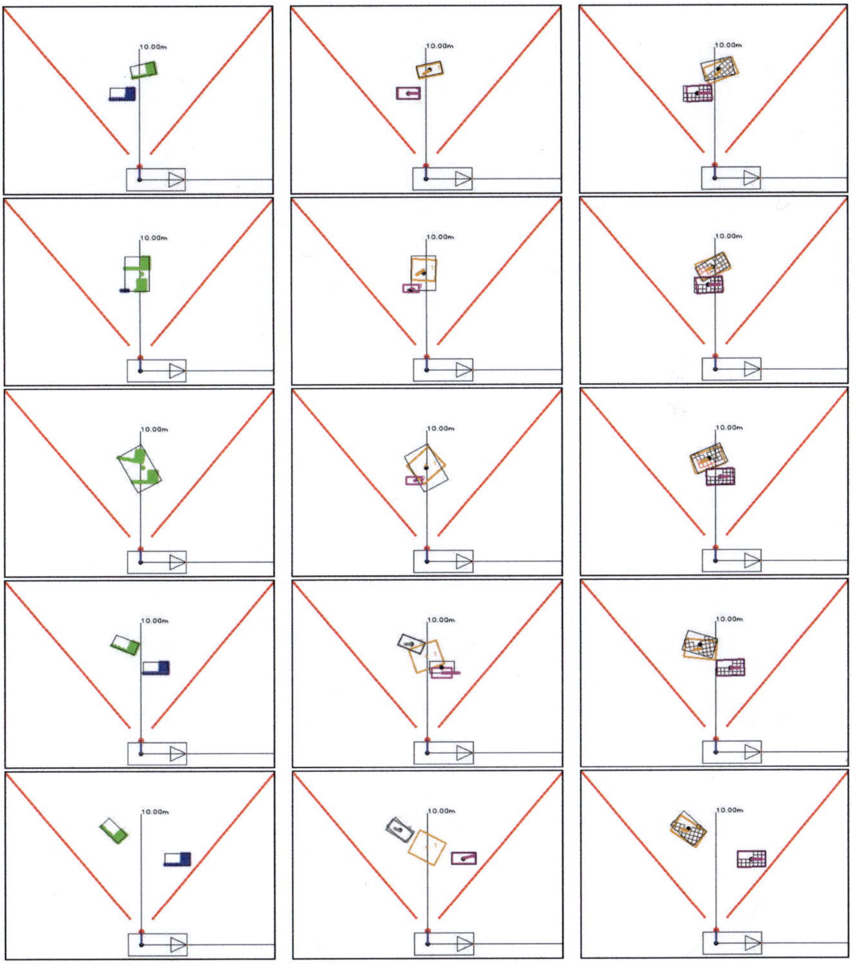

(a) Simulated clusters **(b)** Tracking results: classical approach **(c)** Tracking results: FBPDATA

Figure 6.15: Tracking results for a simulated scenario with splitting and merging point clouds (top view; frames 8, 9, 10, 11, 13).

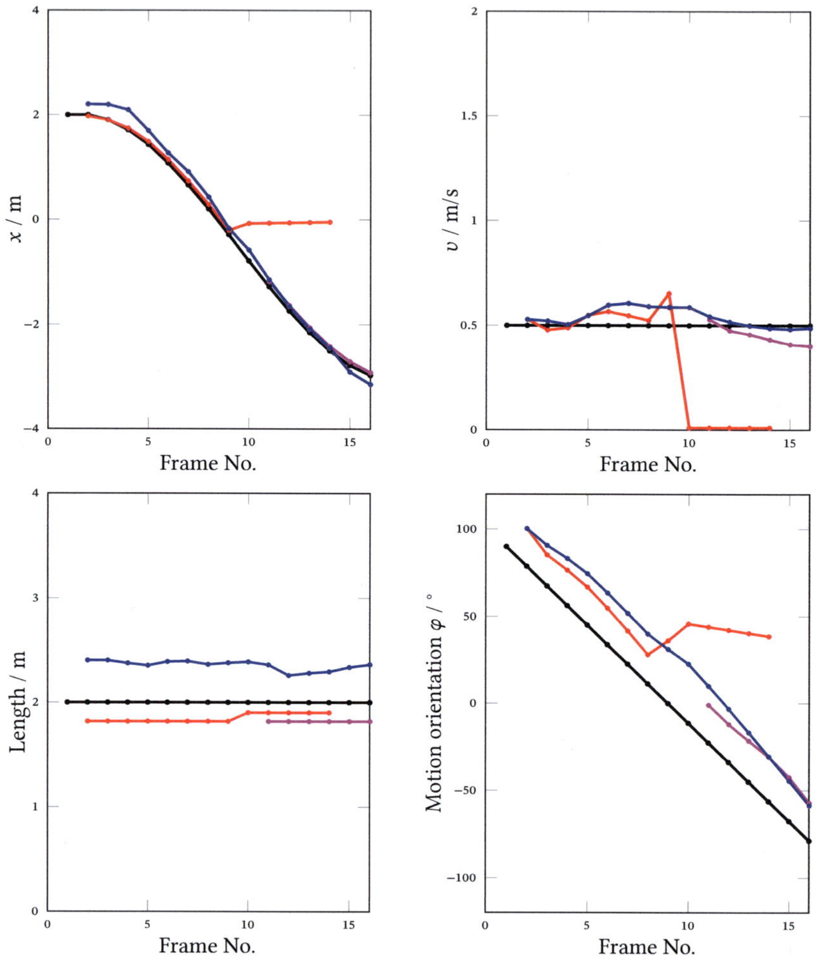

Figure 6.16: Simulated Split & Merge scenario: plots of the lateral position x, speed v, length l, and motion orientation angle φ of the upper object: classical approach (red and magenta), FBPDATA (blue) and ground truth (black).

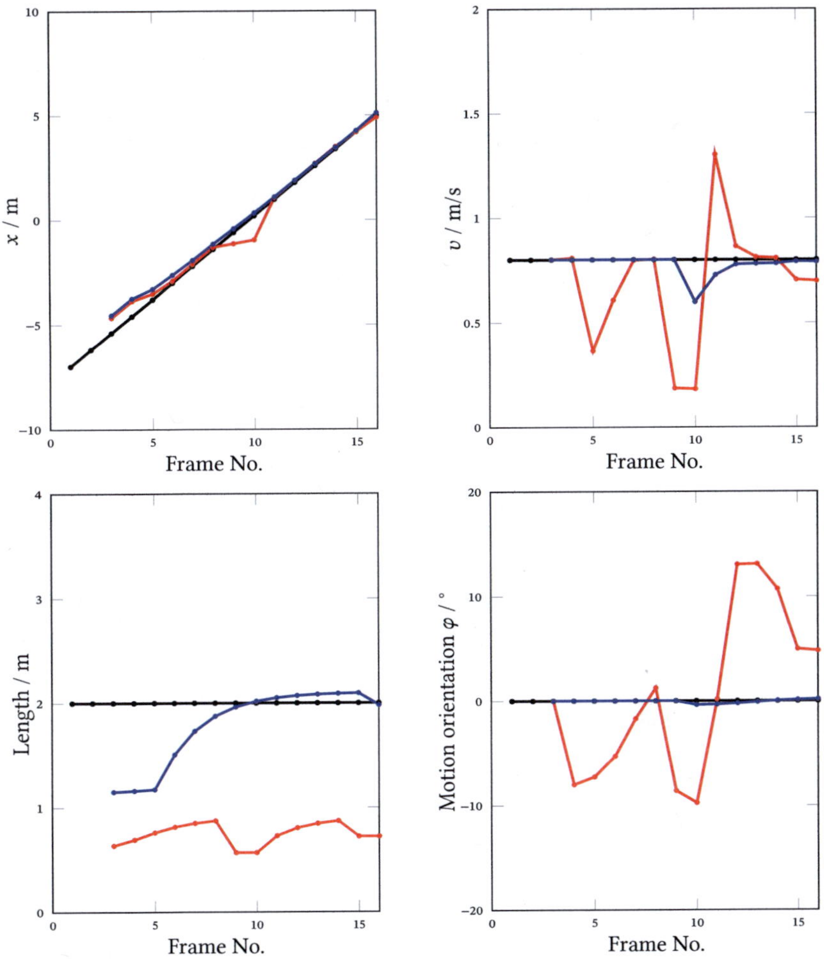

Figure 6.17: Simulated Split & Merge scenario: plots of the lateral position x, speed v, length l, and motion orientation angle φ of the lower object: classical approach (red), FBPDATA (blue) and ground truth (black).

6.7 Robustness evaluation

We conducted several experiments to evaluate the robustness of the proposed approach with regards to impact of noise and missing correspondences. For noise robustness evaluation we added white Gaussian noise to the 3D position of the simulated points in each frame and computed variance of all relevant object parameters. Section 6.7.1 discusses the results of this evaluation. The robustness with regard to point tracking failures, namely missing point correspondences, was evaluated in a similar way by randomly deleting multiple points in each frame. Results of this evaluation are discussed in Section 6.7.2.

6.7.1 Noise robustness

Figures 6.19 – 6.22 show exemplary results of the noise robustness evaluation for the 13th frame of the occlusion sequence from Section 6.5. The 13th frame is a particularly interesting example since it is one of the frames in which the rear object starts to be occluded by the object in the foreground as shown in Figure 6.18.

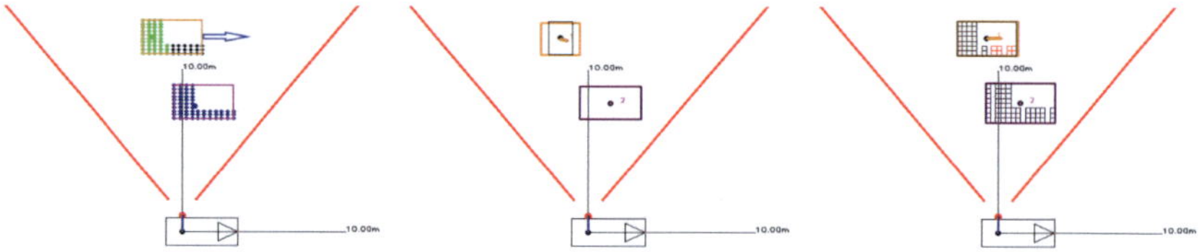

(a) Simulated point clusters (green and blue) and ground truth objects

(b) Tracks provided by the classical approach

(c) Tracks provided by FBPDATA

Figure 6.18: Simulated occlusion scene, Frame 13: Simulated clusters and ground truth objects (a) and tracking results of the classical approach (b) and FBPDATA (c) (no noise added).

The standard deviation of noise added to the points was steadily varied from 0.1 m to 0.9 m. For each step we performed 50 repetitions. In Figures 6.19, 6.20, 6.21, and 6.22 the resulting mean and standard deviation of the estimates of object position, speed, motion orientation, box orientation, length, and width of the rear object are plotted for different added noise values.

As expected, increasing noise leads to increasing variance of the estimates of object position, velocity, dimensions and orientation for both approaches. Especially in the case of length, width and geometric orientation both approaches show a comparable behavior: noisy point positions lead to growing object dimensions and almost random orientation of the object box.

However, one can see a great difference regarding variances of object position and velocity estimates of both approaches. The variances of the FBPDATA estimates are less then those of the classical approach.

One thing that has to be explained right away is the strong bias of the estimates of the object length, lateral position, and lateral velocity in the classical approach. They are due to the lacking occlusion handling of the classical approach. In Frame 13, only a part of the rear object is detected (clearly seen in Figure 6.18b). Corrupted object detection leads to a strong underestimation of the object length, lateral position and lateral velocity compared to FBPDATA, which "reconstructs" the correct measurement. This effect can also be seen in the simulation without added noise, as discussed in Section 6.5.

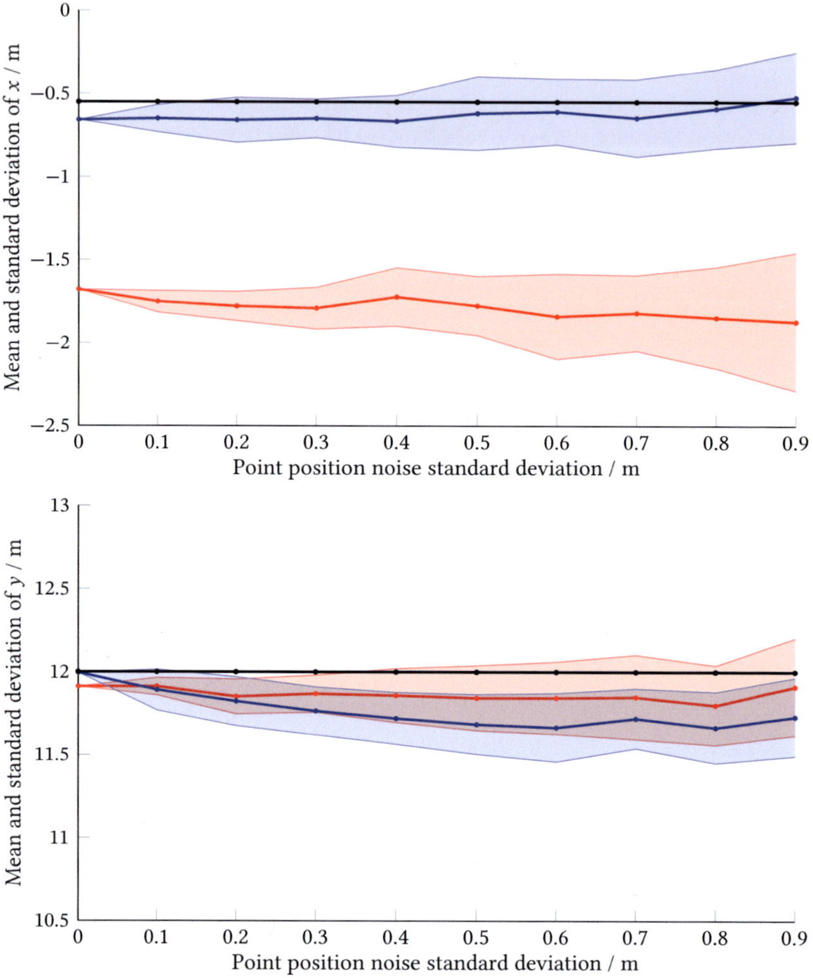

Figure 6.19: Simulated occlusion scenario with added noise: plots of mean and standard deviation of the position of the rear object in dependence on standard deviation of added noise: classical approach (red), FBPDATA (blue) and ground truth (black).

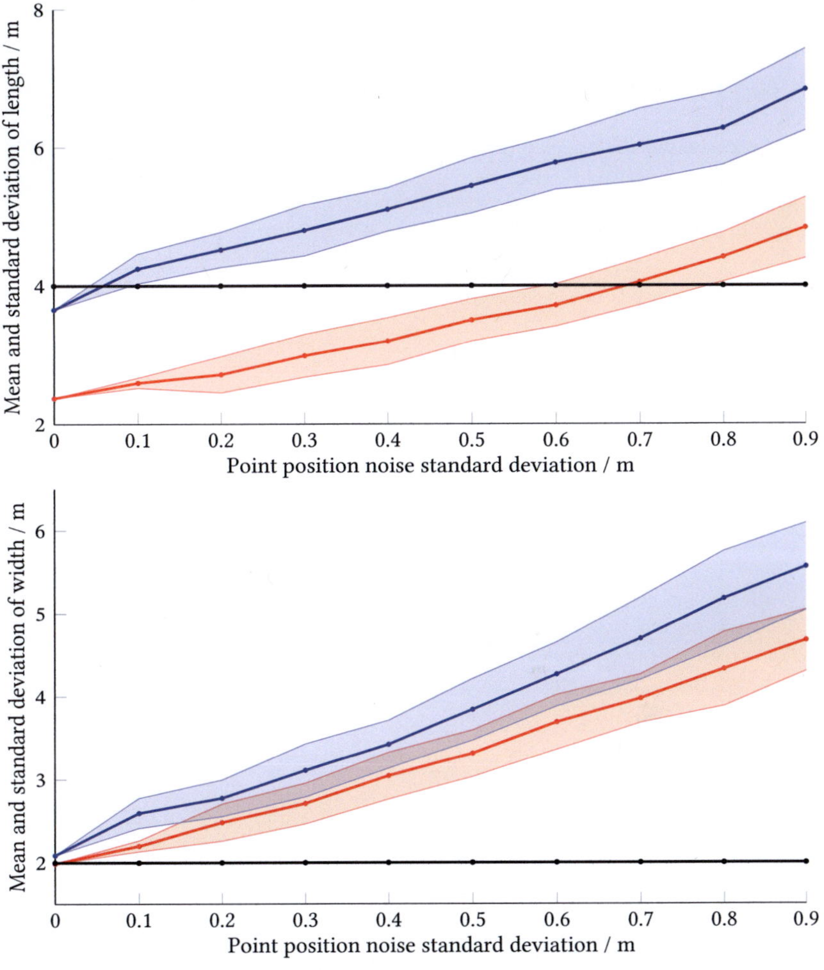

Figure 6.20: Simulated occlusion scenario with added noise: plots of mean and standard deviation of the dimensions of the rear object in dependence on standard deviation of added noise: classical approach (red), FBPDATA (blue) and ground truth (black).

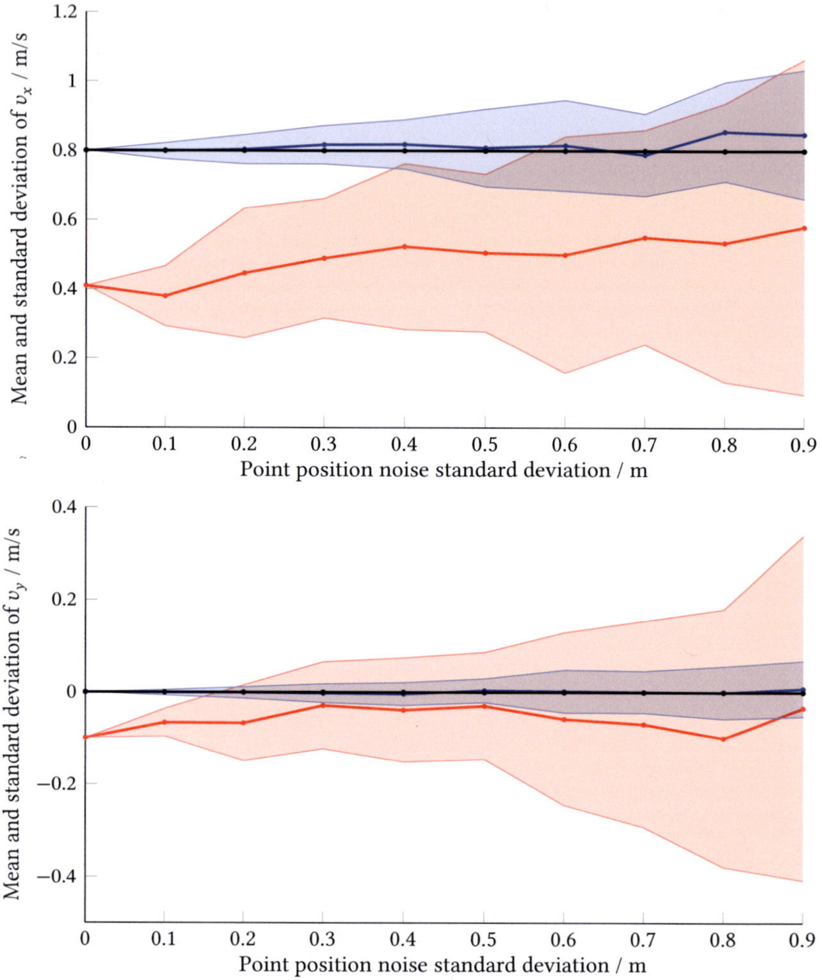

Figure 6.21: Simulated occlusion scenario with added noise: plots of mean and standard deviation of the velocity components of the rear object in dependence on standard deviation of added noise: classical approach (red), FBPDATA (blue) and ground truth (black).

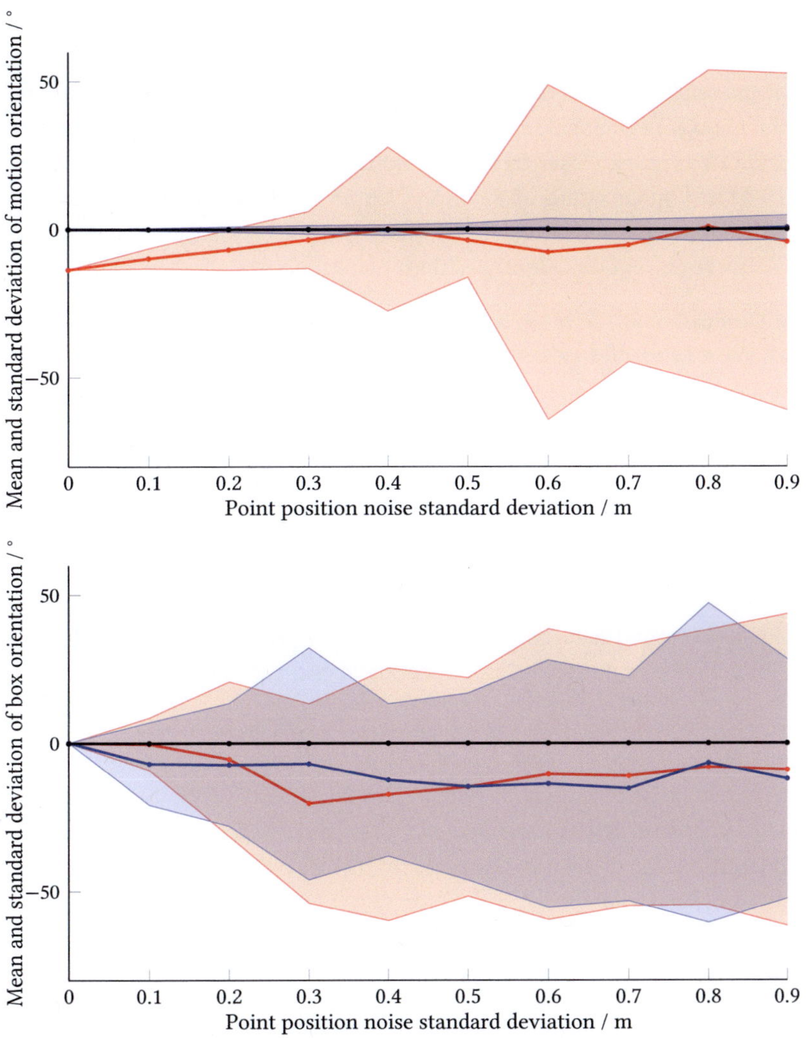

Figure 6.22: Simulated occlusion scenario with added noise: plots of mean and standard deviation of the motion orientation and the geometric orientation of the rear object in dependence on standard deviation of added noise: classical approach (red), FBPDATA (blue) and ground truth (black).

In case of the lateral object position the major effect is, in fact, the bias of the mean value estimation of the classical approach (red hose). This is due to the fact that the centroid of the visible points is tracked, which in Frame 13 is far behind the real object centroid. In contrast to this, lateral object position estimated by FBPDATA is much closer to the ground truth value. A small bias is due to the grid-related quantization of the object length estimation that provides the basis for the lateral position estimate. Besides, the FBPDATA shows a slightly lower variance regarding the lateral position.

Longitudinal object position is estimated quite well by both approaches. A general bias towards smaller values is due to the L-shaped simulation of the respective point cloud, or more specifically due to unequal impact of positive and negative values of added longitudinal noise on the longer part of the L-shape. Positive y values of the added noise pull the corresponding points away from the bounding box border towards the object center. Shifts of individual points towards object center, however, do not lead to any major changes in the object shape. In contrast, in case of negative values, points are pulled out of the bounding box. This causes changes in object shape in the respective area and leads to an estimated rotation of the object box and reduced longitudinal position. In FBPDATA this effect is even slightly increased due to the aforementioned grid-related quantization effects.

The major difference with regard to variance can be observed for the velocity components v_x and v_y. Both lateral and longitudinal velocity components show much less variance in case of FBPDATA than in case of the classical approach. As stated before, here too, estimates of the classical approach show a strong bias (underestimation of velocity) whereas FBPDATA estimates are extremely close to the ground truth values.

6.7.2 Missing point correspondences

Missing point correspondences between frames were modeled by randomly deleting simulated points in each frame. Each point could be deleted with a probability P_{del} that we varied from 0.1 to 0.6. Again, for each P_{del} value, 50 runs were executed.

Figures 6.23, 6.24, 6.25, and 6.26 show results of this evaluation for the 13th frame of the aforementioned occlusion sequence. Again, mean and standard deviation of object position, speed, motion orientation, box orientation, length, and width of the rear object are plotted for different values of P_{del}.

The results are comparable to those of the noise robustness evaluation with respect to the estimated object position. Other parameters behave quite differently. Contrary to the previous experiment, deletion of individual points has almost no effect on the estimation of object position and dimensions for both evaluated approaches. The same holds for the estimated object velocity. In the case of FBPDATA there is no influence at all – even a few tracked points suffice for a correct velocity estimation. This also means a correct estimation of the motion direction. The impact on the orientation of the object bounding box is much less than in the experiment with added noise. In the case of FBPDATA it starts to vary only for $P_{del} > 30\%$.

Overall, one can state that FBPDATA provides a stable, robust tracking despite missed correspondences and is less sensitive to noise than the classical approach.

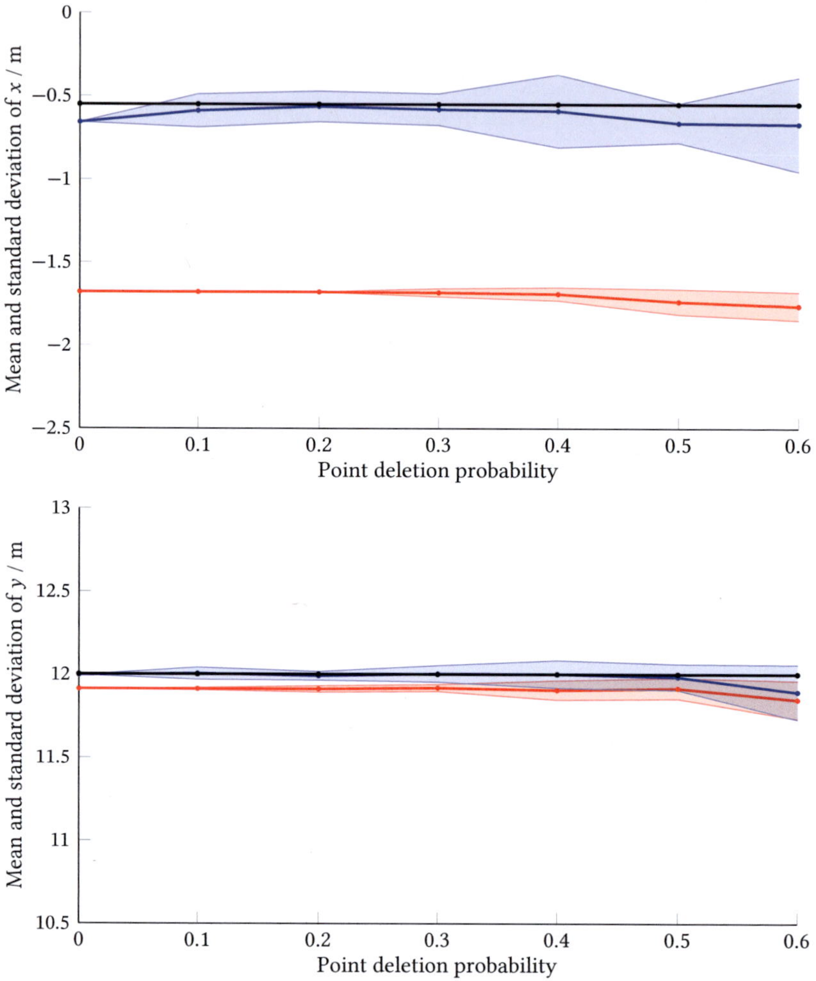

Figure 6.23: Occlusion scenario with missing point correspondences simulation: plots of mean and standard deviation of the position of the rear object in dependence on point deletion probability P_{del}: classical approach (red), FBPDATA (blue) and ground truth (black).

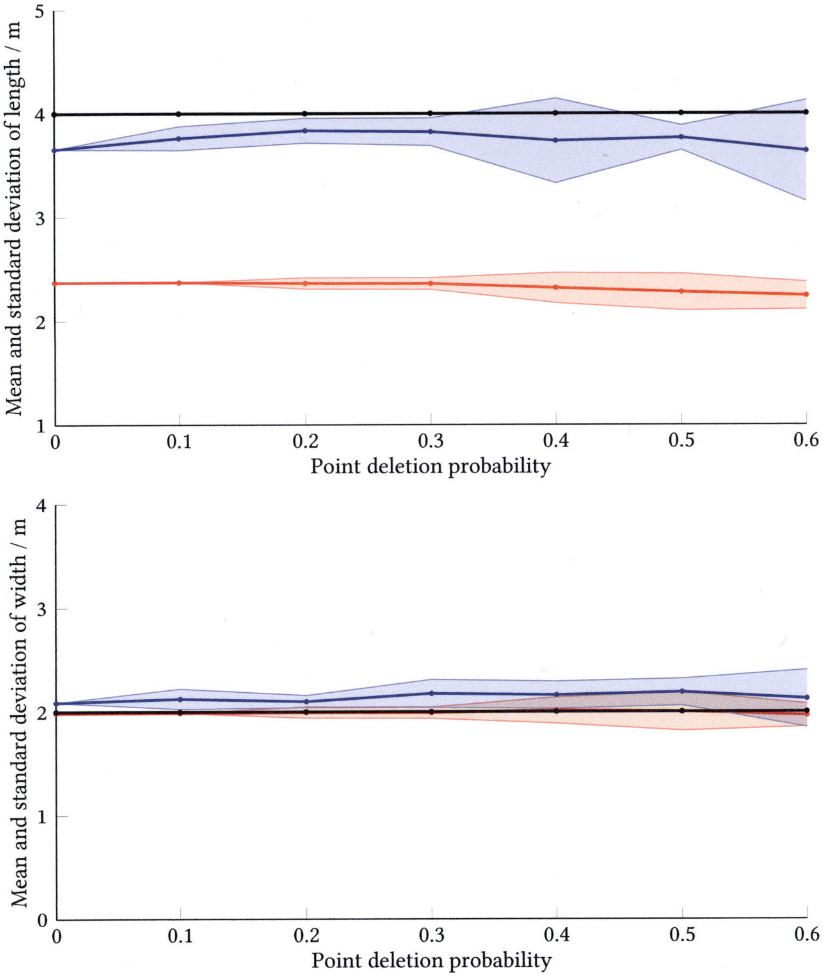

Figure 6.24: Occlusion scenario with missing point correspondences simulation: plots of mean and standard deviation of the dimensions of the rear object in dependence on point deletion probability P_{del}: classical approach (red), FBPDATA (blue) and ground truth (black).

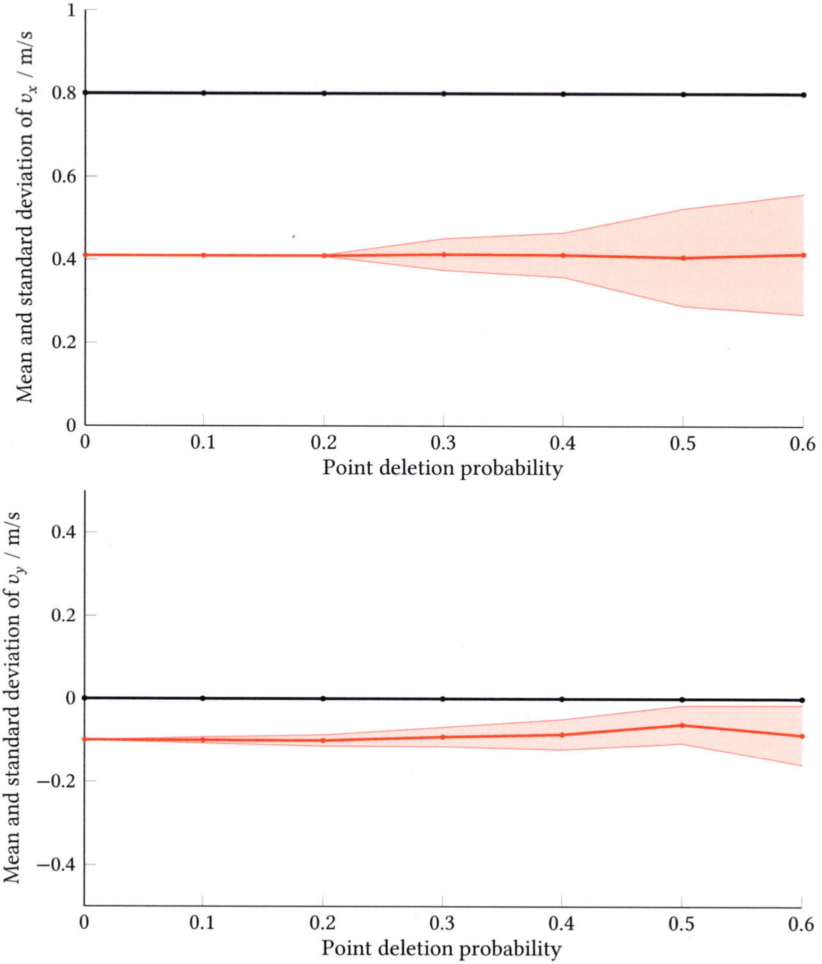

Figure 6.25: Occlusion scenario with missing point correspondences simulation: plots of mean and standard deviation of the velocity components of the rear object in dependence on point deletion probability P_{del}: classical approach (red), FBPDATA (blue) and ground truth (black).

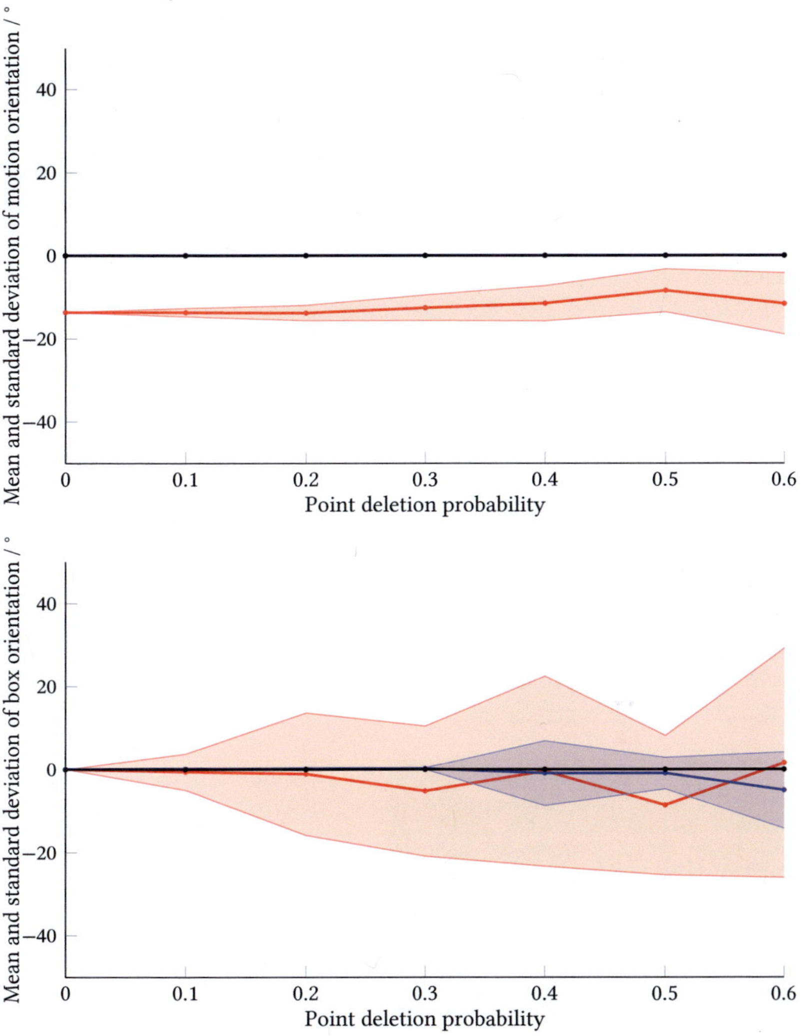

Figure 6.26: Occlusion scenario with missing point correspondences simulation: plots of mean and standard deviation of the estimated motion orientation and the box orientation of the rear object in dependence on point deletion probability P_{del}: classical approach (red), FBPDATA (blue) and ground truth (black).

6.8 Real world scenario: Dynamic occlusion

For the evaluation of our approach on the real-world data we focused on typical scenarios that challenge object trackers. We perform our evaluation based on video sequences obtained using a TYZX stereo camera [Woo06]. In contrast to the aforementioned MOT performance evaluation which operates in the 2D image domain [Gei12], we perform our evaluation based on the ground truth measured directly in the 3D space, hence allowing to evaluate not only the performance of the object detection and data association but also the state estimation in 3D, including object velocities, which are crucial in a pre-crash application.

Figure 6.27 shows frames from a real-world sequence involving two relevant objects. The foreground object is a person who is crossing the field of view of the camera, while the car in the background remains stationary. The motion of the person causes a dynamic occlusion of different car portions starting from the rear end. As soon as the person starts occluding the car, only the front part of the latter can be detected (partial detection). After 9 frames the rear part of the car starts showing again, while the front part is still visible. This leads to two separately detected parts (split detection). Later on, only the rear portion of the car is visible, while the front part becomes occluded (partial detection). Finally, the entire car becomes visible again.

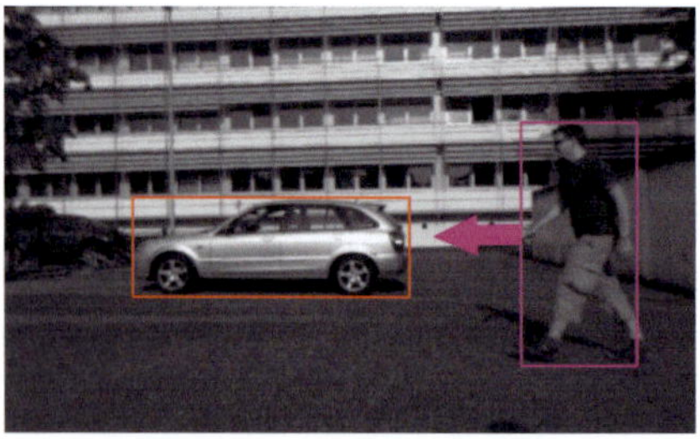

(a) Image of the left camera

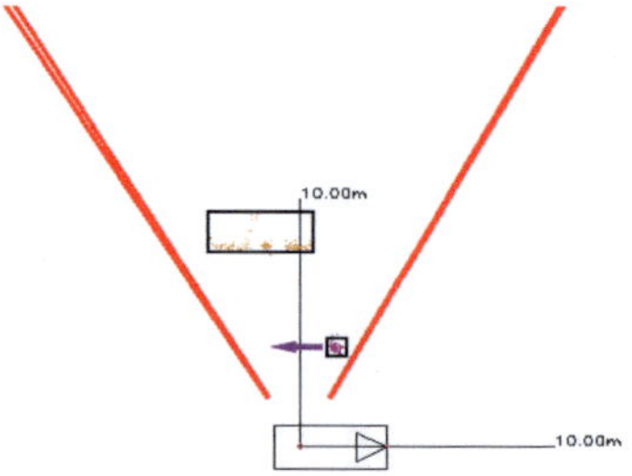

(b) Top view: point clusters and ground truth objects

Figure 6.27: Real world sequence: pedestrian walking in front of a car.

This scenario is equivalent to the commonly observed pattern for the side-looking camera, where a relatively thin object in the foreground (a pedestrian, a pole etc.) is occluding a relevant object in the background. We chose a sequence with a stationary camera and a stationary background object in order to better focus on the achieved algorithm results related to handling occlusions and occlusion-related partial and split detections.

Figure 6.28 shows clustering results as well as the results of object tracking achieved by both approaches. The left column shows the results produced by the clustering algorithm in the top view projection. The middle column shows object detection and tracking results of the classical approach (thin black and thick colored cuboids). In the right column, tracking results of FBPDATA are visualized. In addition to the tracked objects, the images show occupied grid cells of both foreground and background objects, the appearance mask of the foreground object (as a semi-transparent overlay), and occupied grid cells of the background object that are recognized to be occluded (red).

In Figure 6.29 object position, length, speed, and dynamic orientation of the rear object are plotted. From Frame 19 on, the person in the foreground starts occluding the car. Only a part of the points belonging to the rear object are detected in the consecutive frames. The centroid of the respective point cloud moves to the left. Application of the classical approach leads to a decrease of the estimated lateral object position (x); the estimated object centroid starts moving to the left gaining speed. Short after the rear part of the car starts showing again, a new object is created (cyan box). As the respective point cloud increases in size, its centroid moves to the left and the object also gains speed. Starting from Frame 45 and further on, the orange track receives no detection and finally gets deleted in Frame 47.

In contrast to that behavior, FBPDATA keeps the occluded object parts and reconstructs the correct object extent despite the occlusion. The original object position is maintained as well. Later on, when the split detection is obtained, both detected point clouds are correctly associated to the orange track allowing for the correct update of the track position, speed, and extent.

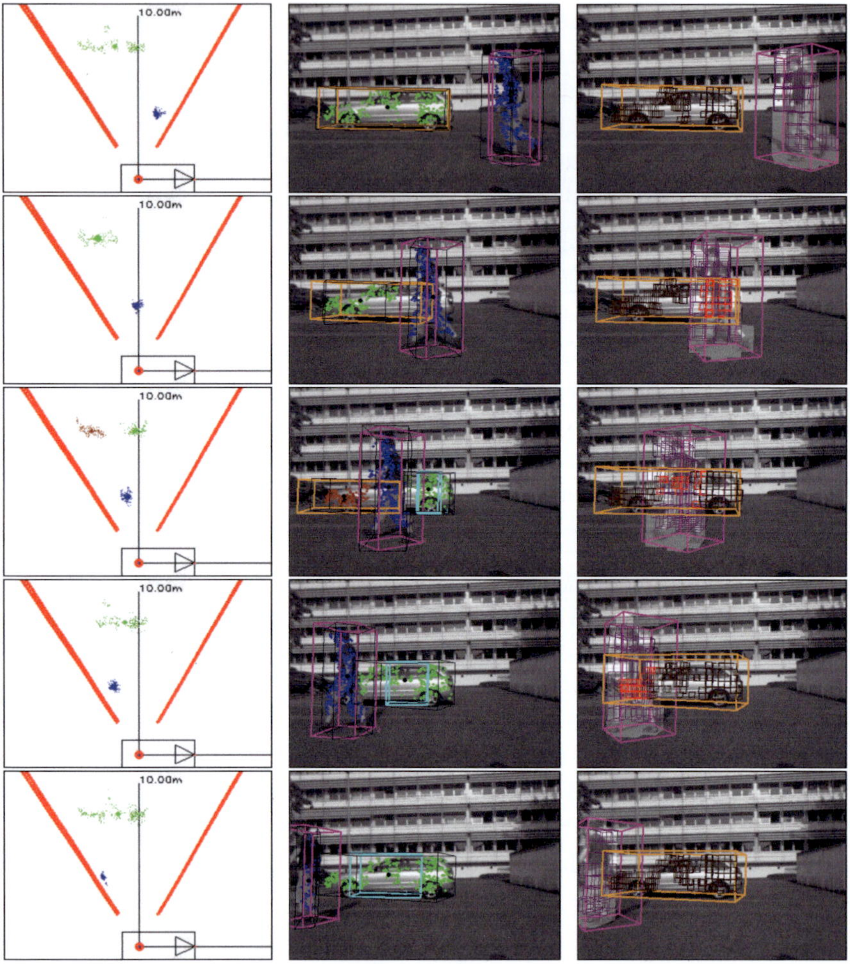

(a) Results of clustering

(b) Tracking results: classical approach

(c) Tracking results: FBPDATA

Figure 6.28: Tracking results for a real-world scene with a dynamic occlusion (top view; frames 7, 28, 37, 48, 58).

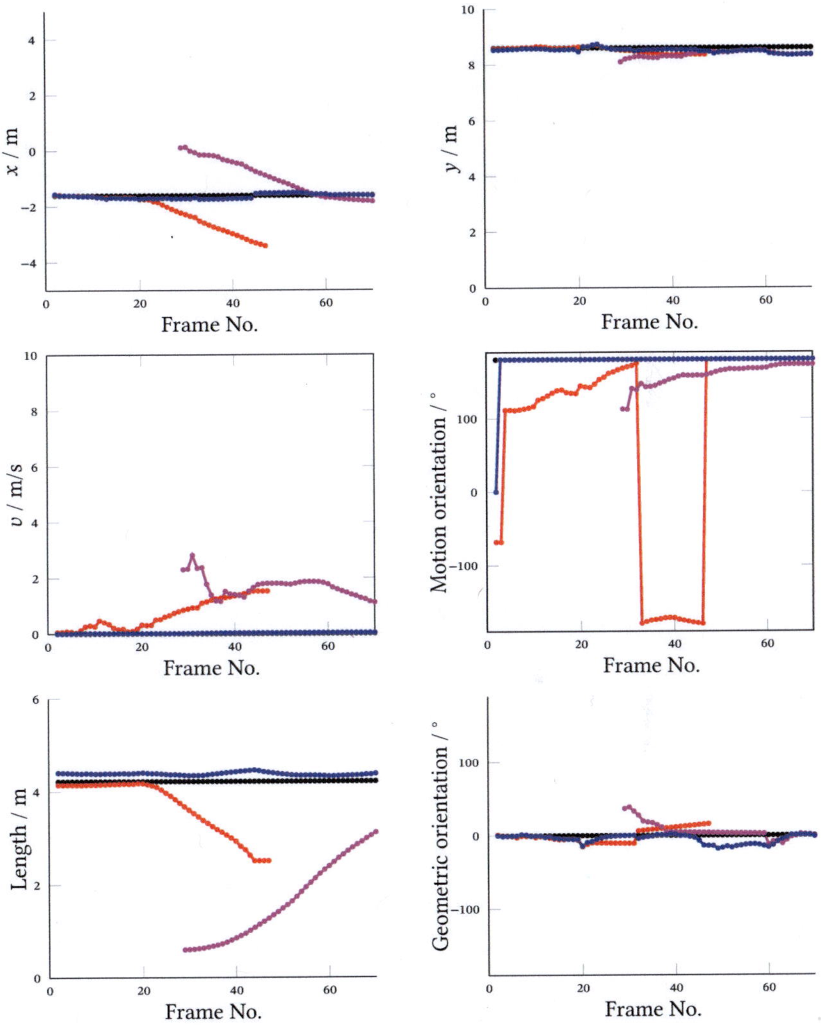

Figure 6.29: Dynamic occlusion scenario: plots of the lateral position x, speed v, length l and motion orientation angle φ of the upper object: classical approach (red and magenta), FBPDATA (blue) and ground truth (black).

7 Conclusion and outlook

In this thesis, an approach for video-based tracking of multiple extended objects has been presented, which is capable of coping with noisy, split, merged, incomplete and missed detections. In contrast to many object tracking systems, the proposed approach does not require any additional knowledge and does not make any assumptions about object appearance in the image domain. Object detections are derived solely on the basis of clustered 3D points. No pre-learned appearance information is assumed for object detection.

The side pre-crash safety system developed within the EU project APROSYS serves as the motivation for this strategy. The restrictions of the side view lead to the development of a stereo-video-based system which is based on a few reasonable assumptions, such as the object rigidity and the "flat world" assumption. This system has been described in detail. The description covers camera modeling, optical flow computation, depth perception, point tracking in 3D, object detection, data association, and object state estimation.

The focus of the thesis was laid on counteracting data association and tracking errors that occur due to corrupted detections. We first gave a detailed introduction to object tracking and its subtasks and provided basics of object state estimation and data association. We analyzed the problem of corrupted detections and identified the major weaknesses of the classical tracking-by-detection scheme. As a result, we formulated a data association and object tracking approach based on the detection-by-tracking paradigm.

The proposed approach consists of several concepts for improving video-based object tracking in cases of corrupted detections.

First, we make a distinction between a measurement and a detection. Data association is performed using raw detections and is based on knowledge about the previous affiliation of individual feature points to the detected objects from previous frames.

In contrast to most classical tracking approaches which follow the tracking-by-detection paradigm, in our approach measurements are not directly derived from detections but are "reconstructed" from the associated detections. The feature-based reconstruction of object dynamics offers a solution to the problem of erroneous object state estimation in cases of split, merged and partial detections as well as in case of detections which are bloated due to clutter. A grid-based object object extent representation in 3D offers a compromise between a coarse and a fine-granular modeling the objects' extent and facilitates a detailed occlusion modeling, which is realized by computing appearance masks and occlusion masks for the tracked objects. This information allows to reconstruct object extent in case of partial and split detections and thus to provide an adequate occlusion handling. Object reference point is filtered taking into account the estimated object dimensions. The problem of false positives (clutter-based detections) and false negatives (missed detections) is handled within a probabilistic data association scheme with object existence and observability modeling. We make a distinction between three different causes for missed detections and two causes for unassociated detections and incorporate the respective likelihoods into the state estimation process. Explicit object existence and observability modeling allows for realization of the Track-Before-Detect track management scheme that is based on a sound probabilistic footing.

The approach has been evaluated based on simulated and real world data. The selected sequences covered critical scenarios in terms of deficient object detection. We succeeded in improving object position and velocity estimation and managed to prevent track losses in case of occlusions and merged and split detections.

For tracking applications that have to cope with the above-mentioned effects of corrupted detections and allow tracking on the feature point level, the presented approach offers a much-needed enhancement which has the potential to increase detection and tracking performance in problematic scenarios and to significantly improve the overall system robustness. But also an integration of the proposed feature-based data association and measurement reconstruction scheme into frameworks that use appearance-based 2D detections and point clustering based 3D detections (i.e., [Oše17]), might considerably improve their performance in complicated scenarios.

The applicability of the proposed approach has been demonstrated based on a stereo-video based object detection and tracking framework that was designed for a side-looking pre-crash application. Adapting the framework for a front-looking perspective or integrating the tracking module into another object detection framework would allow to compare the tracking performance with other state-of-the-art MOT approaches.

The area of application, however, has not necessarily to be restricted to stereo cameras and to ADAS applications. Parts of the proposed approach have already been successfully utilized for improving tracking performance in other applications, such as e.g., indoor surveillance application [Ste12], maritime surveillance [Teu11], and vehicle tracking in Wide Area Motion Imagery (WAMI) data [Teu15, Teu16].

In the current version of the framework we used a very simple model for distribution of object birth, clutter, etc. Collecting more data and learning distributions for object births, splits, merges, and deaths from data is necessary to achieve good results in a specific application.

We consider several enhancements to the presented approach. One of them is utilization of more sophisticated interest point detectors and descriptors, such as SIFT [Low04] or SURF [Bay06], instead of optical flow (or in addition to it) for feature point tracking and particularly for re-identification of object parts re-appearing after an occlusion. Other reasonable enhancements are integration of the stixel representation [Pfe11], Dense6D [Rab10], and scene flow [Vog15] as the underlying data input.

Bibliography

[Ach04] ACHLER, Ofer and TRIVEDI, Mohan Manubhai: "Camera Based Vehicle Detection, Tracking, and Wheel Baseline Estimation Approach". In: *Proceedings of the 7th IEEE Intelligent Transportation Systems Conference.* 2004, pp. 743–748.

[Ach04] ACHLER, Ofer and TRIVEDI, Mohan Manubhai: "Vehicle Wheel Detector using 2D Filter Banks". In: *IEEE Intelligent Vehicles Symposium, 2004.* 2004, pp. 25–30.

[Amd06] AMDITIS, Angelos; FLOUDAS, Nikolaos; POLYCHRONOPOULOS, Aristomenis; BANK, Dirk; VAN DEN BROEK, Bas and OECHSLE, Fred: "Sensor data fusion for LATERAL SAFE applications". In: *Proceedings of the 13th ITS World Congress and Exhibition.* London / UK, 2006, pp. 8–12.

[Amd08] AMDITIS, Angelos; FLOUDAS, Nikolaos; KAISER-DIECKHOFF, Uwe; HACKBARTH, Thomas; VAN DEN BROEK, Bas; MIGLIETTA, Maurizio; DANIELSON, Lars; GEMOU, Maria and BEKIARIS, Evangelos: "Integrated Vehicle's Lateral Safety: The LATERAL SAFE Experience". In: *IET Intelligent Transport Systems* 2.1 (2008), pp. 15–26.

[And08] ANDRILUKA, Mykhaylo; ROTH, Stefan and SCHIELE, Bernt: "People-Tracking-by-Detection and People-Detection-by-Tracking". In: *2008 IEEE Conference on Computer Vision and Pattern Recognition.* 2008, pp. 1–8.

[APR10] APROSYS - Advanced PROtection SYStems: An Integrative Project in the 6th Framework Programme. 2010. URL: https://trimis.ec.europa.eu/project/advanced-protection-systems (visited on 12/12/2017).

[Aru02] ARULAMPALAM, M. Sanjeev; MASKELL, Simon; GORDON, Neil and CLAPP, Tim: "A Tutorial on Particle Filters for Online Nonlinear/Non-Gaussian Bayesian Tracking". In: *IEEE Transactions on Signal Processing* 50.2 (2002), pp. 174–178.

[Bac10] BACHMANN, Alexander: "Dichte Objektsegmentierung in Stereobildfolgen". PhD thesis. Karlsruhe, Hannover, and Karlsruhe: KIT, 2010.

[Bad09] BADINO, Hernán; FRANKE, Uwe and PFEIFFER, David: "The Stixel World - A Compact Medium Level Representation of the 3D-World". In: *Proceedings of the 31st DAGM Symposium on Pattern Recognition.* Berlin, Heidelberg: Springer-Verlag, 2009, pp. 51–60.

[Bar00] BAR-SHALOM, Yaakov and BLAIR, William Dale, eds.: Multitarget-Multisensor Tracking: Applications and Advances. Boston: Artech House, 2000.

[Bar08] BARTH, Alexander and FRANKE, Uwe: "Where Will the Oncoming Vehicle be the Next Second?" In: *Proceedings of the IEEE Intelligent Vehicles Symposium.* 2008, pp. 1068–1073.

[Bar09] BARTH, Alexander and FRANKE, Uwe: "Estimating the Driving State of Oncoming Vehicles From a Moving Platform Using Stereo Vision". In: *IEEE Transactions on Intelligent Transportation Systems* 10.4 (2009), pp. 560–571.

[Bar09] BARTH, Alexander; PFEIFFER, David and FRANKE, Uwe: "Vehicle Tracking at Urban Intersections Using Dense Stereo". In: *3rd Workshop on Behaviour Monitoring and Interpretation.* Ed. by BMI. 2009, pp. 47–58.

[Bar10] BARTH, Alexander and FRANKE, Uwe: "Tracking Oncoming and Turning Vehicles at Intersections". In: *Proceedings of the 13th International IEEE Conference on Intelligent Transportation Systems.* 2010, pp. 861–868.

[Bar75] BAR-SHALOM, Yaakov and TSE, Edison: "Tracking in a Cluttered Environment with Probability Data Association". In: *Automatica* 11 (1975), pp. 451–460.

[Bar78] BAR-SHALOM, Yaakov: "Tracking Methods in a Multitarget Environment". In: *IEEE Transactions on Automatic Control.* Vol. 23. 1978, pp. 618–626.

[Bar88] BAR-SHALOM, Yaakov and FORTMANN, Thomas E.: Tracking and Data Association. Vol. 179. Mathematics in science and engineering. Orlando: Academic Press, 1988.

[Bar92] BAR-SHALOM, Yaakov, ed.: Multitarget-Multisensor Tracking: Applications and Advances. Vol. 2. Boston and London: Artech House, 1992.

[Bar93] BAR-SHALOM, Yaakov and LI, Xiao-Rong: Estimation and Tracking: Principles, techniques, and software. Boston and London: Artech House, 1993.

[Bar94] BARRON, John L.; FLEET, David J. and BEAUCHEMIN, Steven S.: "Performance of Optical Flow Techniques". In: *International Journal of Computer Vision* 12.1 (1994), pp. 43–77.

[Bat09] BATZ, Thomas; WATSON, Kym and BEYERER, Jurgen: "Recognition of dangerous situations within a cooperative group of vehicles". In: *Proceedings of the IEEE Intelligent Vehicles Symposium.* 2009, pp. 907–912.

[Bau10] BAUM, Marcus; GHEŢA, Ioana; BELKIN, Andrey; BEYERER, Jurgen and HANEBECK, Uwe D.: "Data association in a world model for autonomous systems". In: *2010 IEEE Conference on Multisensor Fusion and Integration.* 2010, pp. 187–192.

[Bay06] BAY, Herbert; TUYTELAARS, Tinne and VAN GOOL, Luc: "SURF: Speeded Up Robust Features". In: *Lecture Notes in Computer Science* 3951 (2006), pp. 404–417.

[Bel12] BELKIN, Andrey; KUWERTZ, Achim; FISCHER, Yvonne and BEYERER, Jrgen: "World Modeling for Autonomous Systems". In: *Innovative Information Systems Modelling Techniques.* Ed. by KALLONIATIS, Christos. InTech, 2012, pp. 137–158.

[Bet96] Betke, Margrit; Haritaoglu, Esin and Davis, Larry S.: "Multiple vehicle detection and tracking in hard real-time". In: *Proceedings of the IEEE Intelligent Vehicles Symposium.* 1996, pp. 351–356.

[Bla04] Blackman, Samuel S.: "Multiple Hypothesis Tracking for Multiple Traget Tracking". In: *IEEE A&E Systems Magazine.* Vol. 19. 2004, pp. 5–18.

[Bla99] Blackman, Samuel S. and Popoli, Robert: Design and Analysis of Modern Tracking Systems. Boston: Artech House, 1999.

[Bob16] Bober, Isaac: External airbags reduce side-impact collision force by 30%. 16.02.2016. url: https://practicalmotoring.com.au/car-news/external-airbags-reduce-side-impact-collision-force-by-30/ (visited on 10/16/2017).

[Bou19] Boudette, Neal E.: "Tesla's Self-Driving System Cleared in Deadly Crash". In: *The New York Times* (2017-01-19).

[Bra94] Brauckmann, Michael E.; Goerick, Christian; Gross, Jürgen and Zielke, Thomas: "Towards All Around Automatic Visual Obstacle Sensing for Cars". In: *Proceedings of the IEEE Intelligent Vehicles Symposium.* 1994, pp. 79–84.

[Bro04] Brox, Thomas; Bruhn, Andrés; Papenberg, Nils and Weickert, Joachim: "High Accuracy Optical Flow Estimation Based on a Theory for Warping". In: *Computer Vision - ECCV 2004.* Lecture Notes in Computer Science. Springer, 2004, pp. 25–36.

[Bro71] Brown, Duane C.: "Close-range camera calibration". In: *PHOTOGRAMMETRIC ENGINEERING* 37.8 (1971), pp. 855–866.

[Bro98] Brookner, Eli: Tracking and Kalman filtering made easy. New York: John Wiley & Sons, 1998.

[Büc03] Bücher, Thomas; Curio, Cristobal; Edelbrunner, Johann; Igel, Christian; Kastrup, David; Leefken, Iris; Lorenz, Gesa; Steinhage, Axel and Seelen, Werner von: "Image processing and behavior planning for intelligent vehicles". In: *IEEE Transactions on Industrial Electronics* 50.1 (2003), pp. 62–75.

[Bue09] BUEHLER, Martin; IAGNEMMA, Karl and SINGH, Sanjiv, eds.: The DARPA Urban Challenge: Autonomous Vehicles in City Traffic. Vol. 56. Springer Tracts in Advanced Robotics. Berlin, Heidelberg: Springer-Verlag, 2009.

[Cha05] CHANG, Peng; CAMUS, Theodore and MANDELBAUM, Robert: "Stereo-Based Vision System for Automotive Imminent Collision Detection". In: *Proceedings of the IEEE Intelligent Vehicles Symposium.* 2005, pp. 274–279.

[Cha11] CHALLA, Subhash; MORELANDE, Mark R.; MUŠICKI, Darko and EVANS, Robin J.: Fundamentals of Object Tracking. Cambridge University Press, 2011.

[Cha84] CHANG, Kuo Chu and BAR-SHALOM, Yaakov: "Joint Probabilistic Data Association for Multitarget Tracking with Possibly Unresolved Measurements and Maneuvers". In: *IEEE Transactions on Automatic Control.* 1984, pp. 585–594.

[Che95] CHENG, Yizong: "Mean Shift, Mode Seeking, and Clustering". In: *IEEE Transactions on Pattern Analysis and Machine Intelligence* 17.8 (1995), pp. 790–799.

[Col92] COLLINS, Joseph B. and UHLMANN, Jeffrey K.: "Efficient Gating in Data Association with Gaussian Multivariate Distributed States". In: *Transactions on Aerospace and Electronic Systems.* 1992, pp. 909–916.

[Cou03] COUÉ, Christophe; FRAICHARD, Thierry; BESSIÈRE, Pierre and MAZER, Emmanuel: "Using Bayesian Programming for multi-sensor multi-target tracking in automotive applications". In: *2003 IEEE International Conference on Robotics and Automation (Cat. No.03CH37422).* IEEE, 2003, pp. 2104–2109.

[Cox96] COX, Ingemar J. and HINGORANI, Sunita L.: "An Efficient Implementation of Reid's Multiple Hypothesis Tracking Algorithm and its Evaluation for the Purpose of Visual Tracking". In: *IEEE Transactions on Pattern Analysis and Machine Intelligence.* Vol. 18. 1996, pp. 138–150.

[Dai16] Daimler AG: PRE-SAFE® Impulse side. 2016. url: http://techcenter.mercedes-benz.com/en/pre-safe-impulse-side/detail.html (visited on 10/16/2017).

[Dan02] Dang, Thao; Hoffmann, Christian and Stiller, Christoph: "Fusing Optical Flow and Stereo Disparity for Object Tracking". In: *Proceedings of the IEEE Intelligent Transportation Systems Conference.* Singapore, 2002, pp. 112–117.

[Dan05] Dang, Thao and Hoffmann, Christian: "Fast Object Hypotheses Generation Using 3D Position and 3D Motion". In: *2005 IEEE Computer Society Conference on Computer Vision and Pattern Recognition (CVPR'05).* IEEE, 2005, pp. 56–61.

[Dan07] Danescu, Radu; Nedevschi, Sergiu; Meinecke, Marc-Michael and Graf, Thorsten: "Stereovision Based Vehicle Tracking in Urban Traffic Environments". In: *Proceedings of the IEEE Intelligent Transportation Systems Conference.* 2007, pp. 400–404.

[Dem04] Demonceaux, Cédric; Potelle, Alex and Kachi-Akkouche, Djemâa: "Obstacle detection in a road scene based on motion analysis". In: *IEEE Transactions on Vehicular Technology* 53.6 (2004), pp. 1649–1656.

[Día03] Díaz, Javier; Ros, Eduardo; Mota, Sonia; Botella, Guillermo; Cañas, Antonio and Sabatini, Silvio P.: "Optical Flow for Cars Overtaking Monitor: The Rear Mirror Blind Spot Problem". In: *10th Int. Conference on Vision in Vehicles.* 2003, pp. 1–8.

[Día08] Díaz, Javier; Ros Vidal, Eduardo; Rotter, Alexander and Mühlenberg, Martin: "Lane-Change Decision Aid System Based on Motion-Driven Vehicle Tracking". In: *IEEE Transactions on Vehicular Technology* 57.5 (2008), pp. 2736–2746.

[Dic07] Dickmanns, Ernst Dieter: Dynamic Vision for Perception and Control of Motion. London: Springer-Verlag, 2007.

[Dic94] Dickmanns, Ernst Dieter; Behringer, Reinhold; Dickmanns, Dirk; Hildebrandt, Thomas; Maurer, Markus; Thomanek, Frank and Schiehlen, Joachim: "The Seeing Passenger Car 'VaMoRs-P'". In: *Proceedings of the IEEE Intelligent Vehicles Symposium*. 1994, pp. 68–73.

[Elf89] Elfes, Alberto: "Using occupancy grids for mobile robot perception and navigation". In: *Computer* 22.6 (1989), pp. 46–57.

[Est96] Ester, Martin; Kriegel, Hans-Peter; Sander, Jörg and Xu, Xiaowei: "A density-based algorithm for discovering clusters in large spatial databases with noise." In: *Proceedings of the Second International Conference on Knowledge Discovery and Data Mining*. 1996, pp. 226–231.

[Far00] Farneback, Gunnar: "Fast and Accurate Motion Estimation using Orientation Tensors and Parametric Motion Models". In: *Proceedings of the 15th International Conference on Pattern Recognition*. Vol. 1. 2000, pp. 135–139.

[Fis12] Fischer, Yvonne; Baum, Marcus; Flohr, Fabian; Hanebeck, Uwe D. and Beyerer, Jürgen: "Evaluation of tracking methods for maritime surveillance". In: *Proceedings of SPIE: Defense, Security, and Sensing*. Vol. 8392. SPIE Proceedings. SPIE, 2012, pp. 839208-1 - 839208-11.

[Fis81] Fischler, Martin A. and Bolles, Robert C.: "Random Sample Consensus: A Paradigm for Model Fitting with Applications to Image Analysis and Automated Cartography". In: *Communications of the ACM* 24.6 (1981), pp. 381–395.

[Fle02] Fleischer, Klaus; Nagel, Hans-Hellmut and Rath, T. M.: "3D-Model-Based-Vision for Innercity Driving Scenes". In: *Proceedings of the IEEE Intelligent Vehicles Symposium*. Vol. 2. 2002, pp. 477–482.

[For80] Fortmann, Thomas E.; Bar-Shalom, Yaakov and Scheffe, Molly: "Multi-Target Tracking Using Joint Probabilistic Data Association". In: *Proceedings of 19th IEEE Conference on Decision and Control*. 1980, pp. 807–812.

[For83] Fortmann, Thomas E.; Bar-Shalom, Yaakov and Scheffe, Molly: "Sonar Tracking of Multiple Targets Using Joint Probabilistic Data Association". In: *IEEE Journal of Oceanic Engineering* 8.3 (1983), pp. 173–183.

[Fra00] Franke, Uwe and Joos, Armin: "Real-time stereo vision for urban traffic scene understanding". In: *Proceedings of the IEEE Intelligent Vehicles Symposium 2000.* 2000, pp. 273–278.

[Fra05] Franke, Uwe; Rabe, Clemens; Badino, Hernán and Gehrig, Stefan: "6D Vision: Fusion of Motion and Stereo for Robust Environment Perception". In: *DAGM Symposium.* Pattern Recognition. Vienna, 2005, pp. 216–223.

[Fra05] Franke, Uwe; Rabe, Clemens; Badino, Hernán and Gehrig, Stefan: "6D-Vision: Fusion of Stereo and Motion for Robust Environment Perception". In: *Lecture Notes in Computer Science* 3663 (2005), pp. 216–223.

[Fre11] Frese, Christian and Beyerer, Jurgen: "A comparison of motion planning algorithms for cooperative collision avoidance of multiple cognitive automobiles". In: *2011 IEEE Intelligent Vehicles Symposium (IV).* 2011, pp. 1156–1162.

[Gan04] Gandhi, Tarak and Trivedi, Mohan Manubhai: "Motion Based Vehicle Surround Analysis Using an Omni-Directional Camera". In: *IEEE Intelligent Vehicles Symposium, 2004.* 2004, pp. 560–565.

[Gan05] Gandhi, Tarak and Trivedi, Mohan Manubhai: "Parametric ego-motion estimation for vehicle surround analysis using an omnidirectional camera". In: *Machine Vision and Applications* 16.2 (2005), pp. 85–95.

[Gan07] Gan, Guojun; Ma, Chaoqun and Wu, Jianhong: Data Clustering: Theory, Algorithms, and Applications. Philadelphia / Pa.: SIAM, 2007.

[Gan07] Gandhi, Tarak and Trivedi, Mohan Manubhai: "Video Based Surround Vehicle Detection, Classification and Logging from Moving Platforms: Issues and Approaches". In: *Proceedings of the IEEE Intelligent Vehicles Symposium.* 2007, pp. 1067–1071.

[Gei] GEIGER, Andreas; LENZ, Philip; STILLER, Christoph and URTASUN, Raquel, eds.: KITTY Object Tracking Evaluation. URL: http://www.cvlibs.net/datasets/kitti/eval_tracking.php (visited on 06/30/2017).

[Gei12] GEIGER, Andreas; LENZ, Philip and URTASUN, Raquel: "Are we ready for Autonomous Driving? The KITTI Vision Benchmark Suite". In: *Conference on Computer Vision and Pattern Recognition (CVPR).* 2012, pp. 3354–3361.

[Gen04] GENOVESIO, Auguste and OLIVO-MARIN, Jean-Christophe: "Split and Merge Data Association Filter for Dense Multi-Target Tracking". In: *Proceedings of 17th International Conference on Pattern Recognition.* 2004, pp. 677–680.

[Ghe08] GHEŢA, Ioana; HEIZMANN, Michael and BEYERER, Jürgen: "Object oriented environment model for autonomous systems". In: *Proceedings of the second Skövde Workshop on Information Fusion Topics, Skövde Studies in Informatics.* 2008, pp. 9–12.

[Ghe10] GHEŢA, Ioana; HEIZMANN, Michael; BELKIN, Andrey and BEYERER, Jürgen: "World Modeling for Autonomous Systems". In: *KI 2010: Advances in Artificial Intelligence: 33rd Annual German Conference on AI, Karlsruhe, Germany, September 21-24, 2010. Proceedings.* Ed. by DILLMANN, Rüdiger; BEYERER, Jürgen; HANEBECK, Uwe D. and SCHULTZ, Tanja. Berlin, Heidelberg: Springer Berlin Heidelberg, 2010, pp. 176–183.

[Gib29] GIBBS, Samuel: "Google's self-driving car: How does it work and when can we drive one?" In: *The Guardian* (2014-05-29).

[Gri07] GRINBERG, Michael and WILLERSINN, Dieter: "Bildverarbeitung für Pre-Crash-Anwendungen". In: *Bildverarbeitung in der Mess- und Automatisierungstechnik.* Ed. by PUENTE LEÓN, Fernando and HEIZMANN, Michael. VDI-Berichte. Düsseldorf: VDI-Verlag, 2007, pp. 303–309.

[Gri09] Grinberg, Michael; Ohr, Florian and Beyerer, Jürgen: "Feature-Based Probabilistic Data Association (FBPDA) for Visual Multi-Target Detection and Tracking under Occlusions and Split and Merge Effects". In: *Proceedings of the 12th International IEEE Conference on Intelligent Transportation Systems.* 2009, pp. 291–298.

[Gri10] Grinberg, Michael; Ohr, Florian; Willersinn, Dieter and Beyerer, Jürgen: "Feature-Based Probabilistic Data Association and Tracking". In: *Proceedings of the 7th International Workshop on Intelligent Transportation (WIT 2010).* 2010, pp. 29–34.

[Gri12] Grinberg, Michael; Schneider, Nick; Pagel, Frank; Manger, Daniel and Willersinn, Dieter: "Towards Video Processing in Vehicles under Adverse Weather Conditions". In: *SPIE Optical Systems Design: Detectors and Associated Signal Processing V.* 2012, p. 855020.

[Hac17] Hackel, Timo; Savinov, Nikolay; Ladicky, Lubor; Wegner, Jan D.; Schindler, Konrad and Pollefeys, Marc: "Semantic3D.net: A new Large-scale Point Cloud Classification Benchmark". In: *ISPRS Annals of Photogrammetry, Remote Sensing and Spatial Information Sciences* IV-1/W1 (2017), pp. 91–98. URL: https://www.isprs-ann-photogramm-remote-sens-spatial-inf-sci.net/IV-1-W1/91/2017/isprs-annals-IV-1-W1-91-2017.pdf.

[Han00] Handmann, Uwe; Kalinke, Thomas; Tzomakas, Christos; Werner, Martin and Seelen, Werner von: "An image processing system for driver assistance". In: *Image and Vision Computing* 18.5 (2000), pp. 367–376.

[Har88] Harris, Chris and Stephens, Mike: "A Combined Corner and Edge Detector". In: *Proceedings of the 4th Alvey Vision Conference.* Manchester / UK, 1988, pp. 147–151.

[Hor81] Horn, Berthold K. P. and Schunck, Brian G.: "Determining optical flow". In: *Computer vision* 17 (1981), pp. 185–203.

[Jan17] JANAI, Joel; GÜNEY, Fatma; BEHL, Aseem and GEIGER, Andreas: Computer Vision for Autonomous Vehicles: Problems, Datasets and State-of-the-Art. 2017. URL: http://arxiv.org/pdf/1704.05519v1 (visited on 06/27/2017).

[Jün09] JÜNGLING, Kai and ARENS, Michael: "Detection and tracking of objects with direct integration of perception and expectation". In: *12th International Conference on Computer Vision Workshops*. IEEE, 2009, pp. 1129–1136.

[Kae02] KAEMPCHEN, Nico; FRANKE, Uwe and OTT, Rainer: "Stereo Vision Based Pose Estimation of Parking Lots Using 3D Vehicle Models". In: *Proceedings of the IEEE Intelligent Vehicles Symposium*. 2002, pp. 459–464.

[Kae05] KAEMPCHEN, Nico; WEISS, Kristian; SCHAEFER, Michael and DIETMAYER, Klaus: "IMM Object Tracking for High Dynamic Driving Maneuvers". In: *Proceedings of the IEEE Intelligent Vehicles Symposium*. 2005, pp. 825–830.

[Kal60] KALMAN, Rudolf E.: "A new approach to linear filtering and prediction problems". In: *Journal of Basic Engineering* 82.1 (1960), pp. 35–45.

[Kal98] KALINKE, Thomas; TZOMAKAS, Christos and SEELEN, Werner von: "A Texture-based Object Detection and an Adaptive Model-based Classification". In: *Proceedings of the IEEE Intelligent Vehicles Symposium*. 1998, pp. 341–346.

[Kha05] KHAN, Zia; BALCH, Tucker and DELLAERT, Frank: "Multitarget Tracking with Split and Merged Measurements". In: *2005 IEEE Computer Society Conference on Computer Vision and Pattern Recognition (CVPR'05)*. Vol. 1. IEEE, 2005, pp. 605–610.

[Koc14] KOCH, Wolfgang: Tracking and Sensor Data Fusion. Berlin, Heidelberg: Springer Berlin Heidelberg, 2014.

[Kol96] KOLLNIG, Henner and NAGEL, Hans-Hellmut: "Matching Object Models to Segments from an Optical Flow Field". In: *Computer Vision — ECCV '96*. Ed. by BUXTON, Bernard and CIPOLLA, Roberto. Vol. 1065.

Lecture Notes in Computer Science. Springer Berlin / Heidelberg, 1996, pp. 388–399.

[Kol97] KOLLNIG, Henner and NAGEL, Hans-Hellmut: "3D Pose Estimation by Directly Matching Polyhedral Models to Gray Value Gradients". In: *International Journal of Computer Vision* 23 (1997), pp. 283–302.

[Krü95] KRÜGER, Wolfgang; ENKELMANN, Wirfried and RÖSSLE, Susanne: "Real-time Estimation and Tracking of Optical Flow Vectors for Obstacle Detection". In: *Proceedings of the IEEE Intelligent Vehicles Symposium.* 1995, pp. 304–309.

[Kum06] KUMAR, Pankaj; RANGANATH, Surendra; SENGUPTA, Kuntal and WEIMIN, Huang: "Cooperative Multitarget Tracking With Efficient Split and Merge Handling". In: *IEEE Transactions on Circuits and Systems for Video Technology.* Vol. 16. 2006, pp. 1477–1490.

[Kur90] KURIEN, Thomas: "Issues in the Design of Practical Multi-target Tracking Algorithms". In: *Multitarget multisensor tracking: Advanced applications.* Ed. by BAR-SHALOM, Yaakov. Artech House radar library. Norwood, Mass.: Artech House, 1990, pp. 43–83.

[Lak02] LAKSHMANAN, Sridhar; RAMARATHNAM, Nirmala and YEO, Teck Beng Desmond: "A Side Collision Awareness Method". In: *Proceedings of the IEEE Intelligent Vehicles Symposium.* Vol. 2. 2002, pp. 640–645.

[Lee16] LEE, Byungjae; ERDENEE, Enkhbayar; JIN, Songguo and RHEE, Phill Kyu: "Multi-Class Multi-Object Tracking using Changing Point Detection". In: *Computer Vision – ECCV 2016 Workshops: Amsterdam, The Netherlands, October 8-10 and 15-16, 2016, Proceedings, Part II.* Ed. by HUA, Gang and JÉGOU, Hervé. Lecture Notes in Computer Science. Cham: Springer International Publishing, 2016, pp. 68–83.

[Lei04] LEIBE, Bastian; LEONARDIS, Aleš and SCHIELE, Bernt: "Combined Object Categorization and Segmentation with an Implicit Shape Model". In: *ECCV'04 Workshop on Statistical Learning in Computer Vision.* 2004.

[Lei07] LEIBE, Bastian; CORNELIS, Nico; CORNELIS, Kurt and VAN GOOL, Luc: "Dynamic 3D Scene Analysis from a Moving Vehicle". In: *Proceedings of the 2007 IEEE Conference on Computer Vision and Pattern Recognition.* 2007, pp. 1–8.

[Lei07] LEIBE, Bastian; SCHINDLER, Konrad and VAN GOOL, Luc: "Coupled Detection and Trajectory Estimation for Multi-Object Tracking". In: *2007 IEEE 11th International Conference on Computer Vision.* IEEE, 2007, pp. 1–8.

[Lei08] LEIBE, Bastian; LEONARDIS, Aleš and SCHIELE, Bernt: "Robust Object Detection with Interleaved Categorization and Segmentation". In: *International Journal of Computer Vision* 77.1-3 (2008), pp. 259–289.

[Lim11] LIM, Young-Chul; LEE, Chung-Hee; KWON, Soon and KIM, Jonghwan: "Event-driven track management method for robust multi-vehicle tracking". In: *2011 IEEE Intelligent Vehicles Symposium (IV).* 2011, pp. 189–194.

[Low04] LOWE, David G.: "Distinctive Image Features from Scale-Invariant Keypoints". In: *International Journal of Computer Vision* 60.2 (2004), pp. 91–110.

[Luc81] LUCAS, Bruce D. and KANADE, Takeo: "An Iterative Image Registration Technique with an Application to Stereo Vision". In: *International Joint Conference on Artificial Intelligence.* Vol. 81. 1981, pp. 121–130.

[Ma09] MA, Yunqian; YU, Qian and COHEN, Isaac: "Target tracking with incomplete detection". In: *Computer Vision and Image Understanding* 113.4 (2009), pp. 580–587. URL: http://www.sciencedirect.com/science/article/pii/S1077314209000058.

[Mag11] MAGGIO, Emilio and CAVALLARO, Andrea: Video tracking: Theory and practice. Wiley Online Library, 2011.

[Mah07] MAHLER, Ronald P. S.: Statistical Multisource-Multitarget Information Fusion. Artech House information warfare library. Boston: Artech House, 2007.

[Mäh07] MÄHLISCH, Mirko; RITTER, Werner and DIETMAYER, Klaus: "Decluttering with Integrated Probabilistic Data Association for Multisensor Multitarget ACC Vehicle Tracking". In: *Proceedings of the IEEE Intelligent Vehicles Symposium.* 2007, pp. 178–183.

[Mäh08] MÄHLISCH, Mirko; SZCZOT, Magdalena; LÖHLEIN, Otto; MUNZ, Michael and DIETMAYER, Klaus: "Simultaneous Processing of Multitarget State Measurements and Object Individual Sensory Existence Evidence with the Joint Integrated Probabilistic Data Association Filter". In: *Proceedings of the 5th International Workshop on Intelligent Transportation (WIT2008).* Hamburg, 2008, pp. 117–122.

[Mah36] MAHALANOBIS, Prasanta Chandra: "On the Generalized Distance in Statistics". In: *Proceedings of the National Institute of Sciences of India* 2.1 (1936), pp. 49–55.

[Mak14] MAKRIS, Alexandros and PRIEUR, Clementine: "Bayesian Multiple-Hypothesis Tracking of Merging and Splitting Targets". In: *IEEE Transactions on Geoscience and Remote Sensing* 52.12 (2014), pp. 7684–7694.

[Mel09] MELZ, Tobias; SEIPEL, Björn; KOCH, Thorsten; ZIMMERMANN, Eric; MUNTEAN, Vlad; TANDLER, Joachim; WILLERSINN, Dieter and GRINBERG, Michael: "A New Pre-Crash System for Side Impact Protection". In: *Vision Zero International.* Launch Issue. UKIP Media & Events, 2009, pp. 134–139.

[Men15] MENZE, Moritz and GEIGER, Andreas: "Object scene flow for autonomous vehicles". In: *2015 IEEE Conference on Computer Vision and Pattern Recognition (CVPR).* IEEE, 2015, pp. 3061–3070.

[Met06] METZLER, Jürgen; GRINBERG, Michael and WILLERSINN, Dieter: "Assessment of the FOE for Side Impact Alert". In: *Proceedings of the 3rd International Workshop on Intelligent Transportation (WIT 2006).* Hamburg, 2006, pp. 71–75.

[Mey94] MEYER, François G.: "Time-to-collision from first-order models of the motion field". In: *IEEE Transactions on Robotics and Automation* 10.6 (1994), pp. 792–798.

[Mic11] Michalke, Thomas Paul; Stein, Fridtjof and Franke, Uwe: "Towards a closer fusion of active and passive safety: Optical flow-based detection of vehicle side collisions". In: *2011 IEEE Intelligent Vehicles Symposium (IV)*. 2011, pp. 181–188.

[Mit04] Mitschke, Manfred and Wallentowitz, Henning: Dynamik der Kraftfahrzeuge. 4., neubearb. Aufl. Berlin: Springer, 2004.

[Mon09] Monari, Eduardo; Maerker, Jochen and Kroschel, Kristian: "A Robust and Efficient Approach for Human Tracking in Multi-camera Systems". In: *Sixth IEEE International Conference on Advanced Video and Signal Based Surveillance*. IEEE, 2009, pp. 134–139.

[Mor88] Moravec, Hans: "Sensor Fusion in Certainty Grids for Mobile Robots". In: *AI Mag* 9.2 (1988), pp. 61–74.

[Muk15] Mukhtar, Amir; Xia, Likun and Tang, Tong Boon: "Vehicle Detection Techniques for Collision Avoidance Systems: A Review". In: *IEEE Transactions on Intelligent Transportation Systems* 16.5 (2015).

[Mun09] Munz, Michael; Mählisch, Mirko and Dietmayer, Klaus: "A Probabilistic Sensor-Independent Fusion Framework for Automotive Driver Assistance Systems". In: *Proceedings of the 6th International Workshop on Intelligent Transportation (WIT2009)*. Hamburg, 2009.

[Mun57] Munkres, James: "Algorithms for the Assignment and Transportation Problems". In: *Journal of the Society for Industrial and Applied Mathematics* 5.1 (1957), pp. 32–38.

[Muš02] Mušicki, Darko and Evans, Robin J.: "Joint Integrated Probabilistic Data Association - JIPDA". In: *Proceedings of the 5th International Conference on Information Fusion*. 2002, pp. 1120–1125.

[Muš92] Mušicki, Darko; Evans, Robin J. and Stanković, Srdjan: "Integrated Probabilistic Data Association (IPDA)". In: *Proceedings of the 31st Conference on Decision and Control*. Tucson / Arizona, 1992, pp. 3796–3798.

[Muš94] Mušicki, Darko; Evans, Robin J. and Stanković, Srdjan: "Integrated Probabilistic Data Association". In: *IEEE Transactions on Automatic Control*. 1994, pp. 1237–1241.

[Ned05] Nedevschi, Sergiu; Danescu, Radu; Marita, Tiberiu; Oniga, Florin; Pocol, Ciprian; Sobol, Stefan; Graf, Thorsten and Schmidt, Rolf: "Driving Environment Perception Using Stereovision". In: *Proceedings of the IEEE Intelligent Vehicles Symposium.* 2005, pp. 331–336.

[Ohn15] Ohn-Bar, Eshed and Trivedi, Mohan Manubhai: "Learning to Detect Vehicles by Clustering Appearance Patterns". In: *IEEE Transactions on Intelligent Transportation Systems* 16.5 (2015), pp. 2511–2521.

[Oše17] Ošep, Aljoša; Mehner, Wolfgang; Mathias, Markus and Leibe, Bastian: "Combined Image- and World-Space Tracking in Traffic Scenes". In: *International Conference on Robotics and Automation.* 2017.

[Ott08] Ottlik, Artur and Nagel, Hans-Hellmut: "Initialization of Model-Based Vehicle Tracking in Video Sequences of Inner-City Intersections". In: *International Journal of Computer Vision* 2008.80 (2008), pp. 211–335.

[Pea01] Pearson, Karl: "On Lines and Planes of Closest Fit to Systems of Points in Space". In: *Philosophical Magazine and Journal of Science* 2.11 (1901), pp. 559–572.

[Pfe11] Pfeiffer, David and Franke, Uwe: "Towards a Global Optimal Multi-Layer Stixel Representation of Dense 3D Data". In: *Proceedings of the British Machine Vision Conference.* BMVA Press, 2011, pp. 51.1–51.12.

[Rab07] Rabe, Clemens; Franke, Uwe and Gehrig, Stefan: "Fast detection of moving objects in complex scenarios". In: *Proceedings of the IEEE Intelligent Vehicles Symposium.* 2007, pp. 398–403.

[Rab10] Rabe, Clemens; Müller, Thomas; Wedel, Andreas and Franke, Uwe: "Dense, Robust, and Accurate Motion Field Estimation from Stereo Image Sequences in Real-Time". In: *Computer Vision – ECCV 2010.* Ed. by Hutchison, David et al. Vol. 6314. Lecture Notes in Computer Science. Berlin, Heidelberg: Springer Berlin Heidelberg, 2010, pp. 582–595.

[Rei79] REID, Donald B.: "An Algorithm for Tracking Multiple Targets". In: *IEEE Transactions on Automatic Control.* Vol. AC-24. 1979, pp. 843–854.

[Ren15] REN, Shaoqing; HE, Kaiming; GIRSHICK, Ross and SUN, Jian: "Faster R-CNN: Towards Real-Time Object Detection with Region Proposal Networks". In: *Advances in Neural Information Processing Systems 28.* Ed. by CORTES, C.; LAWRENCE, N. D.; LEE, D. D.; SUGIYAMA, M. and GARNETT, R. Curran Associates, Inc, 2015, pp. 91–99.

[Ric15] RICHERT, Julien; BOGENRIEDER, Ralf; MERZ, Uwe and SCHÖNEBURG, Rodolfo: "PRE-SAFE® Impuls Seite - Vorauslösendes Rückhaltsystem bei drohendem Seitenaufprall - Chance für den Insassenschutz, Herausforderung für Umfeldsensorik". In: *Fahrzeugsicherheit - Sicherheit 2.0.* Ed. by VDI GESELLSCHAFT FAHRZEUG- UND VERKEHRSTECHNIK. VDI-Berichte. Düsseldorf: VDI-Verlag, 2015, pp. 255–266.

[Rod06] RODEHORST, Volker and KOSCHAN, Andreas: "Comparison and Evaluation of Feature Point Detectors". In: *Proceedings of the 5th International Symposium Turkish-German Joint Geodetic Days "Geodesy and Geoinformation in the Service of our Daily Life".* 2006.

[Rüh08] RÜHL, Steffen; GRINBERG, Michael and WILLERSINN, Dieter: "Empirical evaluation of motion models for a side-looking driver assistance system". In: *Proceedings of the 5th International Workshop on Intelligent Transportation (WIT2008).* Hamburg, 2008, pp. 19–24.

[Ryb10] RYBSKI, Paul E.; HUBER, Daniel; MORRIS, Daniel D. and HOFFMAN, Regis: "Visual Classification of Coarse Vehicle Orientation using Histogram of Oriented Gradients Features". In: *Proceedings of the IEEE Intelligent Vehicles Symposium.* 2010, pp. 921–928.

[Sav17] SAVAL-CALVO, Marcelo; MEDINA-VALDÉS, Luis; CASTILLO-SECILLA, José María; CUENCA-ASENSI, Sergio; MARTÍNEZ-ÁLVAREZ, Antonio and VILLAGRÁ, Jorge: "A Review of the Bayesian Occupancy Filter". In: *Sensors (Basel, Switzerland)* 17.2 (2017).

[Sch12] SCHNEIDER, Nick; GRINBERG, Michael; PAGEL, Frank; MANGER, Daniel and WILLERSINN, Dieter: "Fahrzeugtracking unter widrigen Witterungsbedingungen". In: *Forum Bildverarbeitung 2012.* Ed. by PUENTE LEÓN, Fernando and HEIZMANN, Michael. 2012, pp. 291–301.

[Sch13] SCHUMANN, Arne; BAUML, Martin and STIEFELHAGEN, Rainer: "Person tracking-by-detection with efficient selection of part-detectors". In: *2013 10th IEEE International Conference on Advanced Video and Signal Based Surveillance.* IEEE, 2013, pp. 43–50.

[Sei05] SEIPEL, Björn and KOCH, Thorsten: "Aktive Systeme zur Verbesserung des Seitenaufprallschutzes von PKW". In: *Innovativer Kfz-Insassen- und Partnerschutz.* Ed. by VDI-GESELLSCHAFT FAHRZEUG- UND VERKEHRSTECHNIK. Vol. 1911. VDI-Berichte. VDI-Verlag, Düsseldorf, 2005, pp. 115–135.

[Shi94] SHI, Jianbo and TOMASI, Carlo: "Good Features To Track". In: *Proceedings of the IEEE Conference on Computer Vision and Pattern Recognition.* 1994, pp. 593–600.

[Sim06] SIMON, Dan: Optimal state estimation: Kalman, H∞, and nonlinear approaches. Hoboken / NJ: Wiley-Interscience, 2006.

[Sin91] SINGH, Ajit: Optic flow computation: a unified perspective. IEEE Computer Society, 1991.

[Siv09] SIVARAMAN, Sayanan and TRIVEDI, Mohan Manubhai: "Active Learning Based Robust Monocular Vehicle Detection for On-Road Safety Systems". In: *Proceedings of the IEEE Intelligent Vehicles Symposium.* 2009, pp. 399–404.

[Siv11] SIVARAMAN, Sayanan. and TRIVEDI, Mohan Manubhai: "Combining Monocular and Stereo-Vision for Real-Time Vehicle Ranging and Tracking on Multilane Highways". In: *14th International IEEE Conference on Intelligent Transportation Systems (ITSC).* 2011, pp. 1249–1254.

[Siv13] SIVARAMAN, Sayanan and TRIVEDI, Mohan Manubhai: "Integrated Lane and Vehicle Detection, Localization, and Tracking: A Synergistic Approach". In: *IEEE Transactions on Intelligent Transportation Systems* 14.2 (2013), pp. 906–917.

[Siv13] SIVARAMAN, Sayanan and TRIVEDI, Mohan Manubhai: "Looking at Vehicles on the Road: A Survey of Vision-Based Vehicle Detection, Tracking, and Behavior Analysis". In: *IEEE Transactions on Intelligent Transportation Systems* 14.4 (2013), pp. 1773–1795.

[Son07] SONG, Kai-Tai and CHEN, Hung-Yi: "Lateral Driving Assistance Using Optical Flow and Scene Analysis". In: *Proceedings of the IEEE Intelligent Vehicles Symposium.* 2007, pp. 624–629.

[Ste12] STEPHAN, Thomas and GRINBERG, Michael: "Probabilistic Handling of Merged Detections in Multi Target Tracking". In: *Proceedings of the IEEE Ninth International Conference on Advanced Video and Signal-Based Surveillance (AVSS).* 2012, pp. 355–361.

[Sun02] SUN, Zehang; MILLER, Ronald; BEBIS, George and DIMEO, David: "A Real-Time Precrash Vehicle Detection System". In: *Proceeding of the 6th IEEE Workshop on Applications of Computer Vision.* 2002, pp. 171–176.

[Sun04] SUN, Zehang; BEBIS, George and MILLER, Ronald: "On-Road Vehicle Detection Using Optical Sensors: A Review". In: *Proceedings of the 7th IEEE Intelligent Transportation Systems Conference.* 2004, pp. 585–590.

[Sun06] SUN, Zehang; BEBIS, George and MILLER, Ronald: "On-Road Vehicle Detection: A Review". In: *IEEE Transactions on Pattern Analysis and Machine Intelligence* 28.5 (2006), pp. 694–711.

[Sun14] SUN, Deqing; ROTH, Stefan and BLACK, Michael J.: "A Quantitative Analysis of Current Practices in Optical Flow Estimation and the Principles Behind Them". In: *International Journal of Computer Vision* 106.2 (2014), pp. 115–137.

[Tan06] TANDLER, Joachim; PREIS, Christian; WILLERSINN, Dieter and GRINBERG, Michael: "Side Pre-Crash Sensing System Specification". In: *Proceedings of the IEEE Intelligent Vehicles Symposium.* Tokyo / Japan, 2006, pp. 377–382.

[Tan08] TANDLER, Joachim; WILLERSINN, Dieter and GRINBERG, Michael: Characterised Sensing System Prototype (Side Sensing). APROSYS website, 2008. URL: http://www.aprosys.com/Documents/deliverables/FinalDeliverables/AP%20SP62%200035%20D624%20-%20July%202008.pdf (visited on 08/11/2011).

[Tan08] TANDLER, Joachim; ZIMMERMANN, Eric; MUNTEAN, Vlad; SEIPEL, Björn; KOCH, Thorsten; WILLERSINN, Dieter; GRINBERG, Michael; MAYER, Christian and DIEZ, Monica: "A new pre-crash system for side impact protection". In: *International Journal of Crashworthiness* 13.6 (2008), pp. 679–692. URL: http://www.informaworld.com/10.1080/13588260802411499.

[Tay08] TAY, Christopher; MEKHNACHA, Kamel; YGUEL, Manuel; COUÉ, Christophe; PRADALIER, Cédric; LAUGIER, Christian; FRAICHARD, Thierry and BESSIÈRE, Pierre: "The Bayesian Occupation Filter". In: *Probabilistic Reasoning and Decision Making in Sensory-Motor Systems.* Ed. by BESSIÈRE, Pierre; LAUGIER, Christian and SIEGWART, Roland. Vol. 46. Springer Tracts in Advanced Robotics Series. Springer, 2008, pp. 77–98.

[Teu10] TEUTSCH, Michael and KRUGER, Wolfgang: "Classification of small boats in infrared images for maritime surveillance". In: *2010 International WaterSide Security Conference.* 2010, pp. 1–7.

[Teu11] TEUTSCH, Michael; KRÜGER, Wolfgang and BEYERER, Jürgen: "Fusion of Region and Point-Feature Detections for Measurement Reconstruction in Multi-Target Kalman Tracking". In: *14th International Conference on Information Fusion.* 2011, pp. 881–888.

[Teu15] TEUTSCH, Michael: Moving Object Detection and Segmentation for Remote Aerial Video Surveillance. Vol. 18. Karlsruher Schriften zur Anthropomatik. Karlsruhe: KIT Scientific Publishing, 2015.

[Teu16] TEUTSCH, Michael and GRINBERG, Michael: "Robust Detection of Moving Vehicles in Wide Area Motion Imagery". In: *Proceedings of the 29th IEEE Conference on Computer Vision and Pattern Recognition Workshops: 26 June-1 July 2016, Las Vegas, Nevada.* Los Alamitos, California: Conference Publishing Services, IEEE Computer Society, 2016, pp. 1434–1442.

[Thr05] THRUN, Sebastian; BURGARD, Wolfram and FOX, Dieter: Probabilistic robotics. Cambridge and Mass.: MIT Press, 2005.

[Thr98] THRUN, Sebastian: "Learning metric-topological maps for indoor mobile robot navigation". In: *Artificial Intelligence* 99.1 (1998), pp. 21–71.

[Tid07] TIDEMAN, Martijn; VAN DER VOORT, Mascha C.; VAN AREM, Bart and TILLEMA, Frans: "A Review of Lateral Driver Support Systems". In: *Proceedings of the IEEE Intelligent Transportation Systems Conference.* 2007, pp. 992–999.

[Tou06] TOULMINET, Gwenaëlle; BERTOZZI, Massimo; MOUSSET, Stéphane; BENSRHAIR, Abdelaziz and BROGGI, Alberto: "Vehicle Detection by Means of Stereo Vision-Based Obstacles Features Extraction and Monocular Pattern Analysis". In: *IEEE Transactions on Image Processing* 15.8 (2006), pp. 2364–2375.

[Ulm94] ULMER, Berthold: "VITA II - Active Collision Avoidance in Real Traffic". In: *Proceedings of the IEEE Intelligent Vehicles Symposium.* 1994, pp. 1–6.

[Ung11] UNGER, Christian; WAHL, Eric and ILIC, Slobodan: "Efficient stereo matching for moving cameras and decalibrated rigs". In: *2011 IEEE Intelligent Vehicles Symposium (IV).* 2011, pp. 417–422.

[Ved99] VEDULA, Sundar; BAKER, Simon; RANDER, Peter; COLLINS, Robert and KANADE, Takeo: "Three-dimensional scene flow". In: *Proceedings of the Seventh IEEE International Conference on Computer Vision.* Vol. 2. IEEE, 1999, pp. 722–729.

[Vog13] Vogel, Christoph; Schindler, Konrad and Roth, Stefan: "Piecewise Rigid Scene Flow". In: *2013 IEEE International Conference on Computer Vision*. IEEE, 2013, pp. 1377–1384.

[Vog15] Vogel, Christoph; Schindler, Konrad and Roth, Stefan: "3D Scene Flow Estimation with a Piecewise Rigid Scene Model". In: *International Journal of Computer Vision* 115.1 (2015), pp. 1–28.

[Wan05] Wang, Junxian; Bebis, George and Miller, Ronald: "Overtaking vehicle detection using dynamic and quasi-static background modeling". In: *2005 IEEE Computer Society Conference on Computer Vision and Pattern Recognition (CVPR'05)*. IEEE, 2005, p. 64.

[Wan07] Wang, Chieh-Chih; Thorpe, Charles; Thrun, Sebastian; Hebert, Martial and Durrant-Whyte, Hugh: "Simultaneous Localization, Mapping and Moving Object Tracking". In: *The International Journal of Robotics Research* 26.9 (2007), pp. 889–916.

[Wat12] Watson, Kym; Frese, Christian; Batz, Thomas and Beyerer, Jürgen: "Cooperative Group of Vehicles and Dangerous Situations, Recognition of". In: *Encyclopedia of Sustainability Science and Technology*. Ed. by Meyers, Robert A. New York, NY: Springer New York, 2012, pp. 2463–2489.

[Wei15] Weinmann, Martin; Urban, Steffen; Hinz, Stefan; Jutzi, Boris and Mallet, Clément: "Distinctive 2D and 3D features for automated large-scale scene analysis in urban areas". In: *Computers & Graphics* 49 (2015), pp. 47–57.

[Wei16] Weinmann, Martin: Reconstruction and analysis of 3D scenes: From irregularly distributed 3D points to object classes. Switzerland: Springer, 2016.

[Wei17] Weinmann, Martin; Jutzi, Boris and Mallet, Clément: "GEOMETRIC FEATURES AND THEIR RELEVANCE FOR 3D POINT CLOUD CLASSIFICATION". In: *ISPRS Annals of Photogrammetry, Remote Sensing and Spatial Information Sciences* IV-1/W1 (2017), pp. 157–164.

[Wil] WILLOW GARAGE INC.: OpenCV – Open Source Computer Vision Library. URL: http://opencv.org/.

[Wil88] WILLIAMS, McKay: "PROMETHEUS – The European research programme for optimising the road transport system in Europe". In: *IEE Colloquium on Driver Information.* London, 1988, pp. 1–9.

[Woo06] WOODFILL, John Iselin; GORDON, Gaile; JURASEK, Dave; BROWN, Terrance and BUCK, Ron: "The Tyzx DeepSea G2 Vision System, A Taskable, Embedded Stereo Camera". In: *Embedded Computer Vision Workshop.* 2006, pp. 126–132.

[Woo07] WOOCK, Philipp; PAGEL, Frank; GRINBERG, Michael and WILLERSINN, Dieter: "Odometry-Based Structure from Motion". In: *Proceedings of the IEEE Intelligent Vehicles Symposium.* 2007, pp. 1112–1117.

[Wu07] WU, Bo and NEVATIA, Ram: "Detection and Tracking of Multiple, Partially Occluded Humans by Bayesian Combination of Edgelet based Part Detectors". In: *International Journal of Computer Vision* 75.2 (2007), pp. 247–266.

[Xia15] XIANG, Yu; ALAHI, Alexandre and SAVARESE, Silvio: "Learning to Track: Online Multi-object Tracking by Decision Making". In: *2015 IEEE International Conference on Computer Vision (ICCV).* IEEE, 2015, pp. 4705–4713.

[Xia17] XIANG, Yu; CHOI, Wongun; LIN, Yuanqing and SAVARESE, Silvio: "Subcategory-Aware Convolutional Neural Networks for Object Proposals and Detection". In: *2017 IEEE Winter Conference on Applications of Computer Vision (WACV).* IEEE, 2017, pp. 924–933.

[Zha00] ZHANG, Zhengyou: "A Flexible New Technique for Camera Calibration". In: *IEEE Transactions on Pattern Analysis and Macine Intelligence.* 2000, pp. 1330–1334.

[Zha98] ZHAO, Liang and THORPE, Chuck E.: "Qualitative and Quantitative Car Tracking From a Range Image Sequence". In: *Proceedings of the IEEE Conference on Computer Vision and Pattern Recognition.* Santa Barbara / CA, 1998, pp. 496–501.

[Zie92] ZIELKE, Thomas; BRAUCKMANN, Michael and SEELEN, Werner von: "Intensity and Edge-Based Symmetry Detection Applied to Car-Following". In: *Computer Vision — ECCV '92*. Ed. by SANDINI, G. Vol. 588. Lecture Notes in Computer Science. Berlin / Heidelberg: Springer, 1992, pp. 865–873.

[Zom91] ZOMOTOR, Adam: Fahrverhalten: Kräfte am Fahrzeug, Bremsverhalten, Lenkverhalten, Testverfahren, Meßtechnik, Bewertungsmethoden, Versuchseinrichtungen, aktive Sicherheit, Unfallverhütung. 2nd ed. Würzburg: Vogel, 1991.

Publications

[1] GRINBERG, Michael: “Feature-Based Probabilistic Data Association and Tracking - a novel approach capable of tracking objects under splits, merges and occlusions”. In: *Proceedings of the 2009 Joint Workshop of Fraunhofer IOSB and Institute for Anthropomatics, Vision and Fusion Laboratory.* Vol. 7. Karlsruher Schriften zur Anthropomatik. Karlsruhe: KIT Scientific Publishing, 2010, pp. 159–173.

[2] GRINBERG, Michael: “Data Association for Multi-Target-Tracking”. In: *Proceedings of the 2010 Joint Workshop of Fraunhofer IOSB and Institute for Anthropomatics, Vision and Fusion Laboratory.* Vol. 7. Karlsruher Schriften zur Anthropomatik. KIT Scientific Publishing, 2011, pp. 165–186.

[3] GRINBERG, Michael and OHR, Florian: “Handling of Split-and-Merge Effects and Occlusions using Feature-Based Probabilistic Data Association”. In: *Intelligent Robots and Computer Vision XXVII: Algorithms and Techniques. Proceedings of SPIE-IS&T Electronic Imaging.* Vol. 7539. 2010, 75390F 1–12.

[4] GRINBERG, Michael; OHR, Florian and BEYERER, Jürgen: “Data Association for Visual Multi-Target Tracking under Splits, Merges and Occlusions”. In: *Autonome Mobile Systeme.* Ed. by DILLMANN, Rüdiger; BEYERER, Jürgen; STILLER, Christoph; ZÖLLNER, J. Marius and TOBIAS GINDELE. Springer, 2009, pp. 193–200.

[5] GRINBERG, Michael; OHR, Florian and BEYERER, Jürgen: “Feature-Based Probabilistic Data Association (FBPDA) for Visual Multi-Target Detection and Tracking under Occlusions and Split and Merge Effects”.

In: *Proceedings of the 12th International IEEE Conference on Intelligent Transportation Systems.* 2009, pp. 291–298.

[6] Grinberg, Michael; Ohr, Florian; Willersinn, Dieter and Beyerer, Jürgen: "Feature-Based Probabilistic Data Association and Tracking". In: *Proceedings of the 7th International Workshop on Intelligent Transportation (WIT 2010).* 2010, pp. 29–34.

[7] Grinberg, Michael; Schneider, Nick; Pagel, Frank; Manger, Daniel and Willersinn, Dieter: "Towards Video Processing in Vehicles under Adverse Weather Conditions". In: *SPIE Optical Systems Design: Detectors and Associated Signal Processing V.* 2012, p. 855020.

[8] Grinberg, Michael and Willersinn, Dieter: "Bildverarbeitung für Pre-Crash-Anwendungen". In: *Bildverarbeitung in der Mess- und Automatisierungstechnik.* Ed. by Puente León, Fernando and Heizmann, Michael. VDI-Berichte. Düsseldorf: VDI-Verlag, 2007, pp. 303–309.

[9] Höpken, Mark; Grinberg, Michael and Willersinn, Dieter: "Modeling Depth Estimation Errors for Side Looking Stereo Video Systems". In: *Proceedings of the IEEE Intelligent Vehicles Symposium.* Tokyo / Japan, 2006, pp. 31–35.

[10] Melz, Tobias; Seipel, Björn; Koch, Thorsten; Zimmermann, Eric; Muntean, Vlad; Tandler, Joachim; Willersinn, Dieter and Grinberg, Michael: "A New Pre-Crash System for Side Impact Protection". In: *Vision Zero International.* Launch Issue. UKIP Media & Events, 2009, pp. 134–139.

[11] Metzler, Jürgen; Grinberg, Michael and Willersinn, Dieter: "Assessment of the FOE for Side Impact Alert". In: *Proceedings of the 3rd International Workshop on Intelligent Transportation (WIT 2006).* Hamburg, 2006, pp. 71–75.

[12] Rühl, Steffen; Grinberg, Michael and Willersinn, Dieter: "Empirical evaluation of motion models for a side-looking driver assistance system". In: *Proceedings of the 5th International Workshop on Intelligent Transportation (WIT2008).* Hamburg, 2008, pp. 19–24.

[13] Schneider, Nick; Grinberg, Michael; Pagel, Frank; Manger, Daniel and Willersinn, Dieter: "Fahrzeugtracking unter widrigen Witterungsbedingungen". In: *Forum Bildverarbeitung 2012.* Ed. by Puente León, Fernando and Heizmann, Michael. 2012, pp. 291–301.

[14] Stephan, Thomas and Grinberg, Michael: "Probabilistic Handling of Merged Detections in Multi Target Tracking". In: *Proceedings of the IEEE Ninth International Conference on Advanced Video and Signal-Based Surveillance (AVSS).* 2012, pp. 355–361.

[15] Tandler, Joachim; Preis, Christian; Willersinn, Dieter and Grinberg, Michael: "Side Pre-Crash Sensing System Specification". In: *Proceedings of the IEEE Intelligent Vehicles Symposium.* Tokyo / Japan, 2006, pp. 377–382.

[16] Tandler, Joachim; Willersinn, Dieter and Grinberg, Michael: Concepts for data fusion / track handover from the image to the radar subsystem. APROSYS website, 2006. url: http://www.aprosys.com/Documents/deliverables/FinalDeliverables/AP%20SP62%200029%20D623%20-%20July%202008.pdf (visited on 08/11/2011).

[17] Tandler, Joachim; Willersinn, Dieter and Grinberg, Michael: "Data Analysis of the APROSYS Side Pre-Crash Sensing System". In: *Proceedings of the IEEE Intelligent Vehicles Symposium.* 2007, pp. 926–930.

[18] Tandler, Joachim; Willersinn, Dieter and Grinberg, Michael: Characterised Sensing System Prototype (Side Sensing). APROSYS website, 2008. url: http://www.aprosys.com/Documents/deliverables/FinalDeliverables/AP%20SP62%200035%20D624%20-%20July%202008.pdf (visited on 08/11/2011).

[19] Tandler, Joachim; Zimmermann, Eric; Muntean, Vlad; Seipel, Björn; Koch, Thorsten; Willersinn, Dieter; Grinberg, Michael; Mayer, Christian and Diez, Monica: "A new pre-crash system for side impact protection". In: *International Journal of Crashworthiness* 13.6 (2008), pp. 679–692. url: http://www.informaworld.com/10.1080/13588260802411499.

[20] Teutsch, Michael and Grinberg, Michael: "Robust Detection of Moving Vehicles in Wide Area Motion Imagery". In: *Proceedings of the 29th IEEE Conference on Computer Vision and Pattern Recognition Workshops: 26 June-1 July 2016, Las Vegas, Nevada.* Los Alamitos, California: Conference Publishing Services, IEEE Computer Society, 2016, pp. 1434–1442.

[21] Willersinn, Dieter; Tandler, Joachim; Mayer, Christian; Grinberg, Michael; Seipel, Björn; Koch, Thorsten; Zimmermann, Eric and Muntean, Vlad: "Entwicklung und Test eines Pre-Crash-Sensorsystems für Seitenkollisionen". In: *Integrierte Sicherheit und Fahrerassistenzsysteme.* Ed. by VDI Gesellschaft Fahrzeug- und Verkehrstechnik. VDI-Berichte. Düsseldorf: VDI-Verlag, 2008, pp. 345–359.

[22] Woock, Philipp; Pagel, Frank; Grinberg, Michael and Willersinn, Dieter: "Odometry-Based Structure from Motion". In: *Proceedings of the IEEE Intelligent Vehicles Symposium.* 2007, pp. 1112–1117.

[23] Woock, Philipp; Pagel, Frank; Grinberg, Michael and Willersinn, Dieter: "On the Feasibility of Odometry-Based Structure from Motion". In: *Proceedings of the 4th International Workshop on Intelligent Transportation (WIT).* Hamburg, 2007.

List of Figures

Acronyms

ABS	Anti-lock Braking System
ADAS	Advanced Driver Assistance System
APROSYS	Advanced PROtections SYStems
BM	Bicycle Model
BOF	Bayesian Occupancy Filter
BOFUG	Bayesian Occupancy Filter Using Groups
BOFUM	Bayesian Occupancy Filter Using prior Map knowledge
CAM	Constant Acceleration Model
CAN	Controller Area Network
CDKF	Central Difference Kalman Filter
CNN	Convolutional Neural Network
CRF	Conditional Random Field
CVM	Constant Velocity Model
CVRR	Computer Vision and Robotics Research Lab
CYCAM	Constant Yaw Rate Constant Acceleration Model
CYCVM	Constant Yaw Rate Constant Velocity Model
CYM	Constant Yaw Rate Model
DARPA	Defense Advanced Research Projects Agency
DBSCAN	Density-Based Spacial Clustering of Applications with Noise
EBA	Emergency Brake Assist
EKF	Extended Kalman Filter

Euro NCAP	European New Car Assessment Programme
FBPDATA	Feature-Based Probabilistic Data Association and Tracking Algorithm
FOE	Focus of Expansion
FoV	Field of view
FP6	6th RTD Framework Programme
GDBSCAN	Generalized Density-Based Spacial Clustering of Applications with Noise
GNN	Global Nearest Neighbor
GUI	Graphical User Interface
HMM	Hidden Markov Model
HOMHT	Hypotheses-Oriented MHT
ICR	instantaneous center of rotation
IEKF	Iterative Extended Kalman Filter
IES	German: Lehrstuhl für Interaktive Echtzeitsysteme, Vision and Fusion Lab at the KIT
IMM	Interacting Multiple Models
IOSB	German: Fraunhofer-Institut für Optronik, Systemtechnik und Bildauswertung, Fraunhofer Institute of Optronics, System Technologies and Image Exploitation
IPDA	Integrated Probabilistic Data Association
JIPDA	Joint Integrated Probabilistic Data Association
JPDA	Joint Probabilistic Data Association
KF	Kalman Filter
KHYS	Karlsruhe House of Young Scientists
KIT	Karlsruhe Institute of Technology

LDWS	Lane Departure Warning System
LSE	Least square error
MCMC	Markov Chain Monte Carlo
MC-MOT	Multi-Class Multi-Object Tracking
MD	Merged Detection
MDB	Mobile Deformable Barrier
MDP	Markov Decision Process
MHT	Multi-Hypotheses Tracking
MOT	Multi-Object Tracking
NCAP	*see* Euro NCAP
NN	Nearest Neighbor
OF	Optical Flow
PCA	Principle Component Analysis
PDA	Probabilistic Data Association
pdf	Probability Density Function
PF	Particle Filter
pmf	Probability Mass Function
RANSAC	RAndom SAmple Consensus
R-CNN	Recurrent Convolutional Neural Network
ROI	Region of Interest
RTD	Research Technology & Development
SD	Split Detection
SfM	Structure from Motion
SHT	Single Hypotheses Tracking
SIFT	Scale-Invariant Feature Transform
SLAM	Simultaneous Localization and Mapping
SMC	Sequential Monte Carlo
SMCM	Sequential Monte Carlo Methods

SP Subproject
SURF Speeded Up Robust Features

TBD Track-Before-Detect
TM Track Merge
TOMHT Track-Oriented MHT
TS Track Split
TTC Time to Collision

UCSD University of California, San Diego
UKF Unscented Kalman Filter

VID Video Exploitation Systems
VUT Vehicle Unter Test

WAMI Wide Area Motion Imagery

A Evaluation of motion models

The evaluation of the motion models described in Section 5.8.2 was done with data taken both in a controlled environment (crash site) and in regular traffic scenes. In the following, evaluation of two video sequences will be presented. The first one was taken in a crash site. The underlying scenario was a side crash. It was performed similar to a EURO NCAP side crash test using a crash barrier shown in Figure A.1. The ground truth acquisition system of the crash site allowed for a precise quantitative evaluation of the object velocity. The crash barrier (CB) was heading straight for the sensor-carrying platform at the speed of 5.6 m/s as shown in the Figure A.2 (a).

Figure A.1: Pictures of the crash test conducted at the CIDAUT crash site in Valladolid.

The second scenario was taken on a special track where a round-about situation was simulated as shown in Figure A.2 (b). For this scenario there was approximate ground truth available which allowed for a qualitative analysis of the model performance. The vehicle under test (VUT) was standing while another vehicle (bullet vehicle, BV) was driving the depicted trajectory at approx. 8 m/s.

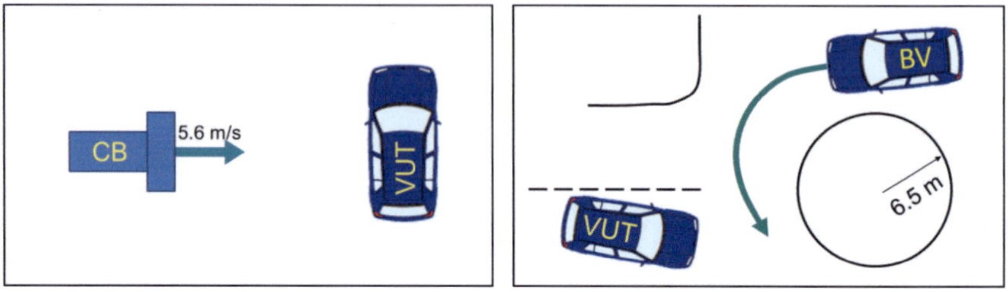

(a) EURO NCAP side crash scenario

(b) Round-about-Scenario

Figure A.2: Test constellation for the crash scenario and the round-about scene.

Object position measurements from the stereo video sensing system had the update rate of approximately 42 Hz. Figure A.3 shows some images taken by one of both video cameras.

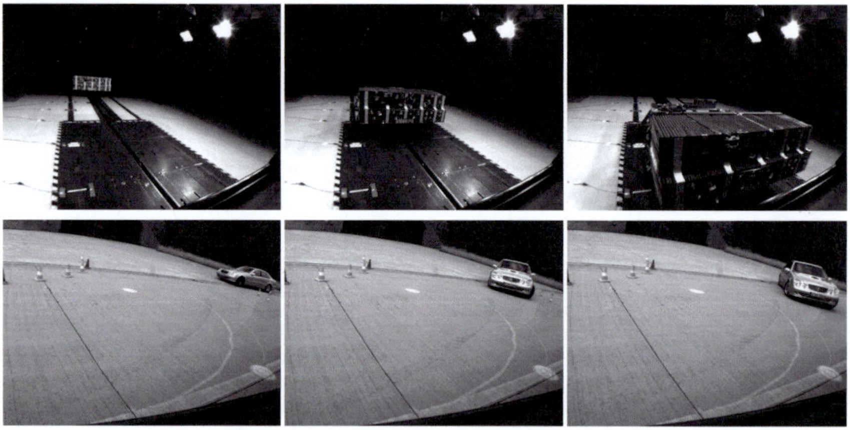

Figure A.3: Selected images of the APROSYS camera taken during the crash test (upper row) and during the track test (lower row).

In the crash sequence, all models yielded good object position estimation. As shown in Figure A.4, object distance was estimated correctly by all models. At the beginning of the sequence, a light oscillation of the lateral position could be observed, but, as it can be seen in Figure A.5, with more measurements available it becomes stable. The constant heading model with constant velocity yields in the most stable estimation of the motion direction. The estimation using bicycle model overshoots and needs more time for convergence. The constant yaw rate model performs slightly better than the bicycle model.

In Figure A.6 the estimated object speed is shown. All models show a good tendency already after a few frames. The object speed was initialized with a very small value. This facilitates a slightly faster convergence of the estimated driving direction. The difference between the initial and the real value has to be corrected by the filter. Models with explicit acceleration estimation tend to do this by assigning the object an acceleration which can be seen in Figure A.7. This is not correct and leads to oscillation of the object speed. The acceleration starts to decrease after correct object speed is reached but the sequence is too short for reaching the correct value for both acceleration and speed. Models without explicit acceleration estimation do not oscillate but need more time to reach the correct speed value.

A closer look at the object detection results of the crash sequence has shown that when the crash barrier approaches, the size estimate of the video object becomes larger. This is due to the fact that occluded object points become visible which leads to a shift of the estimated center of gravity and thus to slightly underestimated velocity.

Figures A.8 (a), (b) and (c) show object trajectories obtained for the round-about scenario with different models. When using constant heading model, after a short transient phase, the trajectory is estimated correctly, however later in the turn, linear motion is predicted for several frames before it can be corrected by the filter (visualized by blue arrow). This can lead to prediction of non-existing collisions, which could often be experienced. When using the bicycle model, the motion direction change is also detected too late. The resulting position offset leads to a stronger steering estimation which yields in a full rotation of the estimated object. Besides, the bicycle model is very sensitive to the parameter settings of the Kalman Filter and generally tends to oscillate. The path estimated with the constant yaw rate model meets the driven path best. The obtained trajectory is smoother than those of the other models. As expected, the explicit acceleration estimation leads to additional uncertainty of the velocity and position estimation. The observation time is too short for a proper estimation. This leads to worse results.

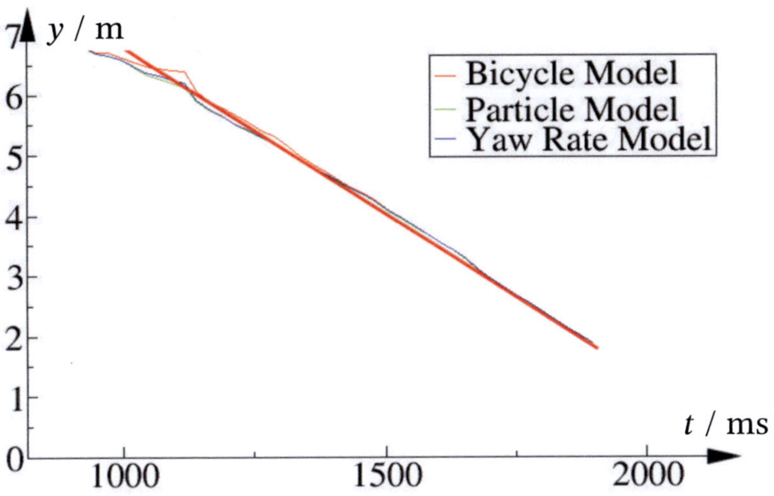

(a)

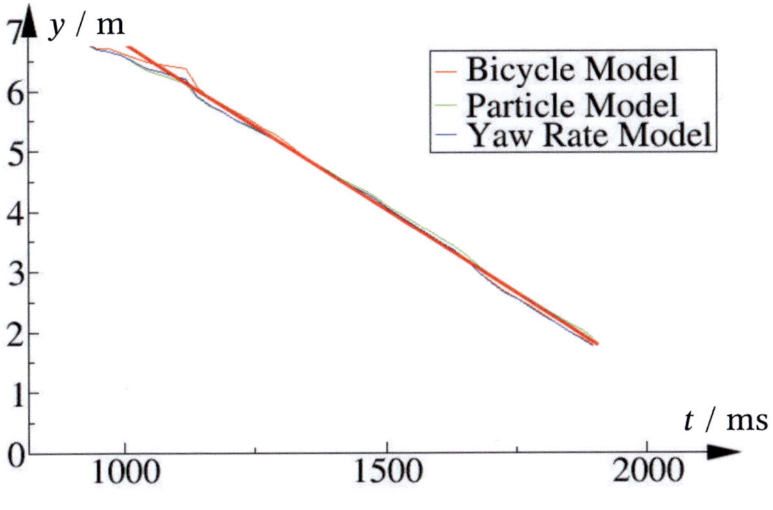

(b)

Figure A.4: Object distance estimation for models without (a) and with (b) explicit acceleration modeling. Thick red line shows the ground truth.

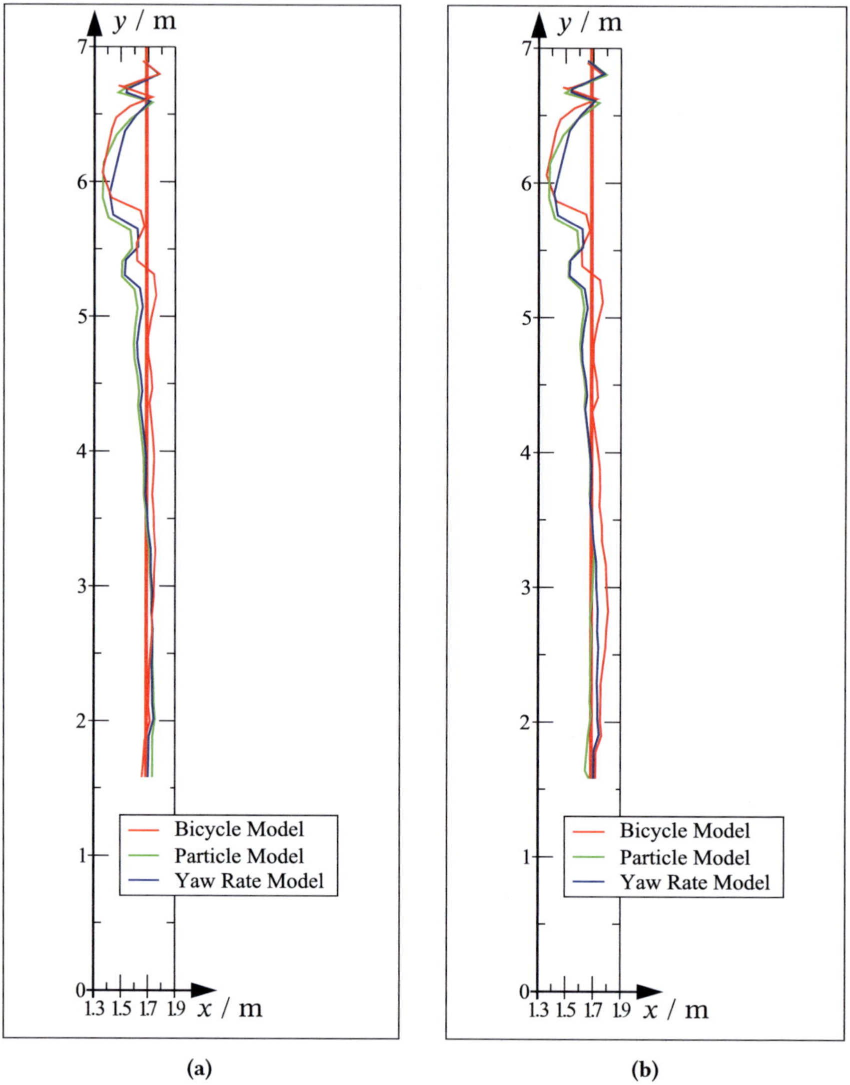

Figure A.5: Estimated object trajectory for models without (a) and with (b) explicit acceleration modeling. Thick red line shows the ground truth.

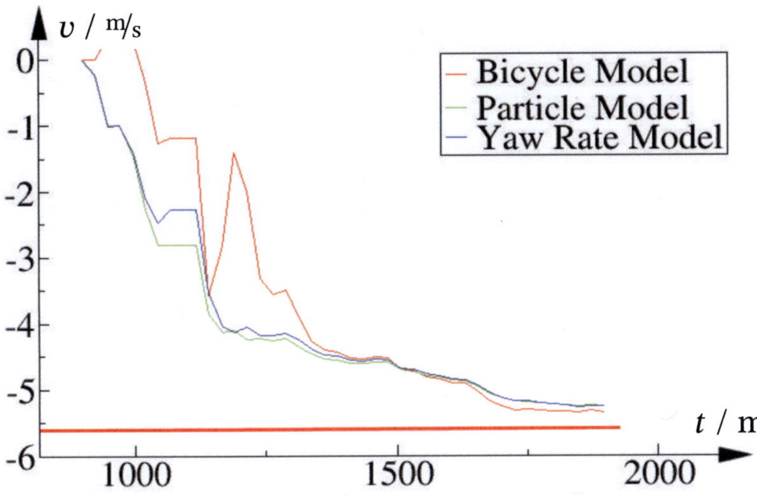

(a)

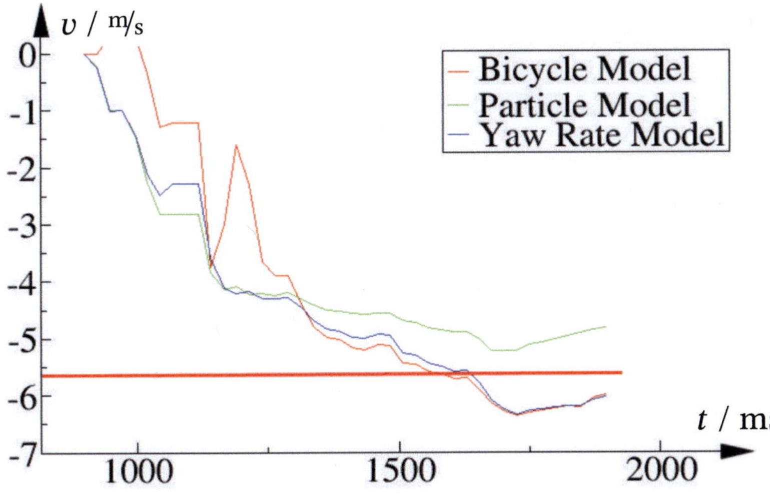

(b)

Figure A.6: Estimated object speed for models without (a) and with (b) explicit acceleration modeling. Thick red line shows the ground truth.

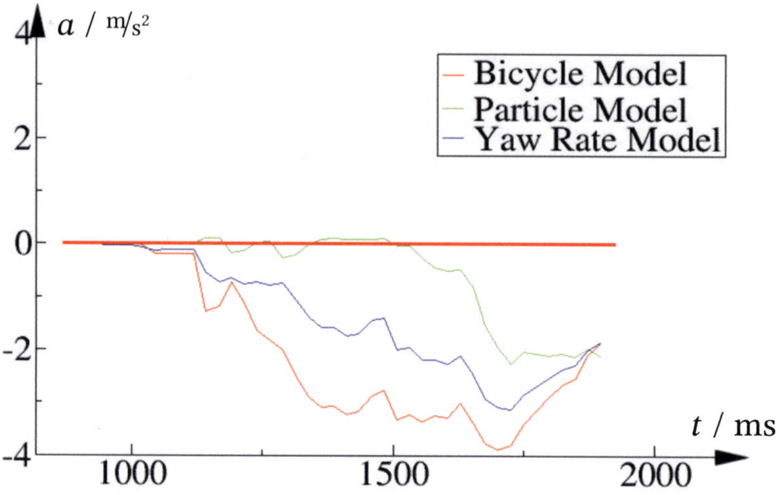

Figure A.7: Estimated object acceleration of the models with explicit acceleration modeling. Thick red line shows the ground truth.

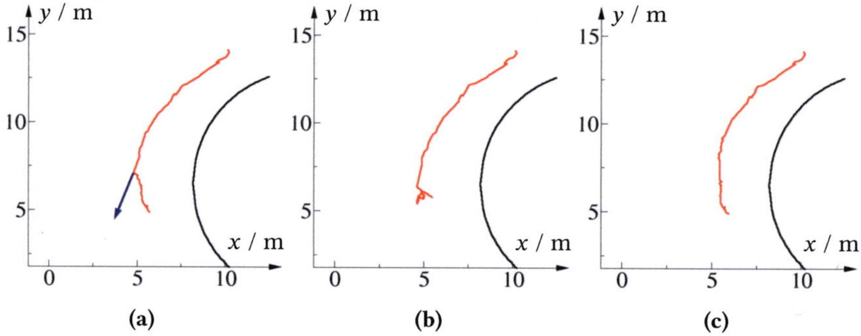

Figure A.8: Trajectories obtained for the roundabout sequence using different motion models: constant heading model with constant velocity (a), bicycle model with constant velocity (b), constant yaw rate model with constant velocity (c).

Karlsruher Schriftenreihe zur Anthropomatik (ISSN 1863-6489)

Herausgeber: Prof. Dr.-Ing. habil. Jürgen Beyerer

Die Bände sind unter www.ksp.kit.edu als PDF frei verfügbar oder als Druckausgabe bestellbar.

Band 9 Thomas Bader
Multimodale Interaktion in Multi-Display-Umgebungen. 2011
ISBN 3-86644-760-8

Band 10 Christian Frese
Planung kooperativer Fahrmanöver für kognitive Automobile. 2012
ISBN 978-3-86644-798-1

Band 11 Jürgen Beyerer, Alexey Pak (Hrsg.)
Proceedings of the 2011 Joint Workshop of Fraunhofer IOSB and Institute for Anthropomatics, Vision and Fusion Laboratory. 2012
ISBN 978-3-86644-855-1

Band 12 Miriam Schleipen
Adaptivität und Interoperabilität von Manufacturing Execution Systemen (MES). 2013
ISBN 978-3-86644-955-8

Band 13 Jürgen Beyerer, Alexey Pak (Hrsg.)
Proceedings of the 2012 Joint Workshop of Fraunhofer IOSB and Institute for Anthropomatics, Vision and Fusion Laboratory. 2013
ISBN 978-3-86644-988-6

Band 14 Hauke-Hendrik Vagts
Privatheit und Datenschutz in der intelligenten Überwachung: Ein datenschutzgewährendes System, entworfen nach dem „Privacy by Design" Prinzip. 2013
ISBN 978-3-7315-0041-4

Band 15 Christian Kühnert
Data-driven Methods for Fault Localization in Process Technology. 2013
ISBN 978-3-7315-0098-8

Band 16 Alexander Bauer
Probabilistische Szenenmodelle für die Luftbildauswertung. 2014
ISBN 978-3-7315-0167-1

Band 17 Jürgen Beyerer, Alexey Pak (Hrsg.)
Proceedings of the 2013 Joint Workshop of Fraunhofer IOSB and Institute for Anthropomatics, Vision and Fusion Laboratory. 2014
ISBN 978-3-7315-0212-8

Die Bände sind unter www.ksp.kit.edu als PDF frei verfügbar oder als Druckausgabe bestellbar.

Band 18	Michael Teutsch **Moving Object Detection and Segmentation for Remote Aerial Video Surveillance.** 2015 ISBN 978-3-7315-0320-0
Band 19	Marco Huber **Nonlinear Gaussian Filtering: Theory, Algorithms, and Applications.** 2015 ISBN 978-3-7315-0338-5
Band 20	Jürgen Beyerer, Alexey Pak (Hrsg.) **Proceedings of the 2014 Joint Workshop of Fraunhofer IOSB and Institute for Anthropomatics, Vision and Fusion Laboratory.** 2014 ISBN 978-3-7315-0401-6
Band 21	Todor Dimitrov **Permanente Optimierung dynamischer Probleme der Fertigungssteuerung unter Einbeziehung von Benutzerinteraktionen.** 2015 ISBN 978-3-7315-0426-9
Band 22	Benjamin Kühn **Interessengetriebene audiovisuelle Szenenexploration.** 2016 ISBN 978-3-7315-0457-3
Band 23	Yvonne Fischer **Wissensbasierte probabilistische Modellierung für die Situationsanalyse am Beispiel der maritimen Überwachung.** 2016 ISBN 978-3-7315-0460-3
Band 24	Jürgen Beyerer, Alexey Pak (Hrsg.) **Proceedings of the 2015 Joint Workshop of Fraunhofer IOSB and Institute for Anthropomatics, Vision and Fusion Laboratory.** 2016 ISBN 978-3-7315-0519-8
Band 25	Pascal Birnstill **Privacy-Respecting Smart Video Surveillance Based on Usage Control Enforcement.** 2016 ISBN 978-3-7315-0538-9
Band 26	Philipp Woock **Umgebungskartenschätzung aus Sidescan-Sonardaten für ein autonomes Unterwasserfahrzeug.** 2016 ISBN 978-3-7315-0541-9

Die Bände sind unter www.ksp.kit.edu als PDF frei verfügbar oder als Druckausgabe bestellbar.

Band 27 Janko Petereit
Adaptive State × Time Lattices: A Contribution to Mobile Robot Motion Planning in Unstructured Dynamic Environments. 2017
ISBN 978-3-7315-0580-8

Band 28 Erik Ludwig Krempel
Steigerung der Akzeptanz von intelligenter Videoüberwachung in öffentlichen Räumen. 2017
ISBN 978-3-7315-0598-3

Band 29 Jürgen Moßgraber
Ein Rahmenwerk für die Architektur von Frühwarnsystemen. 2017
ISBN 978-3-7315-0638-6

Band 30 Andrey Belkin
World Modeling for Intelligent Autonomous Systems. 2017
ISBN 978-3-7315-0641-6

Band 31 Chettapong Janya-Anurak
Framework for Analysis and Identification of Nonlinear Distributed Parameter Systems using Bayesian Uncertainty Quantification based on Generalized Polynomial Chaos. 2017
ISBN 978-3-7315-0642-3

Band 32 David Münch
Begriffliche Situationsanalyse aus Videodaten bei unvollständiger und fehlerhafter Information. 2017
ISBN 978-3-7315-0644-7

Band 33 Jürgen Beyerer, Alexey Pak (Eds.)
Proceedings of the 2016 Joint Workshop of Fraunhofer IOSB and Institute for Anthropomatics, Vision and Fusion Laboratory. 2017
ISBN 978-3-7315-0678-2

Band 34 Jürgen Beyerer, Alexey Pak and Miro Taphanel (Eds.)
Proceedings of the 2017 Joint Workshop of Fraunhofer IOSB and Institute for Anthropomatics, Vision and Fusion Laboratory. 2018
ISBN 978-3-7315-0779-6

Band 35 Michael Grinberg
Feature-Based Probabilistic Data Association for Video-Based Multi-Object Tracking. 2018
ISBN 978-3-7315-0781-9